"AND ALL YOUR CHILDREN
SHALL BE LEARNED"

"AND ALL YOUR CHILDREN SHALL BE LEARNED"

Women and the Study of Torah in Jewish Law and History

Shoshana Pantel Zolty

Jason Aronson Inc.
Northvale, New Jersey
London

Excerpt from THE ESSENTIAL TALMUD by Adin Steinsaltz, copyright © 1976 by Bantam Books, reprinted by permission of Bantam Books, a division of Bantam, Doubleday, Dell Publishing Group, Inc., and Weidenfeld and Nicolson, publishers.

This book was set in 10 pt. Schneidler by Lind Graphics of Upper Saddle River, New Jersey, and printed by Haddon Craftsmen in Scranton, Pennsylvania.

Library of Congress Cataloging-in-Publication Data

Zolty, Shoshana.
  "And all your children shall be learned" : women and the study of
Torah in Jewish law and history / by Shoshana Zolty.
      p. cm.
  Includes bibliographical references and index.   301.412
  ISBN 1-56821-029-9
  1. Women, Jewish–Religious life–History. 2. Jewish religious
· education of girls–History. 3. Women in Judaism–History.
  4. Women Jewish scholars–History. 5. Jewish learning and
scholarship–History. I. Title.
  BM726.Z65   1993
  296.6'8'082–dc20   93-1229

Manufactured in the United States of America. Jason Aronson Inc. offers books and cassettes. For information and catalog, write to Jason Aronson Inc., 230 Livingston Street, Northvale, New Jersey 07647.

For My Beloved Children
Aviva, Yehuda, Elisheva, Méira, Daniella, and Ayala
וְכָל בָּנַיִךְ לִמּוּדֵי ה'
"And all Your children shall be learned of the Lord."

– Isaiah 54:13

Contents

PREFACE   xiii

ACKNOWLEDGMENTS   xix

1 ON TORAH, THE HALAKHIC (JEWISH JUDICIAL)
   SYSTEM, AND A PHILOSOPHY OF JEWISH EDUCATION   1

   Judaism Defined   2

   Basic Theological Premises   3

   The Torah   4

   Post-talmudic Literature and the Halakhic (Jewish Judicial) System   8

   Philosophy of Jewish Education   13

2 THE ROLE AND STATUS OF THE JEWISH WOMAN
   AS VIEWED IN TRADITIONAL JUDAISM   19

   The Creation of Man and Woman and the Need to Relate   20

   Woman as Individual   25

   The Ideal of the Jewish Family   28

   Attitudes toward Women   31

Work Outside the Home and the Concept of Self-Fulfillment   35

Status of Women in Jewish Law (*Halakhah*)   39

3 THE STUDY OF TORAH BY WOMEN IN HALAKHIC
(JEWISH LEGAL) AND EXTRA-HALAKHIC LITERATURE   55

Talmudic Jurisprudence   55

Study of Torah by Women in Pre-Twentieth-Century
Legal Sources   57

Study of Torah by Women in Twentieth-Century Legal Sources   65

The Halakhic Issue in Light of Halakhic Processes   71

Study of Torah by Women in Extra-halakhic Sources   89

4 A HISTORICAL SURVEY OF JEWISH EDUCATION FOR
WOMEN: PART I – THE BIBLICAL PERIOD TO
THE MIDDLE AGES   97

Images of Biblical Women   98

Education in Biblical and Second Temple Periods   101

Women's Religious Roles in the Second Temple Period   106

Evidence for Formal Education in the Late Second Temple Period   107

The Mishnaic (or Tannaitic) Period   113

The Talmudic (or Amoraic) Period   124

5 A HISTORICAL SURVEY OF JEWISH EDUCATION
FOR WOMEN: PART II – THE HEGEMONY OF
BABYLONIAN AUTHORITY AND ITS AFTERMATH
IN THE EAST AND WEST   131

Geonic, Post-Geonic, and Islamic Periods   131

    General Background   132

    Education of Women   137

    Women Scholars   140

The Sephardic Centers of Spain, Provence, Italy, and Elsewhere   146

    Spain   146

        General Background   146

Views of Spanish Rabbis Concerning Women and Torah Study 148

Evidence for Education of Women 151

Provence 154

Italy 155

General Background 155

Evidence for Torah Study by Women 157

Women in the Synagogue 158

Women Scholars and Functionaries 159

Religious Literature for Italian Jewish Women 162

Communal Education in the Seventeenth and
Eighteenth Centuries 166

Other Non-Ashkenazic Centers 169

6 A HISTORICAL SURVEY OF JEWISH EDUCATION
FOR WOMEN: PART III – CHRISTIAN EUROPE IN
THE TWELFTH TO FIFTEENTH CENTURIES 171

Twelfth and Thirteenth Centuries 171

General Background 171

Synagogue as a Means of Education 173

Exclusion of Women from Formal Education Enjoyed by Males 176

Informal Education and the Existence of Women Scholars 177

Passing References to the Testimony of Women
Concerning Jewish Law 183

Fourteenth and Fifteenth Centuries 184

Prominent Women 184

Education and the Average Woman 187

7 A HISTORICAL SURVEY OF JEWISH EDUCATION
FOR WOMEN: PART IV – CHRISTIAN EUROPE IN THE
SIXTEENTH TO EIGHTEENTH CENTURIES 189

Sixteenth Century 189

The Ascendancy of Eastern Europe 189

Prominent Jewish Women in the Sixteenth Century   193

Religious Literature for Women   196

Seventeenth Century   202

Women Scholars   202

Literature for Women and the Attitude toward
Knowledge for Women   208

Evidence for Education of Women   212

Devotional Prayers for Women   213

Women Printers   213

Eighteenth Century   215

Woman Scholars   215

Devotional Literature   219

Forms of Education   223

8 A HISTORICAL SURVEY OF JEWISH EDUCATION FOR
   WOMEN: PART V – THE LATE EIGHTEENTH- AND
   NINETEENTH-CENTURY JEWISH WORLD   227

General Background   227

Jewish Education   231

France   231

Italy   231

England   232

Germany   234

Eastern Europe   238

The Balkans, Islamic States, and Other Countries
Influenced by the Alliance Israélite Universelle   241

Palestine   242

United States of America   243

Women Scholars   246

Hasidic Women   247

Lithuanian and Russian Women Scholars   252

Women Scholars around the World   255

Women Writers   257

9 **THE ESTABLISHMENT OF UNIVERSAL JEWISH
    EDUCATION FOR WOMEN: THE BETH JACOB
    EDUCATIONAL MOVEMENT**   263

Background   264

Sarah Schenirer – Founder of *Bais Ya'akov*: A Model in Educational
Leadership   274

Establishment and Development of *Bais Ya'akov*   276

Ideology and Curriculum of the Beth Jacob Schools   289

Matrix of Change   296

Analysis and Conclusion   297

AFTERWORD   301

BIBLIOGRAPHY   311

INDEX   327

Preface

Some current feminist writings examine areas of male exclusivity to propose remedies for women who wish to gain equal rights and power. This seemingly righteous endeavor looks at the enclaves of male establishments to find the "male-only decay" growing at their core, a decay that predictably taints as heretics those who seek the light and fresh air of egalitarianism. As a result, traditional forms of Judaism, which delineate sharply the turf of the male leadership role from the female nonleadership role, bear much of the weight of feminist attacks and, expectedly, if not appropriately, Jewish authorities look upon feminists as meddlers, troublemakers, and ignoramuses. Generally these polemics against the bastions of Orthodox Judaism come from those outside of them. The critics, male and female, wish to account for what they regard as centuries of unfair treatment of women by blaming the Orthodox Jewish "patriarchal" society for the plight of women today and throughout history, not only in Judaism but apart from it as well. Picking something here and something there, they weave a tapestry of horror. This onslaught has been met by apologists on the inside, both men and women. Explaining away the "heres" and "theres" of the critics, they choose their own heres and theres to paint a glorious mural spanning the ages—a picture of love, happiness, well-being, and self-fulfillment for all.

The thrust and parry of the rhetoric cloud the real issues. That some statement is in itself a polemic or an apology need not detract from its truthfulness or its falseness. These criteria must remain independent of the uses to which they are put. Evidence of male exclusivity need not mean necessarily that women are deprived because they are excluded, but it does signal cause for closer examination. The essence of this matter is not in the heres and theres of any side in the debate. The debate, as debate, can be set aside. The valid points made by the debaters usefully plot the rising or falling curve of concern for women, but they say little about the issue that traditional Judaism focuses on. That issue does not concern the views of feminists or nonfeminists. The question that counts must be phrased in language that is intelligible within the tradition. When a religious system purports to bring sanctity to one's way of life by laying out vehicles, namely religious obligations, for experienced relationship with the transcendent, the real question to address is the one that asks how women gain access to such vehicles. Whether or not the same vehicles are used for women as for men, or whether the vehicles used by women are numerous or complex is irrelevant to the discussion. The nature of women's obligations must be identified. To do less is to ignore the center of traditional Judaism; to do more is to impose one's value system unjustly.

Justifiable gender differentiation should not, however, prevent direct investigation when the very hub of Jewish civilization is at issue. This book concerns the exceptional vehicle by which Jewish men have interacted with the transcendent and from which women have been, and still are, for the most part, excluded—study of the Oral Tradition. Study of the Oral Tradition is embedded in a series of works, mostly of an obtuse, complex legal nature. "Learning," as it is called, happens usually in groups in large halls set aside for the purpose, and male status is measured by attainments in this lifelong pursuit. The issue here concerns whether this vehicle ought to serve women as well. Research into the social and intellectual history of "learning" shows that, for the most part, women were indeed excluded for one reason or another. Although some few women of elite rabbinic families had mastered and still today master the Oral Tradition texts, most women have achieved their contact with the transcendent in other ways, usually connected with the home. During the past half century, women have begun, in a formal manner, to study Written Hebrew Scriptures and their commentaries, leaving the question of the study of the Oral Tradition open to a renewed halakhic (Jewish legal) investigation.

What price would be paid in reopening the issue, and what gains could be had? The question is more than academic. New calls for such study can be heard softly from present-day rabbis, although not from most, and a number of traditional women already engage in study of these texts, thus paving the way for change by creating a new reality.

The greatest price in reawakening this issue would be the further polarization of traditional Jews. Today Orthodox Jews are bitterly divided on political questions such as the status of the modern state of Israel, the value of secular education, support for non-Orthodox communal institutions, community standards of ritual supervision, and many other issues. Clearly, further division would be disastrous and strain to the breaking point the tense relations within the Orthodox communities. No doubt, any clarification of the halakhic position in regard to women's study of the Oral Law texts would yield strongly divergent opinions. Those who would oppose women's study of these texts would rightly point out that Orthodox Judaism has maintained its basic structures for well over a thousand years if not longer; some would claim much longer. To weaken that structure because of some social fad that would radically alter the nature of Jewish study would be an act of treachery. The very fiber of Jewish religious rhythms would be lost forever. No gains could warrant this, for women assuredly have their own avenues to religious fulfillment, and historically they have formed the backbone of traditional Jewish survival. Within that view there is no need to open a matter that, it would seem, has been clearly defended by *Halakhah* for centuries.

Those who would argue for a renewed investigation and change, if halakhically acceptable, would see that the study of the Oral Tradition texts are the substance of the totality of Jewish religious culture. That study is the study of the movements of Jewish civilization, and as such it embodies the Jewish soul. Jewish women, and indeed Orthodox Judaism as a whole, could only gain by having this soul as part of themselves. One could assert that 50 percent of the resources for this soul are lying dormant. In our modern age, the question about why intensifies. One might suppose that sophisticated "modern-Orthodox" women who have professions will find their tradition boring if they do not have the intellectual stimulation of engaging in "learning," and their values, shaped as they are by the larger society, will never come to be shaped by their own heritage.

Questioning the exclusion of women is not a challenge to Jewish tradition but is actually in line with the most noble aspect of the tradition. We are constantly called upon to attempt understanding and to act in line with such efforts. We cannot shake off our responsibility to understand and therefore to question, to reopen the issue, and to act within the halakhic guidelines we discover.

This work charts the positive developments that could contend the time has now come to consider the issue. The halakhic sources, the more positive views of scholars toward women, and the slow but steady growth of educational opportunities for women throughout the ages indicate the issue is pertinent now. Apart from the problem of whether Orthodox Judaism can embrace any movements in the stream of secular society, the question, "How much Torah study for women?" presents itself from within the forceful stream of the tradition itself. The response awaits the community's clearer articulation of the question. This work is that articulation.

Since the purpose of my study is to enunciate the flow of attitudes concerning Jewish women's participation in the traditional curricula and to note the successes of those who managed to participate, a number of concerns must be dealt with here. I assume that men and women are equally capable of reading and understanding Jewish texts–intelligence is not a central issue. Those who have considered it as such must be examined. The history of women's involvement in Jewish learning is embedded in many sources, sources that are far from unified in their approaches and that speak with many voices in many cultures in many ages. These voices are of prime importance, and their views must be weighed. When nonsense can be identified, it can safely be dismissed. Orthodox Judaism has no truck with fools. My purpose is descriptive. But description quickly leads to inferences, to agendas, to prescriptions. The final prescription of how much Torah study for women is not mine to make, but it is mine to define and illuminate the ingredients for such advocacy. Once the facts are assembled, the human decision-making processes of traditional Judaism work themselves into clear positions. Like much else in this tradition, no one definitive prescription will universally be held, but in time some kind of consensus will emerge from the forces that guide the faith. There is an ever-growing literature, popular and professional, that is struggling to probe the past to find keys to the future. My focus, unlike that of others, centers on the issue of education for women. No other issue strikes at the heart of a woman's role in Jewish civilization as does the question, "How much Torah study for women?"

Given the goal of my research, it is important to state at the outset what I am *not* doing. This is not a feminist study for the purpose of condemning or congratulating, nor is it a historical inquiry into the political movements that have affected Jewish life, nor is it a philosophical argument to support one position and not another. It is one person's study of the intersection of Jewish learning (i.e., the totality of Jewish learning) and women throughout the ages in many places and what she can share with others about this study.

Historical research, perhaps more so than any other type, brings home to the researcher how completely dependent she is on the work of countless others who have gone before her. Without the makers or observers of history who were willing to record the events of their day and put down their impressions of people and places, and without the work of others who were willing to preserve, catalog, and store what has been written, a study of this magnitude, which crisscrosses the world and traverses centuries, would have been impossible. The sources of this study are wide and varied. I essentially see my contribution in this area of scholarship as a collator, gathering into one place what I have found in many, in the hope that this work can be used by scholars and students as a springboard for further research and analysis in this field. And, of course, it is my wish that the interested layperson will find much of value in these pages as well. For women, in particular, I endeavored to provide a glimpse into a historical past that included women, for it is important that we know of our past within the context of the general history of our people.

I am only too well aware of the magnitude of the subject and my own limitations. I alone bear the onus of any errors in translations, fact or interpretation that may be present in the work. As for any goals of research and analysis I may have left unfulfilled in this area of scholarship, I can take consolation from the words of the sages: "You are not required to complete the task, yet you are not free to withdraw from it" (*Pirkei Avot* 2:21).

In embarking upon this search to clarify the issue of Jewish education for women, I look back to the generations that carried the Orthodox tradition to me and I see in my children those who will carry it further. I am brought face-to-face with the thought of who will carry what and where and how, and especially I am full of wonder—will my children now be able to hear the question?

Acknowledgments

The conditions under which any individual writes a book – energy, time, support systems, health, material security – demand much from the individual and from those around her. The work involved in writing a book intersects with the other paid and unpaid work we do, and the process is structured by our own personal biographies in ways that cannot be predicted and often cannot be controlled. Through these processes, I have been variously supported, inspired, challenged, and educated by my family, friends, and colleagues. It is they whom I wish to acknowledge with gratitude.

In acknowledging those who have contributed to the writing of this book, I am especially and greatly indebted to Prof. Herbert Basser for his detailed and patient evaluation of the entire manuscript. There is not a chapter in this work that has not benefited from his reasoned suggestions and endless dedication to a project he believed in. His many acts of friendship, freely extended again and again, contributed to the success of this undertaking. In a similar vein, I owe a debt of gratitude to Rabbi Benjamin Hecht for the time and effort he invested in his critical reading of the manuscript and for exposing other sources that needed to be taken into account.

Other sources of inspiration and guidance were Professors Sylvia Barack Fishman, Clive Beck, Eliezer Birnbaum, and Martin Lockshin; Rabbi Dr. Bezalel Safran; Rabbi Dr. Joel Wolowelsky; and Toby Klein Greenwald.

I should also like to acknowledge the unstinting cooperation of Yeshiva University librarians Zalman Alpert and Chaim Gottschalk; Moshe Kolodny, head archivist at Agudath Israel of America; and Toronto librarian Anna Liberman for assisting me in locating source materials or for generously allowing me extended usage of books, understanding that family responsibilities would entail my working largely at home. Thanks are also due to Emmanuel Diena for entrusting me with the loan of many volumes from his extensive private collection of Judaica and for helping to trace hard-to-find works. For assistance in the translation of French and German works, I am indebted to Lilly Heller, Helen Gellis, and Herb Basser.

My heartfelt thanks go to Hebrew University lecturer Deborah Weissman for implanting in me the idea to write a book of this nature. I was attending a seminar of hers in Jerusalem a number of years ago when she casually remarked, "Somebody should write a book on the history of Jewish women's education." Little did Debbie know that a member of her audience would take her suggestion seriously. Her unpublished master's dissertation on the Beth Jacob movement was a valuable resource in my compiling the chapter on that topic.

I would also like to express a debt of gratitude to Arthur Kurzweil, editor in chief at Jason Aronson, for his unfailing cooperation and enthusiasm and for the care he devoted to the publication of this work. Nor should I omit a word of acknowledgment to Muriel Jorgensen, director of editorial production, and Sanford Robinson, copy editor, who rendered valuable editorial assistance in the final stages of this work.

The process of writing a book of this nature is usually considered one of research and study – a process involving the mind. To complete this book, however, has required an equal measure of support from the heart, and for that a debt of gratitude is owed to my family. To my husband, David, who shared with me my moments of inspiration and frustration and who contributed ideas and encouragement, and to my delightful children, who took much pride in "Mommy's book" and generously tolerated my self-absorption at times, I am forever indebted.

To my deceased parents, Rabbi Meyer and Mrs. Ayala Pantel, I dedicate this work, because they, more than anyone, showed me how to work hard, and they set an example of high standards to achieve. My father, an outstanding *talmid hakham*, and my mother, a genuine "Woman of Valour" and *ishah hakhamah*, were an inspiration in my particular choice of subject, for the study of Torah and its application permeated my childhood home. I wish they were here to take credit for their influence.

To the One Above, who provided me with the resources necessary to accomplish this task, there are insufficient words of thanks.

"How great is the reward to them who perform generous acts."

– *Yalkut Shimoni*, Ruth

1

On Torah, the Halakhic (Jewish Judicial) System, and a Philosophy of Jewish Education

In this work, I aim to provide an extensive backdrop against which one may measure issues of continuity and progress in the area of Jewish education for women. In so doing, I have covered the education of women over many centuries in seeking to discover where and when women knew how much. A number of works have dealt with the history of Jewish education, but very few pages in those works have been devoted to the education of women. Occasionally one finds reference to the topic, and, albeit rarely, a monograph is indeed dedicated to this subject; yet, overall, the picture remains sparse and incomplete. The result is that the forces that have shaped the education of Jewish women have never been adequately described, analyzed, and interpreted. This work is dedicated to that task. It is predicated upon the axiom that the best view of the topic of the history and philosophy of traditional Jewish education for women is that of the Orthodox female viewer herself. The guesswork about which tensions are at play in the subjects of that study can be somewhat eliminated by the filter of a "fellow sister" of these subjects in interpreting the data to get at "the inside story."

To speak knowledgeably on the topic of religious education for Jewish women, we must first engage in discussion regarding the philosophy and content of Jewish education in general. It is a commonplace that a philosophy of education is founded on a philosophy of life.[1] Consequently, an under-

---

1. See, for example, Chapter 24, "Philosophy of Education," in John Dewey, *Democracy and Education* (New York: Macmillan, 1916), pp. 321–332.

standing of Jewish educational philosophy and content must be prefaced by an acquaintance with the basic principles of the Jewish religion, as well as with its sacred literature and legal (halakhic) structure, which together constitute the cornerstone of religious education and circumscribe life within Orthodox Judaism.[2]

JUDAISM DEFINED

Judaism itself has two distinct and equally legitimate meanings. Sometimes it denotes a full civilization: "the total actualities, past and present, of the historic group of human beings known as the Jewish people."[3] In this sense, it embraces the history, culture, language, land, religion, and social institutions of the Jewish people. Equally, Judaism may stand for only the religious aspect of that civilization. In that significance, Judaism may be conceived of as a religion that seeks to teach the proper relationship between person and God, and between person and person. In truth, both of these elements are intertwined and woven together, "animated by a common spirit reaching into and penetrating one another, no more to be isolated than the parts of a body."[4] Nevertheless, it is in the latter sense that I shall use the term "Judaism" in this work, as our topic focuses on religious education.

Judaism is based on theological and moral concepts, which are expressed in the daily performance of commandments (mitzvot, mitzvah in singular). As Samuel Belkin, noted rabbi and scholar and past president of Yeshiva University, says:

> Judaism was never overly concerned with doctrine. It desired rather to evolve a
> corpus of practices, a code of religious acts, which would establish a mode of

---

2. The term "Orthodoxy" was first coined early in the nineteenth century. With the beginning of the Reform movement it became necessary to find a distinctive name for the main body of Judaism, which advocated the status quo in Jewish tradition and observance and which resisted the attempts of the Reformers to institute changes and of the nonreligious elements to formulate a secular theory of Judaism. The Reformers originally employed the name "Orthodox" in a derogatory sense to designate the traditionalists, yet it stuck and in fact was adopted by the latter group. See David Rudavsky, *Modern Jewish Religious Movements* (New York: Behrman House, 1967, 1979), p. 109.

3. Milton Steinberg, *Basic Judaism* (New York: Harcourt Brace Jovanovich, 1947), p. 3.

4. Ibid., p. 4. For a philosophical analysis of how national identity and religious belief merge within Judaism see "Religion and Nation," in Isaac Breuer, *Concepts of Judaism* (Jerusalem: Israel Universities Press, 1974), pp. 29–36. See also Benjamin Hecht, "Crisis in Jewish Identity," Parts I–IV, *Nishma* 4–7 (April 1988–April 1990).

religious living. True, these acts and practices stem from basic theological and moral concepts, but most significantly, these theological theories of Judaism always remain invisible, apprehensible only through the religious practices to which they gave birth. . . . In Judaism, articles of faith and religious theories cannot be divorced from particular practices . . . the theology of Judaism is contained largely in the *Halakhah*–in the Jewish judicial system–which concerns itself not with theory but primarily with practice. . . .[5]

Unlike those religions that consider faith as the primary goal and the key achievement, Judaism deems the act of faith as only a first step, a foundation for the call to action. The essential response of a Jew is not simply to believe, not even simply to feel the spirit, but rather to meet the demands of the *mitzvot*, the commandments, "accepting that faith is a necessary step for meeting the true objective defined in action."[6]

BASIC THEOLOGICAL PREMISES

Orthodox Jews believe in the existence of God. For them God is the creator of the world who revealed the Torah to Israel as their covenantal bond with Him. On this basis God bestows His providence upon His people. As Hayim Donin, popular expositor of Jewish law states: "In some spiritual fashion God communicated His Will and His commandments to the creature whom He endowed with free will, but whom He called to be His obedient servant."[7] Orthodox Judaism accepts that God revealed Himself to the entire Israelite nation at Mount Sinai. As well, they maintain that there were subsequent revelations to the Prophets of Israel. To quote the twelveth-century philosopher and theologian Maimonides (1135–1204): "Not because of the signs that Moses performed did Israel believe in Moses . . . but at the Revelation on Mount Sinai, when our own eyes, and not a stranger's saw; and when our own ears, and not any one else's heard. . . . Thus, they to whom Moses was

---

5. Samuel Belkin, *In His Image* (New York: Abelard-Scheiner, 1966), pp. 15–16. The emphasis that Judaism places on duties and conduct rather than creed prompted another leader of traditional Judaism in America to declare: "[Traditional] Judaism has never been concerned about shadings in belief. It has found room for every type of Jew from the most rationalistic to the most mystical" (David de Sola Pool, "Judaism in the Synagogue," in *The American Jew*, ed. Oscar Janowsky [New York: Harper & Row, 1972], p. 35).

6. Benjamin Hecht, "Crisis in Jewish Identity," Part III, *Nishma* 6 (June 1989): 2. For an understanding of the role that faith and dogma play within Judaism, see J. David Bleich, *With Perfect Faith: The Foundations of Jewish Belief* (New York: Ktav, 1983).

7. Hayim Donin, *To Be a Jew* (New York: Basic Books 1972), p. 24.

sent were the attestors to his prophecy. . . .[8]

Says Leo Jung, prolific German and American rabbi and philosopher: "The one theoretical, metaphysical basis of Jewish life is the faith in revelation, the divine origin of the Torah. . . . And even this is not a dogma in the usual sense of the word, because its theoretical acceptance, not reinforced by a life in accordance with the Torah, has no saving power in Judaism."[9] Hence, the foundation of Jewish Law lies in the faith that the Torah, which is its basis, is the word of God. Yet, for the duties that follow from the Sinaitic Covenant to be binding, the consent of the people was regarded as an essential prerequisite.[10] As Zev Falk points out:

> The revelation at Mount Sinai, though originating from the transcendent sphere, has no meaning without appeal to man. If therefore, man thinks in anthropocentric and rational categories, there must be some link between this form of thinking and its divine counterpart. There could be no message from God to man without an effective axis of communication.[11]

The Torah has ultimate significance to Orthodox Jews because they see it as a record of God's reaching out to people. The Torah is viewed by the traditional Jew as a record not of human spiritual genius but of God's Will communicated to mortal and finite people.

THE TORAH

What is commonly understood by the term Torah? The word itself is a Hebrew noun derived from the verb that means "to guide" or "to teach"; hence Torah is unified in both meaning and function, both signifying and acting as an instructional model. Orthodox Jews use the term Torah in a variety of ways. In its restricted use, Torah refers to the Five Books of Moses,

---

8. Maimonides, *Mishneh Torah, Hilkhot Yesodei Hatorah* (Fundamentals of the Torah) 8:1

9. "Major Aspects of Judaism," in *Judaism in a Changing World*, ed. Leo Jung (New York: Holt-Rinehart, 1954), pp. 3–4.

10. *Shabbat* 88a.

11. Zev Falk, *Law and Religion* (Jerusalem: Mesharim, 1981), p. 47. There are various philosophical understandings regarding the nature of the relationship between God and the Jews at Sinai. They are beyond the scope of this work; suffice it here to say that rather than simply commanding the Jews at Sinai to follow the dictates of the Torah, God wished an acceptance of the Torah by the people. See further Joseph Judah Bloch, *Shi'urei Da'at* (Bnei Brak: Nezach, n.d.), vol. 3, pp. 166f; Abraham Fishelis, *Kol Ram* (New York: Moriah, 1969), vol. 3, p. 373, and Abraham Besdin, *Reflections of the Rav* (Hoboken, NJ: Ktav, 1992), vol. 1, pp. 89–98. See also Benjamin Hecht, *Study Materials on Kabbalat Ha-Torah* (Toronto and New York: Nishma, 1991).

believed to have been written down by Moses under divine prophecy during the forty-year period after the exodus of the Jews from Egypt. The Five Books of Moses, along with the entirety of Hebrew Scriptures, is also referred to as *Torah Shebikhtav*, or the Written Torah. In a broader sense, the whole body of Jewish law and learning may be encompassed by the term "Torah." The Torah, particularly in its narrower connotation, is in a sense the constitution of the Jewish people. Yet this constitution was promulgated not by people but by God. Hence it is viewed as absolute in its scriptural form and cannot be altered, for "I am the Lord, I change not" (Malakhi 3:6). But it may be subject to further elucidation through human analysis. The study of Jewish texts entails interpreting and expounding this constitution as diligently as scientists study natural phenomena, testing hypotheses and advancing knowledge.

In addition to the Pentateuch (the Five Books of Moses), the books of the Hebrew Bible also consist of the Prophets and the Hagiographia, or Sacred Writings (e.g., the Psalms). Written over a period of many centuries, these books convey the teachings of the prophets in the context of the Jews' history over a period of about seven hundred years following their entrance into the Land of Israel under the leadership of Joshua following Moses' death. They tell of the prophets' vision of God and of their insistent and adamant denunciation of corruption in the moral, ethical, and social domains; of their ongoing struggles to promote greater allegiance among the people to God's teachings; and of their struggles against the many false prophets and priests, who so often misled the people and turned them away from their ancestral practices. The Five Books of Moses, the Prophets, and the Writings are together referred to by Jews as the *Tanakh* and by non-Jews as the Old Testament—but, to Jews, have always constituted the *only* testament.

By Torah, traditional Jews also mean the Oral Torah, or *Torah Shebe'al Peh*, "which Moses received at Sinai and transmitted to Joshua and Joshua to the Elders and the Elders to the Prophets and the Prophets to the People of the Great Assembly"[12] and so on through the generations. Orthodox Jews also have regarded much of the substance of the Oral Law to have been implied in the biblical revelation from the outset, and it was held that they could still be reconstructed from the biblical text by an ingenious method of hermeneutical reinterpretation.[13] Thus the Oral Law is considered to be as equally valid and significant as the Written Torah.[14]

---

12. *Mishnah Avot* 1:1.

13. For a basic outline of this chain of tradition and the hermeneutical methods of interpretation used by the rabbis, see Salo Baron and Joseph Blau, *Judaism: Postbiblical and Talmudic Period* (Indianapolis: Bobbs-Merrill, 1954), pp. 102–108. See also Adin Steinsaltz, *The Talmud: The Steinsaltz Edition, A Reference Guide* (New York: Random House, 1989), pp. 147–154.

14. For an in-depth analysis of the concept of *Torah Shebe'al Peh*, its nature, manner of transmission, etc., see Benjamin Hecht, "Torah Shebe'al Peh," *Nishma* 6 (Fall 1989).

The Oral Torah includes traditional laws not found in Scriptures, the finer points of the commandments, the details of the general principles contained in the Scriptures, and the ways by which the commandments were to be applied. For example, the Torah forbids "work" on the Sabbath. What constitutes "work"? How shall "work" be defined for purposes of the Sabbath? Except for several references to such tasks as gathering wood, kindling fire, cooking, and baking, the Written Torah does not say. The Oral Torah does. Thus, as Chaim Schimmel states in *The Oral Law*,

> If one were to search out a people who follow literally the Bible's behest, one might be led to [the Samaritans or the Karaites] but never to the Jewish people. They do not now follow the literal word of the Bible, nor have they ever done so. They have been fashioned and ruled by the verbal interpretation of the written word, more particularly by the "Torah," which embraces both the written and the oral law.[15]

Traditional Jews claim that the Oral Tradition was passed down through the generations. Discussions surrounding the Oral Law have been recorded from the third century until today. The first written records of rabbinic *Halakhah*,[16] as Jewish law is called, are found in the *Mishnah* (lit., repeat or study), which seems to date from the turn of the second-century C.E. The *Mishnah* in turn became the cornerstone for the *Gemara* (lit., tradition; completed c. 500 C.E.). The *Gemara* consists of scriptural exegesis, traditional lore, and legal debates conducted by various sages in commenting on and elucidating the laws of the *Mishnah*. *Mishnah* and *Gemara* together make up the Talmud (lit., study, learning).[17]

It should be noted that a certain portion of the Talmud deals not with *Halakhah*, that is, problems of law and legal norms, but with the area known as *Aggadah* (lit., sayings). It includes biblical homiletics and exegesis (referred to as *Midrash*), discussions of theology and ethics, stories and parables, historical descriptions, and practical advice.[18] To paraphrase Gerson Cohen, Jewish

---

15. Chaim Schimmel, *The Oral Law* (Jerusalem and New York: Feldheim, 1978), p. 19.

16. The term *Halakhah* is derived from the Hebrew root word *halakh*, meaning "to go," "to walk," for the *Halakhah* delineates the path for the Jew to follow. It is often used in a more specialized sense, "that which goes from the past to the future"—tradition.

17. There are two Talmuds: the Jerusalem Talmud, composed primarily of the teachings of the Palestinian sages and edited by a number of scholars in Tiberias and Caesarea around 400 C.E., and the more influential Babylonian Talmud, which contains the teachings of the sages of Babylonia, edited by Rabbi Ashi and his disciples in Sura around 500 C.E..

18. For a general outline of the main aspects of *Aggadah* see Zevi Hersh Chajes, *The*

historian and scholar, "If law was the heart and body of Judaism, *Aggadah* was its lifeblood and marrow."[19]

A renowned talmudic scholar, Adin Steinsaltz, describes the Talmud's impact on the Jewish people as "immeasurable." He writes as follows:

> Throughout the generations, Jewish education demanded considerable knowledge of the Talmud, which functioned as the basic text of study. . . . Indeed, much of post-talmudic Jewish literature consists of commentaries, reworkings, and new presentations of the Talmud. Even those areas that were not directly related to the Talmud drew upon it and were sustained by it, and there is hardly a work in any area of Judaism that does not relate to it.[20]

The Torah, whether written (the Bible) or oral (the Talmud), is the teaching that directs a person how to live. Although it speaks primarily to Israel, it also has directives for all people. It is concerned with every aspect of human life. Ritual laws, generally thought of as religious observances, are only part of the total complex of commandments. Ceremonies and rituals are important to traditional Jews because they help them lead a godly life. In the words of American Jewish educator and professor David Rudavsky, "They are symbols intended to alert the Jew to his religious obligations."[21] Thus, for example, many Jews affix the *mezuzah*[22] to the doorpost of the Jewish home as a reminder to all, as they enter and leave, of their sacred duty to God and to fellow-persons.

Orthodox Jews practice their faith in order to perfect their human relationships and society. Hence, in addition to the ritual laws, the commandments of the Torah also cover the entire range of human and social behavior, whether in business, family, or social relationships. The Torah aims at defining behaviors proper to each of life's circumstances in accordance with its concepts of both justice and mercy in its concern to establish civil and criminal codes of law. Even the nonlegal and nonstatutory sections (the *Aggadah*) of Torah have exerted much influence in these definitions. For an observant Jew, Judaism

---

Student's Guide Through the Talmud (New York: Philipp Feldheim, 1960), pp. 139f. For examples of the rich religious and ethical content of some of these nonlegal discourses, the reader may wish to read five midrashic excerpts in Salo Baron and Joseph Blau, *Judaism: Postbiblical and Talmudic Period,* pp. 120–131, 201–208.

19. Gerson Cohen, "The Rabbinic Heritage," in *Great Ages and Ideas of the Jewish People,* ed. Leo W. Schwarz (New York: Random House, 1956), p. 180.

20. Adin Steinsaltz, *The Strife of the Spirit* (Northvale, NJ: Jason Aronson, 1988), p. 82.

21. Rudansky, *Modern Jewish Religious Movements,* p. 100.

22. A *mezuzah* is a parchment, generally placed in a small wooden or metal case, upon which is written the quintessential prayer of a Jew: "Hear, O Israel! The Lord our God, the Lord is One" (Deuteronomy 6:4).

makes little distinction between the secular and the sacred, for every phase of human activity is to be hallowed. As Steinsaltz remarks, "Rather than constituting itself an ideal for the monastic life, say, or a guide for any other sort of separation from the reality of the world, Torah works in precisely the opposite fashion, introducing more content and meaning into the trivial details of the life of the world."[23] Similarly, Falk states, "Judaism, as a system of lifestyle, regulates most of a person's behavior. It regards every single act as meaningful to the spiritual condition of man."[24] Thus, for example, the physical act of eating is sanctified by a benediction; the table becomes a consecrated altar of God when an ordinary meal is accompanied by a discussion of sacred matters. Hence, Judaism is closely identified and integrated with life by means of its laws and precepts. As summed up by Rabbi Samson Raphael Hirsch, foremost exponent of Orthodoxy in nineteenth-century Germany: "In Israel [the Jewish people], religion is not only an addition to life, or a part of life, but it is life itself."[25]

POST-TALMUDIC LITERATURE AND THE HALAKHIC (JEWISH JUDICIAL) SYSTEM

After the Talmud was completed, matters frequently arose over the centuries about which the *Halakhah* – the Jewish law – was inconclusive or unclear or about which no legal precedent existed. The "responsa," or formal answers of the many rabbis and scholars through the generations, up to and including the present time, as well as the many post-talmudic works, were collected and circulated and have become part of the vast array of legal and religious works of Judaism. These applications are an integral part of the entire body of religious jurisprudence. The rabbis understood their authority to process Jewish law in terms of Deuteronomy 17:10–11: "And you shall observe and do according to all that they shall teach you. According to the law which they shall teach you and according to the judgement which they shall tell you, you shall do."[26]

Although the words of the Torah are seen as immutable, the application of its many laws and regulations is subject to the decision-making processes of rabbinic authorities. As Yeshiva University professor of Jewish law David Bleich states, "Once revealed, the Torah does not remain in the heavenly domain. Man is charged with interpretation of the text, resolution of doubts,

23. Adin Steinsaltz, *The Thirteen Petalled Rose* (New York: Basic Books, 1980), pp. 94–95.

24. Falk, *Law and Religion*, p. 215.

25. Samson Raphael Hirsch, *Horeb: A Philosophy of Jewish Laws and Observances*, trans. Dayan I. Grunfeld (New York, London, and Jerusalem: Soncino Press, 1962), p. 571.

26. See *Berakhot* 19b.

and application of the provisions of its law to novel situations."[27] Thus the
Torah is and always has been a living law, constantly applied by a living
people to real conditions that were often changing. The duly ordained
rabbinic authorities had the legislative right to enact positive[28] and restrictive

---

27. David Bleich, *Contemporary Halakhic Problems* (New York: Ktav, 1977), p. xiv.
The *Gemara* (*Bava Metzia* 59b) presents a vivid illustration of the idiom "*lo ba-shamayim
hi*" ("The Torah is not in heaven," Deuteronomy 17:10-11) in an aggadic story
concerning a dispute between Rabbi Eliezer and the talmudic sages regarding a point of
ritual law. Rabbi Eliezer refused to be overridden by the view of the majority. After
failing to convince the sages through rational arguments, R. Eliezer then invoked
supernatural miracles to convince his colleagues that he was right:

"On that day Rabbi Eliezer brought forward every imaginable argument, but they
did not accept them. Said he to them: 'If the law is as I say, let this carob tree prove it!'
Thereupon the carob tree was torn a hundred cubits out of its place. . . . 'No proof can
be brought from a carob tree,' they retorted. Again he said to them: 'If the law is as I say,
let the stream of water prove it!' Whereupon the stream of water flowed backward.
'No proof can be brought from a stream of water,' they rejoined. Again he argued: 'If
the law is as I say, let the walls of the schoolhouse prove it.' Whereupon the walls
inclined to fall. But Rabbi Joshua rebuked them, saying: 'When scholars are engaged in
a *halakhic* dispute, what have you to interfere?' Hence they did not fall in honor of
Rabbi Eliezer; and they are still standing thus inclined" (*Bava Metzia* 59b).

When Rabbi Eliezer saw that his colleagues were not moved to accept his position
as a result of the miraculous "hints" of divine support, he appealed directly to God to
confirm his view: "Again he said to them: 'If the law is as I say, let it be proved from
heaven!' Whereupon a heavenly voice cried out: 'Why do you dispute with Rabbi
Eliezer, seeing that in all matters the law is as he says!' But Rabbi Joshua arose and
exclaimed: 'It is not in heaven' [Deuteronomy 30:12]. What did he mean by this? Said
Rabbi Jeremiah: 'That the Torah had already been given at Mount Sinai; we pay no
attention to a heavenly voice, because Thou has long since written in the Torah at
Mount Sinai, "After the majority must one incline" ' [Exodus 23:2]. Rabbi Nathan met
[the prophet] Elijah and asked him: 'What did the Holy one, blessed be He, do at that
moment?' He replied: 'He laughed saying: "My children have defeated Me, My
children have defeated Me" ' (ibid.)."

This story teaches us that the interpretation of the *Halakhah* has been entrusted to
the human intellect, and, accordingly, human intellect must proceed in its own
dispassionate manner, uninfluenced by supernatural phenomena. As philosopher
David Hartman comments, "Allowing for such supernatural intrusions would un-
dermine the central role of study and rational debate in the development and elaboration of the law. . . . One may understand this text in the light of the covenantal
emphasis on human responsibility." (See David Hartman, *A Living Covenant: The
Innovative Spirit in Traditional Judaism* [New York: Free Press, 1985], p. 33. The English
translation of this *aggadah* is taken from Hartman.)

28. The positive ordinances were intended to improve and advance one of the
following: (1) religion, (2) the family, (3) national consciousness, and (4) society. (See
Schimmel, *The Oral Law*, pp. 83-84.) As an example, early German rabbis forbade the
practice of polygamy even though it had not been prohibited by the Written or Oral
Law. [This decree is usually attributed to Rabbi Gershom ben Judah of Mayence (c.

ordinances.[29] Moreover, they were also given the right to judiciously explore the law and to apply it innovatively as the need arose.[30] Legitimacy is accorded to those rules that are developed in accordance with accepted procedures.[31] There are also guidelines within the Oral Tradition regarding qualifications and eligibility for religious leadership. As Donin points out, "All different religious decisions by authoritative, ordained scholars must be capable of justification and defense under the halakhic rules of interpretation. It must be based on sound religious scholarship."[32]

Rabbi Walter Wurzberger, American Jewish thinker and writer, elaborates:

> Even though, with the disappearance of a supreme religious authority, it was inevitable that there would develop divisions of opinions concerning matters of religious observance, it must be realized that these differences were always within the framework of commonly shared assumptions regarding the divine authority of the Torah. Because there existed a common universe of discourse it was possible to speak of halakhic disagreement.[33]

940–1028), but see Jeremy Cohen, *"Be Fertile and Increase, Fill the Earth and Master It": The Ancient and Medieval Career of a Biblical Text* (Ithaca and London: Cornell University Press, 1990), p. 177 and n. 36.] In fact, a number of such ordinances laid particular emphasis on the welfare of women; they were enacted to protect the interests of young girls and to secure the position of married women. (See for example, *Ketubot* 51a.)

29. Negative ordinances were generally intended to guard against the transgression of a *mitzvah*. Thus, for example, although biblically there is no prohibition of mixing milk and chicken, treating chicken as meat, in regard to these laws, was legislated by the Rabbis in an attempt to guard against the accidental mixing of meat and milk.

30. An example of such innovation is the *Prozbul* enacted by Hillel (d. 10 C.E.). According to *Halakhah*, the laws of *Shemitah* (the seventh year of the halakhic agricultural cycle) provide that all debts are to be released or remitted in this year (Deuteronomy 15:1–3). In view of this law, creditors were becoming reluctant to lend money and face the possibility of loss through the *Shemitah* mechanism. To avoid the financial hardship arising from the lack of credit, Hillel introduced a legal device, the *Prozbul*, to circumvent the law of release.

According to the laws of *Shemitah*, a debt over which a Jewish court was given custody was not subject to release. By so instructing the populace to join the courts into the loan procedure through the *Prozubul*, Hillel presented an innovative, yet halakhically acceptable, method of dealing with the problem of lack of credit (*Mishnah Shvi'it* 10:3). For a further discussion of the permissibility of Hillel's innovation, see *Gittin* 36a. See especially Tosafot ad loc. See further Schimmel, *The Oral Law*, pp. 127–128.

31. Schimmel's book, *The Oral Law*, provides excellent insight into the workings of Jewish law; how the *Halakhah* views its own origin and how it evolved in Rabbinic times; how the scholars created and developed the Law and how they applied it in changing circumstances. It also explains the procedures utilized by the sages in interpreting the law.

32. Donin, *To Be a Jew*, p. 32

33. Walter S. Wurzberger, "Plural Models and the Authority of *Halakhah*," *Judaism* 20:4 (Fall 1971): 393.

The "common universe of discourse," as Wurzberger describes it, is a unique system of action determination, abounding and delighting in fine dialectic argumentation in which many positions are advanced. Unlike most systems of moral direction, however, the discussion does not focus on value issues but rather on textual analysis and the cutting investigation of the word. The Divine Will is not revealed in values that are then placed into action through *mitzvot*, but rather, God's Will is directly expressed in the words of the command itself. Clarification of His Will, therefore, rests in attempting to first fully and completely understand these words of action. Throughout the centuries, the process of learning placed the word, from within both the Written and Oral traditions, under the microscope, subject to the most piercing of minds, in the attempt to clarify God's direction. The myriad of viewpoints that could be expressed through this concentration and exploration of detail was not considered a weakness in the transmission; rather, it further revealed the Divine Wisdom that could express such broad complexity of thought within the limits of the finite word.[34]

In the realm of theory the various positions are correct; in matters of practice, in terms of *psak Halakhah*, or definitive halakhic ruling, there must be a means of deciding between the conflicting views; otherwise legal anarchy would result. To this end, *Halakhah*, as a legal system, includes criteria of *psak* – criteria of judicial determination. Bleich comments, "While these may produce decisions which are of absolute binding authority the view set aside is not of undiminished importance insofar as the study and pursuit of Torah [are] concerned. . . . Definitive *'psak Halakhah'* is a matter of practical necessity, but not a reflection upon transcendental validity."[35] The criteria of *psak*, however, fall within the process of all learning. It is a determination made not through value analysis but through the text.[36]

It must be noted that sound religious scholarship and acceptance of the

34. See Michael Rosensweig, "Personal Initiative and Creativity in Avodat Hashem," *The Torah U-Madda Journal* 1 (1989): 72–90.

35. Bleich, *Contemporary Halakhic Problems*, p. xv.

36. This is a most significant point, which may be illustrated by the following example. In the realm of abortion, *Halakhah* has a spectrum of opinions. We would expect the arguments in support of the variant opinions to mirror the arguments in contemporary society between pro-life and pro-choice adherents. A review of the halakhic literature, however, shows that these value arguments are not the consideration. Rather, the various opinions revolve around the textual analysis of pertinent biblical and talmudic passages, with a focus on the clarification of the legal definitions. For elaboration, see Bleich, *Contemporary Halakhic Problems*, pp. 325–371, and Basil F. Herring, *Jewish Ethics and Halakhah for Our Time* (New York: Ktav and Yeshiva University Press, 1984), pp. 25–45. While a personal value may be instrumental in motivating someone to investigate a halakhic issue, "the actual determination of a *halakhah* must be approached objectively based on the sources." See Benjamin Hecht, "Emotional Identity and Halakhah," *Nishma* Update (June 1991).

authority of Torah and the *Halakhah* are not the sole qualifications of eligibility for religious leadership. Exemplary character and concern for social
justice are necessary preconditions as well. Schimmel,[37] in describing the
greatness of the interpreters of tradition, remarks that their greatness did not
lie in any particular office or appointment they occupied or held, nor did it rest
entirely on intellectual superiority or erudition. Nobility of character was of
the essence. To paraphrase the Talmud: "If the teacher is like an angel of God,
seek Torah from that person, and if not, do not seek Torah from that
person."[38] Ultimately, in Judaism it is recognition by the halakhic population
at large of the "holder of authority" that is, according to Falk, the essence of
authority.[39] If the people were to lose trust in the holder of authority, that
leader's authority would come to an end.

In summation, traditional Jews accept the authority of *Halakhah*, recog-
nizing that divine revelation forms the basis for the life pattern of *Halakhah* as
it is applied to the changing conditions of each land and age. What makes this
difficult for the modern mind to accept, explains Wurzberger, "is the conviction that religious behavior is utterly worthless unless it stems from a personal
faith commitment. Hence we would like to think that *Halakhah* should be
viable enough to accommodate a variety of religious needs and experiences."
But, he continues, "we fail to take account of the fact that if we view *Halakhah*
purely as the concretization of a personal faith we simply remake it in our
own image." To reduce *Halakhah* to a purely subjective domain would be a
flagrant misreading of the essential character of halakhic Judaism, which
insists that the "subjectivity of a personal faith operates in dialectical tension
with objectively binding halakhic norms."[40]

For a final insight into the workings of Jewish Law and elaborating on
Wurzberger's words, some mention of the writings of the renowned contemporary Jewish philosopher Rabbi Joseph Ber Soloveitchik on this subject may
be relevant:

> Because even God has renounced authority in the domain of halakhic interpre-
> tation, the halakhic Jew takes on full responsibility for the elaboration and
> progressive refinement of these laws. The halakhic Jew, with this vote of
> confidence, is therefore able to rise above the anxiety, helplessness, and awe of
> human existence by setting standards and norms to otherwise unpredictable
> religious feelings. Halakhah thus becomes the objectification of religion into
> clearly defined principles and into a fixed pattern of lawfulness.[41]

---

37. Schimmel, *The Oral Law*, pp. 162–163.
38. *Haggigah* 15b.
39. Paraphrasing Falk, *Law and Religion*, p. 143.
40. Wurzberger, "Plural Models and the Authority of the *Halakhah*," p. 392.
41. This is actually a paraphrase from an article entitled "The Lonely Man of Faith

PHILOSOPHY OF JEWISH EDUCATION

We have delved briefly into some basic aspects of Orthodox Judaism: its
theological principles, its literature, and its judicial system. With that as a
background we can now turn to the educational aspects of the philosophy of
Judaism. Although the previous discussion carried educational implications, it
is not sufficient to let the matter rest there. A complete appreciation of Jewish
education requires greater scrutiny into its pedagogical philosophy, characteristics, and requirements.

The highest Jewish aim, wrote first-century Jewish historian Flavius Josephus, is "to educate our children well."[42] Indeed, that aim has been in the
forefront of Jewish civilization from the earliest days of nationhood until the
present day. Not unlike members of a modern democratic society, ancient
Jews had already realized the value of education in the preservation and
perpetuation of their institutions. Indeed, education historians Julius Maller
and Robert Ulich claim that the survival of Jews and Judaism is in large
measure due to the continuous emphasis, throughout Jewish history, on the
transmission of ideas and practices from one generation to another.[43]

Thus if Judaism were to be described as a circumference, then education
would be its pivot.[44] Jewish education has comprised far more than the
teaching and learning of religious law, custom, and ritual. It has been the
doctrine of a people – ethnic as well as religious – and a way of life that sought
to dictate the behavior of the Jew in every instance. Hence, says education
historian Nathan Drazin, "Jewish education was never something extraneous
to life or merely an instrument that served to prepare for life and that later
could be discarded when its utility was exhausted. Jewish education was
rather synonymous with life. It unfolded life, giving it direction and
meaning."[45] For that reason, Torah has often been described as an *Eitz Hayim*

Confronts the *Ish Ha-Halakhah*," *Tradition* 16:2 (Summer 1976): 74–75, in which the
author, M. Sosevsky, synthesizes and summarizes Rabbi Soloveitchik's writings: "*Ish
Ha-Halakhah*," *Talpiot* (New York) 1:3–4 (1944), translated into English by Lawrence
Kaplan, *Halakhic Man* (Philadelphia: Jewish Publication Society of America, 1983);
"Confrontation," *Tradition* 6:2 (Spring 1964): 5–29; and "The Lonely Man of Faith,"
Tradition 7:2 (Summer 1965): 5–67.

42. Flavius Josephus, *Against Apion* 2, 18, trans. H. St. J. Thackeray (Cambridge,
MA: Harvard University Press, 1926).

43. Julius B. Maller, "The Role of Education in Jewish History," in *The Jews: Their
History, Culture, and Religion*, ed. Louis Finkelstein (Philadelphia: Jewish Publication
Society of America, 1949), p. 896; Robert Ulich, *Three Thousand Years of Educational
Wisdom* (Cambridge, MA.: Harvard University Press, 1954), p. 644.

44. See further, Menachem Lubinsky, "Jewish Education in the 80s," *Religious
Education* 75:6 (Nov.–Dec. 1980): 654.

45. Nathan Drazin, *History of Jewish Education from 515 B.C.E. to 22 C.E.* (Baltimore:

("tree of life"),[46] that is, a teaching for life. Embodied in that concept is the insistence that the Torah is not to be an esoteric pursuit, detached from life and indifferent to its problems. On the contrary, its significance and value lie, in part, in its contribution to solving vital problems and enhancing human well-being.

Not only was education synonymous with life; it was also something that was obligatory. It stemmed from the Torah law "And you shall teach them to your children," which appears in the Pentateuch, with variation, in several places.[47] Ulich, speaking about the Jewish religion, says, "In this kind of religion in which the practical and the theoretical elements were so closely fused with each other, instruction was not, as is often with us, a matter of individual promotion, but a sacred duty."[48]

It is in the fulfillment of this sacred duty that we encounter another concept of Jewish education, that of *Torah Lishmah*, the study of Torah for its own sake. In this view, study is regarded also as an end, an act in its own right, and not only a means, a guide to knowledge of the commandments.[49] This aspect of Jewish education is to be the fulfillment of the directive "You shall meditate on it day and night."[50] Torah study is actually regarded by some as worthier than observance of the *mitzvot* (commandments) in that the first, aside from its intrinsic worth, leads to the second by its very nature.[51] The talmudic sages, in what was apparently designed to serve as a model for education in all generations, defined the ideal person as one who studies the Bible and the *Mishnah*, attends upon scholars, is honest in business, and speaks gently to people.[52] There are two types of Torah scholars that have evolved in modern times. The first is the rabbi who deals with the practical application of *Halakhah* to guide the community in accordance with the principles and laws found in traditional sources. The second is the scholar who elucidates the problematics of traditional texts. The latter is described by Adin Steinsaltz:

> Study of Torah undoubtedly serves numerous practical purposes, but these are not the crucial objectives. Study is not geared to the degree of importance or the

Johns Hopkins University Press, 1940), p. 12.

46. See Proverbs 3:18.

47. Deuteronomy 7:6, 11:19, 31:12.

48. Robert Ulich, *Three Thousand Years of Educational Wisdom*, p. 644.

49. The exact definition of the word *lishmah* is the subject of much discussion and debate. For a nuanced presentation, see Norman Lamm, *Torah Lishma: Torah for Torah's Sake in the Works of Rabbi Hayim of Volozhin and His Contemporaries* (Hoboken, NJ: Ktav, 1989).

50. Joshua 1:8.

51. *Kiddushin* 40b.

52. *Yoma* 86a.

practical potential of the problems discussed. Its main aim is learning itself. Likewise, knowledge of Torah is not an aid to observance of law but an end in itself. This does not mean that the Talmud is not concerned with the values contained in the material studied. On the contrary, it is stated emphatically that he who studies Torah and does not observe what he studies would better never have been born. A true scholar serves as a living example by his way of life and conduct. But this is part of the general outlook of the Talmud; for the student poring over the text, study has no other end but knowledge. Every subject pertaining to Torah, or to life as related to Torah, is worthy of consideration and analysis, and an attempt is always made to delve into the heart of the matter. In the course of study, the question of whether these analyses are of practical use is never raised. We often encounter in the Talmud protracted and vehement debates on various problems that try to examine the structure of the method and to elucidate the conclusions deriving from it. The scholars invested all this effort despite the fact that they knew the source itself had been rejected and was of no legislative significance. This approach also explains why we find debates on problems that were relevant in the distant past and were unlikely ever to arise again. . . . It sometimes occurs, of course, that problems or debates once thought impractical or irrelevant gain practical significance in some later age. This is a familiar phenomenon in the sphere of pure science. But this development is of little consequence to the talmudic student, as, from the onset, his sole objective has been to solve theoretical problems and to seek the truth.[53]

Joseph Lookstein, American educator and homilist, in outlining the goals for modern Jewish education, lists five common themes regarding education that were present in many periods of Jewish existence.[54] The first is the universality of Jewish education. It was nationalized and made the common property of all Israel, so that it lost its connection with a particular class and became relevant to human life apart from all social restrictions. Aristocrat and commoner, affluent and humble, rich and poor, clergy and layperson, all could enjoy the "inalienable right" and opportunity of education in many, though not all, periods and places of residence in Jewish history. (It remains to be seen whether women enjoyed this right as well. Was it indeed universal?)

Lookstein's second characteristic concerns "maximalism," which is to say that the study of Torah is not limited to prescribed learning hours and formal institutions. Its prescription was said to stem from Joshua 1:8, "And you shall meditate on it by day and by night," and also from Deuteronomy 6:5–9, "And you shall speak of them when you sit in your house and when you

---

53. Adin Steinsaltz, *The Essential Talmud* (New York: Bantam Books, 1976), pp. 5–6.

54. Joseph H. Lookstein, "Goals for Jewish Education," in *Judaism and the Jewish School,* ed. Judah Pilch and Meir Ben-Horin (New York: Bloch, 1966), pp. 214–215. See also Eliezer Ebner, *Elementary Education in Ancient Israel* (New York: Bloch, 1956), pp. 20–24, who writes similarly.

walk by the way and when you lie down and when you rise up." In fact, religious instruction from the Rabbinic period onward was to begin almost with the ability of a child to speak. Halakhic authorities[55] declared that the father should teach the child the verses in Deuteronomy: "Moses charged us in the Torah, as the heritage of the Congregation of Jacob" (33:4), and "Hear, O Israel! The Lord is our God, the Lord is One" (6:4). Torah study was to be considered obligatory until the last breath of life. Maimonides stated, "He is duty bound to study Torah to the day of his death. . . ."[56]

Hence, Simon Greenberg, in "Lifetime Education as Conceived and Practiced in the Jewish Tradition," makes a distinction between education and study.[57] He defines education as the acquiring of knowledge or skills. Once a specific body of knowledge or skills is mastered, one goes on to some new body of knowledge or new skills. Study of Torah as a lifetime preoccupation, however, implies that one never really masters the Torah as a body of knowledge. Greenberg states, "Education implies activity in preparation for the work of life. Study of Torah implies that that is *the* work of life" (cf. Drazin, p. 13). According to talmudic tradition, Rabbi Yochanan Ben Zakkai, the great sage who was chiefly responsible for shaping the Rabbinic tradition after the destruction of the Temple by the Romans in 70 C.E., admonished his pupils, "If you have learned much Torah, claim no special merit for it, for that is the purpose for which you are created."[58]

Lookstein's third theme is religious motivation. For the rabbis, Jews were expected to engage in Jewish study not because of any compulsory requirement that originated in some secular agency but because God willed it. They said that the Torah required it.

The fourth theme of religious education, according to Lookstein, is to inculcate reverence for it. The learned individual and not the wealthy person is to be the aristocrat in Judaism. The teacher and not the professional or businessperson is to occupy the topmost rung of the social ladder. The Talmud goes so far as to state that "one who teaches his friend's child Torah, it is as if he has given birth to the child."[59] The rabbis ordained that when one meets a great scholar, Jewish law requires that a special blessing be made over that person. There is a custom that when a child first starts learning Torah, a drop of honey is placed on the letters so that the child's first impression of

---

55. See, for example, Maimonides, *Mishneh Torah, Hilkhot Talmud Torah* (Laws of Torah Study) 1:6.

56. Ibid., chap. 1. para. 10.

57. Simon Greenberg, "Lifetime Education as Conceived and Practiced in the Jewish Tradition," *Religious Education* 68:3 (May–June 1973): 341.

58. *Avot* 2:8.

59. *Sanhedrin* 19b.

Torah will be sweet. Another custom is to kiss a religious book as one closes it after it is used. And old, withered pages of religious works are not discarded but consigned for burial. This is Jewish education: to revere and respect an ancient heritage through the divine teachings and subsequent interpretation by generations of scholars.

The last theme in Lookstein's schema concerns religious, national, and ethical concepts, the practical consequences of an educated life. Lookstein states, "It was not enough to bring man near to God, nor was it sufficient to bind the Jew faster to his people. It was necessary to mold the Jew into a better person. . . . The corrupt scholar is detested even if he is pitied."[60]

The home was considered the educational foundation for the moral and religious development of the child[61]; thus the first educational environment for a Jew was the family. Indeed, the family was the major educational institution mentioned in the Bible. The rabbinic interpretation of "And you shall teach them diligently to your children"[62] conceived of education as a function to be carried out within the home. It was the family that was responsible for instilling religious and cultural beliefs in the child. Daily activities such as eating and washing were imbued with religious significance. Ceremonies, especially on holidays, were family oriented. Some rituals were designed to reinforce cultural beliefs mythically and symbolically. Children received training in ethical behavior and concern for social justice. Shoshana Matzner-Beckerman states in *The Jewish Child: Halakhic Perspectives*, "The realm of early childhood education has remained in the sphere of the home as the basis for the child's emerging conception of the world around him."[63] From the age of six or seven onward, education was relegated to the school.

In sum, the Jews' enormous devotion to education is due to the fact that they believe themselves to have a subject matter worthy of such devotion. Even today pious Jews see God's love for Israel in the fact that the Jews find themselves in the possession of the Torah, the content of which they cannot conceive as being the product of a finite mind. They find it worthy of a lifetime of study and of endless restudy of texts until they are thoroughly mastered. Greenberg views this as largely due to the character of the texts, which have an intrinsic intellectual and spiritual appeal to all ages and all levels of intellectual attainment.[64] The texts that have attracted study over the ages are the entire Hebrew Scriptures with medieval commentaries, the *Mishnah*,

---

60. Lookstein, "Goals for Jewish Education," p. 215.

61. See chap. 8, "Early Childhood Education," in Shoshana Matzner-Beckerman, *The Jewish Child: Halakhic Perspectives* (New York: Ktav, 1984), for elaboration.

62. Deuteronomy 7:6

63. Matzner-Beckerman, *The Jewish Child: Halakhic Perspectives*, p. 125.

64. Greenberg, "Lifetime Education in the Jewish Tradition," p. 343.

the Talmud, Rabbinic *Midrash*, legal codes, and responsa. William Brickman, in "Education for Eternal Existence: The Philosophy of Jewish Education," emphasizes the motivation for Jewish education as follows:

> The philosophy of Jewish education may be said to be built upon the belief in a personal God, a revealed truth, and the teaching of this truth. By exercising his free will toward the fulfillment of the Divine precepts, each individual, no matter of what group, may attain immortality. The will to do presupposes knowledge of what to do, obtainable only through proper instruction.[65]

Knowledge and action—these are the twin purposes of Jewish education, a system that "has outlasted every other system whatsoever [and that is consequently] . . . the most successful educational experiment ever staged in the history of education."[66]

We have examined the traditional rabbinic view of Torah study by discussing the essential components of that view. In fine, we have looked at rabbinic concepts of divine revelation, human freedom to interpret within the guidelines of the Oral Tradition, and the value of extensive learning for the inculcation of rabbinic truths and values. We have briefly considered the formal requirements of rabbinic leadership, and we have sketched the rabbinic educational ideal. We may now ask, if Jewish education is indeed so fundamental, then what has been its status vis-à-vis women, both in theory and in reality, throughout the generations? The answer to that question forms the inquiry of this work.

---

65. William Brickman, "Education for Eternal Existence: The Philosophy of Jewish Education," in *Judaism and the Jewish School*, ed. Judah Pilch and Meir Ben-Horin (New York: Bloch, 1966), p. 207.

66. Frederick Eby and Charles F. Arrowood, *The History and Philosophy of Education: Ancient and Medieval* (New York: Prentice-Hall, 1940), p. 157.

2

The Role and Status of the Jewish Woman as Viewed in Traditional Judaism

In the previous chapter we have seen the great import which Judaism attributes to religious education and the high esteem in which it is held. Before proceeding to examine religious education as it pertains to the Jewish woman, it would be useful to give brief but serious attention to the role and status of women in Judaism as seen from rabbinic perspectives. In other words, prior to an analysis of the halakhic and extrahalakhic attitudes toward the education of women, progressive trends regarding the general position of women in Judaism will be looked at. Such a survey enables us to appreciate the variations within the minds of modern halakhic decisors. By evaluating the areas in which scholars have projected what appear to be enlightened and unenlightened views of women, we will be able to understand the issue of "how much Torah study for women" with greater clarity. Most important, this chapter will lay the groundwork for determining the flux of opinions which will be discussed throughout this work.

This chapter deals with concern for issues pertaining to women among modern rabbinic thinkers. It will be of interest to examine some views regarding the creation of woman, the purposes of marriage, and the ideal of the Jewish family. Positive apologetic trends from the Middle Ages to the present regarding women's aptitudes will be explored, as will mechanisms for self-fulfillment and personal satisfaction. Finally, issues of some discontent in the social/religious treatment of women today will be raised.

Although no claims can be made in this chapter regarding the comprehensive view of the role and status of women in traditional Judaism,[1] it is important to note here that over the last several centuries, a fair amount of rabbinic speculative and exegetical literature has been predicated on a highly positive image of women in the intellectual and social sphere. Further concern has been raised to translate these positive attitudes into halakhic norms in the educational sphere, as will be demonstrated in the following chapter. In fact, regardless of the perception of women, leading decisors, over the ages, continuously protected the status of women. Jewish law granted increasing protections, safeguards, and expansion of rights to women in response to the changing needs of women over time.[2]

THE CREATION OF MAN AND WOMAN AND THE NEED TO RELATE

Every Sabbath eve, the observant Jewish family recites the last chapter of Proverbs, a tribute to the ideal woman in Judaism. The picture of womanly achievement as depicted in "The Woman of Valor" at the end of the book of

---

1. Eliezer Berkovits, however, has suggested a provocative view of the status of women in *Jewish Women in Time and Torah* (Hoboken, New Jersey: Ktav, 1990). Briefly, Berkovits views the status of women in Jewish tradition as comprising two phases: the Torah-tolerated one and the Torah-guided and Torah-instructed one. On the first and lowest level, he claims, woman is not recognized as possessing her own personality. This nonpersonal stage, essentially determined by the social and economic conditions of an early society, was not much different from what could be observed in the non-Jewish cultures of the time. It was a condition that the Torah tolerated, but was not instituted by Torah teaching and Torah values. The second phase, which Berkovits terms the personal status of the woman, acknowledged the value and dignity of the female personality in a world in which the woman has her own vitally important place because of her own life-related nature. This second phase, contends Berkovits, was taught and demanded by Torah ideals. It even led to halakhic innovations out of concern for the rights and welfare of women.

One may of course argue about the merits of this critical historical scheme (the traditional view would posit that women have consistently been taken seriously, both legally and socially, and that apparent restrictions are in fact a reflection of women's privileged status), but Berkovits's view is in any case reminiscent of Maimonides' historical account of sacrifices in the *Guide of the Perplexed* 3:32 (which Nahmanides in his commentary on Leviticus 1:9 disputes). A comprehensive discussion of the tension between the historical and "metahistorical" strands in Jewish intellectual history would make for a fascinating study.

2. For some examples, see Maimonides, *Mishneh Torah, Hilkhot Ishut* 10:7; 12:2; 16:17; and 20:1.

Proverbs[3] presents us with one model of a praiseworthy woman in Judaism. In commenting on this panegyric to the Jewish woman, the German Bible commentator and philosopher Rabbi Samson Raphael Hirsch (1808–1888) attempts to define the Jewish woman and postulates as follows:

> What is this Jewish woman? She is the trusted and beneficent friend of her husband, whose heart rests securely in hers and finds in her its highest acquisition. She is the independent leader and controller of the house. But she is also more than this. She is not content merely to utilize the earnings of her husband for the good of the household, for the sustenance and comfort of its members. She takes an active part herself, and seeks by her own work to increase the prosperity of the house. Of her own free will she makes herself a partner in her husband's toil and labor. Work is her element, good deeds her joy, wisdom sits on her lips and by word and deed she teaches self sacrifice and love.[4]

Hirsch uses some verses in the Book of Genesis to express his notion of the equality of the Jewish woman. Genesis 1:27 records together the creation of woman and the creation of man in the image of God: "And God created man [the human being] in His image, in the image of God did He create him [the human being], male and female He created them."

Hirsch comments on this verse as follows:

> Though all living creatures were created in two sexes, this fact is stressed only in the case of man in order to state the verity that both sexes, male and female, were created to be equally close to God, and equally in His image. This equality is expressed in a particularly striking manner by the transition from the singular "oto" ["(did He create) him"] to the plural "otam" ["(created He) them"]. The one Adam-creature, made in the image of God, has been created in two sexes which only together can effectuate the concept of "Adam" in its entirety.[5]

Thus, from the outset, the Bible, according to Hirsch's interpretation, gives one of the oldest and finest expressions concerning the female sex. It declares that man and woman are of the same excellence and nobility; God created both man and woman in His own image; and both are invested with the authority to subdue the earth and all its living creatures.[6] In Hirsch's worldview, the equality of man and woman is firmly established.

---

3. Proverbs 31:10–31.

4. Samson Raphael Hirsch, *Judaism Eternal*, vol. 2, trans. Dayan I. Grunfeld (London: Soncino Press, 1960), p. 89.

5. Samson Raphael Hirsch, *Commentary on Genesis* 1:27, vol. 1 of *The Pentateuch: Commentary on the Torah*, trans. Issac Levy (London: Judaica Press, 1989).

6. Genesis 1:28.

Maurice Lamm, in *The Jewish Way in Love and Marriage,*[7] explains that the first chapter in Genesis is the record of physical creation. Adam and Eve were natural beings, akin to the animals that surrounded them. But in the second account of Creation (Genesis 2:21–24), Adam and Eve were endowed with spiritual dimensions. "They rose above the natural environment, had metaphysical yearnings, and could relate to God."[8] In Genesis 1, man and woman were simply *"Ha-Adam"*; in Genesis 2, they were marriage partners. Humanity thus traces its history to the second chapter of Genesis, wherein God provides the motivation for the creation of woman, and therefore the purpose of marriage: *"lo tov heyot ha-Adam levado"* – "It is not good for man to be alone."[9] Umberto Cassuto, Italian historian and biblical and Semitic scholar, states similarly:

> In the first account which belongs to the physical world the text emphasizes the sexual aspect of the relationship of the husband to his wife: "Male and female He created them" (Genesis 1:27); in the second chapter, which belongs to the moral world, the text emphasizes in particular the moral aspect of this relationship, "a help-meet for him" (Genesis 2:18).[10]

Thus, far from being merely an expedient economic institution created by society, marriage in the Jewish perspective makes its appearance within the natural order of creation, not as a law promulgated by Moses nor as a legal sanction, but as a blessing from God. It is seen as such because it enables humanity to overcome loneliness. According to contemporary philosopher Rabbi Joseph Ber Soloveitchik,[11] Genesis 2:18 reads "heyot *ha-Adam levado*" rather than "lihiyot *ha-Adam levado*." This verse does not imply simply that "it is not good for man to be alone," in a physical, utilitarian aloneness, needing assistance. Rather, the verse is to be interpreted as "it is not good for man to be *lonely*." Being "lonely" means spiritual solitude, as one can feel lonely even in a crowd. As Rabbi Soloveitchik states:

> "To be" is a unique in-depth-experience . . . unrelated to any function or performance. "To be" means to be the only one, singular and different, and consequently lonely. For what causes man to be lonely and feel insecure if not

---

7. Maurice Lamm, *The Jewish Way in Love and Marriage* (San Francisco: Harper & Row, 1980), p. 123.

8. Ibid.

9. Genesis 2:18.

10. Umberto Cassuto, *Commentary on Genesis* 2:18, trans. Israel Abrahams (Jerusalem: Magnes Press, Hebrew University, 1961). (The author was a twentieth-century Italian Jewish Bible commentator.)

11. Joseph Ber Soloveitchik, "The Lonely Man of Faith," *Tradition* 7:2 (Summer 1965): 27.

the awareness of his uniqueness and exclusiveness. The "I" is lonely, experiencing ontological incompleteness . . . because there is no one who exists like the "I" and because the modus existentiae of the "I" cannot be repeated, imitated, or experienced by others.[12]

Hirsch carries the theme of *lo tov*, "it is not good" further, suggesting that man's need for woman goes beyond the assuagement of loneliness. She is needed to work with him in accomplishing the human being's ultimate purpose, perfecting the world. In Hirsch's words:

Everything cannot be "good" as long as man is alone. The goal of perfection which the terrestrial world is to attain through man cannot be attained in full as long as man is alone. The completion of good was not man but woman; only woman could bring that to man and to the world. This verity was absorbed so deeply by . . . our Rabbis that they taught us: "Only through his wife can man become truly 'man,' "[13] only husband and wife together can comprise "Adam." The task is too great for either to perform alone and must be shared by another.[14]

And so, in order to effect the full accomplishment of humanity's purpose, God created woman. The woman is to be his *ezer kenegdo*, a "help-meet" opposite him (Genesis 2:18). Hirsch states:

Even a superficial glance at this term suffices to see that it defines the true dignity of women's position. It does not carry any implication of sexual relationship. All it indicates is that woman was placed into the sphere of man's activities. . . ."*Ezer kenegdo*" does not imply that woman is to be subordinate to man; actually, it connotes complete equality between man and woman, on a footing of independent parity. The woman is to stand at man's side *kenegdo*, on the same level, in a parallel position. . . .[15]

---

12. Ibid. Also see classical commentators Moses ben Nahman (Nahmanides), *Commentary on Genesis* 2:18 (Spain, thirteenth century); Bahya ben Asher, *Midrash Rabbenu Bahya* (New York: Keter, 1945) on Genesis 2:18 (Spain, thirteenth and fourteenth centuries).

13. See *Yevamot* 62b–63a.

14. Hirsch, *Commentary on Genesis* 2:18.

15. Hirsch, *Commentary on Genesis* 2:18. A number of earlier commentaries also view this term as implying equality between the sexes. See, for example, the commentaries on Genesis 2:18 or 2:20 of Hezekiah ben Manoah (France, thirteenth century) (*Hizkuni* [Vilna, 1875]); Yitzhak Ibn Latif, *Tzror Hamor* (North Africa, thirteenth century) ("Tzror Hamor," in *Kerem Hemed* 9, ed. Adolph Jellinke [1856], pp. 154–159); Issac Arama, *Akedat Yitzhak* (Spain, fifteenth century) (*Akedat Yitzhak* [Lemberg, 1808]); Ovadiah ben Jacob Sforno (Italy, fifteenth and sixteenth centuries), (*Commentary on Genesis*, trans. Ralph Pelcovitz [New York: Mesorah, 1987]); Moshe Alshekh (Safed,

Similarly, the fifteenth-century commentary of *Akedat Yitzchak* states that "Adam's help-meet . . . will be fashioned in a way that will enable her to become his full partner in all his tasks," and that the love between them "will exist from a position of absolute equality."[16]

How was the creation of woman intended to help man accomplish the "goal of perfection which the terrestrial world is to attain?"[17] Moshe Meiselman, in *Jewish Women in Jewish Law*,[18] comments on the verse "It is not good that man be alone" that the word "good" is both an ethical and a practical judgment. From a practical perspective, man is a social being who craves contact with others; but he also requires marriage for another dimension of his life: his ethical completion. In Meiselman's words: "Completion and perfection of the human personality occur when man and woman live for each other, give to each other, and function together as one unit."[19]

This idea was already anticipated by the twelfth-century scholar Rabbi Abraham ben David (called by the acronym of his name, Rabad),[20] who notes that the verse "Therefore shall man leave his father and his mother and cleave to his wife and they shall be one flesh" (Genesis 2:24) follows immediately upon the creation of Eve (Genesis 2:21–23). Rabad comments that the manner of creation defines the proper relationship within marriage. The basic attitude of marital partners to each other must be one of *hesed* (loosely translated as acts of kindness). *Hesed* is the "character trait which Judaism felt must underlie all interpersonal relationships. It is the basis of all Jewish ethics."[21] *Hesed* is the ability to surpass limitations of "me-ism" and to shift the focus of concern to

---

sixteenth century) (*Torat Moshe* [Warsaw, 1879]); and Naftali Z. Y. Berlin, *Ha'amek Davar* (Lithuania, nineteenth century) (*Ha'amek Davar* [Jerusalem, 1938]). See also Phyllis Trible, "Depatriarchalizing in Biblical Interpretation," in *The Jewish Woman: New Perspectives*, ed. Elizabeth Koltun (New York: Schocken, 1976), p. 223, who comments, "The word *neged* which joins *ezer* connotes equality: a helper who is a counterpart."

16. Arama, *Akedat Yitzhak* on Genesis 2:20. Other medieval commentaries see this term as connoting woman's subservience to man. See the commentaries on Genesis 2:18 of David Kimhi (known by his acronym *Radak*, France, twelfth and thirteenth centuries) (*Perushei Rabbi David Kemhi al ha-Torah*, with introduction, notes, and references by Moses Kamelhar [Jerusalem: Mossad Harav Kook, 1970]; Bahya ben Asher, *Midrash Rabbenu Bahya*; and Don Isaac Abrabanel (Spain, fifteenth century) (*Perush al ha-Torah* [Tchernowitz, 1860]). Also see Roslyn Lacks, *Women and Judaism: Myth, History and Struggle* (New York: Doubleday, 1980), p. 14.

17. Hirsch, *Commentary on Genesis* 2:18.

18. Moshe Meiselman, *Jewish Women in Jewish Law* (New York: Ktav, 1978), p. 22.

19. Ibid., p. 10.

20. Abraham ben David, *Ba-al ha-Nefesh* (Jerusalem: Mosad Harav Kook, 1964), see introduction. (The writer is of twelfth-century France; the book is a code of law related to women.)

21. Meiselman, *Jewish Women in Jewish Law*, p. 10.

another human being–to "give" to another out of a sense of closeness and identification with the other's needs. The story of creation, continues Rabad, tells humanity that the ideal marriage is the one in which man treats his wife as he would himself, because in a very real sense she is a part of him. Hence, states the Talmud, "a man should love his wife as himself and honor her more than himself."[22] However, *hesed* is demanded of the woman as well as the man. "The marriage relationship is the paradigm of *hesed* for in marriage one is continually required to focus on and to be as sensitive to the other's needs as one would be to one's own."[23]

WOMAN AS INDIVIDUAL

The story of creation of man and woman as understood by traditional commentators indicates their assumption that the two beings were to act together as one. This is a fundamental principle that guides Judaism in its view of the sexes, of how man and woman should interact. There remains a fundamental question of how we are to look at each of these two beings, man and woman, as separate individuals.

In commenting on the manner of creation of woman, Sforno (c. 1470–c. 1550) addresses the question as to why woman was created from a part of man (i.e., his rib [Genesis 2:22]), rather than independently, as were the females of all the other animal species. His answer further reinforces the theme of equality between man and woman, which a number of commentators view these biblical passages to imply, as we have already seen: "that she may have the form of man and his faculties [qualities], differing from him only in the physical vessels [i.e., sex], this being the difference between them; [otherwise] both have the possibility for the [attainment of] perfection, [be the measure] abundant or meager."[24]

In Genesis 3 we are confronted by the story of humanity's first sin, and the consequences of that transgression. "By the sweat of your brow shall you eat bread" (Genesis 3:19), God decrees for man. As for woman, God proclaims (Genesis 3:16): "In pain shall you give birth to children . . . and he [the husband] will rule over you." How can we understand the pronouncement of "he will rule over you" in light of what has hitherto been said? According to a contemporary scholar and biblical commentator, Nahum Sarna,[25] it is quite clear from the description of woman in Genesis 2:18, 23 that the ideal

---

22. *Yevamot* 62b.

23. Meiselman, *Jewish Women in Jewish Law*, p. 11.

24. Sforno, *Commentary on Genesis* 2:22, trans. Ralph Pelcovitz.

25. Nahum Sarna, *The Torah Commentary* (Philadelphia and New York: Jewish Publication Society of America, 1989), commentary on Genesis 3:16.

situation, which thus far had existed, was the absolute equality of the sexes. The new state of male dominance is regarded as an aspect of the deterioration in the human condition that resulted from defiance of Divine Will. The implication of Sarna's position would be that humanity, by acting in consort with the Divine Will, has the opportunity to rectify this imperfect state of affairs and bring the world to a position in which ideal relationships can once again prevail. As Hirsch remarks, in a society not governed by Torah principles and laws, woman's dependence on man becomes a social reality. However, if Jews live a life governed by Torah law, this will reestablish man and woman "in an equal God-serving calling of being priests to God."[26]

Traditional Jewish thought clearly views the woman as equal to man. The dominant perception, however, is that the woman's role is distinct from the man's. It is basic to the thinking of the rabbis that every creature under the sun has a unique mission to fulfill.[27]

The story of creation concludes with the Bible's role definition for woman: "And Adam called his wife Eve, for she was the mother of all life" (Genesis 3:20). Names assigned in the Bible are regarded not as the mere giving of an arbitrary title but, rather, as an essential part of role definition. Thus to give Eve the name "mother of all life" is to assign to her that task as her "fundamental, though not necessarily exclusive, role."[28]

According to the *Midrash*,[29] this role definition results from the nature of creation. Eve was created from a part of Adam's body that is private in two senses: first, that it is generally clothed, and second, that it is located beneath the skin. Thus implicit in woman's creation was a command that she develop a specific trait of the human personality to its maximum, namely, the capacity for *tzniut* (loosely translated as "modesty"). Its use by the prophet Micah (6:8) *"Ve-hatzneya lekhet im Elohekha"*—"And walk privately with thy God," has become paradigmatic: in its extended use, as *tzniut*, it is considered the foundation of Jewish values and one of the fundamental underpinnings of the Jewish family. *Tzniut* means modesty, simplicity, reserve, and humility; it relates to indecent speech or action, dress and appearance, covert or overt behavior. It is "conceived as humility and human decency, in counterdistinc-

---

26. Hirsch, *Commentary on Genesis* 3:16.

27. See, for example, Malbim, Meir Loeb ben Yehiel Michael, *Ha-Torah ve-ha-Mitzvah* (New York: MP Press, 1974), commentary on Genesis 2:20, and Abraham Isaac Kook, *The Lights of Penitence, Lights of Holiness, Essays, Letters and Poems,* trans. Ben Zion Bokser (New York and Toronto: Paulist Press, 1978), p. 230.

28. Meiselman, *Jewish Women in Jewish Law,* p. 11.

29. *Genesis Rabbah* 18:2. Meiselman, *Jewish Women in Jewish Law,* p. 11, cites this *midrash*.

tion to *pritzut*—the frivolous breaking of the moral code of conduct."[30] But most important, it refers to privacy. When anyone, male or female, serves God, he or she must concentrate on the inner dimensions of his or her personality. As Meiselman states: "*Tzniut* is the inner dimension of one's striving, which is the essence of the Jewish heroic act."[31] It is this trait of personality that woman was counseled to develop to its highest degree.

Modesty in action, in behavior, in dress, and in social relationships enables both the man and the woman to maintain accurate perspectives on each other and to refrain from sexual exploitation. As Yisrael Miller explains in *In Search of the Jewish Woman*,[32] when a man meets a woman (or vice versa) in a situation devoid of *tzniut*, he cannot properly relate to her as a person who incidentally happens to be female. She becomes a female who incidentally happens also to be a person, and sometimes even the "person" vanishes and she remains simply an object for self-gratification. *Tzniut* "is not intended to stamp out masculinity and femininity, but to keep them from being exploited and from being wrenched out of the context of the total personality."[33] Dignity comes not from exposure and indecent exhibition, but from discretion and the assurance that the human being will be considered a private, sensitive being, to be respected and not exploited—an objective consonant with feminist goals.

In Jewish tradition the categories of public and private roles are considered to be not exclusive but, rather, different points of initial emphasis. Meiselman's words on this subject are significant:

> Public and private are necessary aspects of the lives of both men and women. Neither sex is restricted to either area, but tradition did say that the private sphere should be the dominant area of a woman's life. However, even a man, whose primary involvement may be public, was reminded that his highest achievements are the acts that he does in private.[34]

---

30. Menachem M. Breyer, *The Jewish Woman in Rabbinic Literature: A Psychosocial Perspective*, vol. 1 (Hoboken, NJ: Ktav, 1986), p. 235.

31. Moshe Meiselman, "Women and Judaism: A Rejoinder," *Tradition* 15:3 (Fall 1975): 55.

32. Yisrael Miller, *In Search of the Jewish Woman* (New York: Feldheim, 1984), pp. 125–126.

33. Ibid., p. 126. It is significant, though beyond the scope of this discussion, to point out that there are laws (the Jewish family purity laws) that provide safeguards against women's becoming mere sex symbols. The interested reader may wish to read Tamar Frankiel, *The Voice of Sarah: Feminine Spirituality and Traditional Judaism* (San Francisco: Harper Collins, 1990), pp. 79–83, or Norman Lamm, *A Hedge of Roses* (New York: Feldheim, 1966).

34. Meiselman, *Jewish Women in Jewish Law*, p. 15. Meiselman provides examples (pp. 12–14) to demonstrate how, even among the male figures of the Bible, the high

What of contemporary society, wherein women are increasingly taking on the public roles previously assigned to men? Need there be a loss of this virtue? Not if *tzniut* is defined more in terms of its characteristics and not its role limits. As a contemporary Orthodox Jewish woman thinker explains:

> *Tzniut* is both absolute and relative; absolute in modes of behavior, dress, [and] speech, and relative in all those things as well. In certain communities at certain times, a woman did not initiate actions . . . or venture forth into public places. . . . What is today perfectly acceptable behavior in the [observant] community in speech, dress and action was unheard-of in other generations. Furthermore, what is permissible in one community is not permitted in another.[35]

One can act in a public capacity but be continually cognizant of the need to preserve the sanctity of the inner human being from assault by the coarseness of daily life.

THE IDEAL OF THE JEWISH FAMILY

The need for the creation of two sexes has been discussed, and the Jewish view of how the two sexes are to interrelate and how they are to function as individuals has briefly been touched upon. In Judaism, the dominant forum for the dynamics of this relationship has been the family. Jewish tradition has long recognized the family as the social unit best equipped to foster a healthy dynamic of male–female relationships. It is here, in the family, that the tradition views most positively the contributions of women.

Jewish community, states Reuven Bulka, Canadian psychologist and rabbi, is Jewish family: the fate of one is the fate of the other. Judaism's genesis was in the family, and as the family expanded and proliferated, it was redeemed, and as a collective family, received the Torah at Sinai.[36]

"Certainly, within the history and tradition of Jews," writes contemporary sociologist Chaim Waxman, "the family has been the most prominent institution involved in ethnoreligious identity formation and the transmission of ethnoreligious norms and values."[37] There is a prevailing misconception that the synagogue is the focus of Judaism. On the contrary, the center of

points in their moral life occur in private. See chapters 4 and 5 in Solomon Ashkenazi's *Ha-Ishah ba-Aspaklariah ha-Yehudit* (Tel Aviv: Yizra'el, 1955), on the topic of *tzniut*.

35. Blu Greenberg, *On Women and Judaism* (Philadelphia: Jewish Publication Society, 1981), p. 51.

36. Reuven Baulka, "The Jewish Family: Realities and Prospects," *Jewish Life* 6 (Spring–Summer 1982): 25–34.

37. Chaim I. Waxman, *America's Jews in Transition* (Philadelphia: Temple University Press, 1983), p. 160.

Jewish life, the strongest formative Jewish influence – continuous and permeating – and the bastion of Jewish survival for so many centuries of exile have been the home and family. As one writer describes it, "the 'Jewish home' represents the life-giving sustenance of faith, fortitude and hope, which have always been the hallmark of the Jewish household. It serves as a viable model for the Jewish heritage and spirituality; it is the haven for the ideals and aspirations of the Jewish family."[38] In Judaism, the family is not only the necessary instrument for biological succession but also a prime instrument for the transmission of cultural values and practices. The home and family are central to many religious ceremonies such as the Sabbath, the Passover eve gathering around the table to recount the birth of freedom, the week of thanksgiving spent in the harvest booth at Sukkot, the lighting of the candles at Chanukah, or the convivial gatherings that characterize Purim. A Jewish home colored by historical tradition is pervaded by such influences not occasionally but day and night, from the outward doorpost to its innermost privacy. It is a place in which one lives, not a retreat to which one comes to sleep.

Pnina Nave-Levinson describes Judaism as a "powerful matriachate half hidden under apparent male authority."[39] It is in the home that the influence of women is most strongly exercised. The Jewish woman is the "creator, molder and guardian of the Jewish home . . . its soul."[40] Her role as significant educator of her children to Jewish values is inscribed in the Jewish tradition. As Meiselman writes, it is no small task to create a Jewish home. "It requires much more than the burden of childbearing, child rearing and menial household tasks, because to create a Jewish home is to create a new link in the chain of Jewish existence and tradition. It is no easy task to form children in the Jewish mold and prepare them to become Jewish adults."[41] While providing for the physical needs of the family is generally a necessary component of a Jewish woman's job, her paramount role is that of teacher and guide. It is from the mother primarily that the child learns the fundamental concepts and principles of Judaism.

It should be emphasized, however, that whereas the *Halakhah* mandates the father to teach his children Torah, women are expressly exempt from that obligation.[42] Indeed, in all instances in *Halakhah* concerning the education of children for *mitzvot*, the law specifically mentions the father's

---

38. Breyer, *The Jewish Woman in Rabbinic Literature: A Psychosocial Perspective*, vol. 1, p. 243.

39. Pnina Nave-Levinson, "Women and Judaism," *European Judaism* 15:2 (Winter 1981): 25.

40. Meiselman, *Jewish Women in Jewish Law*, p. 16.

41. Ibid.

42. *Kiddushin* 29a; Maimonides, *Mishneh Torah, Hilkhot Talmud Torah* (Laws of Torah Study) 1:1.

responsibility.[43] As Rachel Biale points out in *Women and Jewish Law*,[44] it is in the realm of midrashic literature, memoirs, and sentimental and polemical writings that the woman's role in the education of her children is emphasized, and where she is regarded as having the responsibility for the child's primary spiritual and moral learning. The image of the Jewish woman as bearer of the tradition in the home "is grounded in popular ethos and is not based on the requirements of the *Halakhah*."[45]

This is not a matter that can be easily overlooked. Even though midrashic literature contains much evidence to defend a Jewish outlook that gives utmost significance to the maternal role for women, the exclusion of women from the halakhic obligation does present a question to a theory of this nature. It is generally understood within Jewish thought that the commands of God are a reflection of the true essence and being of the one commanded. In the traditional Jewish view, the true will of the one commanded is to follow the Will of God.[46] Further, God's commands are in line with, and the greatest indicator of, the true nature of the one commanded.[47] An exemption from halakhic obligation would seem to support the argument that involvement in parenting[48] is not an essential aspect of the female personality. Considering the midrashic literature, a conclusion of that nature is also problematic. A full investigation of the matter must include a resolution to the question about why women are not obligated in parental commands.[49]

---

43. See, for example, *Arakhin* 2b, *Succah* 42a; Maimonides, *Mishneh Torah*, Laws of Forbidden Foods 17:28; *Shulhan Arukh, Orah Hayim, Hilkhot Shabbat* 343.

44. Rachel Biale, *Women and Jewish Law* (New York: Schocken, 1984), p. 30.

45. Ibid.

46. See *Kiddushin* 50a.

47. This idea is supported by numerous verses in the Bible when the fulfillment of the *mitzvot* is connected with intrinsic benefit to people. See, for example, Deuteronomy 30:11–15. See also Malbim, commentary on Deuteronomy 30:11. This benefit is not perceived as arising from a potential reward external to the essence of the person but is considered intrinsic to the very behavior itself. See *Avot* 1:3. This model of the commandments, that God is directing a person toward behavior that is intrinsically beneficial, is sometimes referred to as *"rofeh ha-metzuvah al ha-holeh,"* as a doctor who is treating his patients. See Joseph Judah Bloch, *Shi'urei Da'at*, vol. 3 (Bnei Brak: Netzach, p. d.), p. 166.

48. Women's exclusion from parenting obligations extends beyond educational matters to include almost every area of parental duty. They are excluded from the commandment to procreate (see *Sefer ha-Hinukh, mitzvah* 1). They also have limited responsibility in providing sustenance for their children (see Joseph Caro, *Shulhan Arukh, Even ha-Ezer* 82:5). It is most interesting to note, however, that although a divorced woman cannot, generally, be compelled to provide nourishment and support for her children, even for the very young, she is given the prima facie right to custody even with the father's continuing to pay for support.

49. In attempting to answer this question, Meiselman, *Jewish Women in Jewish Law*,

ATTITUDES TOWARD WOMEN

It is perhaps because of the woman's importance in molding the Jewish family that the role of wife and mother is lauded and regarded so highly in Judaism. Instructive are the positive attitudes enunciated in Scriptures, in the Talmud, and in subsequent traditional literature. In the Book of Proverbs we read, "Hearken, my child, to the discipline of your father and do not forsake the Torah teachings of your mother."[50] Two talmudic passages read, "Anyone without a wife dwells without blessing, without Torah, without good, without joy, and without peace. . . ."[51] and "No matter how short your wife is, lean down and take her advice."[52]

The role of the wife places moral obligations on her husband. The sages thus teach: "A man should ever be careful of his wife's honor, for blessing comes to their home only for her sake."[53]

In his legal code, Maimonides formulates this supralegal obligation:

> The sages command us that a man should honor his wife more than himself. He should love her as himself. If he has money he should increase her portion. He should not cast fear over her. He should speak quietly with her, and not be melancholy or short-tempered. Similarly they command the woman to honor her husband very much. . . . This is the way of the daughters and sons of Israel, in their union, and in this manner, their sojourn will be beautiful and praiseworthy.[54]

---

p. 32, writes: "A woman's decision to marry is totally optional, as is a man's decision to dedicate himself totally to the learning of Torah. A person's ultimate task is totally optional, and he may choose the level of his service." This approach, however, presents many problems. For example, the underlying assumption that an "ultimate task is totally optional" may be challenged. We may also wish to note that a man's decision to dedicate himself to learning is, at least, built upon the obligation of a minimum level of study; the man would still be working within a category whereby he is commanded. This would not be so for the woman. For another approach in addressing this question, see further Rabbi Hecht.

50. Proverbs 1:8.

51. *Yevamot* 62b–63a.

52. *Bava Metzia* 59a.

53. *Sanhedrin* 22a–b.

54. Maimonides, *Mishneh Torah, Hilkhot Ishut* (Laws of Marriage) 15:19, 20. In outlining the nature of the honor accorded to a husband by his wife, Maimonides states, "the fear of him should be upon her, and all her work should be done in accordance with his instruction; he should be in her eyes like a prince or a king who may act as he desires. . . ." It is difficult to understand why Maimonides did not see the tension between these two commands. How does one practically reconcile the instruction to a husband to love and honor his wife more than himself with the instruction to his wife to fear him and to be subordinate to all his needs? How to

The tenth-century exilarch and philosopher Rabbi Saadiah Gaon writes, "A man . . . must honor his wife and give her full freedom. Anyone who treats his wife as a maidservant shows that he possesses a gross character. He himself is fit to be nothing more than a servant, ruled by others."[55]

On commenting on woman's character and personality traits, the Talmud has this to say: "The daughters of Israel are refined,"[56] "Women are compassionate,"[57] and "It is not the way of woman to sit idle."[58]

The status of women as mothers may be judged by the following examples. When Rabbi Judah ha-Nasi, editor of the Mishnah, sensed that his death was approaching, he said, "I need my sons." When his sons arrived, he said to them, "Take extreme care regarding the honor of your mother."[59] Of Rabbi Joseph it is told that when he heard the footsteps of his mother, he said, "I shall stand before the *Shekhinah* [Divine Presence] that has arrived."[60]

Lest we conclude that the talmudic references to women were unanimously favorable, statements exist in the literature that do not portray women in a positive light. Informative are the following: "Whoever follows his wife's advice descends into hell,"[61] "Women's minds are light,"[62] and "Women are greedy, eavesdroppers, lazy, and envious."[63]

Of further interest is the fact that many of these derogatory statements appear to contradict some of the more positive assertions. Illustrative are the two contradictory statements, quoted earlier, which appear in the same passage in the Talmud[64]: "No matter how short your wife is, lean down and take her advice" and "Whoever follows his wife's advice descends into hell." The talmudic editors attempted to reconcile the contradiction in two possible ways. One suggestion was that the former referred to household affairs, the

---

resolve this tension in Maimonides' attitude to women deserves further serious treatment. One may either opt for a conservative approach, which stresses the spouses' capacity for self-sacrifice in relation to each other, or if one is inclined to adopt Berkovits's critical historical suggestion, *op. cit.* (p. 56), one may regard Maimonides' statement as evidence for what Berkovits claims to be a continued manifestation of features deriving from the Torah-tolerated impersonal status of women existing alongside women's Torah-directed personal status (see n. 1).

55. Quoted in Rabbi Hasdai Crescas, *Or Hashem* (Vilna, 1904), essay 6, chap. 14 (Spain, fourteenth-century; philosophical treatise).

56. *Nedarim* 61a.

57. *Megillah* 14b.

58. *Ketubot* 5:6.

59. *Ketubot* 103a; cf. Berkovits, *Jewish Women in Time and Torah*, p. 44.

60. *Kiddushin* 31a; cf. Berkovits, *Jewish Women in Time and Torah*, p. 44.

61. *Bava Metzia* 59a.

62. *Kiddushin* 80b; *Shabbat* 33b.

63. *Nedarim* 31b.

64. *Bava Metzia* 59a.

latter to worldly matters. The second approach was that the former referred to worldly matters, the latter to spiritual matters.[65] Women, it would seem, are to be lauded when they function within the important realms of home care and child rearing. Men, however, are to be the administrators of the society and its religious conduct. It appears that in matters infringing on these male roles in society, the judgment about women is generally severe.

This conclusion, however, in itself has sources that provide challenge. Although the Talmud may declare that in spiritual matters a woman's advice should not be followed, there are numerous cases that point to the strength of the female in spiritual matters. In *Genesis Rabbah* 17:7, the case is presented of a pious couple who divorced, each of whom then remarried individuals who were considered wrongdoers. The *Midrash* relates that the evil woman turned the pious man into an evildoer, while the pious woman turned her new husband into a righteous individual, for "everything arises from the woman."

This portrait of women's possessing moral courage and spiritual strength is further reinforced by midrashic and rabbinical depictions of women in the Bible. It is the women whose memory is cherished by the nation when the Jewish people were enslaved in Egypt, for it was they who kept the spirits of the men up and the hope of redemption alive.[66] It was the midwives who had the courage of defy Pharaoh's cruel policy of extinguishing the babies' lives at birth (Exodus 1:15–20) and "to confront a king with the boldness of a woman who fears God more than man."[67] When Amram despaired of bearing children in Egypt (and from his example as leader, many other men despaired as well), the *Midrash* tells us, it was his daughter Miriam who convinced him not to bring about the extinction of the Jewish people out of overreaction to despair.[68] "In the merit of righteous women," claims the *Midrash*, "our ancestors were redeemed from Egypt."[69]

The *Midrash* further informs us that in the wilderness following the Israelites' exodus from Egypt, women refused to contribute toward the project to build the golden calf.[70] Lest this be attributed to parsimonious character, the *Midrash* reminds us that the women were more generous than the men when called upon to bring offerings for the Tabernacle.[71] When God sought to transmit the Torah to his people, it was the women he calls first (Exodus 19:3). The *Midrash* advances the interpretation that women are mentioned

---

65. Ibid.
66. *Exodus Rabbah* 1:16; *Sotah* 11b.
67. Hirsch, *Judaism Eternal*, p. 80.
68. *Exodus Rabbah* 1:17.
69. *Sotah* 11b.
70. *Pirkei d'Rabbi Eliezer*, ed. D. Luria (Warsaw, 1852), chap. 45.
71. *Exodus Rabbah* 35:29.

before men because they are usually quick to fulfill commandments.[72]

While the approaches introduced by the Talmud, in its reconciliation of the two statements regarding the advice of women, must be considered significant, it is obvious that in light of the full spectrum of opinions found within talmudic and midrashic literature, a simple understanding of a division of the sexes into household and worldly functions or worldly and spiritual functions does not stand. We may also wish to consider the fact that the Talmud itself recognizes that not all statements regarding women necessarily apply to all women. There are times that the Talmud applies to only one type of woman an assertion regarding women. It occasionally uses this method to reconcile apparent contradictions in statements by declaring that one statement applies to one type of woman, and the other statement pertains to another type.[73] In toto, however, the importance of the woman's role, it would seem, does center on her place within the family and the home.

Beyond the matter of mere attitudes regarding the importance of women's role in the home and family, there are specific laws in the Torah governing the obligations of man and woman to each other in marriage. They are numerous and beyond the scope of this work, but the following example from Scripture is enlightening: Concerning the newlywed man it stipulates (Deuteronomy 24:5), "He shall not go out in military service, nor shall he be subjected to anything associated with it; he shall be exempt for the sake of his home for one year, and he shall gladden his wife." The Torah states that the man shall "gladden his wife" and not, as we might have expected, "be glad with his wife." He may be happy, but this is no obligation. The obligation is to make his wife happy. Rabbi Leo Levi poses the question as to how personal sentiment, such as the gladdening of a newlywed bride, can take precedence over military service.[74] His answer reflects the paramount importance the Torah ascribes to the family: "The foundations of a healthy and strong family structure are laid during the first year of marriage. In viewing the family as the fundamental national unit, this too, is a 'national duty' and clearly one of even greater importance than military service."[75]

What of the father's role and responsibility within the home? Is the mother to be solely responsible for her children's upbringing? Because Judaism places such a high value on family life, both husband and wife are expected to

---

72. *Mekhilta Yitro* 19:3; *Exodus Rabbah* 28:2.

73. Illustrative are the two contradictory statements in *Yevamot* 63b: "Whoever finds a woman (wife) finds a great good" and "I find more bitter than death the woman." These statements are not meant to be blanket statements: The Talmud understands each as applying to a particular type of woman.

74. Leo Levi, "Man and Woman in Torah Life," *Jewish Life* 41 (Spring 1974): 44.

75. Levi jokingly adds that in effect, it is the Torah that originated the slogan "Make love, not war."

participate in it. In contemporary society, fathers are taking an increasingly greater role in household tasks and the physical care of children. The Orthodox Jewish way of life offers women the possibility of finding a mate they can regard as an involved parent, even a partner in the maintenance of home life, and it provides men with a source of identity beyond the sphere of work. One professional woman, an Orthodox Jew, explains: "A man who is secure in his religious identity, who has the breadth of vision and the inner harmony that comes with Torah learning, has always been ready for partnership in marriage. . . . "[76] A difference in degree is called for, but the idea and practice of partnership are already there in the tradition. Indeed, many Jewish women who were raised in non-Orthodox homes but are now embracing an Orthodox Jewish life-style claim that they are able to make demands upon men as husbands and fathers in ways they believe less possible in the secular world.[77]

Sociologists believe that the erosion of family life has contributed considerably to the breakdown of values and norms, to alienation and violence in contemporary society.[78] In fact, recent scientific research confirms what Jewish tradition has always maintained: the family is the most potent socializing and civilizing force available to us; it is also the single strongest determinant of religious commitment, values, and educational achievement.[79] It is in appreciation of this fact that Judaism holds its women in high esteem.

WORK OUTSIDE THE HOME AND THE CONCEPT OF SELF-FULFILLMENT

That the bearing and rearing of children are not the sole purposes and only options of Jewish women's existence and that, like men, women "can advance in the moral and intellectual field," is illustrated by the fifteenth-century Spanish Talmudist Isaac Arama (1420–1494) in his philosophic commentary on the Pentateuch, entitled *Akedat Yitzhak*. In Genesis (30:1–2),

---

76. Rivkah Blau, "What Are Observant Jewish Women Really Thinking," *Jewish Action*, Holiday Issue 2 (1986): 70.

77. See Debra Renee Kaufman, *Rachel's Daughters: Newly Orthodox Jewish Women* (New Brunswick, NJ, and London: Rutgers University Press, 1991), pp. 10–11. See also Lynn Davidman, *Tradition in a Rootless World: Women Turn to Orthodox Judaism* (Berkeley, CA: University of California Press, 1991), pp. 117–118.

78. See, for example, Gershon Kranzler, "The Changing Orthodox Jewish Family," *Jewish Life* 3 (Summer/Fall 1978): 23.

79. See, for example, Harold S. Himmelfarb, "The Non-Linear Impact of Schooling: Comparing Different Types and Amounts of Jewish Education,"*Sociology of Education* 50 (April 1977): 114–132. Cited in Greenberg, *On Women and Judaism*, p. 13.

Rachel, barren and childless, appeals in her misery to her husband, Jacob: "Give me children or else I die." The following verse states, "Jacob's anger was kindled against Rachel and he said, 'Can I take the place of God, who has denied you the fruit of the womb?' " Arama offers an explanation for Jacob's anger based on his conception of the creation of woman and the names given her:

> The two names "woman" (Isha) and "Eve" indicate two purposes. The first teaches that woman was taken from man, stressing that like him you may understand and advance in the intellectual and moral field just as did the matriarchs and many righteous women and prophetesses and as the literal meaning of Proverbs 31 about "the woman of valor" indicates. The second alludes to the power of childbearing and rearing children, as indicated by the name Eve–the mother of all living. A woman deprived of the power of childbearing will be deprived of the secondary purpose and be left with the ability to do evil or good like the man who is barren. Of both the barren man and woman, Isaiah (56:5) states: "I have given them in My house and in My walls a name that is better than sons and daughters," since the offspring of the righteous is certainly good deeds (see Rashi on Gen. 6:9). Jacob was therefore angry with Rachel when she said, "Give me children or else I die," in order to reprimand her and make her understand this all-important principle that she was not dead in the matter of their joint purpose in life because she was childless, just the same as it would be, in his case, if he were to have been childless.[80]

Contemporary Torah educator Nechama Leibowitz comments on Rabbi Arama's interpretation as follows:

> Jacob's anger is here explained as being directed at Rachel's forgetting the true and chief purpose of her existence, which, according to the Akedat Yitzhak, is no different from that of her partner, the man's. "Like him you may advance in the intellectual and moral field as did the matriarchs and many righteous women. . . ." She in her yearnings for a child saw her whole world circumscribed by the second purpose of woman's existence (according to the Akedat Yitzhak "the secondary purpose"!) to become a mother. Without it her life was not worth living. "Or else I die." This was a treasonable repudiation of her function, a flight from her destiny and purpose, shirking the duties imposed on her, not by virtue of her being a woman, but by virtue of her being a human being.[81]

---

80. Issac Arama, Akedat Yitzhak, Commentary on Genesis (30:1–2). Quoted in Nechama Leibowitz, Studies in Genesis (Jerusalem: World Zionist Organization, 1985), p. 334.

81. Nechama Leibowitz, Studies in Genesis, p. 335. Of more limited application, the twelfth-century philosopher and theologian Maimonides, in his major philosophic treatise, Guide of the Perplexed (3:51), links Miriam to Aaron and Moses, when speaking of the intellectual perfection attained by each in their service of God at the time of their

In actuality the rabbis did not forbid a woman's efforts outside the home, whether these were in business, the professions, or a trade. The many observant women who today are participating fully in the work force as businesswomen, teachers, lawyers, doctors, and so forth[82] have antecedents in earlier times: medieval Jewish women[83] and nineteenth-century eastern European women[84] often engaged in commercial activities. A responsum of the medieval period on problems involving women includes the statement: "Nowadays, it is commonplace for women to engage in business."[85]

Not only could a woman be employed but also the Talmud engages in discussion about the rights and obligations of a working woman.[86] If a woman wanted to keep all her earnings, she had to reimburse her husband for her food, but the husband was still required to pay for her clothing and

---

deaths. Menachem Kellner regards this linkage as evidence for Maimonides' recognition of women's equal potential to attain intellectual and moral perfection. Maimonides writes, "The philosophers have explained that the bodily faculties impede in youth the attainment of most of the moral virtues, and all the more those of pure thought, which is achieved through the perfection of the intelligibles that lead to passionate love of Him. . . . For it is impossible that it should be achieved while the bodily humors are in effervescence. Yet in the measure in which the faculties of the body are weakened and the fires of the desires quenched, the intellect is strengthened, its lights achieve a wider extension, its apprehension is purified, and it rejoices in what it apprehends. The result is that when a perfect man is stricken with years and approaches death, this apprehension increases very powerfully; joy over this apprehension and a great love for the object of apprehension become stronger, until the soul is separated from the body at that moment in this state of pleasure. Because of this the Sages have indicated, with reference to the deaths of Moses, Aaron, and Miriam, that the three of them died by a kiss. . . . Their purpose was to indicate that the three of them died in the pleasure of this apprehension due to the intensity of passionate love. . . ." (Quoted from Menachem Kellner, *Maimonides on Human Perfection* [Atlanta: Scholars Press, 1990], pp. 4–5.)

82. See, for example, Kranzler, "The Changing Orthodox Jewish Family," pp. 32–33.

83. See, for example, Judith R. Baskin, "Jewish Women in the Middle Ages," in *Jewish Women in Historical Perspective* (Detroit: Wayne State University Press, 1991), pp. 103–104; Mordechai Breuer, "Jewish Women in the Middle Ages," *Jewish Digest* 29 (October 1983): 63–64; and Cecil Roth, "Outstanding Jewish Women in Western Europe," in *The Jewish Library: Women*, ed. Leo Jung (London and New York: Soncino Press, 1970), pp. 151–163.

84. See, for example, Charlotte Baum, "What Made Yetta Work? The Economic Role of Eastern European Jewish Women in the Family," *Response* 7:2 (Summer 1973): 33–38.

85. Rabbi Meir ben Barakh of Rothenberg (thirteenth century), *Responsa of Maharam*, ed. R. N. Rabinowitz (Lemberg, 1860), sec. 57.

86. Meiselman, *Jewish Women in Jewish Law*, p. 82. Sources on the Talmud's view of women's working are from Meiselman.

personal needs. The Talmud is vague as to whether a woman who joins the work force is still liable for a certain amount of housework.[87] Some scholars have obligated her to pay the entire household expense.[88] Others have exempted her from normal household duties, such as child care, cooking, and washing.[89] Those scholars have ruled that such duties become the husband's responsibility and expense. The practice in contemporary rabbinic courts is a compromise between the two positions.[90] The decision between dependence and independence was left exclusively to the woman. She alone decided whether or not she wished to work outside the home and what she would do with her earnings.[91] All this is to indicate that work outside the home by women was and is considered by rabbinical authorities an acceptable activity.

However, it must be emphasized that work, in the mind of rabbis, as the only means of self-definition and self-fulfillment is not the Jewish way for women or for men. As for women working outside the home in contemporary society, some women interpret women's liberation only in terms of their own personal needs, narrowly defined. Phyllis Chesler's words are instructive: "Women must try to convert the single-minded ruthlessness with which they yearn for, serve, and protect a mate or biological child into the 'ruthlessness' of self-preservation and self-development."[92] The result of such an attitude is a denial that there can be self-fulfillment in the process of giving to others. But any relationship of intimacy, whether a marriage or parent–child relationship, if it is to blossom requires "the surrender of some of the self – disclosing, sharing, making compromises, yielding . . . a measure of sacrifice."[93] Contemporary Jewish sociologist Daniel Elazar echoes a more balanced view: "I would argue that the pursuit of individual passions ends up, in the last analysis, as empty or unsatisfying. It is only in commitment to something larger than oneself that one fulfills one's real needs and achieves truly human dimensions."[94]

---

87. *Ketubot* 63a.

88. See the glosses of Rabbi Abraham ben David, *Hasagot ha-Ravad al Mishneh Torah* (in Alfasi section) to *Ketubot* 63a (southern France, twelfth century); and the commentary of Rabbi Solomon ben Abraham ibn Aderet (the Rashba), ad loc. (Spain, thirteenth century).

89. Tosafot, ad loc. (analyses of talmudic topics by medieval French and German scholars; they are printed alongside the text of the Talmud in the standard edition of the Talmud).

90. Meiselman, *Jewish Women in Jewish Law*, p. 82.

91. Ibid.

92. Phyllis Chesler, *Women and Madness* (New York: Avon, 1973), p. 282.

93. Greenberg, *On Women and Judaism*, p. 16.

94. A symposium among Jewish historians, sociologists, feminists, etc. "Does Judaism Need Feminism?" *Midstream* 32 (April 1986): 40.

A study by Bahr and Day in 1978 implies that it is not women's working outside the home that affects the family as much as the attitude of women who work. If the work is an escape from the family it can be harmful, but if it is an expression of responsibility for the family, then it need not be an impediment to the family's flourishing.[95] This view is possible with regard to Orthodox women (as well as men) who work outside the home. If a career is only a secondary consideration and remains subservient to the primary dedication of building a Jewish home, then a career is certainly not inconsistent with Jewish ideals. As already mentioned, many Orthodox women today are professionals. They are university trained and educated. Their salaries are not secondary salaries but vital incomes for their families' financial viability. Though many will state that they work out of economic necessity, they see in their job personal fulfillment as well and regard their role at work as complementing their role at home.[96] Nevertheless, despite all sorts of activities outside the home, Judaism still sees the woman's ideal centered in the home, creating and guarding the Jewish home, and imparting to children a life-style of Torah. In Judaism it is the ethic of self-transcendence rather than self-fulfillment, the notion of sharing and outer-directed concern, that is the essential dynamic in human relations, especially husband–wife and parent–child relations. In Bulka's words, "One gives up a little bit of the self in order to make the lot of others better, but in that process an entire environment is enhanced, and often to the benefit of the self-transcenders. . . ."[97]

The notion of outer-directed concern can be enlarged to include the idea of marriage as expressing a shared destiny with one's partner in life. This is best developed, says Bulka, in a coherent Jewish life-style "which has a futuristic focus to it and in which marriage is oriented toward the ultimate destiny of the Jewish people."[98]

STATUS OF WOMEN IN JEWISH LAW (*HALAKHAH*)

From much of what has been said one might infer that Judaism does accord a high degree of respect to women, and that many women are secure and content with their status within the *Halakhah* and Jewish society. There are,

---

95. This study is cited (unfortunately without sources) by Reuven Bulka in "The Jewish Family: Realities and Prospects," p. 31.

96. For elaboration on this and other areas of involvement, both secular and religious, of Orthodox women in today's world, both in North America and Israel, see Joshua Berman, "Balancing the Bimah: The Diaspora Struggle of the Orthodox Feminist," *Midstream* 36:6 (August/September 1990): 20–24.

97. Bulka, "The Jewish Family: Realities and Prospects," p. 32.

98. Ibid.

nonetheless, a number of women who, owing to a variety of factors, do not share those feelings. The issues that present a challenge to the role of women must also be recognized and investigated.

Before proceeding with a review of some areas of concern,[99] we should recognize the gap that often exists between the ideal and social reality, between the *Halakhah* and life itself. Rachel Biale, in her analysis of women and Jewish law, acknowledges that "the *Halakhah* was probably more permissive and more generous to women than life itself. . . . A gap between common practices, folk beliefs, and popular attitudes on the one hand, and formal legal principles on the other, is a feature of all organized societies governed by law."[100] What often troubles some women are actually insensitive actions or remarks that are foreign to authentic Jewish tradition. This is one reason why a sound Jewish education is so vital; all Jewish men and women need to be educated as to the equal value of women and men in the eyes of God.

One issue in which a sense of injustice arises is the disadvantaged position of women in several matters of Jewish civil and family law. One trenchant example is the Jewish divorce process.[101] Briefly, according to biblical law, divorce, it seems, is a unilateral action on the part of a husband. Within the Talmud, however, we see that this right of the husband was greatly curtailed. The laws regarding the Jewish bill of divorce, the *get*, were sufficiently complicated that the Jewish court would have to be included in the procedure and thereby ensure a level of justice. The husband would also be reluctant to divorce his wife without the court's permission and the waiving of the wife's right to the *ketubah*,[102] for he would then be subject to paying his wife an extensive sum of money. The Talmud also recognized the wife's right to initiate the divorce procedure. While the actual action of divorce, the giving of the *get*, had to be directed from the husband to the wife, the wife could approach the court and, with justifiable cause, petition the court to compel the

---

99. This topic has already been examined extensively in the literature of the Jewish women's movement and will be dealt with briefly here. The interested reader may wish to read the previously cited works by Berkovits, Berman, Biale, Levi, and Meiselman, as well as Getsel Elinson's book *Serving the Creator: Women and the Mitzvot*, vol. 1 (Jerusalem: World Zionist Organization, 1986), for a more in-depth examination of the status of women in *Halakhah*.

100. Rachel Biale, *Women and Jewish Law*, p. 7.

101. Other seeming injustices in Jewish civil law include women's not being permitted to appear as witnesses in Jewish courts of law (with some exceptions) and not being permitted to hold executive office. For elaboration, see the previously cited works by Berkovits, Berman, Biale, Ellinson, Levi, and Meiselman.

102. The *ketubah* is the Jewish marriage contract, which includes, among other provisions, that upon divorce or the husband's death the wife is to receive a significant sum of money. See Maurice Lamm, *The Jewish Way in Love and Marriage*, pp. 197–206.

husband to issue a *get*.[103] Rabbis, in the course of ten centuries, further addressed the potential inequality of women within the divorce laws. Rabbi Gershom ben Judah of Mayence (c. 940–1028) instituted that a woman cannot be divorced against her will.[104] Nevertheless one is still left with the heartbreaking case of the *agunah* (deserted wife). This occurs when the husband disappears, leaving no evidence of his death or when he becomes permanently mentally incapacitated or when the courts are powerless to compel the husband to grant a divorce, and there is no way of releasing the wife from her marriage bond. Though attempts have been made to resolve this problem,[105] more assertive and concerted effort is necessary, especially in an age when divorce is more prevalent among Jews than it has been in most periods of history.

Though most observant women have been able to discover a life of fulfillment and religious growth within the existing patterns of *Halakhah*, for a number of women another area of discontent is the sense of being deprived of opportunities for positive religious identification. As expressed in Chapter One, the life of any traditional Jew is guided, even dictated, by the *mitzvot* (the commandments). The great majority of the *mitzvot* apply equally to men and women – from the universal prohibition "Thou shalt not murder" to the rigorous particulars of the laws of Sabbath and *kashrut* (kosher food). In fact, one may say that there is virtually no differentiation between men and women in the area of moral accountability covered by the negative commandments (except those that are gender related). There is a distinction between men and women, however, in regard to certain positive commandments. An investigation of one area of differentiation in the performance of positive

---

103. *Bava Batra* 48a. See also David Amram, *The Jewish Law of Divorce* (New York: Hermon Press, 1968), pp. 54–62. This solution worked somewhat better until the Enlightenment (late eighteenth and the nineteenth century) and the loss of Jewish judicial autonomy. Because of the absence of judicial autonomy, this process of compulsion does not function. Even in Israel, where the rabbinic courts are empowered to impose various pressures, such as imprisonment, the religious judges are reluctant to impose them.

104. See Edwin Samuel, "Gersohn Ben Judah Me'or Ha'Bolah," *Encyclopedia Judaica*, vol. 7, pp. 511–513.

105. For example, the Ontario government in 1988 passed a law stating that if there are any impediments (such as religious) to remarriage on the part of either spouse, then the couple's case, if brought to the secular court system, may be tossed out of court. Rabbis and feminists worked closely with government officials to have this law passed. Lack of Jewish judicial autonomy necessitates the rabbis having to turn to the secular courts for cooperation and assistance.

In former times, rabbis, among them some of the greatest halakhic authorities, have struggled to solve the *agunah* problem in attempting, with great courage and sincere concern, to introduce solutions.

commandments may serve as a model of how Jewish thought approaches such distinctions. Women are obligated in almost all positive commandments that are independent of time, but they are exempt from some, though not all, time-bound positive commandments.[106]

Various commentators advance a rationale for women's exemption from some of the commandments. Rabbi David ben Yosef Abudarham (fourteenth-century Spain) suggests a practical consideration: Women are excused from time-bound commandments because of their familial responsibilities. When women are overwhelmed by demands by their husband and small children, the performance of some of the *mitzvot* at set times might constitute an excessive burden for them. Abudarham writes:

> If she would perform the commandment of the Creator and leave aside [her husband's] commandment, woe to her from her husband! If she does her husband's commandment, and leaves aside the Creator's, woe to her from her Maker! Therefore, the Creator has exempted her from his commandments, so that she may have peace with her husband.[107]

In analyzing Abudarham's position, Rachel Biale, a contemporary Jewish feminist, regards it as exemplifying a conflict between the commands of God and the demands of a husband. "Interestingly, it is God who 'bows out' of the competition, allowing the husband's commands to prevail. Presumably God is less given to small jealousies and power struggles and can afford to lay some of his requirements aside in order to preserve peace."[108] This, in Biale's view,

---

106. For example, women are exempt from the obligation to dwell in a *sukkah* (a booth) on the Feast of Tabernacles and from the duty to take up a palm branch (*lulav*) on that holiday. They are also exempt from the commandment of hearing the *shofar* (ram's horn) blown on the New Year (Rosh Hashanah). Aside from the above *mitzvot*, which are particular to certain holidays, women are also exempted from three *mitzvot* that are time bound and generally carried on every day: the obligation to wear fringes (*tzitzit*) when wearing a four-cornered garment, the obligation to don phylacteries (*tefillin*) while praying in the morning, and the recitation of the *Shma*, the quintessential statement of Jewish belief, at prescribed times in the morning and evening. (Women are obligated to pray in general, however, within guidelines different from men's. See Ellinson, *Serving the Creator*, vol. 1, pp. 168–211, for elaboration.) Nevertheless, there are several time-bound positive *mitzvot* that are incumbent upon women, such as eating unleavened bread (*matzoh*) on Passover, as well as several positive *mitzvot* from which women are exempt (such as procreation and the study of Torah), although these are not time bound, and which, therefore, according to the general principle, should have been expected to be applicable to women.

107. David ben Yosef, *Sefer Abudarham* (Warsaw, 1878), sec. 111, "The Blessing over [Fulfilling] the Commandments" (Spain, fourteenth-century; this book is an explanation of customs, including the blessings, prayers, and their laws).

108. Biale, *Women and Jewish Law*, p. 14.

underscores a profound point:

> The halakhic and religious position of women is strained by a tension between two views of women. God, in the "rivalry" of our text, holds a fundamental theological and ethical position which recognizes no stratification of human beings, no inferiority of women to men. All persons are of equal value, spiritually and morally, and all human life is equally sanctified. On the other hand, the husband represents an attitude grounded in daily life and social reality, where there are distinctions of religion, class, learning, and of course gender. . . . While in ultimate moral and spiritual terms a woman's role is equal to a man's, her concrete, day-to-day life is marked by subservience to men.[109]

Biale regards this tension as exemplified in the two accounts of creation in Genesis. She views the first as indicative of woman's having been created equally with man "in God's image," and the second—in contrast to the positive views of some of the commentators we have studied—of woman's being created to meet man's needs.

In contrast to this more deprecative perception by Biale, several modern writers have echoed Abudarham's position in a more positive vein, focusing on the practical considerations of the woman's domestic role in society. Rabbi Saul Berman writes in "The Status of Women in Halakhic Judaism":

> The underlying motive of exemption would be [not] the attempt to unjustly deprive women of the opportunity to achieve religious fulfillment. . . . Rather, exemption would be a tool used by the Torah to achieve a particular social goal, namely to ensure that no legal obligation would interfere with the selection by Jewish women of a role which was centered almost exclusively in the home.
>
> It is admittedly very difficult for an American raised with almost a sense of sanctity of individual rights to accept a stance which gives not only primacy to the social goal, but then assigns to the individual a status which would encourage the achievement of the goal. Yet, that is exactly what Jewish law seems to do. Placing its emphasis on the communal need for the maintenance of strong family units as the central means of the preservation of the Jewish community both physically and spiritually, the law ensures that nothing will interfere with that goal.[110]

Berman views exemption as a function of the private and public nature of a particular ritual. Because Jewish society prescribed that woman function primarily in the private realm of the home, the rabbis did whatever was in their interpretive power to prevent women from being summoned into the

---

109. Ibid.

110. Berman, "The Status of Women in Halakhic Judaism," in *The Jewish Woman: New Perspectives,* ed. Elizabeth Koltun (New York: Schocken, 1976), pp. 121–122.

public sector. That is why women are exempt, for example, from the obligation to testify in court or to participate in communal worship.

Noam Zohar, Jerusalem thinker and writer, presents an intriguing insight into the reason for the exemption of women from time-bound commandments.[111] Zohar considers the literary structure of the first chapter of *Mishnah* tractate *Kiddushin*. He discovers that the first half of the chapter shares the same linguistic formulas and contains an ordered list of acquisitions. The list begins with the acquiring of wives and ends with the acquiring of movable items. Zohar posits that the principle behind the list is that of control. Men have very limited control over their wives but maximum control over movable objects. Appended to the list is a statement that is linguistically and substantively separate from the list. The statement implies that God is the true owner of all. Following this is a second list, linguistically similar to the statement, which posits God as the Supreme Controller. This second list orders the hierarchy showing to whom and where commandments apply. It is here that the *Mishnah* states that women are exempt from time-bound commandments; men are obligated to keep these. Another such ordered pair delineates an exemption from certain commandments for those who dwell outside the Land of Israel in lesser holiness.[112] Zohar demonstrates that this list is dependent upon the first list. Those who are higher on the social scale, that is, those who are more free from control, have larger obligations for commandments. He illustrates that those who have fewer obligations are deemed to have less sanctity. Furthermore, he shows that the editor of the *Mishnah* added a humane touch to this state of affairs by claiming that the fulfillment of one commandment is redemptive.

Zohar penetrates the structure of the chapter by indicating that holiness is a function of freedom, not of intellectual superiority. That freedom is dependent on the degree of control that one has over oneself. The key to his insight is the weight he attaches to the statement that bridges the two lists. God as Commander requires more of those who are free to serve him. Those who have their time occupied with other obligations lack the time ingredient to spend in the realms of holiness and are therefore exempt from time-bound commandments. Zohar supports his contention with references to companion compositions of the *Mishnah*, which implicitly refer to the relationship between holiness and exemption from time-bound commandments.[113]

---

111. Noam J. Zohar, "Women, Men and Religious Status: Deciphering a Chapter in Mishnah," in *Approaches to Ancient Judaism*, ed. Herbert Basser and Simha Fishbane, vol.5 (Atlanta: Scholars Press, 1993), chap. 2.

112. Compare *Mishnah Kelim* 1:6.

113. See *Mishnah Horayot* 3:6–7 and Maimonides' explicit comments to it. See also *Sifrei* Numbers 115.

Zohar concludes his essay by calling for a new redemptive vision as a guide for halakhic teaching and practice:

> The Hebrew word for "husband" (ba'al) is the same as for "owner"; but redemption must spell the fading of this acquisitive aspect, and the concomitant emergence of women as full partners in the realm of holiness. "And in that day – declares the Lord – You will call (me) Ishi [= my man], And no more will you call me Ba'ali [= my master]" (Hosea 2:18).

Zohar's analysis gives credence to Abudarham's rationale in that he has provided a comprehensive argument to support the contention that it is difficult to serve two masters. What Zohar accomplishes is the argument for women's exemption to be looked at in the light of relative social positioning. This approach is more dynamic than Abudarham's and requires further discussion.

Meiselman points out that a number of authorities disagree with Abudarham's position, maintaining that he takes no cognizance of the fact that unmarried women or women who have no household tasks are also exempt from these mitzvot. Those authorities, however, offer no explanation for the exemption but regard it as "part of the basic fabric of Jewish law to which the question 'why?' is inapplicable."[114]

Other writers – those who defend the role of women in Jewish Orthodoxy – have elevated the principle of exemption beyond mere practical considerations. They view women's exemptions from various commandments as evidence of the greater ease with which women achieve spiritual goals. In a spiritual sense, women are perceived as requiring fewer reminders in their service to God. Hirsch writes:

> The Torah did not impose time-bound positive mitzvot upon women because it did not consider them necessary to be demanded from women. These mitzvot are meant, by symbolic procedures, to bring certain facts, principles, ideas and resolutions afresh to our minds from time to time to spur us on afresh and to fortify us to realize them to keep them. God's Torah takes it for granted that our women have greater fervor and more faithful enthusiasm for their God-serving calling and that their calling runs less danger in their case than in that of men from the temptations which occur in the course of business and professional life. Thus they have no need for such periodic reminders.[115]

This explanation is in line with the concept formulated by Rabbi Judah Loew (Maharal, sixteenth-century Prague). He writes that women are closer to the

114. Meiselman, Jewish Women in Jewish Law, p. 43.
115. Hirsch, Commentary on Leviticus 23:43.

calm state of the World to Come and therefore can earn it with less effort.[116]

Other contemporary rabbis have attempted to attribute women's exemption from time-bound laws to women's possession of their own biological clock. Because of menses, women are more attuned to the passage of time and do not require certain *mitzvot* that mark time. Men, however, do need such commandments to sensitize them to the cosmic dimension of time.[117]

Whatever the reasons may be, a woman *is* allowed to perform optionally almost all the *mitzvot* from which she is exempt. As Adin Steinsaltz states, "The fact that women were not obliged to perform many of the positive precepts was regarded as an exemption rather than a ban. . . . Those women who sincerely wished it were permitted to undertake additional *mitzvot*."[118] Thus, in effect in regard to the time-oriented commandments as well as in other matters, women are given the choice by *Halakhah* of either fulfilling the Divine Command or not. In analyzing this issue, Canadian rabbi and educator Benjamin Hecht suggests a cogent approach.[119] Allowance for choice for women should be compared to the obligatory nature of these commands for men. The issue is not whether or not the action is performed but rather the motivation, the cause for action. It is within this realm of motivation that the Torah distinguishes between men and women, demanding different thought and emotional processes leading to the performance of the command. The man must respond to obligation, to a sense of duty or necessity in performance. In having a choice, the woman can investigate the results of the action, the meaning of the *mitzvah*, and the personal spiritual or other benefit in its performance. This approach is demanding of further investigation in a broad area of matters where the *Halakhah* differentiates between the sexes.

In practice, women in contemporary society have undertaken many of these time-bound commandments, undoubtedly because of their perception that something is missing in the fullness of the religious experience, particularly in those *mitzvot* related to the holidays. The major exceptions seem to be the donning of *tzitzit* (four-cornered fringed garment) and *tefillin* (phylacteries).[120] Thus, to some extent the dissatisfaction of women today is

---

116. Rabbi Judah Loew (Maharal), *Drush al ha-Torah*, included in *Sifrei Maharal* (New York: Judaica Press, 1969), p. 27 (central Europe, sixteenth century; this work consists of philosophic and religious insights on the Torah).

117. See Greenberg, *On Women and Judaism*, p. 84.

118. Adin Steinsaltz, *The Essential Talmud* (New York: Bantam Books, 1976), p. 139.

119. Based on personal discussion with the author.

120. For a discussion of the laws of *tzitzit* and *tefillin* as they pertain to women, see Ellinson, *Serving the Creator*, pp. 95–108. In medieval Ashkenazic literature, we note that Rabbi Moshe ben Jacob of Coucy (thirteenth century), author of *Sefer Mitzvot Gadol*, reports that his teacher R. Yehudah of Paris (1166–1224) ordered his wife to

psychological. The trend in our society is to limit the spectrum of differences based on gender. Role distinction of any nature, for many legitimate reasons, is subjected to intense scrutiny. It is therefore not surprising that for some women any type of distinction, even an exemption in the realm of time-oriented commandments, implies a lack of equality.

It should be noted, however, that role distinction is a significant factor within Judaism and it is not exclusive to gender. *Kohanim* (priests from the tribe of Levi) were singled out for special duties and privileges in the Holy Temple (and were supported by the community) from which non-*Kohanim* were forbidden. Similarly, the Levites were ordained with certain rights and responsibilities that were not to be undertaken by any other Jew. These special roles were not meritocratic. They were divinely decreed to be hereditary; this was to be the optimum way of serving God. They did not reflect a person's level of learning, observance, wealth, or community participation. Whereas, then, role distinction exists, "Judaism does not make the value of a personality dependent upon the amount of its responsibilities or the size of its task but only upon the conscientious fulfillment of the duties assigned."[121] The *Midrash* states to that effect, "The Divine Spirit rests upon a person, whether male or female, according to the person's action."[122]

In a 1990 address in Jerusalem, Israeli supreme court justice Menachem Alon offered a legal perspective on the question of role distinction, specifically as it relates to the notion of equality between the sexes in Judaism:

------

wear *tzitzit*. Rabbi Mordecai ben Hillel, in *Hilkhot Tzitzit* 949, adds that this woman wove the *tzitzit* under her husband's direction. In the standard edition of *Minhagei Maharil* (Jerusalem: Makhon Yerushalayim, 1989), p. 588 (fourteenth–fifteenth centuries), there is mention that Rabbanit Bruna of Magenza wore *tzitzit* at all times. Prof. Robert Werman of the Hebrew University of Jerusalem, who has communicated these sources, notes that he has heard that some Italian women of rabbinic families of the eighteenth century wore both *tallit* (prayer shawl) and *tefillin* during prayer. However, there is an early strand of rabbinic thought that reacts against this trend. See Targum Jonathan to Deuteronomy 22:5. Also see Rabbi Moses Isserles's glosses to *Shulhan Arukh, Orah Hayim* 38:3. Nevertheless, Werman notes that Rabbi Isaac ben Samuel (France, twelfth century), Rabbi Solomon Ibn Adret (Rashba, Spain, thirteenth century), and others have maintained that if women carry out a custom, the rabbis should let them do it even though the idea has not been widely accepted. Rabbi Moshe Feinstein, leading decisor of the late twentieth century, also permits the donning of *tzitzit* by a woman but considers the woman's motivation a primary factor. If her desire is to elevate herself in service to God, she may do so. If, however, her motivation is to challenge the overriding authority of the classical *Halakhah*, Rabbi Feinstein categorically declares that she is not performing a *mitzvah*. (For elaboration, see Moshe Feinstein, *Responsa Igrot Moshe, Orah Hayim*, Part 4 [Bnei Brak, 1982], sec. 49.) The donning of *tefillin* is discouraged by normative *Halakhah* today, as per Isserles.

121. Eli Munk, *The World of Prayer* (New York: Feldheim, 1953), vol. 1, pp. 27–28.

122. Shimon Ashkenazi, *Yalkut Shimoni* (Vilna, 1910) on Judges 4.

As far as equality is concerned, I would like to point out that there is a major principle in law which distinguishes "discrimination" which is invalid from "distinction" which is valid, such that one must treat every person equally unless there are material differences between them which are real and relevant to the issue. The critical question is, of course: when are the differences between men and women "real" and "relevant" so as to justify "discrimination" and make it into "distinction"? It can be immediately assumed that the list of differences in the world of *Halakhah* will not correspond to that in a secular legal system; this results from the philosophy of *Halakhah*, which is different from the philosophy of someone who does not see himself subject to the observance of Torah and *mitzvot*. For example, giving birth, nursing and the daily relationship between mother and child in its early days, without any intermediary, is a halakhic value, and if as a result the woman is exempted from observing the *mitzvot* which require particular acts to be done at particular times, this is not a negative discrimination but a positive distinction. Moreover [according to *Halakhah*] a woman is entitled – if she so wants – to observe the *mitzvot* which require particular acts to be done at particular times. . . . The equality of a woman does not depend on her becoming a man; her equality and respect derive from the social outlook of the woman's living within the framework of the *Halakhah* and the world of Torah and *mitzvot*, as determined and developed in every generation, as is required by the principle of tradition and transition, working together as one.[123]

This is not to say that there are no areas of practical concern. Unfortunately, because of women's exempted status, some men may not take women's voluntary acceptance of these *mitzvot* as seriously. Whereas within the halakhic system, the obligatory nature of the man's *mitzvah* will give him preference in a question of performance,[124] there is no doubt that a woman's performance is considered meritorious[125] and of lasting worth.

---

123. Menachem Alon, in an address delivered in Jerusalem on January 1, 1990, before the World Emunah Congress.

124. For example, if there is only one person available to blow the *shofar* on Rosh Hashanah and there is a choice between whether he should go to one hospital to blow the *shofar* for a sick man or to another hospital to blow the *shofar* for a sick woman, all things being equal and given the impossibility of doing both, *Halakhah* would require he blow the *shofar* for the male.

125. Maimonides, *Mishneh Torah, Hilkhot Talmud Torah* (Laws of Torah study) 1:13. The merit of a woman's performing an optional *mitzvah* is less than that of a man's performing that same *mitzvah*. The idea underlying this principle may be psychological. A person's nature is to be "oppositional"; hence, once one is told that one must do something, one approaches the task with some reluctance. On the other hand, one who is not commanded does not feel this way because if one wishes not to, one need not fulfill it. In addition, one who is commanded is under stress and worries lest he or she transgress the commandment. (See commentary of Tosefot on *Kiddushin* 31a.

One area of practical import that is a sore point for some Jewish women is their halakhic exclusion from certain aspects of public worship. Although the woman's voluntary performance is significant, her choosing to perform *mitzvot* from which she is exempt does not raise her to the halakhic status of those obliged to do so. Therefore she would be unable to discharge a man's obligation in such *mitzvot*. This would mean, for example, that she would not be permitted to blow the *shofar* on behalf of a man on Rosh Hashanah. Similarly, women are prohibited from being included in a *minyan*—a quorum of ten male adults, aged 13 years or over, necessary for public worship and certain other religious ceremonies, and they are barred from *aliyah la-Torah*, the ceremonial act whereby members of the congregation "go up to the Torah" during the public reading of the Torah on Mondays, Thursdays, and Sabbaths to read or, more often, to recite the blessings over the Torah and then have a reader read aloud for them.[126] A response to this concern has been made by the network of women's prayer groups that have been established across North America and in Israel. These groups meet on a monthly to bimonthly basis to hold morning services for women only. Yet, since the first women's prayer group met at Lincoln Square Synagogue in New York City in 1972, many halakhic challenges have been raised throughout the Orthodox camp concerning the innovation.[127] In any event, it must be recognized that these groups do not have the status of a *minyan*; cannot, as such, completely parallel the public worship of men; and fall short for women who consider any form of distinction between the sexes as problematic.

Returning to Professor Alon's philosophic point, we are led to consider the contributions of women within their own social and religious avenues mandated by *Halakhah* and *mitzvah*. These avenues may well be as fulfilling and rewarding as other avenues are for men. The avenues are different but not of lesser import. Alon's point is further illustrated by Mary Shoub in her essay "Jewish Women's History: Development of a Critical Methodology."[128]

See also Yehiel M. Epstein, *Arukh ha-Shulhan*, vol. 5 [Warsaw, 1884], *Yoreh De'ah* 246:19–20.)

126. For an exposition of this topic, see Berman, "The Status of Women in Halakhic Judaism"; Ellinson, *Serving the Creator*, chap. 7; and Meiselman, *Jewish Women in Jewish Law*, chap. 20. Also see Biale, *Women and Jewish Law*, section on Prayer and Torah Reading, pp. 17–29. See especially her treatment of the concept of *kvod ha-tzibur* (the esteem of the congregation), an aspect tied in with these exclusions.

127. See, for example, N. Wolpert, A. Braunspiegel, M. Willig, J. Parnes, and Z. Schachter, "Teshuvah be-Din Nashim be-Tefilah, be-Kriat ha-Torah, be-Hakafot," *Hadarom* 54 (Sivan 5745 [1985]): 49–53. For one who argues that women's prayer groups do not contravene *Halakhah*, see Avraham Weiss, *Women's Prayer Groups: A Halakhic Analysis of Women's Prayer Groups* (Hoboken, NJ: Ktav, 1990).

128. Mary Shoub, "Jewish Women's History: Development of a Critical Method-

Women's participation in Judaism, Shoub believes, must be studied from a gender-specific viewpoint. As women and men are halakhically responsible for the performance of different *mitzvot*, their roles must differ concerning religious participation. Consequently, religious participation by women should be measured surrounding the home, not the synagogue. Marion Kaplan, professor of history and writer on the social history of Jewish women, agrees with the conception of the centrality of the home for Jewish women's religiosity:

> Family life and the religious observance of the Sabbath, holidays and dietary laws were clearly women's domain. Women's relationship to their religion and to their Jewish community, then, should be measured in a way different from men's: that is, by the extent of their maintenance of "Jewishness" in the home and by their social contact with family and other Jews.[129]

Tamar Frankiel, a scholar of comparative religion and an Orthodox Jew, does just that in her recent work *The Voice of Sarah*.[130] Probing the intimate connection between traditional Judaism and authentic feminine spirituality, she illustrates how Jewish tradition affirms an eminently feminine approach to religious experience and observance. Frankiel discloses how the seasonal and traditional women's rituals make Judaism a religion deeply attuned to women's growth. Her discussions of salient issues—food, sexuality, inwardness, and feminine concepts of God—open fresh outlooks on women's self-understanding. Frankiel asserts that women "must learn to understand feminine spirituality on its own terms, for only then can [they] begin to evaluate [their] present situation in Judaism with attention to its inner depths."[131]

Debra Renee Kaufman, in a recent book, *Rachel's Daughters: Newly Orthodox Jewish Women*, discovers that this line of reasoning is operative when studying *ba'alot teshuvah*—women undergoing religious conversional experiences and espousing Orthodox Judaism. A feminist and a sociologist, she was interested to determine whether women experience Orthodoxy in the way in which they are theologically described in male-oriented literature.[132] In her study, she relied not "on historical abstractions to explain a woman's 'place' in Jewish orthodoxy, but rather upon [the] immediate and concrete experiences"[133] of

---

ology," *Conservative Judaism* 35 (Winter 1982): 41–42.

129. Marion Kaplan, "Tradition and Transition: The Acculturation, Assimilation and Integration of Jews in the Kaiserreich, a Gender Analysis." Unpublished paper, in Shoub, "Jewish Women's History," p. 42.

130. Frankiel, *The Voice of Sarah*.

131. Ibid., pp. 44–45.

132. Kaufman, *Rachel's Daughters*, p. 69.

133. Ibid.

the 150 women she interviewed. Kaufman was intrigued by those American *ba'alot teshuvah* who had come of age during the counterculture and the birth of the women's movement but who, in the 1970s and 1980s, embraced a seemingly patriarchal society. Disillusioned and threatened by the pursuit of personal fulfillment over commitment and obligation, the women under study claim that Jewish Orthodoxy replaces the "masculine ethos" of aggression and self-importance with a "feminine ethos" that stresses modesty and community. The *ba'alot teshuvah* find a "moral community of both public and private virtue," which provides them with a moral framework in which to make decisions. But the "ultimate attraction" of Jewish Orthodoxy for these women is their discovery of a "setting in which values of the private sphere and those associated with female and family are publicly shared, respected, and, most important, acted upon."[134] The specialness of woman and the importance of her sphere of activity within Orthodox Judaism were stressed throughout the interviews. The women asserted that their "return" to Orthodoxy "put them in touch with their own bodies, in control of their own sexuality, and in a position to value the so-called feminine virtues of nurturance, mutuality, family, and motherhood."[135] For *ba'alot teshuvah*, says Kaufman, sexuality and motherhood are communal acts. The women link the feminine and the female with the sacred and spiritual meaning of life, turning their devalued status in the secular world into a high-status aspect that the Orthodox community confers.[136]

These *ba'alot teshuvah*, while rejecting feminism, maintain a gender consciousness that incorporates aspects of feminist ideology, and, in the course of the interviews, they often used feminist rhetoric to explain their lives. One woman summed up her feelings as follows: "I love being a woman in this tradition. The Jewish people, the Torah, and the *Shekhinah* (the indwelling of God) are all feminine in the way I see Judaism. All the most important things that can happen to you in life–loving, birthing, working–are put into a feminine framework."[137] Many of the women who were interviewed were undisturbed by women's exemptions from certain *mitzvot*. They generally view these exemptions as indicative of woman's greater self-discipline and innate spiritual sensibility. They experience their female and familial roles as inextricably linked to their religious role. "No woman," Kaufman attests, "doubts her theological equality in Orthodox Judaism." One of the women

---

134. Ibid., p. 35.

135. Ibid., p. 8.

136. Similarly, Lynn Davidman, in her study of *ba'alot teshuvah*, concludes that Orthodox definitions of gender and clear guidelines for a nuclear family life are major factors in Orthodoxy's appeal to modern individuals. See *Tradition in a Rootless World*, chap. 5.

137. Kaufman, *Rachel's Daughters*, quoted on p. 51.

declared, "I am glad that women do not have to obey the time-bound commandments. It is so much more meaningful for me to be spontaneous in my prayers. . . . I like the fact that the men and the women are expected to reach holiness through different means. I think it suits our personalities."[138] Kaufman sums up her findings of *ba'alot teshuvah* as follows: "They do not see their sphere as inferior, but rather as a place where they are free to create their own forms of personal, social, intellectual, and, at times, political relationships."[139]

These *ba'alot teshuvah* celebrate their differences within Orthodoxy. But for other women—the discontented ones—contemporary Orthodox rabbi Saul Berman identifies, sympathizes with, and attempts to propose solutions to the areas of discontent. Nevertheless, he offers a rejoinder:

> When all is said and done, these laws were the total preoccupation of centuries of Jewish sages and scholars. Indeed, these were the very same sages and scholars through whose interpretive skills capital punishment was virtually abolished; through whose legal creativity the task of the transformation and eventual elimination of slavery was accomplished; and through whose social awareness a Jewish social welfare system came into existence which is un-matched to this day for its sensitivity to the feelings of the poor. It has often been suggested that the ethical strength of a legal system and its jurists may be gauged by their treatment of the powerless: the poor, the alien, the widow and the orphan. By any such test, Jewish law and its Rabbinic jurists would stand high, if not at the pinnacle, among the legal systems of the world. It is difficult to conceive of these same jurists' setting out with malice aforethought to subject their own mothers, wives and daughters to the most blatant forms of injustice and inequity. It is crucial, therefore, for us to see these laws and practices through

138. Ibid., quoted on p. 48.

139. Ibid., p. 113. Lynn Davidman, in her research of newly Orthodox women, found that professional women's acceptance of traditional gender roles within Ortho-doxy did not extend to other areas of their lives: although they did not object to their lack of access to full participation in the synagogue, they would strongly object to the same lack in the workplace. She speculates that "because work was not central for them, they felt they did not risk much by insisting on fair treatment. In contrast, the synagogue seemed to offer true fulfillment. Therefore, they did not want to jeopardize their chances by objecting to the system and struggling with it" (*Tradition in a Rootless World*, p. 128).

An alternative possibility for explaining this behavior is that the Orthodox woman will not accept discrimination in the workplace because she does not believe there is legitimate reason for it. But in Orthodox Judaism, given her belief in the divine origin of *Halakhah*, she presumes that there must be some valid reason for male/female distinctions. Aside from investigating possibilities for change from within the system, as this work attempts to do with regard to the study of Torah, the Orthodox woman is more likely to passively investigate divine reasoning for male/female distinctions, rather than engage in vehement fighting for change, as she would do in the workplace.

their eyes if we are ever to achieve a Jewish perspective as to how to proceed in the future.[140]

It may be difficult for us to view these laws through the eyes of our sages, for we cannot replicate their social context to the extent that we can justify or criticize their intentions. However, one may rest assured that the general principles of their process, mainly "to do that which is right in the sight of God,"[141] would be operative. We, in our day, can achieve a Jewish perspective by implementing the rabbis' halakhic system in ways that are sympathetic to their overall goals of justice and equity. It is from this perspective that I will proceed as we come now to dealing with the specific subject at hand, that of religious education and the Jewish woman.

---

140. Berman, "The Status of Women in Halakhic Judaism," p. 117.

141. See Deuteronomy 6:18.

3

The Study of Torah by Women in Halakhic (Jewish Legal) and Extra-Halakhic Literature

Jewish legal sources are useful in probing general trends of Jewish education for women. For the most part, women have been excluded from Torah study by teachers of *Halakhah*, even though Torah study is not a commandment bound by time. In the Mishnaic period, debate is recorded on whether a woman should be precluded from the study of Torah. Nevertheless, there is evidence that in early times women studied both Scripture and *Mishnah*. In this regard *Tosefta Berakhot* 2:12[1] states that even women who are in various states of impurity may study Scriptures and *Mishnah*. From the Middle Ages to the twentieth-century the legal codes and their commentators preclude women from the study of *Mishnah* and its oral traditions and also discourage the study of Written Scriptures and their traditions. In the early part of the twentieth century allowance is made for women to study Written Scriptures because "of the extraordinary needs of the age." As the century progresses, there is evidence, albeit slight, of a more permissive attitude toward women's study of the Oral Law.

TALMUDIC JURISPRUDENCE

The Talmud indicates a variety of approaches to the study of Torah by women. The most important source posits that it is obligatory for fathers to

---

1. The *Tosefta* is a post-mishnaic document that elaborates upon mishnaic themes and is generally dated to the third and fourth centuries C.E. Our statement is also cited in the Jerusalem Talmud *Berakhot* 3:4.

instruct their sons and not their daughters. The Talmud[2] explains the biblical verse "And you shall teach them to your children" (Deuteronomy 11:19) to mean that fathers must teach their sons. The word "children" (*beneikhem*) in Hebrew is said to mean, in this context, sons, and not daughters. According to this source, (1) there is no obligation to teach women Torah, (2) women are under no obligation to teach themselves (to study) Torah, and (3) women are not obligated to teach others. Hence, women are effectively exempted from the cycle of learning and teaching and "remain outside the bond of teaching which connects father and son in every generation."[3] However, the necessary implication of this talmudic passage is that it is permissible, even if not obligatory, for fathers to instruct their daughters. The Italian rabbinical scholar Isaiah ben Elijah di Trani (the Younger, "Riaz"; d. c. 1280) states this implication as follows: "Although the woman is not commanded to study Torah, as it is written: 'And you shall teach them [the laws] to your sons,' meaning, and not to your daughters, nevertheless, if one wishes to teach his daughter, he may do so."[4]

In accordance with further talmudic principles, such instruction for women would be counted as meritorious for them. If a woman studies Torah, it is considered a commendable act and falls within the Talmud's discussion of the optional learning of Torah, wherein the merit is great but of lesser degree than that of an "obligated performer":

> Mar, the son of Rabina said . . . that the person [who voluntarily performs a precept] does not receive the reward of the obligated one but rather of a non-obligated performer [which is less], for Rabbi Hanina said: "Greater is the reward of those who have having been enjoined and do *mitzvot* ("divine commandments") than of those who not having been enjoined and [merely out of free will] do *mitzvot*.[5]

Elsewhere, the discussion focuses on pragmatic considerations. In *Mishnah Sotah* 3:4 we find two opposing viewpoints: On one hand, it is obligatory for fathers to instruct their daughters. This was said in the context of the matter of the adulterous wife: "Ben Azzai said that a man must teach his daughter Torah. . . ." The issues surrounding the statement are beyond the scope of our discussion. Suffice it to note that Ben Azzai argues that it is necessary for a woman to learn Torah, not only so that she can follow the laws but also so that she can understand the mechanisms governing Jewish law and can

---

2. *Kiddushin* 29b; *Berakhot* 2:7, *Eruvin* 10:1.

3. Rachel Biale, *Women and Jewish Law* (New York: Schocken, 1984), p. 33.

4. Several fragments of Isaiah di Trani's works appear in David Sassoon, *Me'at Devash* (Oxford, 1928). This particular quotation is from this book and is excerpted in Simha Assaf, *Mekorot le-Toldot ha-Hinukh be-Yisrael*, vol. 2 (Tel Aviv: Dvir, 1930), p. 95.

5. *Bava Kamma* 38a.

deduce and apply the significant underlying principles. On the other hand, the *Mishnah* records the harsh view of Rabbi Eliezer: "He who teaches his daughter Torah teaches her *tiflut* [variously interpreted as 'distortions' or 'deviations' or 'trivialities']."

An indication of just how strongly Rabbi Eliezer, who discouraged the study of the Torah according to the previously cited *Mishnah*, felt on the subject of teaching women Torah is found in the Jerusalem Talmud.[6] There it is related that the rabbi avoided a question of biblical interpretation put to him by a woman. He answered her sharply, "Woman's wisdom is in the loom," using as a prooftext a biblical passage (Exodus 35:25): "And all the women that were wise-hearted did spin with their hands." When questioned by his son as to his prudence in avoiding her question, considering that Rabbi Eliezer's Levite family were recipients of this wealthy woman's generous annual tithes, he replied, "Better the words of Torah be burned than that they be transmitted to women." (This incident is recounted again in a shortened version in the Babylonian Talmud.[7] Both Talmuds then go on to answer the woman's intelligent question.)

In summation, it appears that the question of women's study of Torah is left open in the *Mishnah*, where a number of views are presented. Subsequently, the *Tosefta* illustrates a positive attitude toward such study. The Babylonian Talmud (*Sotah* 21a), in its final editing, suggests that women are better off aiding their sons and husbands in their study than themselves studying. Women then share the great reward of "male" study as opposed to the substantially lesser merit of their own study. Eliezer Waldenberg suggests that the practice in Palestine was to allow women to study the Oral Tradition, whereas in Babylonia they were discouraged from doing so. In this way, he explains the differences between the Palestinian sources, such as the *Tosefta* on one hand and the Babylonian Talmud on the other.[8] As with most cases, however, it is the Babylonian Talmud that is considered to be more authoritative and serves as the base for the development of *Halakhah* subsequent to the talmudic period. It is, in fact, the prohibitive opinion of Rabbi Eliezer that became the basis of subsequent Jewish law on this subject.

STUDY OF TORAH BY WOMEN IN PRE-TWENTIETH-CENTURY LEGAL SOURCES

Let us now examine the basic laws forbidding and dissuading instructors from teaching women anything beyond what women had to apply in their daily

---

6. *Sotah* 3:4.

7. *Yoma* 66b.

8. See *She'alot u-Teshuvot Tzitz Eliezer* (Jerusalem, 1985), 9:3. Cf. *Tosefta Berakhot* 2:12 and *Berakhot* 22a.

living. Although a door was left open for women to study on their own if they somehow managed to master the linguistic and other formal tools necessary to engage in such private study, instruction for women, meaning formal and comprehensive teaching of the texts and reasoning of the Oral Torah (such as is found in the Talmud), was forbidden. Even such formal instruction in the Written Torah–the Hebrew Bible–was highly discouraged.

In the Middle Ages, Maimonides (1135–1204) codified his impression of the study of Torah for women:

> A woman who studies Torah is rewarded, but not to the same degree as is a man. This is so since she is not commanded. Anyone who does that which one is not commanded to do does not receive the same reward as one who is commanded, but a lesser reward. However, even though she is rewarded, the sages commanded that a man should not teach his daughter Torah. This is because most women are not attuned to study and so will turn the words of Torah into distortions according to the inadequacy of their minds. Our sages said that anyone who teaches his daughter Torah is to be considered as if he had taught her distortions (*tiflut*).[9] This statement refers to the Oral Torah; as for the Written Torah, he ought not to teach her, but if he has done so, it is not "as if he had taught her distortions."[10]

The salient points of Maimonides' position are (1) that there is merit in the study of Oral Torah for women, but the rabbis commanded fathers not to teach their daughters and (2) that there is merit in the study of the Written Law, yet it is recommended that fathers not teach it to their daughters, although this is not prohibited outright.

Though it is apparent that Maimonides' approach is based on talmudic

---

9. It is interesting to note that whereas in the *Mishnah* Rabbi Eliezer's opinion is cited as his own individual view, Maimonides represents it as the blanket statement of "the sages" in general. According to contemporary scholar Isadore Twersky, Maimonides readily acknowledged his tendency to omit names or to make collective references to scholars under the "totally plastic rubric" of "the sages." As Twersky states: "His omission of names . . . was a non-issue according to Maimonides. One could even reverse the tables and contend, as Maimonides did, that anonymity was a virtue, for it bolstered the authoritativeness of the oral tradition by removing any misleading impressions of fragmentation, dissonance, and conflict. It substituted consensus for controversy, general norm for individual opinion. . . . It was not only a literary device but also a polemical-ideological achievement" (*Introduction to the Code of Maimonides [Mishneh Torah]* [New Haven and London: Yale University Press, 1980], pp. 111 and 109).

10. *Mishneh Torah, Hilkhot Talmud Torah* 1:13. This translation follows the understanding of Rabbi Avraham di Boton (Greece, sixteenth century), in his *Lehem Mishnah*, a commentary found in the standard printed editions of Maimonides' *Mishneh Torah*.

sources, there is sufficient departure from talmudic statements on the issue to have demanded the attention of many subsequent scholars. The most striking problems these teachers deal with concern Maimonides' bases for his distinction between (1) the Written Law and the Oral Law and (2) what is preferable and what is not preferable regarding women's study of the Written Law. In seeking to discover Maimonides' sources, interpreters reflect, in their approach, their individual predilections concerning the study of Torah for women.

One approach to explaining Maimonides' distinction between the Written Law and the Oral Law in Torah study for women is based on a passage in tractate *Hagigah* (3a). Here we find that the king of Israel, every seventh year, would assemble the people to relate a passage of the Torah. Rabbi Joel Sirkis (Poland, seventeenth-century), in his *Bayit Hadash* commentary,[11] states:

> Maimonides' distinction between Written and Oral Torah is based on a passage in Tractate *Hagigah*: "Assemble the people, the men, the women, and the children" [Deuteronomy 31:10] – if the men come to learn and the women come to listen, why then do children come?" We see from here that women have an obligation to listen to the Written Torah in order that they will know to perform commandments. Of necessity, we must conclude that when Rabbi Eliezer said, "It is as if he teaches her *tiflut*," he was referring to the Oral Law. Moreover, when Maimonides wrote that it is preferable that a father not teach his daughter [Written Torah] it would seem that he was interpreting this statement. This statement, in the name of Rabbi Elazar ben Azariah, says: "If men come to learn and women come to listen," but it does not say "If men and women come to listen and to learn" (*Hagigah* 3a). Thus it is preferable that women not be taught formally and routinely, but only by informal listening, as need arises. Then it is an obligatory act just as in the injunction to assemble the people in order that they [women] will know to perform commandments. However, learning formally and routinely is to be discouraged, yet if he [a father] does teach her [a daughter] it is not as if he teaches her *tiflut*. Were it to be *tiflut* it would be prohibited to teach her even by informal listening, and it would not be obligatory to assemble women to listen to the Torah. Nevertheless, in regards to commandments which pertain to women, they are obligated to learn them, and therefore, women recite the Torah blessings each day, as is legislated by the *Tur* in *Orah Hayim* 47.

Rabbi Sirkis posits that the distinction that Maimonides drew between the Oral Law and the Written Law (i.e., women are not to be taught the first but only preferably should not be taught the second) is based on the recognition that women were enjoined to listen to the Written Torah at a prescribed

---

11. This commentary appears in the standard printed editions of the *Arba'ah Turim* of Rabbi Yaakov ben Asher. See commentary to *Tur, Yoreh De'ah* 246:6.

ceremony. Maimonides then must have understood that the injunction against the teaching of Torah to women was to be limited to the Oral Law. Rabbi Sirkis believes that in Maimonides' understanding of the talmudic passage in *Hagigah* 3a, he differentiates between the notion of "learning," which is for males, and the notion of "listening," which is for females. "Listening" is said to mean informal instruction regarding pertinent matters.

Rabbi David Halevy, in his commentary of *Turei Zahav*,[12] elaborates on this distinction. He claims that the *Hagigah* passage illustrating "learning" refers to involved and lengthy analysis of Written Torah passages, whereas "listening" suggests attentiveness to the literal, unanalyzed text. He proposes, not entirely convincingly,[13] that when Maimonides stated that it is not preferable for fathers to instruct daughters in the Written Law, he was referring to complex and involved analysis of the text. Both Rabbis Sirkis and Halevy permit the relating of simple, literal material from the Written Law as circumstances require, but not in any formal setting. For the most part, the analyses that these decisors present are consonant with the practices prevalent in their days. Indeed, as Rabbi Halevy notes, such was the common practice in his day. One wonders precisely what Rabbi Menahem Mendel Auerbach (1620–1689) meant by his tantalizing expression "for although they [women] are exempt from the study of the Oral Law, nevertheless they are obligated in the study of the Written Law."[14]

We may now observe that women, as far as *Halakhah* was concerned, were not to be taught Torah in any formal manner. However, the underlying premise of the commentaries recognizes that women did attend synagogue sermons. This observation is corroborated by the notice in the codes that a partition may be erected on the Sabbath, when women come to hear the sermon.[15]

It must not be thought that the issue of practical knowledge for women

---

12. Commentary of *Turei Zahav* on *Shulhan Arukh, Yoreh De'ah* 246:6. (This commentary to the *Shulhan Arukh* was written in seventeenth-century Poland.)

13. Rabbi Elijah of Vilna, in his glosses (*Be'ur haGra*) to *Shulhan Arukh, Yoreh De'ah* 246, derives Maimonides' principle from here and from an alternative source, *Mishnah Nedarim* 35:2 – "But he teaches his sons and his daughters Scriptures." Rabbi Michael Winkler ("Limud Torah la-Nashim," *Otzar ha-Hayim* 5 [1929]: 14) notes that the reading "his daughters" is absent in both early citations of the Mishnah and many manuscripts. Rabbi Winkler derives Maimonides' principle first from *Tosefta, Berakhot* 2:12, which refers to women studying on their own Scriptures and Mishnah, and secondly, from *Tosefta, Pesahim* 10:4, which implies that Scriptures alone may be taught.

14. See commentary of *Ateret Zekenim* to *Shulhan Arukh, Orah Hayim* 47:3.

15. See Rabbi Abraham Gombiner, commentary of *Magen Avraham* (Poland, seventeenth century) to *Shulhan Arukh, Orah Hayim* 315:1, citing Rabbi Mordekhai ben Hillel (Germany, thirteenth century).

was ignored. The complex structures of Jewish civilization had to be mediated to women. The decisors accepted that the standard view of Torah study for women is that of Maimonides. His view is cited authoritatively by the major codes: Rabbi Jacob ben Asher's *Arba'ah Turim* (called simply the *Tur*; Spain, fourteenth century) and Rabbi Joseph Caro's *Shulhan Arukh* (Palestine, six-teenth century).[16] However, Maimonides said nothing concerning what should be taught to women, and this state of affairs had to be corrected. Therefore, Rabbi Moses Isserles (popularly called by the acronym of his name, Rema), the sixteenth-century eastern European scholar, in his glosses to *Shulhan Arukh, Yoreh De'ah* 246:6, officially codified the long-standing opinion that women should study those laws that apply to them. Surely no one could object to the reasoning that if women were responsible for acts, they should learn about them. Many had recognized this to be the case. Some of these earlier authorities were Rabbis Abraham ben David (known as Rabad; Provence, twelfth century), Judah ha-Hasid (Germany, twelfth–thirteenth centuries), Isaac of Corbeil (France, thirteenth century), Jacob Halevi Moellin (Maharil; Germany, fourteenth–fifteenth centuries), Jacob Landau (Agur; Germany, fifteenth century), and Solomon Luria (Maharshal; Poland, six-teenth century). According to these authorities, a woman is obligated to study the laws applicable to her, whereas Rabad and Maharshal require a woman to recite Torah study benedictions on this account.[17] This obligation is conso-nant with the statement in tractate *Yevamot* (109b): "All who are obligated in the performance of a *mitzvah* are obligated in its study, as it is stated, 'that you may learn them and observe to do them' [Deuteronomy 5:1]."

Rabbi Isaac of Corbeil, France, was a thirteenth-century authority on Ashkenazic practices. In his *Sefer Mitzvot Katan* he enumerates the positive and negative precepts that apply to women, stating, "Scrutinizing them in detail will profit the women, as studying Talmud profits the men."[18] Rabbi Isaac insists that women study methodically from a text the *mitzvot* that apply to them, rather than rely solely on oral transmission of the laws. In contrast, it is to be noted that two centuries later, Maharil illustrates the reality that women do not learn from texts:

---

16. See *Yoreh De'ah* 246:6. Interestingly, in quoting Maimonides, the *Tur* makes a significant emendation. Instead of permitting the learning of Written Law, and prohibiting the study of Oral Law, as does Maimonides, this later text does the exact opposite. Most commentators, including Rabbi Caro (see his commentary of *Beit Yosef* on *Tur, Yoreh De'ah* 246), however, attribute it to a printing error, since the author of the *Tur* expressedly indicates that he is quoting Maimonides.

17. See Rabbi Joel Sirkis, *Bayit Hadash (Bah)*, commentary to *Tur, Orah Hayim* 47.

18. Rabbi Isaac Ben Joseph of Corbeil, *Amudei Golah: Sefer Mitzvot Katan* (Satmar, 1935), Introduction. (Actually, this statement is made by a disciple of the author in the introduction to this book.)

Even though women must fulfill negative precepts and those positive precepts not dependent on a set time, they should not be taught systematically, for it is as if they are being taught *tiflut*. . . . And as for the knowledge required for the observance of the *mitzvot*, they can learn the basic principles through tradition. We see in our generation that women are familiar with laws . . . all by means of traditional practice.[19]

Regarding "learning through tradition," we note the words of Judah he-Hasid, who writes in his *Sefer Hasidim* as follows:

One must teach his daughters the *mitzvot*, i.e., the halakhic rulings. The statement in the Talmud that "he who teaches his daughter Torah is as if he taught her *tiflut*" refers only to the depths of learning: the rationale for the *mitzvot* and the mysteries of the Torah; these are not taught to a woman or a minor. However, a woman should be taught the laws concerning the *mitzvot*, for if she does not know the laws of the Sabbath, how can she properly observe the Sabbath? And the same goes for all the commandments in order that she be mindful in their performance. However, it is not permitted for a bachelor to teach girls even if the father were to stand right there and watch over them, so that they are not secluded together. For [even then] his desires or hers might overwhelm them. Rather the father should teach his daughter or his wife.[20]

Sefer Hasidim requires teaching women the legal aspects of Torah so that they know practical duties, especially those laws pertaining to them. What is irrelevant, according to Rabbi Judah he-Hasid, is teaching women the rationale for the commandments and the mystical interpretation of the Torah. Learning for functional purposes rather than for academic objectives is considered valid for women by this scholar. Though he seems to permit the hiring of a male teacher for a girl, he cautions against hiring a bachelor. This is not because of the question of Torah study by women, but because of the danger of sexual temptation by either party. Practical education is obligatory, according to *Sefer Hasidim*.

The codified laws to the effect that women are legally required to study all commandments for which they bear responsibility to perform follows the wording of *Sefer ha-Agur*[21] by the fifteenth-century German rabbi Jacob Landau, who uses the expression that women are "obligated to learn the laws which are applicable to them." Study from books was not universal and seems to have been advocated in the advanced cultural milieu of Provence but not in "Dark Age" Germany.

---

19. Rabbi Jacob Halevi Moellin, *Responsa Maharil* (Cracow, 1881), no. 199.

20. Rabbi Yehudah he-Hasid, *Sefer Hasidim*, ed. R. Margolius (Jerusalem: Mossad Harav Kook, 1957), sec. 313.

21. *Tefillah* 2:5.

Rabbi Moses Isserles's codification authorizing the study of practical commandments for women does not abrogate the medieval ban on public, formal education, but it underscores the importance of education for women, albeit in private matters and in private instruction. Isserles advocated this form of education to be universal. The general tone of the decisors was that the study of the Oral and the Written Law by women was to be highly discouraged.

Rabbi Joshua Falk (Poland, sixteenth–seventeenth centuries), in his *Perishah* commentary to *Tur, Yoreh De'ah* 246:15, proposes that Maimonides' and subsequent codes' concern was for women who lacked the wherewithal to master such study.[22] On the basis of Maimonides' usage of the term "most women," he argues that some women, apparently in the minority, who demonstrate on their own that they could master such study are permitted to engage in the learning of Torah. Hence, it would seem that Falk permits women to study on their own and if successful, would allow fathers to formally instruct their daughters once they know their abilities. It is to be noted that Falk's mother and wife were knowledgeable in aspects of the Oral Law. No one has raised objections to Falk's proposal that talented women may study all aspects of Torah and apparently be taught in a more private manner than men.

Falk's directive finds its echo in the contemporary work *Ma-ayan Ganim*, written by an Italian rabbi, Samuel ben Elhanan Jacob Archivolti:

> Perhaps the words of our Sages, i.e., "Whoever teaches his daughter Torah is as if he teaches her *tiflut*" referred to a father teaching a girl when she is young. This is so even if through her actions it can be recognized that she acts in a pure and upright manner. Certainly under such conditions [her youth] there may be cause for concern since most women are presumed to be light-headed, wasting their time on nonsense. Since the majority of them are so, they sin from their impoverished minds. However, the women who dedicate their hearts to approach the service of God by choosing good for its own sake will surely rise to the summit of the mountain of the Lord and dwell in His holy place, for they are exemplary women. The scholars of their generation should treat them with honor and respect, and encourage them and strengthen their hands by saying, "Go forward and succeed, and may Heaven send you all necessary assistance."[23]

The tenor of Rabbi Archivolti's words might be taken to mean that a father could instruct an older daughter who wishes to dedicate herself to Torah

---

22. This understanding of Maimonides is further clarified by Rabbi Abraham Isaac Kook in *Igrot ha-Reiyah* (Jerusalem, 1922), no. 467 (a collection of letters dealing with philosophical and halakhic subjects; Palestine, early twentieth century).

23. This responsum is quoted in Rabbi Barukh Epstein's *Torah Temimah* (Vilna, 1904), commentary on Deuteronomy 11:18. (*Torah Temimah* is a commentary to and a talmudic and midrashic exegesis on the Pentateuch written in early twentieth-century Russia.)

study. In this regard, Rabbi Archivolti's position is similar to that of Falk. However, it is to be noted that neither of these two rabbis explicitly states that such teaching is permissible, although such implication is reasonable. What is novel on the part of Rabbi Archivolti is that he encourages the leading scholars of the day to support the intellectual aspirations of female Torah students. He states his position as consonant with the prevailing halakhic opinion that most women are not suited for Torah study.

The question of formal instruction for women is nowhere directly addressed but by the eighteenth century, scholars were generally permitting the individual instruction of exceptional women. Rabbi Hayim Joseph David Azulai, popularly referred to as Hida (the acronym of his name), the eighteenth-century Sephardic halakhist and mystic, notes that Beruriah, a scholar mentioned in the Talmud,[24] whose motivation and abilities were recognized, had been taught Torah. He suggests, then, that the sages did not establish a general prohibition against teaching women Torah but had certainly indicated their uneasiness with the concept.[25] And what of a woman who studied on her own? In the nineteenth century, the Hungarian rabbi Yehudah Aszdod stated categorically, "We do not find anywhere that women are prohibited from studying."[26] Undoubtedly, his assertion is based on the fact that the language of the talmudic statements and of Maimonides expressedly refers to a father's teaching a daughter. There is no mention of a prohibition regarding a woman's studying on her own. While self-instruction was not encouraged, neither was it forbidden.[27] Nineteenth-century scholar Rabbi Joseph Babad, in his commentary to Sefer ha-Hinukh, considers learned women's opinions valid in halakhic decision-making processes.[28]

We can now observe that teachers of Halakhah from the twelfth century until the dawn of the twentieth century maintained a single view toward Torah study by women. The eighteenth-century Russian hasidic leader Rabbi

---

24. Eruvin 53a, Pesahim 62b.

25. Rabbi Hayim Joseph David Azulai, Tov Ayin (Husyatin, 1904), sec. 4 (a halakhic treatise, eighteenth century).

26. Yehudah Aszdod, Yehudah Ya'aleh: Responsa (Lemberg, 1873), sec. on Yoreh De'ah 48.

27. This view, however, may not be universal. Both Rabbi David Halevy (Turei Zahav to Shulkhan Arukh, Orah Hayim 47:14) and Rabbi Elijah of Vilna (Biur haGra ad loc.) refer to the injunction against teaching one's daughter and the concept of tiflut while discussing an issue that would pertain to female self-instruction. The modern-day decisor Rabbi Eliezer Waldenberg presents the possibility that these two scholars did not distinguish between a woman's self-instruction and her being taught (Tzizt Eliezer [Jerusalem, 1985]). Rabbi Waldenberg, however, does question this assertion. We can maintain our assumption that most scholars would have permitted self-instruction.

28. See commentary of Minhat Hinukh (Jerusalem, n.d.), Mitzvah 78, sec. 6.

Shneur Zalman of Lyady incorporated this view in his code. He states that women are exempt from the commandment of learning Torah and of teaching it to their children; nor need they support Torah educational institutions (aside from their requirement to give charity). It is preferable that a woman sponsor the males in her family to learn Torah than that she learn Torah herself. The rabbis discourage a man from teaching his daughter Torah, because most women are not suited for such study. Nevertheless, women are obliged to study all laws of the Torah, both biblical and rabbinic, which apply to them.[29]

What does change are the emphasis and the nuance. Fathers are not to instruct their daughters. Talented women may study on their own. Women may be taught laws that apply to them. There are veiled hints suggesting that all of Torah might be taught to exemplary women. However, certain circles still maintained stringent restrictions. We find in the sermons of Rabbi Moses Sofer (the *Hatam Sofer*), leader of Orthodox Jewry in Hungary in the eighteenth and early nineteenth centuries, that girls should merely read "German works in Hebrew letters [Yiddish], based on aggadic tales from the Talmud, but nothing else."[30] Thus, at the turn of the twentieth century, women were not universally knowledgeable, even to the extent that could be permitted within *Halakhah*.

STUDY OF TORAH BY WOMEN IN TWENTIETH-CENTURY LEGAL SOURCES

Rabbi Yehiel Michel Epstein composed an important code of practical Jewish law at the close of the nineteenth and the beginning of the twentieth century. He does not change the basic law, which by this time was completely accepted. However, he does note an important societal innovation concerning the education of women. Whereas throughout previous generations in eastern Europe most women did not know Hebrew and had little resource to study the laws that applied to them but in most instances learned what they needed to know by cultural osmosis, Rabbi Epstein justifies a new practice. It would seem that halakhic guides in the vernacular for women were previously unknown to the women of his native Belorussia (although they existed in other places, as we shall see). "And we have never taught our women from a text. We are only familiar with the custom that a woman teaches her daughter and daughter-in-law the pertinent customs that apply to them." Rabbi Epstein defends the use of the halakhic works in Yiddish that were innovated in his

---

29. *Shulhan Arukh ha-Rav*, vol. 6, Laws of Talmud Torah 1:14.

30. Quoted in Assaf, *Mekorot le-Toldot ha-Hinukh be-Yisrael*, vol. 4, p. 209, from the sermons of Moses Sofer, "Hatam Sofer" (1829).

community. Obviously, objections had been raised to this new practice. He countered by saying that the women of his community were scrupulously concerned to keep *Halakhah*. Certainly, no one should think that the women would decide questionable matters for themselves, on the basis of having read these works. The women, he maintains, would consult rabbinic authorities as they always had in matters of any doubt. He does not entertain the possibility of women's learning directly from the original texts.[31]

As Jewish women in the early twentieth century become the beneficiaries of a secular education, it becomes imperative to ensure that their knowledge of Scripture and rabbinic thought be sufficient to counter the effects of a secular society and ensure the preservation of their identity as Jews. It is this argument—on ex post facto grounds—that paves the way for the universal establishment of formal religious education for girls in every segment of Jewish society.[32] This argument was debated, as early as 1903, at a special rabbinic council of Polish rabbis convened in Cracow. Rabbi Menachem Mendel Landau urged formal education for girls. Opposition was voiced by the chief rabbi of Paltawa on the grounds that this was contrary to *Halakhah*. Rabbi Landau stood his ground and, in fact, Rabbi Landau's suggestion was initially acceptable. However, after vigorous debate, at the end of the day Rabbi Landau's motion was shelved.[33] No solution was set into motion and it seemed as if none were forthcoming. In the meantime, secularist values and ideas continued to encroach upon the minds of young women. A response to the situation was the 1917 founding of the Beth Jacob movement in Poland, a network of schools for girls that subsequently became worldwide, and the 1921 establishment of the *Yavneh* schools for girls in Lithuania. When questioned about the appropriateness of formal religious education for women, Rabbi Israel Meir ha-Cohen (Kagan, 1838–1933; popularly referred to by the name of one of his major works, *Hafetz Hayim*), the leading spiritual leader of eastern Europe, replied that in the past there had been no need to teach girls the tradition institutionally, as they could follow what they saw being practiced in their homes and communities. He wrote:

31. *Arukh ha-Shulhan*, vol. 5, *Yoreh De'ah* 246. See also Simha Fishbane, "In Any Case, There Are No Sinful Thoughts: The Role and Status of Women in Jewish Law as Expressed in the *Arukh ha-Shulhan*," *Judaism* 42:4 (Fall 1993); and Simha Fishbane, "A Response to the Challenge of the Modern Era as Reflected in the Wording of Rabbi Yechiel Mechel Epstein," in *Social Scientific Study of Jews and Judaism*, ed. Simha Fishbane, vol. 2 (Hoboken, NJ: Ktav, 1992), pp. 96–112.

32. See further Chapter Nine.

33. See Jacob Gutman, *Mekitz Nirdamim* (Piotrokow, 1904). Reprint: Copy Corner, Brooklyn, NY, 1992, pp. 51–56. This source contains the collected writings of Rabbi Menahem Mendel Landau and his records of the council debates.

Nowadays, when parental tradition has weakened and we find girls who do not live close to the parental environment, and especially that there are those who have been given a secular education, certainly it is required to teach them the Pentateuch and also the other books of Scripture [the Prophets and Hagiographia], and the ethical instructions of our sages, as in the tractate Avot, and *Menorat ha-Maor* and so on, so that the principles of our holy faith will be strong for them. Otherwise . . . they may stray from the path of God, and transgress all the precepts of our religion.[34]

Here we have for the first time a halakhic decision based on societal needs to permit to girls universal formal instruction of the Written Scripture, without any caveats. Rabbi Kagan took an unprecedented halakhic position, which was noted in justifying the education provided for women at the beginning of the twentieth century. He did not suggest that the times required that girls be trained in the intricacies of talmudic reasoning or traditional legal thought.

A contemporary of the Hafetz Hayim, Rabbi Zekel Bamberger (Kissingen, Bavaria, 1863–1934), rabbinical judge of his district, maintained that it always was permissible to teach women the Written Law. He claimed that preferably the intricate explanations of the Written Law were not to be studied. His claim might have been prompted by the realization that at least some women were studying the Written Bible with intricate commentaries drawn from the Oral Law. These women were students in the Beth Jacob seminary in Cracow. Rabbi Bamberger posited that the accepted prohibitions concerning teaching of Torah to women were applicable only in previous generations, when families dwelt in the same city for long periods and maintained religious traditions within the family. Now that times have changed and women are fluent in the vernacular and secular studies, it is a great *mitzvah* to teach them the curriculum suggested by the Hafetz Hayim. He wrote about his quandary concerning teaching to girls the biblical commentaries of Rashi and the abbreviated Hebrew codes. Bamberger thought that these works ought to be forbidden, because they might well be categorized as Oral Law. On this basis Rabbi Bamberger asked precisely what halakhic works should be taught to women and if it is permissible to teach them from written texts the laws that apply to them. He noted that if this is the case, then girls will understand Hebrew to the extent that they will be able to teach themselves the entire Torah and its commentaries. He observes that whereas it has always been forbidden to teach them such matters, it has always been entirely permissible for them to study on their own. Are we permitted to give them the tools?[35]

---

34. Rabbi Yisrael Meir ha-Cohen Kagan, *Likutei Halakhot* (St. Petersburg, 1918), *Sotah* 20a.

35. Seckel Bamberger, "She'alah be-Inyan Limud Torah la-Nashim," *Otzar ha-*

Rabbi Bamberger's question was addressed by Rabbi Michael S. Winkler, the chief decisor in Copenhagen, who responded that it was most likely that Maimonides meant only to suggest what should or should not be taught but also that it did appear that the later *Halakhah* forbade teaching women. Citing the responsum of the Hafetz Hayim, he agreed that the contemporary situation called for new measures. Rabbi Winkler leaned in the direction that women should not be taught the entire abbreviated codes, but went on to say that there is no problem in teaching them the laws that apply to them from such codes. He proceeded to bless women who, after such study, would, in fact, continue to learn the Oral law on their own. He cites numerous talmudic sources justifying such study.[36]

In theory, the issue of some kind of formal education for women had been addressed by 1930. However, this progress was not universally practiced, for we find, in the 1940s, that Rabbi Zalman Sorotzkin, a leading Lithuanian and Israeli scholar, took arms against those who continued to refuse to educate their daughters. Like the Hafetz Hayim and others, he noted the adverse results of such neglect. In a carefully worded responsum, he maintained that in contemporary society, wherein education is a prerequisite for proper motivation, such education is not only permitted but also required:

> Our age differs from earlier ages. Formerly, Jewish homes followed the *Shulhan Arukh*, and one could learn the entire Torah from experience; there was no need to teach Jewish girls Torah from a text. Now however . . . many homes are totally dissociated from many *mitzvot* and laws of the Torah. Indeed, Jewish girls coming from such homes to attend a religious school are essentially like converts and consequently they must be taught the fundamentals of Judaism and the basic practices. . . . Not only is it permitted to teach Torah to girls in our generation, it is an absolute duty; it is indeed meritorious to found schools for girls and to inculcate in their hearts pure faith and knowledge of Torah and *mitzvot*.[37]

Poetically, Rabbi Sorotzkin proceeds to state that nowadays, one who does *not* teach his daughter Torah is as if he were teaching her *tiflut*, because she is then left to fall prey to the street culture where she imbibes its "immoral

---

Hayim (an irregular periodical that appeared in Rumania in the years 1924–1938); see vol. 4, 1927 (h.d. 5688), pp. 146–148.

36. Michael Winkler, "Limud Torah la-Nashim." *Otzar ha-Hayim*, vol. 5, 1928 (h.d. 5689), pp. 14–15.

37. Rabbi Zalman Sorotzkin, *Moznaim la-Mishpat* (Jerusalem, 1955), vol. 1, responsum 42. The (English) translation of Rabbi Sorotzkin's responsum appears in Gretzel Ellinson, *Serving the Creator* (Jerusalem: World Zionist Organization, 1986), pp. 246–265.

values."[38] Indeed, in his book of homilies, *Ha-De'ah ve-haDibur*, Sorotzkin suggests that the establishment of educational institutions for girls should take precedence over those for boys:

> We find the Bible relating (Gen. 12:8) that Abraham "pitched his tent [*oholoh*] west of Beth-El." The word as written could be read *oholah*, "her tent," meaning that he first pitched his wife's tent and then his own [Rashi ad loc]. According to tradition, these tents were not ordinary tents, but abodes of learning. Thus Abraham, the first patriarch, set up two types of tents of learning: one for women and the second for men. Sarah was engaged in teaching women, propagating the monotheistic idea to her sex, while Abraham was teaching similar religious belief to men. Not by accident did Abraham precede the building of Sarah's tent to his tent, but by design, as a lesson to generations, that an era will come similar to his, when the education of the woman and setting up of "her tent of learning" should take precedence [over] his tent.[39]

Rabbi Sorotzkin defends formal schooling for women in which they will study the Written Law and also study the aspects of the Oral Law that apply to them. He maintains that women should not be taught complex, dialectic matters but must learn to conduct themselves knowledgeably. Rabbi Sorotzkin refers to the curriculum in his previously cited responsum:

> We may have certain reservations as to the Oral Torah but there should be no hesitation about teaching Scripture. . . . Only concerning *pilpul* [i.e., the study of the Oral Torah in dialectical depth] did our Sages declare, "Whoever teaches his daughter Torah etc." [*Sotah* 21b]. Women may study even the Oral Torah; but they should concern themselves with the ultimate formation of the *Halakhah*, rather than with argumentative texts.[40]

Interestingly, we may note that Rabbi Hayim Amkin, a distinguished decisor in eastern Europe whose responsa appeared in the periodical *Otzar ha-Hayim*, had already permitted such dialectical self-instruction.[41] However, Rabbi Sorotzkin avoids coming to a conclusion on the issue of voluntary study of the Oral Law in all of its complexity. This issue, as well as the question of formal

---

38. A contemporary rabbi, Benzion Fuerer, makes the same point in a responsum of his, published in *Noam* 3 (1960): 131.

39. Zalman Sorotzkin, *Ha-De'ah ve-ha-Dibur* (Jerusalem, 1955), vol. 1, Homily 17. See the entire homily for elaboration of Rabbi Sorotzkin's thesis. (Sorotzkin condenses this idea in his responsum in *Moznaim la-Mishpat*.) Also see Homily 3 on the education of women.

40. Sorotzkin, *Moznaim la-Mishpat* 1:42.

41. Amkin writes: "It is permitted for a woman herself to study Torah, even in dialectical depth." Limud Torah la-Nashim," *Otzar ha-Hayim*, vol. 5, 1928 (h.d. 5689), p. 18.

instruction of the Oral Law for women, poses a problem in modern halakhic literature.

Transcending Rabbi Sorotzkin's parameters, Rabbi Ben Zion Fuerer, in an annual collection of halakhic responsa emanating from Jerusalem, suggests that in contemporary times, when many a woman can be found teaching Torah to elementary school boys, "all laws – both those that pertain to her as a woman and those that pertain to her as a teacher of boys – are equally relevant to her [so that she may teach them]."[42] Using the rationale that the commandments that apply to boys will be taught by women, Rabbi Fuerer ingeniously submits that these laws can be categorized as laws that have practical significance for women. Since *Halakhah* requires that practical laws that apply to women must be taught to them, the laws pertaining to young boys whom women will teach are now part of the necessary knowledge a woman must acquire.

Thus, while the general trends in *Halakhah* still fall short of urging the teaching of the Oral Law, the Talmud and its commentaries, to women, we see that the limits of Maimonides' codification and its subsequent understandings are being pushed to extremes by some modern halakhic decisors (see further, additional responsa). This is consonant with a shift in this century in which women are cognizant of greater opportunities yet need to have the door opened still wider. In many ultra-Orthodox circles there is pressure to maintain the status quo with regard to women's traditional roles. Women's issues are dividing centrist and ultra-Orthodox views. It is difficult to see at present any softening in the ultra-Orthodox position. Rabbi Moses Feinstein (d. 1986), who was considered by many Orthodox people to be the decisor par excellence, showed no movement away from the position of the Hafetz Hayim at the turn of the century.[43] The respected decisor Rabbi Eliezer Waldenberg of Jerusalem wrote an extensive analysis of this issue. Although he appears to share the approach of Rabbi Feinstein, his presentation is much more nuanced.[44]

Another Jerusalem rabbi, David Auerbach, in his *Halikhot Beita*, an examination of legal issues pertaining to women, acknowledges that some opinions permit an older girl or woman to study the Oral Law. As he writes, "If it is her will to study Torah with dedicated integrity and her entire intention is to elevate herself in the service of God, she is permitted to study on her own, and even others may teach her."[45] Furthermore, Rabbi Auerbach stipulates that a

---

42. Fuerer, "Limud Torah la-Nashim," p. 31.

43. Rabbi Moshe Feinstein, *Igrot Moshe, Yoreh De'ah*, Part 3 (New York, 1982), sec. 87. (A collection of responsa following the order of the *Shulhan Arukh*.)

44. Eliezer Waldenberg, *She'alot u-Teshuvot Tzitz Eliezer* 9:3 (Jerusalem, 1985).

45. David Auerbach, *Halikhot Beita* (Jerusalem: Machon Sha'arei Ziv, 1983), p. 389. Rabbi Auerbach is the nephew of one of the leading halakhic decisors of this genera-

learned woman who has mastered *Halakhah* may render legal decisions, but she may not act as a judge. His position is supported by the notice in the *Sefer Ha-Hinukh* that refers to "a learned woman who is qualified to render legal decisions." He notes that important decisors have cited the terminology of the *Sefer Ha-Hinukh.*[46]

These legal positions concerning the study of Torah by women are analyzed in a comprehensive and insightful article by Rabbi Moshe Weinberger, who concludes that there are two essential positions.[47] The first prohibits women from the study of Oral Torah and involved study of Written Torah. The second permits women's involved study of Written Torah and individual study of Oral Torah; some permit open enrollment in classes in all areas of Torah, provided the program "constructively caters to the needs of a good number of women in a particular society."[48]

THE HALAKHIC ISSUE IN LIGHT OF HALAKHIC PROCESSES

The modern student of *Halakhah* confronts the specific issue of Torah study for women in the words "The sages commanded a man not to teach his daughter Torah. . . . Anyone who teaches his daughter Torah is to be considered as if he had taught her *tiflut*." This issue is more complicated than first meets the eye. Whereas some consider this injunction to be simply good advice, which may not be legally binding (see further Rabbis Silver and Henkin), others view the directive as a commandment of the rabbis. According to Orthodox principles, such "commandments" can be changed only by as august an assembly as that of the ancient rabbis.[49] An assembly of this nature is not convenable in our age; therefore, it may be argued, an outright rejection of this legislation may not even be contemplated. There is, however, built into the halakhic system some judicial latitude. If the reasoning responsible for the commandment is no longer applicable, in certain circumstances the commandment itself could be deemed no longer binding.[50] Viewing the situation from a wider perspective, we may also consider that ample evidence

tion, Rabbi Shlomo Zalman Auerbach of Jerusalem. The latter's letter of approbation appears in this work.

46. See Auerbach, p. 395 and n. 12. The citation from *Sefer Ha-Hinukh* is from sec. 152.

47. See Moshe Weinberger, "Teaching Torah to Women," *Journal of Halacha and Contemporary Society* 9 (Spring 1985): 19–52.

48. Ibid., p. 52.

49. Maimonides, *Mishneh Torah, Hilkhot Mamrim* 2:1.

50. Rabbi Tziv Hirsh Chajes, *Kol Sifrei Maharitz Chajes,* vol. 1 (Jerusalem, 1958), p. 229.

exists to show that when certain laws became counterproductive because they instigated hatred toward Jews, caused severe economic difficulty, were awkward to the circumstances, were inapplicable to the changing natures of people, or dropped into disuse by the people, then such laws were allowed to fall by the wayside.[51] In our case, mitigating against these forces, which might allow for change, is the strong ensconcing of the law as promulgated by the Hafetz Hayim as established in current Orthodox schools for women.

The institutionalized curriculum allows for the teaching of the Written Law and all its commentaries, the study of all pragmatic materials, and the study of sources that will infuse a law-abiding, value-filled Torah way of life, a *Torat Hayim*. What has not been sufficiently institutionalized is *Torah Lishma*, the idea that the Torah is the "Word of God and, hence, valuable per se; all areas of Torah are significant, for they are all expressive of the Divine Will, whether or not they are relevant in practice."[52] Since the *Torat Hayim* approach has met with success and acceptance, responsible decisors may therefore feel encouraged to maintain a status quo that fulfills the perceived needs of Orthodox Jewry. The question may now be addressed as to whether it is advisable to introduce the notion of *Torah Lishma* into a new type of schooling and if so, what halakhic mechanisms, if any, might best be utilized to accomplish such change.

Halakhah evolves primarily through the careful examination of the wording of accepted decisions. We have seen this process applied by Rabbi Falk (in his *Perishah* commentary), who distinguished between Maimonides' prohibition of teaching Torah to most women and the notion of self-study of Torah by women, which he saw as permissible. Analysis of this nature is an integral component of the halakhic system. It constitutes an aspect of the process referred to as "learning."

One must ask, however, how *Halakhah* responds to a motivation external to the system, such as changing societal mores and attitudes. Rabbi Benjamin Hecht identifies three distinct approaches to innovation spearheaded by outside societal forces.[53] One is to totally reject any change. The specific halakhic action that existed for centuries continues to be deemed appropriate. There is no room for innovation within this view. As we shall see, in regard to women's study of Torah, this approach is accepted by only a small minority of the Orthodox world.

The second approach is to apply the emergency power to set aside certain laws for the general good of Torah. This is sometimes referred to as *"eit la'asot*

51. Ibid.

52. Meiselman, *Jewish Women in Jewish Law* (New York: Ktav, 1978), p. 36.

53. See Benjamin Hecht, "Examining the Ideal," *Nishma* Update (December 1992). It should be noted that overlap between these approaches exists in the halakhic literature.

la-Hashem" ("it is a time to act for God").[54] This principle alludes to the religious implications of a social emergency, and has been used at certain times to mean that in a time of crisis, specific laws may be set aside. The most famous example of this involves the recording of the Oral Law. Although such was specifically forbidden, the alternative – loss of the Oral Law – would have been catastrophic.[55] Implied in this approach is the notion that any change is only a concession, almost a necessary evil, to prevent a worse occurrence from happening. According to that view, it would seem that, regarding women and Torah study, the optimal situation would have been for circumstances not to have changed and for women's education, or lack thereof, to have continued as it did. Practically, following this approach, one will also wish to effect only the minimal changes to accomplish the goal. If the fear of women's desertion of Judaism is alleviated by the study of the Written Law, there is no reason to ever consider teaching the texts of the Oral Law. This view of the emergency power, however, may not necessarily be the only one possible. Although the many Torah works that are being written today would technically fall under the prohibition of writing the Oral Law, we would be hard-pressed to find authors who contemplate that their endeavors are merely a concession and that a more idealistic world would preclude these writing efforts.[56]

The third approach is the probing of a halakhic statement to discover its exact nature and requirements, subsequently determining whether there is any room for adjustment or change or both. *Halakhah* is usually defined in terms of specific actions. At times, a particular behavior is precisely what is demanded, and there is little room for latitude in rendering decisions. At other times, however, the described action is merely the reflection of a desired ideal as manifested within a certain context. A new context, such as a change in societal practice or circumstance, may therefore yield a new, equally valid, formulation of what the *Halakhah* requires. For example, the Talmud states that there is a positive commandment for every man of Israel to write a Torah scroll.[57] Rabbi Jacob ben Asher (fourteenth century) declares, however, that

---

54. *Mishnah Berakhot* 9:5. Whether this permits a violation or a *perceived* violation is a matter that Rabbi Hecht alludes to in his article; it is beyond the scope of our discussion.

55. See *Temurah* 14b. This example also demonstrates that the emergency period may not be limited to a set time but may actually cover all of subsequent history.

56. It is related that the reason that Rabbi Elijah of Vilna's commentaries are so tight and cryptic is that he was conscious of the original prohibition and believed that he was allowed to invoke the emergency power only in the most minimal way.

57. *Sanhedrin* 21b. Women are considered exempt from this commandment based on their exemption from the requirement to study Torah. See however, Rabbi Aryeh Leib Gunzberg, *Sha'agat Aryeh* 35 (Warsaw, 1869), who challenges this assertion. One

the dictate in his times did not mean the writing of a scroll per se, but rather the writing of books for study, such as the Talmud.[58] His contention is that the specific action of writing a scroll is not what is demanded. The requirement, however, does intend the broader ideal, whereby Jews should have works from which to study. When it was forbidden to write any works of Torah, except for the actual scrolls, the *mitzvah* had to be defined in such a manner. Now that other works are written, the commandment can be fulfilled through acquiring these works. The change in circumstances resulted in a modification of how the law is manifested, not in the inherent halakhic ideal. The resultant *Halakhah* is in no way considered any less significant. A determination that a halakhic statement demands an ideal, rather than a specific action, however, requires scrupulous scholarship and must be supported in the sources.

It is within this approach that we can find the greatest flexibility in regard to women's study, especially its promotion in a positive sense. If one could argue, through a careful reading of the sources, that the Rabbinic edict did not apply to women per se but rather to women as characterized by earlier societies and that, therefore, women not so characterized are not subject to the ban, we would have an argument for the further development of women's study that fully meets the criteria of the eternal *Halakhah*. The assertion would be that it was not the specific action of teaching women Torah that was being banned. Rather, the *Halakhah* was representing through these words an ideal that caution should be exercised in teaching the depths of Torah to individuals who may misuse the information because of certain intellectual inabilities, which may or may not be societally induced. Certainly, some things about women's nature and circumstances that were once axiomatic are no longer so. In that regard, some have endeavored to "process" Maimonides' injunction by indicating that the traditional *Halakhah* warrants and sanctions not only self-instruction but actual instruction of the Oral Law to women in modern times.

Rabbi Arthur M. Silver has asked the question anew: "May women be taught Bible, *Mishnah*, and Talmud?" Silver maintains, as some others have before him, that the law that forbids teaching Torah to women is not an absolute rule but only good advice. Therefore, this advice need not be taken when the results would be negative owing to changed circumstances. Silver argues that the Hafetz Hayim (in Silver's view) deemed teaching women Bible a great *mitzvah* on this basis. If we were to follow the Hafetz Hayim's reasoning that Maimonides' advice applied only to previous times, there is no

---

of his arguments centers on the fact that women are commanded to learn the *mitzvot* applicable to them.

58. *Tur, Yoreh De'ah* 270. See also Rabbi Joshua Falk's commentary, *Perishah* ad loc., para. 8. In his companion commentary, *Derishah*, Rabbi Falk states that this precept can be fulfilled by the acquisition of such works.

reason to prohibit the teaching of *Mishnah* today. Silver believes that the Hafetz Hayim probably felt that learning Bible would be sufficient to counteract the heresies of secular studies. Surely the negative influences of today's college and university training in skepticism could not be addressed by the simple curriculum of the Hafetz Hayim. We therefore should encourage the teaching of the Oral Law in depth. Silver concludes that Maimonides would concur with this analysis. Maimonides stated that the study of the laws, including Talmud, was a precondition to the study of natural science and philosophy.[59] Silver attributes this precondition to the need for a solid religious background to withstand the possible negative attraction that study of secular subjects might exert.[60]

Silver's approach is to find the same halakhic justification for all three areas of study. Since the Hafetz Hayim permitted the study of Bible, Silver would extend the reason for that permission to the study of *Mishnah* and Talmud in modern society. The problem with Silver's analysis is his speculation that the Hafetz Hayim considered Maimonides' directive regarding the study of the Oral Law for women as "good advice."[61] Clearly, Maimonides' formulation made it easier to permit teaching Scriptures (removed from the category of *tiflut*) than to permit teaching Oral Torah (solidly within the category of *tiflut*). It is by no means certain that the Hafetz Hayim would have extended his permission to the teaching of the Oral Law to women, even under prevailing circumstances. Also, it is not the case that Maimonides' precondition was based on the fear that secular subjects might contaminate unfortified souls. Nevertheless, Silver's contention has merit as a raison d'être to promote an extension of study of the Oral Law for women, but it is weak in providing halakhic arguments justifying such change.

Another argument may be made for the purposes of deciphering the *Halakhah* to permit the study of Oral Torah for women in modern times. Maimonides noted the injunction that women should not be taught the Oral Law because they would distort the essentials of this Law. To that end, he proposed a Halakhic norm suggesting that there was a legal presumption of incompetence in the ability of women to be disciplined sufficiently to understand such matters accurately. Maimonides, aware that women in fact could be educated,[62] was not able to conceive a halakhic ruling advocating Torah

---

59. *Mishneh Torah, Hilkhot Yesodei ha-Torah* [Laws of Torah Fundamentals] 4:13.

60. See Arthur M. Silver, "May Women Be Taught Bible, Mishnah and Talmud?" *Tradition* 17:3 (Summer 1978): 74–85.

61. It may be that the Hafetz Hayim considered Maimonides' injunction to be law and relied upon the emergency power of "*et la'asot la-Hashem*" to override the law, but only as far as absolutely necessary.

62. See Malmonides, *Teshuvot ha-Rambam,* ed. Joshua Blau, vol. 2 (Jerusalem: Mikestse Nirdamim, 1957), resp. 276.

study for women. He knew that ideally women might study,[63] but for him
the catchword *tiflut* acted as justification for the current practice wherein
women generally did not study. He defined the *tiflut* act as an act of distortion.
Women were not to be trusted in their understanding of complex materials.
Although some take Maimonides to mean that there is an inherent defect in
the physiological makeup of the female mind,[64] such interpretation can be
shown to be weak. Maimonides advises those who give public instruction
touching on esoteric themes to deliberately simplify the material. He notes
that women, youths, and children attend these lectures and that someday
their intellects may become sufficiently perfected to understand these matters
accurately.[65] One might think that women are included in the list as an
example of those who lack understanding but not included among those
whose intellect may become perfected. However, nowhere does Maimonides
preclude all women from intellectual perfection, even if he does preclude most
women. It is therefore reasonable to maintain that Maimonides suggests here
that some women can master esoteric materials. If so, women's minds are not
physiologically defective, for otherwise no woman would be able to gain such
perfection. He includes the biblical Miriam among the philosophic elite.[66]
Further evidence in this regard can be found in Maimonides' list of those who
can learn to worship God with developed intellectual capacity.[67]

In short, Maimonides' legal principle that attributes a problem concerning
the majority of women cannot in any wise mean that women's minds are
defective by nature. One might still argue that Maimonides meant that the
majority of women have defective minds by nature, but it would be difficult
to uphold such an inconsistency in nature. Normally, what is defective is

---

63. See *Mishneh Torah, Hilkhot Yesodei ha-Torah* [Laws of Torah Fundamentals] 4:13,
and *Hilkhot Talmud Torah* 1:13.

64. Other scholars express this notion in more explicit language. Menahem
ha-Meiri, thirteenth-century commentator on the Talmud, writes, "A woman's intelligence is not sufficient for proper understanding, and thinking she has grasped [the
material] she clangs like a bell to show her wisdom to everyone" (*Bet ha-Behirah* [New
York, 1947], commentary on *Sotah* 20a). Meiri advocates that women have priority in
household decisions and that they be highly respected by their families (ibid., commentary on *Bava Metzia* 59a). Even the much-later rabbi Israel Lipschutz, nineteenth-
century German rabbinic commentator on the *Mishnah*, states, "Like tasteless food
without salt, unable to understand the reasoning of the Torah, she ridicules it" (*Tiferet
Yisrael* [Berlin, 1862], commentary on *Sotah* 3:4).

65. Maimonides, *Mishnah with the Commentary of Rabbi Moses ben Maimon*, trans. from
the original manuscript by Joseph David Kafah (Jerusalem: Mossad Harav Kook,
1963), Order *Zeraim* (Introduction), pp. 19–20.

66. Maimonides, *Guide of the Perplexed*, trans. with introduction and notes by
Shlomo Pines (Chicago: University of Chicago Press, 1963), 3:51.

67. *Mishneh Torah, Hilkhot Teshuvah* [Laws of Repentance] 10:5.

abnormal. In fact, we know that Maimonides attributes irrational thinking to undue interference by the imagination faculty, led by physical drives and desires.[68] We are led now to consider the sociological underpinnings of Maimonides' principle.

In Maimonides' time, the place of women in Islamic society was very different from their place in current Western society. Hence, Maimonides expected that women would serve their husbands in ways that seemed excessive even to those who lived in the enlightened Provence of his day.[69] Furthermore, the threatening laxity in some Jewish women's moral propriety moved Maimonides to castigate "women who removed from their hearts and faces the integrity of their mothers, who had been modest and pure in their ways, while they learned to act [in an unbecoming manner].[70] Such behavior, in Maimonides' scheme, would not have been conducive to perfecting the rational faculty. In short, suffice it here to state that an enormous gulf separates our society from that of Maimonides and from that of the entire Middle Ages. We may well accept that in Maimonides' experience the minds of most women were not geared toward the discipline of fine dialectical reasoning. This is the meaning of his observation that *"rov nashim, ein da'atan mekhuvanot lehitlamed."* In Maimonides' society, women did not generally participate in intellectual pursuits. As a result, they were not expected to follow precise scholastic arguments. Thus Maimonides concluded, *"Ela hein motz'in divrei Torah ledivrei havai, lefi aniut da'atan."* That is to say, because of their lack of trained understanding they could not be relied upon to reproduce sophisticated arguments. Lest we think that Maimonides' words have an overly pejorative meaning, we should also recognize that most rabbis used this very expression (*"lefi aniut da'ati"*) to denote their own lack of understanding of complex materials. An entire monograph has been dedicated to the sociological study of *Halakhah*, demonstrating that *Halakhah* does, under such circumstances as we have noted, make allowance for sociological change.[71] That is perhaps why Maimonides stated in this case the reason for his decision. Rabbi Falk, as noted earlier, understood Maimonides to permit teaching the Oral Law to a woman once we could ascertain her determination and ability to master the subject matter. One could therefore propose that a modern decisor could render, in principle, a decision from within the sources permitting the teaching of the Oral Law to women in a society in which the general presumption is that such women are as sophisticated as men in their thinking.[72]

---

68. *Guide of the Perplexed* 3:51.

69. See *Mishneh Torah, Hilkhot Ishut* [Laws of Marriage] 21:3, 10. See objections of Rabbi Abraham ben David (Rabad) in the standard editions of the *Mishneh Torah*.

70. *Teshuvot HaRambam*, ed. Joshua Blau, vol. 2, responsum 242.

71. See Jacob Katz, *Exclusiveness and Tolerance* (New York: Schocken, 1961).

72. The following example may serve as an illustration of this mechanism. In

One reason that one might confuse the formulation of Maimonides with a totally negative view of women's intellectual capabilities is that there is a talmudic statement: *"Nashim da'atan kalot aleihen."*[73] This passage has been taken to mean that women are silly, frivolous, unintelligent, or incapable of being educated. It should be noted that Maimonides does not refer to this passage in his code, but rather states, "The minds of most women are not geared to intellectual discipline." This is a sociological statement, not a medical opinion. The question now arises as to what the talmudic rabbis meant when they said, "The minds of women are *light*."

After carefully studying this statement in context, I have concluded, as does Meiselman,[74] that it has often been misinterpreted and taken out of context. The phrase, used twice in the Talmud and both times in the same context, is saying that women, under intense pressure, will yield [emotionally or sexually] more easily than men. One may object to that assumption and question its veracity. However, the important issue is that the statement has no bearing on the right of women to study Torah. The question of whether general psychological tendencies can be attributed to the sexes is not germane to our discussion. "The minds of women are light" was never used in the Talmud in reference either to intellectual abilities, or to moral character.[75] In fact, we have statements to the contrary that speak in glowing terms of women's intellectual capacities and propensities, such as the following passage from the Talmud: "Rabbi Hisda says . . . this teaches us that women were given greater intelligence/intuition/understanding (*'binah yeteirah'*) than men."[76] It should be

---

regard to the laws surrounding the Passover *seder*, the Talmud states that a woman is not required to recline at the table unless she is a woman of distinction (*Pesahim* 108a). The implication is that most women would not be obligated, whereas a minority, certain women of consequence, would be. Rabbi Mordekhai ben Hillel (thirteenth century) declares, however, that *all* the women of his time are considered to be women of importance and are, consequently, obligated (*Piskei ha-Mordekhai, Peshahim* 108). A status that applied only to a minority of women in the talmudic era was deemed to apply to the majority at a subsequent time, with the resultant effect on the law.

73. *Kiddushin* 80b, *Shabbat* 33b.

74. Meiselman, *Jewish Women in Jewish Law*, p. 41.

75. This is not a blanket statement by the rabbis of the Talmud. It has been a source of distress to many a woman, especially since it has been misinterpreted and cited out of context by students of Talmud. For the Hellenistic background of this phrase, see A. A. Halevi, *Olamah Shel ha-Aggadah* (Tel Aviv: Dvir, 1972), pp. 249–252, who confirms the notion that it means that women can be swayed more easily than men.

76. *Niddah* 45b. Judith Romney Wegner, "The Image and Status of Judaism in Classical Rabbinic Judaism," in *Jewish Women in Historical Perspective*, ed. Judith Baskin (Detroit: Wayne State University Press, 1991), pp. 78–79, complains that traditional apologists use this passage to excuse male predominance in performing many precepts, by claiming that women are intuitively closer to God and have no need for such precepts. She considers that *binah* is more of an animal attribute, like that of the rooster

stated that this has certain halakhic consequences. According to the law, a person who takes an oath (e.g., to abstain from certain enjoyments) is required to keep it if he or she is mature enough to understand the meaning of the obligation that has been self-imposed. Rabbi Judah ha-Nasi is of the opinion that because of her superior intelligence and insight, a girl at the age of twelve is judged to be capable of such understanding, while a boy reaches maturity at the age of thirteen.[77] According to the Talmud, this is consonant with the idea of women's quicker intelligence. There is another opinion: that boys mature at the same age as girls do. The Talmud maintains the principle of women's superior intelligence in its discussion of this other opinion, namely, that male and female have identical ages of majority. The implication of the talmudic passage is that boys are intellectually trained more than girls, so that boys reach maturity at the same age as girls do. The Tosafists[78] grant that boys are more streetwise than girls but were this not the case, we would have to posit that boys would mature at a later age. What is significant here is that talmudic opinion did not state that boys and girls were of equal intelligence. It had to find a reason to advance the boys' level to reach that of the girls at the same age. In point of fact, the *Halakhah* accepts that girls mature one year earlier than boys.[79]

This talmudic passage acknowledges that the difference between the intellectual attainments of males and females is not physiological but societal. Boys receive advance training, are stimulated in their daily contacts, and have more intellectual options than do girls. The Talmud suspects that were matters to be equalized, women might exceed men in intellectual attainment. We have indeed moved a far distance from the assertion that women's minds are incapable of studying Torah.

If not because of intellectual limitation, why else then might women have been discouraged from the totality of Torah study, especially as it pertains to the *Torah Lishma* aspect of learning? An investigation of the term *tiflut* is informative at this point. The Talmud considered the statement of Rabbi Eliezer, who said, "Whoever teaches his daughter Torah teaches her *tiflut.*" This statement was followed by one in which *tiflut* means sexual indulgence.[80] Indeed, the word *tiflut* is used to cover a wide range of meanings having to do with improper or offensive social behavior.[81] The final layer of

---

who is praised for having sufficient *binah* to distinguish night from day. Wegner sees here an "invidious distinction" between male cognition-by-intellect (*hokhmah*) and female cognition-by-instinct (*binah*).

77. *Niddah* 45b.
78. Ad loc.
79. See *Tur, Yoreh De'ah* 233.
80. *Mishnah Sotah* 3:4.
81. See Herbert Basser, "The Meaning of 'Shtuth' Gen. R. 11 in Reference to Mt.

the talmudic discussion connected the idea of such study's being *tiflut* and of *tiflut*'s meaning "sexual indulgence."[82] This translation of *tiflut* as implying immorality was adopted by Rabbi Abahu in the *Gemara*, who, in clarifying Rabbi Eliezer's position, explained that the reason for his stand was based on the verse (Proverbs 8:12) "I, wisdom, have made subtlety (*armimut*) my dwelling," meaning, when wisdom (Torah) enters a person's mind, so enters subtlety.

Rashi,[83] in commenting on this section of the Talmud, explained that according to Rabbi Eliezer and Rabbi Abahu, if a woman will be taught Torah, she will acquire the subtlety to indulge her sexual inclinations and get away with it.[84] Maimonides totally ignored this layer of talmudic discussion in his halakhic codification, but commentators such as Rabbi Joel Sirkis[85] have freely integrated Rashi's contribution with the words of Maimonides, thereby conflating conflicting approaches. Maimonides defines *tiflut* for us as "distorted understanding." He does not think that Rabbi Eliezer would have accused women of devious intentions.

Another approach as to why women were discouraged from Torah study addresses the possible reasoning for the original exemption. A few contemporary writers and scholars have advanced a view that women were released from the obligation of Torah study for the sake of national survival.[86] Success in Torah study–the forging of a *Talmid Hakham*, or scholar-sage–requires considerable commitment, stamina, and time. It is certainly possible for a woman to have outside interests (career, educational pursuits, etc.), as long as her primary commitment is to her family. But if the primary commitment for women were to be the study of Torah, this would, as the sages saw it, be detrimental to the proper functioning of the family. If husband and wife were to involve themselves equally in Torah study, the havoc it would wreak in the family and home would be considerable. Indeed, says early twentieth-century Talmud scholar Rabbi Barukh Epstein, "If women were required to study

---

5:29–30 and 18:8–9," *New Testament Studies* 31 (1985): 150.

82. *Sotah* 21b.

83. Ad loc.

84. See further, Rabbi Jacob Moellin, *Responsa Maharil*, no. 199.

85. Commentary of *Bayit Hadash* to Tur, *Yoreh De'ah* 246:6.

86. See, for example, Naomi Cohen, "Hinukh ha-Bat ve-ha-Ishah," a lecture delivered at a symposium on the topic of women's education in Tel Aviv, 1980; Rabbi Barukh Halevi Epstein, *Mekor Barukh* (Vilna, 1928), p. 1969; Leo Levy, "Man and Woman in Torah Life," *Jewish Life* 41 (Spring 1974): 51–53; and Chana K. Poupko and Devorah L. Wohlgelernter, "Women's Liberation–An Orthodox Response," in *Tradition* 15:4 (Spring 1976): 48–50. See also the commentaries of *Tosafot Rid* (Rabbi Isaiah of Trani the Elder; southern Italy, thirteenth century) (New York, 1945) and *Hiddushei Ha-Ritvah* (Rabbi Yom Tov ben Abraham Ishbili of Seville, Spain, early fourteenth century) (Warsaw, 1879) on *Kiddushin* 34b.

Torah with the same all-consuming intensity of men, the future of the Jewish family would be in great peril.[87] Thus women are called upon to sacrifice part of their Torah-learning potential for the sake of national survival. And though the concept of self-sacrifice may be alien to the modern feminist movement, it is inherent in Jewish thought. Of course, there is room for exception in terms of a woman's becoming a Torah scholar, and women have and are achieving such heights, but if Torah learning (of the *Torah Lishma* type) were to be made mandatory, rather than optional, for women as it is mandatory for men, the survival of the Jewish family would be gravely in doubt.

The foregoing may help us to understand better the note of caution and prudence that is reflected so often in the literature with regard to the study of Torah, and especially the Oral Law, by women. The rabbis may have feared the dangers of superficial knowledge, which might result from the inability of the woman to devote herself in earlier times with the same intensity of commitment to Torah study as the man devotes himself. Further, they may well have been concerned about the Jewish family's survival, if more than a few women were to pursue Torah study with great intensity.

One may assert that concern for the Jewish family's survival – had Torah study been incumbent on women – might have been legitimate in ages when *all* of a woman's time was taken up by home and family (if not by business activities) and when, generally, people married and died at younger ages. What of contemporary times, however, when technological advances and sociological developments have substantially altered women's existential condition?[88] Modern appliances, advances in preschool care, women marrying at later ages, and the reasonable expectation women have of engaging in many active and productive years after their childbearing and child-rearing years are over, have made it feasible to channel spare time and energy into productive, gratifying activity. Might that activity take the form of many women – rather than only the exceptional woman – developing their potential as Torah scholars, if they so desire? That would mean engaging in the vigorous and dialectical study of oral law texts. As radical as this may sound, such forward-looking propositions may now be found in the writings of recognized and responsible Orthodox rabbis.

Contemporary Israeli rabbi Moshe Malka, in his responsa *Mikveh ha-Mayim*, reviews the traditional laws of Maimonides, Falk, and Isserles and notes the current practice to teach women Scriptures, history, ethical works, and the laws pertaining to them. He proceeds to analyze the realistic position of women in modern society. He argues that Rabbi Eliezer of the *Mishnah*

87. Epstein, *Mekor Barukh*, p. 1969.

88. This question is posed by Naomi G. Cohen, "Women and the Study of Talmud," *Tradition* 24:1 (Fall 1988): 28–37.

lived in times when women stayed at home. Today women are involved in every aspect of social and business interaction; they are exposed to ideas and life-styles that are antithetical to the ideals of the Torah. For purely functional reasons, not ideological ones, Rabbi Malka declares that Rabbi Eliezer would want women to study the Oral Law were he alive today. This is the only way to save the Torah way of life, since women are so influential in the lives of their husbands and children. The demons of the wider world must be banned. Implicit in his notice that, up to the era when he wrote, no women had taught Talmud in academies, no women had headed academies, and no women had studied in talmudic institutions is his desire to change this. He explicitly advocates that women be taught the Oral Law, not as some voluntary exercise but as a necessary requisite to protecting the Torah way of life. Women have time for all kinds of nonproductive pursuits and do engage in them. Even in the unlikely event that a few women would distort some of what they learn, this is a very acceptable risk to run and it is outweighed by the huge benefits that would accrue to Jewish life in its entirety. Women must be encouraged to leave their trivial pursuits and engage in serious Torah study. In short, it is our duty to see to it that women are instructed in the Oral Law. Instructive are Rabbi Malka's words:

> Modern woman plays a significant role in society, engaging in scientific research, filling the universities, managing offices and businesses, participating in government and political affairs. Indeed, they are becoming smarter and more developed than men. Surely Rabbi Eliezer would now waive his ban on teaching women even the Oral Torah, so that they might carefully observe all the laws of the Torah affecting their activities and employment. Furthermore, we must intensify their education so that the light of Torah might keep them in the path of the upright. . . .[89]

Rabbi Malka believes that it is incumbent upon the community to prepare girls from childhood to handle the challenges faced by the modern emancipated woman. It is only by receiving a sound religious education from childhood, as well as a thorough knowledge of Jewish law, that her loyalty to a Torah way of life will be secured as she makes her way in the liberated society of today. Rabbi Malka claims that he would not advocate this program if women, in reality, stayed within the confines of their home. His approach is one in which he sees the traditional *Halakhah* as counterproductive to its

---

89. Rabbi Moshe Malka, *Mikveh ha-Mayim* vol. 3, *Yoreh De'ah* 21 (Jerusalem, 1975), p. 146. (A collection of responsa written by the Sephardic chief rabbi of Petah Tikvah, Israel.)

own goal – the preservation of Torah. He realizes that the curricula and place of education for women have changed in this century already.

Malka sees that when it is dysfunctional, the *Halakhah* can, and should, be responsive to change. Such a stance provides arguments to assure women of a complete Torah education, but it lacks the ideological vision necessary to convince others that such a change is in order. Rabbi Menachem Schneerson independently reiterates these arguments but adds an ideological dimension. Whereas Rabbi Malka is a relatively minor decisor, Rabbi Schneerson is a major figure.

Rabbi Menachem Schneerson leads the largest and most influential hasidic group in modern-day Jewry. Lubavitch *hasidim* are noted for their strict adherence to halakhic norms and their dedication to Torah learning. Their rabbi is acknowledged to be one of the great masters of Talmud and *Halakhah* in this generation. His thoughts become the actions of his followers but are also studied by serious Torah scholars everywhere. Rabbi Schneerson, immune to the political pressures that plague many community leaders, has oftened acted as a respected vehicle for manifesting the visions of an ideal Jewish society for many Orthodox Jews. His addresses are widely disseminated and discussed throughout the world.

The views that he espouses concerning Torah study for women show his keen awareness of past *Halakhah*, although he does not dwell on exegesis of his progressive views from within the stated rules.[90] Rather, he establishes a positive tone that vibrates throughout Talmud, *Midrash*, hasidic literature, and other traditional works. Here he finds the justification for advocating that women study all of the Torah that their children study, so that they may help them review their studies. He acknowledges that women are at home more than men or, at least that they, in reality, are the ones with the patience and love, who spend time in the evenings with their children on their lessons. He further observes that all women have the capacity to learn the Oral Torah and that whereas in the past only a select few voluntarily mastered Torah, today all women should do so. He implicitly dismisses the negative views of earlier decisors by advocating both that women study more than only the laws they are obligated to know and that women should study the laws with all the scholastic, dialectic discussions surrounding them. Moreover, women can be taught the entire range of Torah studies, form groups for self-instruction on the intricate texts, and study with their husband the same materials that their

---

90. See his address "Me-Sihat Shabbat Parshat Emor, Erev Lag ba-Omer 5750: Al Devar Hiyuv Neshei Yisrael be-Hinukh u-ve-Limud ha-Torah" ["From the Address Delivered on the Eve of Lag ba-Omer 5750 (May 1990): Concerning the Obligation of Jewish Women in Torah Education and Study"], in *Likutei Sichot* (Hebrew version) 5750 (New York: Mercaz le-Inyanei Hinukh, 1990), pp. 171–175.

husband studies. In short, Rabbi Schneerson argues that women should master the totality of Torah studies. In his words:

> Our analysis shows the following in regards to the study of the Oral Law. Women and girls, without such vigorous Torah studies, would learn a variety of subjects through which "immoral subtlety (armimut)" would possess them. Therefore, it is the case that it is permissible [for women] to study the Oral Law. More than this, according to the very reasoning of the Halakhah, it is really necessary to teach them the Oral Law [emphasis mine]. Women study the laws which apply to them, but additionally should study not only the laws without their reasons, but also study the reasons for the laws. This study should eventually include the fine, dialectical arguments that are in the Torah. For it is in human nature, male and female, to delight in this kind of study. Through this there will develop in them [the women] the proper sensitivities and talents in the spirit of our Holy Torah.[91]

Rabbi Schneerson has divided his address into seven sections. He introduces Section Five, "Taking note that this matter is in the mode of *good innovations*, like those of previous generations," with these words:

> As a result of the above, another benefit accrues with enabling women to continually involve themselves in the learning of their children and husbands. [Traditionally] women received merit for "helping their children learn Scripture in the synagogue, and helping their husbands learn the Oral Law in the *Yeshivah*, and waiting for their husbands until they returned." Beyond this, women are now able to actively encourage them by participating in the actual study.[92]

The rabbi outlines a curriculum through which women might accomplish this goal by beginning with relatively easy materials and progressing to the more difficult ones. He sees that the world is progressing toward its full redemption and wonders how this movement could be accomplished without the entire Jewish population, male and female, being fully saturated with Torah knowledge. This address illustrates a more technical analysis of the issue of Torah study for women than his general statement, which was widely circulated in an English adaptation of his addresses on this matter:[93]

---

91. Ibid., p. 173.

92. Ibid., p. 174.

93. "A Woman's Place in Torah," an adaptation of addresses of the Lubavitcher Rebbe given on May 12 and 19, 1990 (New York: Mercaz le-Inyanei Hinukh, Sihot in English, 1990).

[The Talmud] relates that women should not study the Oral Law. . . . However, the change in a woman's place in society necessitates a change in this perspective as well. Women who are exposed to the sophistication of contemporary society should prepare themselves for such involvement by developing their thinking processes within Torah, studying not only the practical application, but also the motivating purposes, for *mitzvot*.[94]

Here the rabbi acknowledges the changing role of women in society. He recognizes the role that theoretical study of Torah plays in developing one's thinking processes, a necessity when women are immersed in a sophisticated society. He concludes:

Within the context of our society, women are required to function on a more sophisticated level than ever before, occupying professional positions that require higher knowledge. To prepare themselves for such activities, they should develop their thinking processes in Torah, training themselves to think on an advanced level within the framework of Torah. This will set the tone for their behavior in the world at large.[95]

Rabbi Schneerson's declaration may influence the widespread study of Oral Torah among women so that, in the future, such study will be taken for granted. Indeed, in the Lubavitch *Beth Rivkah* high school and seminary system for girls in New York, courses in Oral Law have already been introduced, with the teaching of selected topics in *Mishnah, Gemara, Ein Ya'akov,* and *Tanya* (works culled from the Oral Law).[96] The reality is that a number of schools have already begun to teach the Oral Law to women.[97] Some of these schools employ male instructors, but others hire competent and knowledgeable

94. Ibid., pp. 4–5 n. 9.

95. Ibid., p. 5.

96. *Ein Ya'akov* is a collection of *aggadot* from the Babylonian and Jerusalem Talmuds, written by Rabbi Jacob ben Solomon ibn Habib (1445–1555). To this collection the author added a commentary culled from the commentaries of Rashi and *tosafot* on the Talmud and from the novellas on the Talmud of Nahmanides, Rashbah, Rosh, and other halakhists.

Tanya, written by Rabbi Shneur Zalman of Lyady, founder of *Chabad Lubavitch* Hasidism (eighteenth century), is a mystical analysis of human psychology, of a person's place in the world, and of a person's relationship to the Divine. The work is based essentially on the writings of the master kabbalist Rabbi Solomon Luria on kabbalistic premises and on the interpretation of the Written and Oral Torah.

The information regarding Beth Rivkah's curriculum was conveyed to me by Mrs. Chana Gurewitz, principal of the teachers' seminary in New York. It should also be noted that several Lubavitch communities across the world are offering courses in Talmud to adult women.

97. In actuality, women have been studying aspects of Oral Law for years, as

women to teach Talmud. Undoubtedly, this trend will continue with opposition, but with resolution. *Halakhah* has never envisioned the case in which
women teach women and, so, it does not proscribe such teaching. *Halakhah*'s
usual cases concerned men teaching women. Therefore it is feasible and likely
that those schools in which women teach Talmud to women will proliferate
ahalakhically, creating future generations of women teachers and women
scholars. Even in regard to men teaching women Talmud, it is the case that
often *Halakhah* accepts, and even justifies, within particular parameters, widespread practices that are viewed beneficially.[98] In this case, it would be
premature to guess the future, but indications warrant optimism in this regard.

Evidence of change can be found in the growing number of contemporary
articles and responsa that address this issue, thus expanding the parameters for
women's study of Torah. Whether or not one adopts any or all of these
scholars' insights, it is important to note that rabbinic minds are grappling
with ways to advance for women the study of the Oral Law. New York rabbi
Shlomo Wahrman, addressing the question of a woman who completed a
talmudic tractate, provides a radical interpretation of the issue of Torah study
for women.[99] He draws a distinction between the *study* of Torah, which is

---

many of the commentaries on the Bible that women do study are culled from Oral
Law sources. When I refer here to women's studying the Oral Law, I refer to their
studying directly from the original sources, rather than from biblical commentaries.

The introduction of the study of Oral Law in schools for women may take on one
of two forms. There are schools that approach the subject in the same way as Talmud
is traditionally presented in schools for men. The focus of study is on the talmudic
tractate, with emphasis on the development of skills in talmudic study, so that the
study of Talmud may become a focal part of the student's life. Substantial time may be
devoted to independent study with a partner (*havruta*) in the *Beit Midrash* (study hall).
For schools applying the second approach (and they are in the majority), the use of
talmudic and other Oral Law textual material is subject oriented, with a focus on the
acquisition of relevant information and knowledge rather than skill. The introduction
of Oral Law texts broadens the material that a woman may study on a given subject.
It is not, however, expected that the woman be immersed in Talmud study developing
the skills, so that her study parallels the male's. As such, the introduction of the study
of Oral Law to women in these schools does not mean that the education process of the
two sexes becomes similar. (See subsequent comments by Rabbi Wahrman.) It does
mean, however, that by immersing herself in the study of all relevant textual material
on a given topic, she becomes an active participant in the learning process, rather than
a passive recipient of teacher-centered material. Some schools incorporate aspects of
each of these two approaches into their curriculum.

98. See, for example, Rabbi Tzvi Hirsh Chajes, *Kol Sifrei Maharitz Chajes*; Jacob
Katz, *Exclusiveness and Tolerance*; and Simha Fishbane, "A response to the Challenge of
the Modern Era as reflected in the Wording of Rabbi Yechiel Mechel Epstein," vol. 2.

99. Shlomo Wahrman, "Mitzvat Talmud Torah be-Nashim" [The Commandment of Talmud Study for Women], *Hadarom* 46 (1978): 55–62.

obligatory for men,[100] and the *knowledge* of Torah, which is obligatory for everyone.[101] He suggests that the standard *Halakhah*, discouraging women's study, deals with women's reviewing materials they already know.[102] He claims women were discouraged from this aspect of Torah study except in matters that apply to them. However, he hypothesizes that women must indeed study the whole Torah in order to fulfill their obligation of knowing it. This distinction between learning and knowing (to know, one must have first learned) leads him to many interesting speculations.

Writing in the Fall 1992 issue of *Hadarom*, a journal of Torah thought, Judah Henkin, Jerusalem rabbi and decisor; Ephraim Halivni, New York rabbi; and Abraham Jacob Yuttar, New Jersey rabbi and educator, each lend their own analysis and insights to the issue of Talmud study for women. Rabbi Henkin, espousing the position that it is permissible for women to study Talmud, reviews the pertinent halakhic issues.[103] He notes that *Halakhah* permits self-motivated women to study Oral Law. He goes on to postulate that the difference between the teaching of Oral Tradition to women (forbidden) and the teaching of Written Torah to women (permitted) cannot be maintained any longer. Women, he suggests, were impressed with the written word but skeptical of oral teaching. As a result, they would accept Written Torah as stated, without hesitation, but might have been more hesitant to accept Oral *Halakhah* as authoritative. Nowadays the Oral Tradition is widely accessible in books, and such differentiation is not an accurate portrayal of reality. (It is surprising that the author neglects to mention the fact that oral teachings have been written for well over a thousand years; one must

---

100. Based on the passage in *Kiddushin* 29b, which interprets the verse in Deuteronomy 11:19, *"Velimadetem otam et beneikhem"* ("and you shall teach them to your children"), to mean sons, and not daughters.

101. In his speculative discursus, Wahrman derives the obligation of knowledge of Torah on everyone, both male and female, from the fact that the Talmud (*Kiddushin* 30a) does not make a distinction between sons and daughters when interpreting the verse in Deuteronomy 6:7, *"Ve-shinantem le-vanekha"* ("And you shall teach them diligently to your children"). The Talmud interprets the words *Ve-shinantem* as meaning thorough knowledge of the Torah. This is in contrast to the *mitzvah* of *limud* (study), which involves study for its own sake, regardless of whether or not one acquires additional knowledge thereby. See further, regarding the distinction between knowledge and study, J. Zevin, *Le-Ohr ha-Halakhah: Ba'ayot u-Verurim* (Tel Aviv: Abraham Zioni, n.d.), pp. 204–212.

102. One may question Rabbi Wahrman's contention in that continuous review of one's learning is considered, in Judaism, a necessary component in the acquisition of knowledge. Therefore, if, in Wahrman's view, a woman is obligated in the acquisition of knowledge, then continuous review would be necessary under the mandate of *"ve-shinantem le-vanekha."*

103. Judah Henkin, "Limud Torah le-Nashim," *Hadarom* 61 (Elul 5752 [1992]): 11–19.

assume that he regards modern times as different from the past in that printed books are much more readily available.) In this regard, he concludes, we cannot deny the opportunity to supply motivated women with the finest tools of talmudic scholarship. His decision is based on the recognition that *Halakhah* has no qualms about teaching Oral Tradition to exceptionally motivated women; *Halakhah* recognizes that women can understand for themselves the binding nature of Oral Law; and *Halakhah* acknowledges that teaching women Torah was never an outright prohibition but rather a rabbinic advisement. He contends that Maimonides uses the expression "our sages have commanded us," rather than "our sages have forbidden us." He then goes on to adduce proof that the expression of command concerns good advice rather than legal proscription.

Rabbi Abraham Yuttar, again reviewing the major talmudic and rabbinic sources concerning the study of the Oral Tradition for women, ends his discussion on a sociolegal observation.[104] He notes that Rabbis Schneerson and Soloveitchik favor teaching women *Gemara* (see further Rabbi Soloveitchik). The change of women's status in society has created a de facto situation in which women are immersed in secular pursuits. Rabbi Yuttar, in a similar vein to Rabbi Henkin's, draws a distinction between binding legal precedent and the advisements of the sages, in which category he places women's Torah study. In this regard he points out that sociological perspectives by themselves are insufficient reason to abandon the wellsprings of past tradition. Nevertheless, outstanding sages have the authority to adjust tradition for social realities in order to preserve the pristine sanctity of Torah ideals. Since there is no expressed prohibition against teaching Oral Tradition to women, the Torah giants of our time are well positioned to define this issue as they see fit. Their permission to teach women Talmud is well grounded within the complex sources of *Halakhah*.

Rabbi Halivni traverses the same sources and draws three inferences:[105] (1) Motivated women can indeed pursue the study of Talmud; Rabbi Halivni demonstrates that there is no prohibition against teaching any woman Oral Torah. (2) All women must engage in proficient study of the Oral Law for the purpose of performing commandments according to the fine points of the Oral Law. (3) Family instruction or merely reading the abridged *Shulhan Arukh* is not sufficient to ensure meticulous observance, and he quotes Rabbi Israel Meir Kagan, the Hafetz Hayim, to that effect: "No one can be prevented from violating *Shabbat* unless one has mastered the laws of *Shabbat* through detailed study."[106]

104. Abraham J. Yuttar, "Nashim ve-Talmud Torah: Iyun Halakhahti Tahbiri," *Hadarom* 61 (Elul 5752 [1992]): 38–41.

105. Ephraim Halivni, "Nashim ve-Talmud Torah," *Hadarom* 61 (Elul 5752 [1992]): 25–34.

106. See the Hafetz Hayim's introduction to *Mishnah Berurah*, part 3.

This argument is reminiscent of the thought of Rabbi Aaron Lichtenstein, the *Rosh Yeshivah* ("head of *yeshivah*") of Har Etzion in Israel.[107] He asserts that for a woman to serve as an educator of the coming generation, she needs knowledge as well as a personal commitment to encourage the transmission of tradition. When her learning is intensified, her own commitment and sense of responsibility are deepened. "When something is well learned, it creates personal commitment." There are things that can be known in a general way, but they are not felt existentially, and therefore they do not penetrate one's consciousness. "When laws are not properly studied, a deep impression has been made neither on the intellect nor on the soul." Therefore, in Rabbi Lichtenstein's view, the study of *Torah Shebe'al Peh* must be intensified, with the proper use of all relevant textual materials, so that *Halakhah* becomes a living entity. Merely giving a woman a list of dos and don'ts is insufficient to guarantee wholehearted commitment to a Jewish way of life.

The arguments for advancement in women's Torah education can be divided into two categories. Some, like Rabbi Henkin, present changes in modern society that yield, within proper halakhic parameters,[108] a new understanding of the law regarding women and the study of Torah. Others, like Rabbis Halivni and Lichtenstein, present arguments that seem to be of a timeless nature, indicating that expanded study for women is inherent to the Torah system. One may wonder, if this is so, why these arguments were not presented in earlier years. This may just be a further indication that since the matter of women's study was not of vital concern in previous centuries, scholars did not grapple with the issue to the extent they do in modern times. It may be that the question of "How much Torah study for women?" has been left for our generation to thereby "distinguish itself." This is consonant with the talmudic concept that each generation leaves its mark on Jewish law.[109]

STUDY OF TORAH BY WOMEN IN EXTRA-HALAKHIC SOURCES

Studies indicate that patriarchal societies guard their power structures by drawing tight boundaries around them.[110] These boundaries are celebrated

---

107. See Aaron Lichtenstein, "Fundamental Problems Regarding the Education of the Woman," *Ten Da'at* 3:3 (Spring 1989): 7–8.

108. See above, Rabbi Hecht.

109. See *Hullin* 6b and 7a. On receptivity to intellectual themes in one time period rather than another, i.e., "climate of opinion," see the intriguing discussion of Carl Becker in *The Heavenly City of the Eighteenth-Century Philosophers* (New Haven, CT: Yale University Press, 1932), pp. 1–31.

110. See Kate Millet, *Sexual Politics* (Garden City, NY: Doubleday, 1970), p. 26.

and preserved within the society with an aura of sacredness. When these boundaries become threatened, anxiety results.[111] Hence, women who do gain power must be marginalized because they threaten the boundaries of male power.[112] This is one way by which some contemporary feminist thinkers have chosen to explain the exclusion of Jewish women from Torah study.[113] The implicit claim, when spelled out in detail, supposes that power in Jewish society is a function of knowledge and study. Depriving women of knowledge and study suggests that women be kept out of the bounds of power.

Tamar Frankiel, commenting on gender politics, points out that while it is true that in all periods of Jewish history, men have outnumbered women in public leadership roles, there have been times when it was less unusual for women to rise to the fore.[114] The most notable example took place in the earliest period of Israelite history, approximately a thousand years from the time of Abraham to the destruction of the First Temple, in which both Bible and tradition record the names of many outstanding women.[115] Frankiel posits that power in the spiritual realm comes from God, and it appears to human perception in a variety of forms. These forms make up a kind of continuum. On one end are those forms in which the human ego virtually disappears, as in prophecy. At the other end are those forms in which human beings consciously and actively shape the knowledge, insight, and practice of relating to God. Examples are the intellectually oriented forms of religious law and scholarship, which seem (although, Frankiel claims, appearances may be deceptive) less "inspired." Frankiel advances a number of reasons having to do not with ability but rather with psychological makeup, as to why women more often express themselves on the prophetic or inspired end of the spectrum rather than on the end where conscious, directed, often analytical activity is required. These reasons would explain why women occupied positions of power during the prophetic era of Jewish history. Frankiel believes that these factors are sufficient to explain how feminine spiritual tendencies differ from masculine ones without needing to invoke a powerful patriarchy that intentionally oppresses women. Nevertheless, she concludes, it would be naive to ignore the fact that once certain structures of power and

---

111. Ibid., p. 220.

112. Ibid., p. 38.

113. See, for example, Vanessa Ochs, *Words on Fire* (New York:Harcourt Brace Jovanovich, 1990), pp. 306–307. Also see Judith Plaskow, *Standing Again at Sinai* (San Francisco: HarperCollins, 1990), pp. 14, 28, 46, 71, 75, 110, 169, 211, and 223.

114. See Tamar Frankiel, *The Voice of Sarah: Feminine Spirituality and Traditional Judaism* (San Francisco: HarperCollins, 1990), pp. 41–47.

115. According to the *Midrash* (*Shir Hashirim Rabbah* 4:22) there were as many female prophets as male prophets.

influence have developed, human egos become invested in them and will do almost anything to protect those structures from change.[116] Nonetheless, it is to be noted that Jewish scholars in the Middle Ages were not so narrow-minded as to preclude knowledgeable women from their enterprises, since good resources were always cherished. We will see in the following chapters that talented women did not threaten many important rabbis of the ages. We may conclude that if power issues were important they were not always decisive. Of course, the few exceptions may prove the rule but they too have had their influence. Virtually every responsum concerning the issue of the study of Torah by women refers to at least one or two of these women.

The net result of these "few exceptions" and their impact on some scholars can be appreciated in the works of the nineteenth-century theologian, Bible commentator, philosopher, and educator Rabbi Samson Raphael Hirsch (founder of the Neo-Orthodox movement in Germany, integrating loyalty to Torah and *mitzvot* with modern culture). He considers Torah education for girls necessary in principle, as he believes that in some measure it has always been available to girls. As he states:

> No less [than sons] should Israel's daughters learn the content of the Written Torah and the laws which they are required to perform in their lifetime as daughter and young woman, as mother and housewife. Many times in our history Israel's daughters saved the purity of the Jewish life and spirit. The deliverance from Egypt itself was won by the women; and it is by the pious and virtuous women of Israel that the Jewish spirit and Jewish life can and will again be revived.[117]

Elsewhere, Rabbi Hirsch writes:

> The fact is that while women should not pursue specialized Torah study or theoretical knowledge of the Law, which are primarily the function of the men, such understanding of our sacred literature as can teach the fear of God and the conscientious fulfillment of our duty, and all such knowledge as is essential to the adequate execution of our tasks should indeed form part of the mental and spiritual training not only of our sons, but of our daughters as well. This is indicated also by the commandment pertaining to the Law of Assembly [Deuteronomy 31:12].[118]

---

116. Frankiel, *The Voice of Sarah*, pp. 41–47.

117. Samson Raphael Hirsch, *Horeb: A Philosophy of Jewish Laws and Observances*, trans. Dayan I. Grunfeld (New York, London, and Jerusalem: Soncino Press, 1962), p. 371.

118. Samson Raphael Hirsch, *The Hirsch Siddur* (Jerusalem and New York: Feldheim, 1978), p. 122.

Rabbi Hirsch identifies the "pious" and "virtuous" woman as one who properly observes the laws. This is possible, he implies, only through the acquisition of knowledge necessary for their performance. Since, as the philosopher points out, there have always been pious women throughout Jewish history, in some fashion they received the necessary education to achieve such heights of piety and virtue. Though Rabbi Hirsch deters women from pursuing advanced theoretical knowledge, which he perceives as "primarily" the "function" of men, he advocates women's acquiring any knowledge necessary to ensure (1) their loyalty to Judaism and the values it espouses, and (2) the proper execution of their obligations, in whatever generation they happen to live. Hence, the program of study he advocated for women of his day, when the threat to traditional Jewish survival was ever present, was quite considerable, as we shall see in a subsequent chapter when we examine the curriculum he instituted for girls in his school system.

Rabbi Hirsch alludes to a difference in the intellectual propensities of men and women. Such an approach was common in the intellectual climate of his day and in some ways still persists. Such a view could justify the exclusion of women from the study of the Oral Law. The view that the intellectual strengths of the two sexes are different has implications for the type of Torah study men and women engage in. Regarding the dialectical/argumentative study of the talmudic texts, there seems to be some indication that a number of scholars may consider the man as having greater intellectual strength in this area of study. Those scholars would maintain that women deal better with creative, religious thinking as opposed to rigorous linear thinking.[119] An acceptance of a difference in thinking processes between men and women, however, need not yield the conclusion that women be excluded from the study of Oral Law. Women may very well bring new strengths to this area of study.[120]

A transformation of this kind of thinking can be found in the writings of contemporary rabbi and thinker Joseph Ber Soloveitchik (d. 1993). Rabbi Soloveitchik is considered by many to have been the foremost talmudic scholar of his generation. As a leading Torah educator at Yeshiva University,

---

119. See, for example, Barukh Epstein, *Torah Temimah*, Commentary on Deuteronomy 11:18, and Zalman Sorotzkin, *Moznaim la-Mishpat* 1:42. Compare Mary Field Belenky et al., *Women's Way of Knowing* (New York: Basic Books, 1986); see esp. chap. 6.

120. Women Talmud teachers today maintain that whether or not women have a unique approach to Torah study, the skills and creativity they bring to "learning" can only enhance the study of Oral Law texts. As Jerusalem Talmud teacher Dr. Tamar Ross contends, "We believe that there is still much to be accomplished in the area of Oral Law. This may be the final frontier." Quoted in Toby Klein Greenwald, "Wise Women: Is There a Woman's Approach to Torah Study?" *Kol Emunah* (Winter/Spring 1991): 11.

his effect on thousands of students, including many contemporary rabbis, has been immeasurable. In his published eulogy of a woman friend, he considered the issue of whether the differing obligations of women and men with regard to Torah study affect the nature and character of the Torah's transmission by mothers and fathers to succeeding generations.[121]

According to Rabbi Soloveitchik, there is in Judaism not "one *Massorah* [tradition] and one *Massorah* community – the community of the fathers," but "*two Massorot*, two traditions – the *Massorah* community of the fathers and that of the mothers."[122] References to these two communities are found by the thinker in Exodus 19:3: "Thus shalt thou say to the House of Jacob [i.e., the women] and tell the Children of Israel" (i.e., the men); and in Proverbs 1:8: "Hear, my child, the instruction of thy father [*Mussar avikha*] and forsake not the teaching of thy mother" [*Torat imekha*]. Rabbi Soloveitchik explains that on one hand, the tradition of the fathers is an "intellectual-moral" tradition of law and discipline [*Mussar*]: the intellectual discipline of how to read a biblical or talmudic text – how to comprehend, analyze, conceptualize, classify, and so on, in addition to the moral discipline of what to do, what is morally right, and what is morally wrong. On the other hand, the tradition of the mothers is, according to the philosopher, an "experiential" tradition. In describing the "*Torah*" he learned from his mother, as opposed to the "*Mussar*" he learned from his father, Rabbi Soloveitchik writes:

> Most of all I learned that Judaism expresses itself not only in formal compliance with the law but also in a living experience. She taught me that there is a flavor, a scent and warmth to *mitzvot*. I learned from her the most important thing in life – to feel the presence of the Almighty. . . . Without her teachings . . I would have grown up a soulless being, dry and insensitive.[123]

It seems as if Rabbi Soloveitchik is implying that the tradition of the fathers is the one from which the child will acquire formal knowledge of the law – the "dry," "soulless" component of learning. The tradition of the mothers, on the other hand, is responsible both for the child's acquiring the sensitivity to and the "warmth" and "flavor" of the *mitzvot* and for his or her realization of "the most important thing in life – to feel the presence of the Almighty." Rabbi Soloveitchik continues:

> The laws of *Shabbat* [the Sabbath], for instance, were passed on to me by my father; they are a part of *Mussar Avikha*. The *Shabbat* as a living entity, as a queen,

---

121. Joseph B. Soloveitchik, "A Tribute to the Rebbitzen [rabbi's wife] of Talne," *Tradition* 17:2 (Spring 1978): 73–83.

122. Ibid., p. 76.

123. Ibid., p. 77.

was revealed to me by my mother; it is a part of *Torat Imekha*. The fathers *knew* much about the *Shabbat*; the mothers *lived* the *Shabbat*, experienced her presence, and perceived her beauty and splendor.

The fathers taught generations how to observe the *Shabbat*; mothers taught generations how to greet the *Shabbat* and how to enjoy her twenty-four-hour presence.[124]

Though Rabbi Soloveitchik perceives the tradition of the mothers as an experiential tradition, he nevertheless emphasizes that in order for the woman to properly carry on and transmit this tradition, she must be an *ishah hakhamah*, a wise woman: "A guardian of *Torat Imekha* must be an *Ishah Hakhamah*. Regardless of the fact that the maternal *Massorah* [tradition]is charged with the transmission of living experiences, it cannot succeed in discharging its task if the experiences are not nurtured by wisdom."[125]

Rabbi Soloveitchik defines "wisdom" [*hokhmah*] as connoting (1) innate intelligence, (2) erudition or accumulation of knowledge, and (3) intellectual curiosity. In eulogizing the Rebbetzin of Talne, he refers to her "wonderful mind . . . sensitive to ideas and to abstract problems," and states that "her remarks about theoretical matters were always weighty and to the point." He praises her expert knowledge of Bible and of Jewish customs and observances, as well as "her curiosity to know every aspect of Judaism."[126] The rabbi concludes his eulogy with a suggestion that the requirements for eternal life [*Olam Haba*], which are enumerated in the Talmud, apply equally to women as well as men: "He [or she] who is meek and humble, enters quietly and leaves quietly, *studies the Torah constantly*, and does not claim credit for himself [herself]."[127] Rabbi Soloveitchik considers the constant study of Torah by a woman a prerequisite for eternal life. He may not require of her the necessity of engaging in the elaborate hairsplitting sophistry and dialectical examination of talmudic arguments – the methodology that characterizes the *Torah Lishmah* component of Torah study (although he may make it available to her). But he would surely insist that *Torat Hayim* – Torah for the sake of living a value-filled, law-abiding Torah way of life, even including the acquisition of relevant talmudic textual knowledge – is very much in order. In light of his perception of two *Messorah* traditions, Rabbi Soloveitchik may further demand that the woman bring her own unique approach to thought into her study of Talmud,

---

124. Ibid. Rabbi Soloveitchik – in addition to distinguishing between the tradition of the fathers and the tradition of the mothers – also makes a distinction between one's relationship to God as Father and one's relationship to God as Mother. The interested reader may wish to peruse Lawrence Kaplan's "Religious Philosophy of Rabbi Joseph Soloveitchik," in *Tradition* 14:4 (Fall 1973): 45, 54.

125. Soloveitchik, "A Tribute to the Rebbitzen of Talne," p. 79.

126. Ibid.

127. The talmudic passage is from *Sanhedrin* 88b. Rabbi Soloveitchik takes the liberty of substituting "she" for "he."

thus opening new vistas from a woman's perspective. Indeed, Rabbi Soloveit-chik saw to it that his daughter was educated in the texts of the Oral Tradition, and his granddaughter has followed suit. His son-in-law, Rabbi Aaron Lich-tenstein, advocates universal instruction in Talmud for women, even if they will not dedicate themselves as intensely as men to its study.[128]

Rabbi Soloveitchik and Rabbi Lichtenstein have claimed that since in contemporary times women receive a university secular education, where they are opening up all books in every other world, they must have the same opportunity to study Torah and Talmud.[129] Rabbi Soloveitchik's breadth of scope has resulted in the institution of Torah study for women, including the study of Talmud, in two major North American schools–Maimonides High School in Boston and, more significantly, Stern College in New York. "Quite frankly," writes American rabbi and educator Joel Wolowelsky, "when Jewish newspapers carry a picture of Rav Joseph Ber Soloveitchik giving the inaugural Talmud *shiur* (lesson) in the Stern College *Beit Midrash* (House of Study), the halakhic issue has been settled for the modern Orthodox community."[130]

But even for the many women who do not study Talmud, there is enough Torah that they can and must learn that could fill three lives, let alone one. Since it is impossible to study everything, perhaps the differentiation in learning patterns between the sexes may lie in where each is to begin studies and in which areas each is to develop expertise.[131] One thing is certain, however: that regardless of a woman's area of focus, only by acquiring a sound and thorough Jewish education will she be able to represent with wisdom, greatness, and dignity the *Torat imekha*, and be eligible for member-ship in the entire community of women who have kept the Jewish tradition alive throughout centuries of challenge.

---

128. See Lichtenstein, "Fundamental Problems Regarding the Education of Wom-en," p. 7.

129. Ibid. See also Shlomo Riskin, "Women and Judaism: The Key Issues," in *Orthodoxy Confronts Modernity*, ed. Jonathan Sacks (Hoboken, NJ: Ktav, 1991), p. 90. Rabbi Moshe Kahn, writing on the subject of Jewish education for women, contends, "No self-respecting student would accept the need to always turn to someone else for help because certain areas of a subject have been intentionally kept closed. We run the risk of the brightest young women turning their backs on us intellectually if we persist in containing their Jewish intellectual horizons" (Moshe Kahn, "Jewish Education for Women," *Ten Da'at* 3:3 [Spring 1989]: 11). Considering that a number of Orthodox women today engage in careers ranging from law to medicine to nuclear physics–professions that have engaged their intellect considerably–Rabbi Kahn's concern is legitimate.

130. Joel B. Wolowelsky, "Modern Orthodoxy and Women's Changing Self-Perception," *Tradition* 22:1 (Spring 1986): 78.

131. See Rabbi Moshe Hochman's comment in this regard in Benjamin Hecht, "Women and Judaism: The Question of Learning," *Nishma* Update (September 1992).

4

A Historical Survey of Jewish
Education for Women:
Part I—The Biblical Period
to the Middle Ages

So far I have examined the *attitudes* toward Torah education for women as reflected in centuries of halakhic literature. Let us now explore the historical *reality* as it existed concurrent with these positions. After some discussion of women in the biblical and talmudic periods, the major enquiry will be directed toward the period from the eleventh century up to modern times. In this chapter, as in the next chapters, the patterns of education for women that may have existed—primarily informal ones but not wholly so—will be considered. A major focus of this exploration will be to highlight a number of outstanding Torah-educated women who played active and prominent roles throughout the generations in enhancing or disseminating Torah knowledge for and to others. Other women who actualized their intellectual capabilities and propensities for their own personal Jewish religious growth and development will also be described. In this way, a considerable number of women who have remained relatively unknown to the general Jewish public will be brought to the foreground and accorded a place in history.[1]

The reader should bear in mind at the outset an important qualification

---

1. Judith Plaskow points out that the recovery of history and tradition pertaining to women is especially important in Judaism, in which memory, remembering, and telling the story are a religious obligation. See "Jewish Memory from a Feminist Perspective," in *Weaving the Visions: New Patterns in Feminist Spirituality*, ed. Judith Plaskow and Carol P. Christ (San Francisco: Harper, Collins, 1989), p. 40.

made by Deborah Weissman, a researcher in this field who states, " 'Education' is not one single, easily defined entity," and 'unschooled' is not synonymous with 'uneducated.' " Indeed, she maintains that one of the challenges of studying the history of women's education is the "range of formal and non-formal ways in which the functions of socialization and cultural transmission can be carried out."[2] Thus our definition of education is broad enough to include such activities as women's involvement in religious ritual, synagogue services, and even the publishing of Hebrew books.

IMAGES OF BIBLICAL WOMEN

A survey of portraits of women in biblical narratives provides no scenes of instruction. However, we might assume that girls are incorporated under the term *ben*, which, while meaning "son," often is a generic term to signify any child. In various places in the Bible we find directives concerning informing the *ben* who seeks instruction regarding the historical meaning of the Passover sacrifice.[3] The portrayals of women in the biblical narratives have been subjected to a number of inquiries by contemporary scholars.[4] Some view the biblical world as having been a man's world, patriarchal in social structure and excluding women from legal privileges.[5] At first impression, it does seem as if

2. Deborah R. Weissman, "Education of Jewish Women," in *Encyclopaedia Judaica Yearbook* 1986–1987, p. 29.

3. See, for example, Deuteronomy 6:7. Though we have seen the term *ben* applied only to sons in the context of the study of Torah, the term can also be understood to mean "child," either male or female, in other contexts, even educational ones. *Sefer ha-Hinukh, mitzvah* 21, states that women are equally obligated in the commandment to recount the Passover story and that the term *ben* in this context is all-inclusive.

4. See, for example, Tamar Frankiel, *The Voice of Sarah: Feminine Spirituality and Traditional Judaism* (San Francisco: Harper Collins, 1990), pp. 5–36; Frederick E. Greenspahn, "A Typology of Biblical Women," *Judaism* 32:1 (Winter 1983): 43–50; JoAnn Hackett, "In the Days of Jael: Reclaiming the History of Women in Ancient Israel," in *Immaculate and Powerful: The Female in Sacred Image and Social Reality*, ed. Clarissa W. Atkinson, Constance H. Buchanan, and Margaret R. Miles (Boston: Beacon Press, 1985), pp. 15–38; Susan Niditch, "Portrayals of Women in the Hebrew Bible," in *Jewish Women in Historical Perspective*, ed. Judith R. Baskin (Detroit: Wayne State University Press, 1991), pp. 25–42; Adin Steinsaltz, *Biblical Images: Men and Women of the Book* (New York: Basic Books, 1986); and Phyllis Trible, "Depatriarchalizing in Biblical Interpretation," in *The Jewish Woman: New Perspectives*, ed. Elizabeth Koltun (New York: Schocken, 1976), pp. 217–218.

5. See, for example, Greenspahn, "A Typology of Biblical Women," p. 45; Trible, "Depatriarchalizing in Biblical Interpretation," pp. 217–218; and Niditch, "Portrayals of Women in the Hebrew Bible," pp. 29–31.

the stories of biblical women are deeply embedded in the stories of men or in events pertinent to the entire Jewish people. But a closer reading of the scriptural text reveals clever and resourceful women who used their intelligence and strength to direct pivotal moments within the biblical accounts, at times helping to guarantee the survival of the Jewish people.[6] Within their family contexts, these women shine as people who have unique relationships with God. Though we cannot gauge the degree of education of the women in these narratives, we can appreciate their wisdom and knowledge. Therefore it is of interest to look briefly at some of these women.[7] Their legacy continued to color the portrayals of women to the end of the Second Temple period.[8] It is likely that these are the models that have inspired women throughout the ages to fulfill their deepest religious quests in family contexts.

Abraham's role as the first of the patriarchs looms majestically in Israelite history. The biblical narrative focuses in detail on his family life and his desire for a son and heir. In such matters Abraham consults with Sarah on all major decisions, and in one case Sarah overrides his judgment: "In all that Sarah has said to you, listen to her voice" (Genesis 21:12). Sarah's decision to remove Hagar's and Abraham's son Ishmael from their household receives divine approbation and sets the stage for Sarah's son, Isaac, to continue the Israelite patriarchal line of Abraham. The divine destiny for the nation is thus fulfilled through Sarah.

Rebecca is the wife of Isaac. Troubled in pregnancy, she seeks advice from God (Genesis 25:22–24). She learns that of her twins, the younger (Jacob) is to fulfill the role of Israelite leadership. Isaac, however, desires his older son to take this role. Rebecca manipulates matters so that the divine destiny, which she alone knows about, comes to fruition (Genesis 27). "Both Isaac and Jacob are playing out the drama for which Rebecca has written the script."[9] She also protects Jacob from his older brother, enabling him to continue the role of Israelite leadership (Genesis 27:41f.). Leah and Rachel, the wives of Jacob, hold power associated with fertility and children, and in their shrewd mach-

---

6. Elisabeth Schussler Fiorenza points out that we can, by "rereading the available sources in a different key," rediscover feminine dimensions in our stories and traditions. See "In Search of Women's Heritage," in *Weaving the Visions: New Patterns in Feminist Spirituality*, p. 35.

7. It is beyond the scope of the current discussion to analyze each of the biblical women in detail. My brief discussion also does not include the entire complement of women in the Bible. For a fuller picture of biblical women, Frankiel's book is especially informative.

8. Such portrayals are found in the Apocryphal stories of Judith, Susannah, and Hannah and her seven sons.

9. Greenspahn, "A Typology of Biblical Women," p. 48.

inations fulfill the ultimate divine plan for Jacob's and their children's destiny. The story related in Genesis 30:14–18 describes the birth of Issachar in just such a way.

Moses is born during the enslavement of the Israelites in Egypt. In this period, it was the midwives who had the courage to defy Pharaoh's cruel policy of extinguishing the babies' lives at birth (Exodus 1:15–20) and "to confront a king with the boldness of a woman who fears God more than man."[10] Jewish tradition views Moses as its greatest prophet and hero. The biblical portrayal of his sister, Miriam, depicts her in various stages of her life: first, as the one who watches over her infant brother, Moses, to protect him (Exodus 2:3ff.), and later, as a prophet celebrating the salvation of the Israelites at the miraculous splitting of the Red Sea (Exodus 15:20–21). Her appearance generally signifies divine interaction with the nation, in which she plays a major role.

It is noteworthy that women are able to challenge the rightness of a law taught by Moses. The daughters of Zelophehad, when their father died without male heirs, demanded the right to inherit their father's land, a claim in which God acquiesced: "The daughters of Zelophehad speak rightly . . . " (Numbers 27:2–6).

Deborah's song of triumph (Judges 5) and Hannah's prayer of Thanksgiving (1 Samuel 2:1–10) are perhaps "the noblest outpourings of the God-possessed spirit which adorn the national literature of our people."[11] Hannah, whose heartfelt prayer, with lips moving but no sound emanating, became the preferred mode of Jewish prayer; Deborah, the prophetess, the judge, and with her Jael, the brave woman who slew Sisera the tyrant (Judges 4:18–23); Michal who rescued her husband David from the clutches of King Saul, her father (1 Samuel 19:11–17); the wise woman from Tekoa who brought appeasement to David with regard to his son Absalom (2 Samuel 14); the wise woman of Abel, the counselor and savior of her city (2 Samuel 20:14–22); Ruth, who forsook her native Moab to live a moral life at the side of her bereaved mother-in-law (Book of Ruth); and Esther, who risked her personal safety to effect the rescue of her people (Book of Esther) are only some of the women who appear in Hebrew Scriptures. The lives of ordinary women are largely hidden from us throughout this literature. It is remarkable and fortunate that we find women of stature in biblical stories, so that their paradigm can be instructive for all ages.

There are clear indications in the Bible that women participated in public worship. The first mention of such occurs in Exodus 15:20–21, when Miriam led the women in public celebration and song after the splitting of the Red Sea.

---

10. Samson R. Hirsch, *Judaism Eternal*, trans. I. Grunfeld, vol. 2 (London: Soncino Press, 1960), p. 80.

11. Ibid. p. 43.

We also read of women who assembled to minister at the door of the tent of meeting (Exodus 38:8).[12] When we find that in 1 Samuel 1:12, "Hannah continued to pray before the Lord," we assume that she was doing there what many of her own sex had done before and after her.[13] Although Israelite women did not participate in the Temple choirs at Jerusalem, there is some evidence to show that they sang at the royal court.[14] Others were known for the gifts of prophecy and poetic expression.[15] Such skills may indicate a formal training, learned from experts.[16] Huldah, the prophet, is an example of one woman who attained a high degree of respect for her access to the Divine in biblical times.[17] Living during the reign of Josiah in the latter part of the First Commonwealth, it was she, rather than Jeremiah the prophet, whom the king consulted when he sent to "inquire of the Lord" after he found the copy of the Book of the Law.[18] In a much later period, it was proclaimed that "each generation is redeemed because of the righteous women of that generation."[19]

EDUCATION IN BIBLICAL AND SECOND TEMPLE PERIODS

Present knowledge about education in ancient Israel is sparse. The sources at hand do not allow for a precise chronological description of the development of pedagogical institutions or methodology. It will therefore not be possible to cite passages from the Bible that can be taken as conclusive evidence for the existence of schools. I use the term "school" here as implying a form of professional education, which involved both reading and writing, at a specific location to which young people came and for which fees were paid to a teacher. Evidence from the Bible is largely circumstantial, and some texts say more about literacy in general than about how the ability to read and write

12. See also 1 Samuel 2:22, where reference is again made to "the women who ministered at the entrance of the tent of meeting."

13. The High Priest Eli's shocked response was due to Hannah's method of prayer, not the fact that she was praying.

14. See, for example, 2 Samuel 19:36; Ecclesiastes 2:8. See also Aberbach, Ha-Hinukh ha-Yehudi be-Tekufat ha-Mishnah veha-Talmud (Jerusalem: Rubin Mass, 1982), p. 12.

15. See, for example, Exodus 15:20–21, Judges 5, and 2 Kings 22:14.

16. Encyclopaedia Judaica, vol. 6, p. 398.

17. 2 Kings 22:14–20. There are seven prophetesses mentioned in the Bible: Sarah, Miriam, Deborah, Hannah, Abigail, Hulda, and Esther. Most commentators agree that Rebecca, Rachel, and Leah had some degree of prophecy as well. Tradition has it that there were as many prophetesses as prophets. See Rabbi Aryeh Kaplan, Handbook of Jewish Thought (New York and Jerusalem: Maznaim, 1979), pp. 110–111 and n. 244.

18. 2 Kings 22:13–14.

19. Midrash Zuta to Ruth, ed. S. Buber (Berlin, 1894), p. 54.

was acquired.[20] This is understandable, considering that the Bible may be regarded less as a document detailing the evolution of educational institutions per se, or as describing educational philosophies, than as being in and of itself a philosophy of education; that is, the teachings expressed therein became a philosophy of life and learning for the people of the time and for people in subsequent times. Thus the whole concept of education in the Hebrew Scriptures is one that must be drawn from inference.

The issue here is the context within which education occurred: Did parents assume primary responsibility for educating their children, or did they entrust their children, whether boys or girls, to professional educators? In short, were there schools during the formative period of the monarchy, or, more generally, prior to the first explicit reference to a school, namely, Ben Sira's invitation to acquire an education at his house of study (*Bet ha-Midrash*)[21] in about 200 B.C.E.?

It should be noted that the Bible contains no mention of elementary schools. According to the opinion of a number of historians,[22] the school, functioning as a public institution, did not exist during the whole period covered by biblical literature. It must be taken for granted, however, that the priests, Levites, prophets, and scribes received some kind of formal or systematic instruction,[23] which they in turn transmitted to the people. The evidence clearly points to the existence of literate persons at an early period in Israel.[24]

---

20. See James L. Crenshaw, "Education in Ancient Israel," *Journal of Biblical Literature* 104:4 (December 1985): 602, where he cites August Klostermann's pioneer study of education in Israel, "Schulwesen im alten Israel," in which only three texts are taken as conclusive evidence for schools: Isaiah 28: 9–13, Isaiah 50:4–9, and Proverbs 22:17–21.

21. *Sefer Ben Sira ha-Shalem (Ecclesiasticus)*, ed. M. Segal (Jerusalem: Mossad Bialik, 1958), 51:23.

22. See, for example, E. B. Castle, *Ancient Education and Today* (Baltimore: Penguin Books, 1961), p. 164; E. W. Heaton, *Everyday Life in Old Testament Times* (London: B. T. Batsford, 1956), pp. 79 and 178; Nathan Morris, *The Jewish School* (New York: Jewish Education Committee Press, 1937), p. 4; and Roland de Vaux, *Ancient Israel: Its Life and Institutions* (London: Darton, Longman & Todd, 1961), p. 50.

23. See, for example, 2 Kings 4:38.

24. See James Crenshaw, "Education in Ancient Israel," pp. 603–604, who provides a list of evidence. The evidence includes, among other things, (1) the existence of a city named *Kiryat Sepher* (City of the Book, or City of the Scribe); (2) the story in Judges 8:13–17 about Gideon's enlisting the aid of a local youth to write down the names of the city officials; (3) Isaiah's determination to bind up the testimony and seal the teaching among his disciples (8:16) (scholars have long recognized the existence of a professional group of prophets who gathered around a prophetic leader such as Elijah or Elisha); (4) Job's desire to have the charges against him written on a document so that he could display them and demonstrate his innocence (31:35–37); (5) presumed scribes

Nathan Morris states in *The Jewish School* that it may be assumed that many children received some form of literary instruction.[25] As a rule, the father was the instructor, but sometimes private teachers were engaged for that purpose.[26] Such individual teachers might set up schools of a sort in their own home, but these were the private affairs of their owners and received no support from the community.[27] The publicly controlled elementary school for children did not come into being until after the period of the Bible, and the beginning of the Common Era.

Quite apart from school, the Bible hardly contains a reference even to the regular education of children, if education is to be understood in its modern sense. There are indeed numerous injunctions about "telling," "relating to," and "teaching" children. These were interpreted by later generations as referring to formal elementary education, which had then already become a recognized social institution.[28] Thus the well-known verses in Deuteronomy, "And you shall teach them diligently to your children" (6:7) and "And you shall teach them to your children" (11:19), were made the religious basis of Jewish elementary education. In a general sense, however, these and other passages were meant to convey the transmission of tradition and moral teachings from generation to generation, in whatever formal or informal manner. Indeed, in many books of the Bible this concern for the transmission of knowledge and tradition and the application of ethical principles is emphasized.

It was the family that served as the foremost institution for the dissemination of ideals and the amassed knowledge of society. As William Smith notes in *Ancient Education*, "The outstanding characteristic of Hebrew education during the (pre-exilic) period was its concentration in and about the home and the family."[29] Simon Greenberg, American rabbi and educator, writes:

---

and courtiers in the royal court, particularly in the time of David, Solomon, and Hezekiah; (6) references to parental instruction in Proverbs (especially 4:1–9 and 8:32–36); (7) scattered references to writing (e.g., Isaiah 10:19, Isaiah 29:11–12, Proverbs 3:3, Jeremiah 8:8, Deuteronomy 24:1, Jeremiah 32:12, and Joshua 18:9); and (8) vocabulary for teaching and knowledge, particularly in Deuteronomy and Proverbs.

25. Morris, *The Jewish School*, p. 4.

26. See also Nathan Drazin, *History of Jewish Education from 515 B.C.E. to 220 C.E.* (New York: Arno Press, 1979), p. 45.

27. Thus there came into existence the phrase *tinokot shel bet rabban*, "children of the house of the master" for schoolchildren. (See Drazin, *History of Jewish Education from 515 B.C.E. to 220 C.E.*, p. 45.)

28. See Morris, *The Jewish School*, p. 4.

29. William A. Smith, *Ancient Education* (New York: Philosophical Library, 1955), p. 238.

> The home is mankind's universal educational agency. . . . But the home was
> not used by all groups with equal awareness and effectiveness for transmitting
> the spiritual and ethical teachings and the treasured historic memories of the
> group. The biblical record clearly indicates that among the Jews the home was
> at a very early period *consciously* employed for such educational purposes.[30]

The religious home ceremony was the primary means of conveying cultural
values from one generation to another. The Passover home ritual is found at
the very inception of Israel's national history (Exodus 12:21–27), and other
home rituals were associated with other holidays of the Hebrew calendar.[31]
As to direct religious training, the Bible furnishes us with numerous
examples. We read, for example, of children, both boys and girls, who go
with their parents to the sanctuaries,[32] where they would hear the chanting
of the Psalms and the recounting of those historical episodes that were
connected with each great festivity. We read of mothers teaching their
daughters the lamentations for the dead.[33] At least two historians are of the
opinion that the religious education of girls and boys was more or less on an
equal footing in biblical times.[34] With regard to practical training of a
religious or social nature, the girl is mentioned as well as the boy; and
teaching by the mother is commended equally with instruction by the
father.[35] Instructive, for example, are the following verses from Jeremiah
(9:19) and Proverbs (1:8), respectively: "Indeed, hear, O women, the word of
the Lord, and let your ears receive the word of His mouth"; "Hearken, my
child, to the discipline of your father, and do not forsake the Torah teachings
of your mother."

Women were included in the Law of Assembly, in which the Covenant
was to be reread publicly once every seven years during the Feast of
Tabernacles;[36] indeed, this was the earliest prescription for mass education in
ancient Israel: "Gather the people, men, women, children . . . in order that

---

30. Simon Greenberg, "Jewish Educational Institutions," in *The Jews: Their History,
Culture and Religion*, ed. Louis Finkelstein, vol. 2 (Philadelphia: Jewish Publication
Society of America, 1949), p. 917.

31. See, for example, Deuteronomy 16:10–12 and 1 Samuel 20:5–6.

32. See, for example, Deuteronomy 12:12, 18; 16:11; and 31:12; 1 Samuel 1; and
Nehemiah 12:43.

33. Jeremiah 9:19.

34. See Nathan Morris, *The Jewish School*, p. 28. See also Lorenz Durr, *Das Erziehungswesen im Alten Testament und im Antiken Orient* (Leipzig: J. C. Hinrichs, 1932), p. 113,
where he emphasizes the breadth of learning acquired by daughters, particularly in
Torah.

35. See, for example, Deuteronomy 12:12, Jeremiah 9:19, Joel 3:1, and Proverbs
1:8.

36. Deuteronomy 31:10–13.

they may hear and so learn to revere the Lord, your God, and to observe faithfully every word of His Teaching."[37]

The mother was naturally the girl's primary parental teacher and model (cf. Ezekiel's epigram [16:44], "Like mother like daughter"), as the father was the son's.[38] Besides being instructed in domestic chores and the special skills the mother might possess, the young girl learned of her religious obligations in the informal atmosphere of the home.[39] She was brought up on the virtues of sexual innocence and chastity; violation of her body was considered a great personal and family tragedy.[40] Greenberg states:

> If the Jewish girl until very recent days was most often not sent to receive formal instruction in a school, it was not merely because of a widespread attitude that a girl needed no formal education. It was due rather to the feeling that her mother and home training could provide her with all the instruction she needed to live a good and pious Jewish life. Until very recent times, the expectation was, by and large, fully realized.[41]

At the outset of the period of the Second Temple, a great religious rededication assembly under the leadership of Ezra and Nehemiah was held in Jerusalem, at which time the Mosaic legislation of the Pentateuch was ratified as the constitution of the people.[42] We find that "Ezra brought the Torah before the entire congregation, man and woman . . . and he read from it . . . from [first] light to midday before the men and women and those who have understanding, and the attention of all the nation was to Torah."[43] Women were hence included in efforts made for the advancement of adult religious education.

It was during the period of the Babylonian exile and in the early years of the Second Commonwealth that the synagogue (Bet ha-Knesset) took root among Jewish society. It was here that the scribes, a learned class devoted to the interpretation of the sacred books, taught the law to the body of people. "The synagogues became centers of social and religious life," writes E. B. Castle in Ancient Education and Today, "but their chief function was to act as popular universities [at first for adults and at a much later time for children], a kind of extra-mural department of the main university, which was the newly built Temple at Jerusalem."[44] In this early postexilic period appear the first

---

37. Deuteronomy 31:12.
38. See, for example, Exodus 10:2, 12:26, 13:8; and Deuteronomy 4:9, 6:7, 20f.
39. Encyclopaedia Judaica, vol. 6, p. 397.
40. See, for example, Genesis 34:25f. and 2 Samuel 13: 1f.
41. Greenberg, "Jewish Educational Institutions," pp. 918–919.
42. Nehemiah 8–10.
43. Nehemiah 8:2–3.
44. Castle, Ancient Education and Today, p. 166.

hesitating attempts at the creation of an elementary educational terminology.[45] The teacher is referred to as a *maven* ("one who causes to understand") and *maskil* ("one who causes to be wise").[46] There is reference to the term *melamed* (the teacher),[47] which became permanently established in Jewish educational terminology, and the pupil is denoted by a word that has remained in general usage to the present time, *talmid*.[48]

WOMEN'S RELIGIOUS ROLES IN THE SECOND TEMPLE PERIOD

Especially on the Sabbath and festivals, women participated in the prayers in the Temple in Jerusalem and in all the synagogues in the land of Israel and in the Diaspora, in both Second Temple and subsequent times.[49] These gatherings at the Temple and at synagogues supplied an important means of religious education for them. Although they did not lead public services or read publicly from the Torah,[50] they did participate in all traditional prayers and listened to the Torah reading and to the explanation of the weekly portion and the Prophets.[51] They were also present at the sermons delivered on Sabbath and prior to the festivals.[52] In fact, if we can grant some continuity in practice, which in this case seems reasonable, we can learn from one *midrash* that, in the period following the destruction of the Second Temple, some women were more diligent than their husband in attending these scholarly sermons. We

45. See Morris, *The Jewish School*, p. 10, who notes this phenomenon.

46. *maven*–Ezra 8:16, 1 Chronicles 25:8, and 2 Chronicles 35:3. *maskil*–Daniel 11:33, 12:3; and 2 Chronicles 30:22.

47. *melamed*–Psalms 94:10 and 119:99.

48. *talmid*–1 Chronicles 25:8.

49. See, for example, *Avodah Zarah* 38b and *Sotah* 22a. In *Sotah* 22a the reference is to a woman who used to attend synagogue services *daily*. See also I. M. Elbogen, *Ha-Tefilah be-Yisrael* (Tel Aviv: Dvir, 1972), pp. 350–352. See also Ross S. Kraemer, "Jewish Women in the Diaspora World of Late Antiquity," in *Jewish Women in Historical Perspective*, ed. Judith Baskin (Detroit: Wayne State University Press, 1991), pp. 48–49.

50. According to the *Tosefta* (*Megillah* 3, 5) a woman could be one of the seven readers required for the public reading of the Torah on the Sabbath, but the Rabbis later discontinued the practice and declared that a woman should not read publicly (*Megillah* 23a). This insistence upon a more thorough segregation of the sexes at public gatherings is due to the strict standards of womanly modesty that the Rabbis imposed (see, for example, *Mishnah Ketubot* 7:6).

51. See Drazin, *History of Jewish Education*, p. 132, for elaboration.

52. See, for example, *Sotah* 1: 4 and *Leviticus Rabbah* 9. See also commentary of Rashi on *Shabbat* 30b; I. M. Elbogen, *ha-Tefilah be-Yisrael*, p. 351; and Moshe Aberbach, *Ha-Hinukh ha-Yehudi be-Tekufat ha-Mishnah veha-Talmud*, pp. 14–16.

read in that *midrash* of a woman whose husband chided her for returning so late on a Friday night from the sermon.[53]

Bernadette Brooten, in her doctoral dissertation, *Women Leaders in the Ancient Synagogue*, suggests that women may have not only participated in synagogue activities but also, in fact, served as leaders in a number of synagogues during the Roman and Byzantine periods. The evidence for this, in Brooten's view, consists of nineteen Greek and Latin inscriptions on ancient synagogues uncovered by archaeologists in which women bear the titles "head of the synagogue," "leader," "elder," "mother of the synagogue," and "priestess." It is Brooten's thesis that these titles were not merely honorific, but functional.[54]

EVIDENCE FOR FORMAL EDUCATION IN THE LATE SECOND TEMPLE PERIOD

Morris sees the development of Jewish popular education as marked by three definite stages.[55] The first is the rise of the synagogue during, or soon after, the Babylonian captivity. The second is the establishment of schools for youths in the period following the Maccabean wars. The third, which will be dealt with briefly here but more extensively in the subsequent section, is the foundation of the public elementary school after the destruction of the Second Temple by the Romans and the downfall of the political state.

Only two statements dealing directly with the establishment of schools for

---

53. *Leviticus Rabbah* 9:9. This woman, who attended the lectures of Rabbi Meir (second century C.E.), which he was in the habit of giving every Friday evening, was so interested in them that she once remained there so long that the candles in her house burnt themselves out. Her husband, who waited at home, so strongly resented having to wait up in the dark for her that he would not permit her to cross the threshold until she gave some offense to the lecturer, which would make him sure that she would not venture to attend his sermons again. When the sage learned of the couple's quarrel, he asked the woman to spit seven times in his face to cure him of an eye affliction. Then he advised her to go back home to her husband and tell him that she had done as he had demanded of her. When his disciples reproved him for having abased the honor and the authority of Torah, Rabbi Meir replied, "There is no sacrifice too great to reconcile husband and wife." What this *midrash* has to say about the lengths to which one should go to keep peace between husband and wife is a poignant ethic. One has to hope that the husband's attitude toward his wife's learning is not reflective of society's attitudes in general at that time. (See Vanessa Ochs, *Words on Fire* [New York: Harcourt Brace Jovanovich, 1990], pp. 125–127, for one approach to analyzing this *midrash*.)

54. Bernadette Brooten, *Women Leaders in the Ancient Synagogue* (Chico, CA: Scholars Press, 1982).

55. Morris, *The Jewish School*, p. 13. See also Drazin, *History of Jewish Education*, p. 37, who delineates three stages in the growth of popular education slightly differently from Morris's delineation.

children have come to us from talmudic sources. One is the brief statement "And he, Simeon ben Shetah, enacted that the children should go to school."[56] The other statement on the origin of the school is in the form of a historical outline:

> Truly, let this man be remembered for good; Joshua ben Gamla is his name, for were it not for him, Torah would have been forgotten in Israel. At first, if a child had a father, his father taught him; if he had no father, he did not learn at all. . . . They then introduced an ordinance that teachers of children be appointed in Jerusalem. . . . But still, he who had a father was brought to Jerusalem and instructed, while he who had no father did not go up there to learn. They therefore ordained that teachers should be set up in every district, to whom children should be sent at the age of sixteen and seventeen years. But because a pupil who was punished by his teacher would rebel and leave school, Joshua ben Gamla at length introduced a regulation that teachers of young children be appointed in each district and town, and that children begin their schooling at the age of six or seven years.[57]

It will be noticed that these two traditions on the origins of the school identify different founders for the school; according to the first, it was Simeon ben Shetah, said to be brother of Queen Salome, who reigned from 76 to 67 B.C.E.; according to the second, it was Joshua ben Gamla, the High Priest, who functioned in this capacity a hundred years later (c. 63–65 C.E.). There is considerable controversy among modern writers who attempt to integrate the school ordinance of Simeon ben Shetah with the *Bava Batra* report and to properly date and categorize the stages in the development of the school system outlined in that report. Some historians are also reluctant to treat the latter tradition as a strictly historical document.[58]

A number of social, religious, and practical factors led to the establishment of schools for children. Teaching had been, as mentioned earlier, a parental concern (except for the specialized training schools for priests, prophets, and scribes). The system was fairly successful, as Nathan Drazin, an educational

---

56. *Ketubot* 8:11.

57. *Bava Batra* 21a.

58. It is beyond the purview of this paper to deal with this controversy. The reader may wish to read Eliezer Ebner, *Elementary Education in Ancient Israel* (New York: Bloch, 1956), pp. 39–42, for the best treatment of this subject. Also see Salo W. Baron, *The Jewish Community*, vol. 3 (Philadelphia: Jewish Publication Society of America, 1945), p. 23 n. 8; Drazin, *History of Jewish Education*, pp. 37–46; M. Guedemann, *Jewish Encyclopedia*, vol. 5, p. 43; Julius B. Maller, "The Role of Education in Jewish History," in *The Jews: Their History, Culture and Religion*, ed. Louis Finkelstein, p. 901; and Morris, *The Jewish School*, p. 17. The historicity of the accounts in the Talmud are doubted by David Goodblatt, "The Talmudic Sources on the Origins of Organized Jewish Education" [in Hebrew], in *Studies in the History of the Jewish People in the Land of Israel* 5 (1980): 83–103.

historian, points out,[59] because being chiefly an agrarian people during the days of the First Temple (and since agriculture is a seasonal occupation), the Jews had sufficient time to advance their own education and to instruct their youth. With the rise, however, of the arts and industries in Israel in the latter part of the Second Commonwealth, many of the people had to work all year round for their livelihood and so found little time for teaching their children and for continuing their own education. Many children were neglected because of their parents' preoccupation with daily work or because the fathers themselves might not have been conversant with the elements of Jewish learning—hence the need for the establishment of schools.

Besides this factor, a cultural-political one played a role in the evolution of schools for children.[60] Beginning with the third century B.C.E., Hellenism made great inroads into Jewish society. Many Jews in Israel fell before the blandishments of this new and attractive culture. The Hellenized Jew became an even more dangerous enemy to the traditional modes of Judaism than the Hellenized Egyptian monarchy that ruled Syria at this time. The attempt by the Syrian king Antiochus Epiphanes to bolster the Hellenized Jew precipitated the fierce nationalistic revolt of the Maccabees[61] in 168 B.C.E. The Talmud attributes the dominance of traditional Jewish education over opposing ideologies to the influence of the Pharisees,[62] headed by Simeon ben Shetah, on Queen Salome Alexandra, his sister. Simeon succeeded in "restoring the Torah to its former glory," establishing schools in Jerusalem and in the district towns and obliging parents to send their children to them.[63] As Eliezer Ebner states in *Elementary Education in Ancient Israel*: "In the struggle for leadership in Jewish life between the Pharisees and Sadducees, the founding of the public school constituted an important move to assure the spread of the Pharisaic teachings among the people."[64] The popularity of

---

59. Drazin, *History of Jewish Education*, p. 40.

60. See Ebner, *Elementary Education in Ancient Israel*, p. 44. See also Aberbach, *Ha-Hinukh ha-Yehudi*, p. 18–19.

61. Maccabee was the additional name given to Judah, son of Matathias, military leader of the revolt against Syria in 168 B.C.E. The name Maccabee is applied loosely to other members of the family, as well as to the Hasmonean dynasty, as a whole.

62. Rabbinic literature considers the Pharisees to be the forerunners of the rabbinic establishment, and the Sadducees as their opponents. The Sadducees were a sect of the latter half of the Second Temple period, composed largely of the wealthier elements of the population who refused to accept the binding authority of the Oral Law, as opposed to the canonical Scriptures, which they adhered to strictly and interpreted literally. Their influence over some of the Hasmonean kings led to the persecution of the Pharisees and their teachings of Oral Tradition.

63. *Kiddushin* 66a.

64. Ebner, *Elementary Education in Ancient Israel*, p. 44.

the Pharisees by the time of Josephus in the first-century C.E. lends credence to this scenario.[65]

Thus, in about 75 B.C.E., for the first time in the history of the Jews, a "two-level" school system came into existence. This consisted of a college in Jerusalem for advanced students and preparatory secondary schools, which were spread throughout the cities in which Jews lived.[66] Drazin believes that the Jerusalem college entailed financial expenditure and was inconvenient for those who resided elsewhere in Palestine, particularly so for orphans ("he who had no father did not go up there and did not learn" [Bava Batra 21a]). Therefore, free and compulsory schooling was established, presumably by Simeon ben Shetah, in the main cities of each district for all male adolescents ("they ordained that teachers should be set up in every district, to whom children should be sent at the age of sixteen or seventeen years" [Bava Batra 21a]).[67] Elementary education was still a matter of parental care in the years prior to the Common Era and the destruction of the Temple in Jerusalem. This is the picture according to later talmudic sources.

Direct evidence that women were taught Torah by both parents in Second Temple times can be found in the apocryphal story of Susanna. This story probably dates from the first century B.C.E. and purports to tell the tale of Susanna and Daniel in the time of the Babylonian Exile. The author relates that "her parents also were upright people and instructed their daughter in the Law of Moses."[68] Here it is stated without hesitation that parents had taught Torah to their daughter. Similarly, in the apocryphal Book of Tobit, it is stated at the beginning that the male Tobit performed the commandments "as Deborah, my grandmother, had instructed me, for I was left an orphan by my father."[69] Here the author indicates that although the primary duty of Torah

---

65. Josephus, *Antiquities*, trans. William Whiston (Grand Rapids, MI: Kregel Publications, 1981), 13:10:6.

66. Some historians regard the school established in Jerusalem as the enactment of Simeon ben Shetah. See, for example, Ebner, *Elementary Education in Ancient Israel*, p. 46, and Aberbach, *Ha-Hinukh ha-Yehudi*, pp. 19–21. Others consider this school as the enactment of the Men of the Great Assembly several centuries earlier. See, for example, Drazin, *History of Jewish Education*, pp. 35–45 and 49–50. Drazin sees in the *Bava Batra* account an outline of the development of the three-level system of Jewish education. The first phase, in his view, refers to the establishment of a central academy of higher learning in Jerusalem, following the demand of the Men of the Great Assembly to "raise up many disciples" (*Mishnah Avot* 1:1). In the setup of the district schools for the 16- and 17-year-old youth, he recognizes the foundation of secondary high schools, which are identified with the enactment of Simeon ben Shetah. The third phase, describing Joshua ben Gamla's enactment, deals with elementary schools.

67. Drazin, *History of Jewish Education*, p. 43.

68. *The Apocrypha*, trans. Edgar J. Goodspeed (New York: Vintage, 1959), p. 349.

69. Ibid., p. 109.

instruction was performed by the father, a woman was equally capable of fulfilling this role.

It is with the establishment of schools beyond the home that the exclusion of girls from the *formal* religious educational process becomes apparent. Drazin and Ebner are of the opinion that it was concern about the possibility of undesirable conduct arising from a coeducational system, rather than a belief in the inferior position of women that led to the exclusion of girls from public instruction at the secondary and later the elementary level.[70] On the other hand, Eliezer Berkovits[71] and Tamar Frankiel[72] claim that women's exclusion from intellectual activity reflected the general position of women in the Hellenistic world. Furthermore, the religious obligation to study Torah was incumbent on men, not on women, as we have already seen. Yet any conclusions we draw must be made in the context of the event as it may have been seen through Jewish societal eyes at the time.

It has become a universally accepted practice, recurrently expressed by writers of the history of education, to note with pride the fact that in the times of Joshua ben Gamla there already existed among Jews a law of compulsory education.[73] Yet a number of present-day historians and thinkers–notably Rabbi Isaac Hutner, mid-twentieth-century leading Orthodox Jewish thinker–disagree with the view that these institutions were of notable worth and pride.[74] Before the existence of compulsory education, Jewish children received their education at home, as we have already seen. It was only after the breakdown of the family, with the occupation of Palestine by foreign powers, that *zwang-schule*, or compulsory schooling, was deemed necessary–for boys, at least. In actuality, the home, which served as the nest for physical and emotional nourishment, was the ideal environment for the transmission of Torah values, ideals, and knowledge. The school system, being by definition a system, an institution outside the family, was a foreign or less natural body for the communication of Torah. "The study of Torah was equated with the study of life, and therefore constrictions of it to a curriculum seemed at best forced or more likely ludicrous."[75]

Some of the aforementioned conclusions about why institutionalized schooling was created only for boys may be built upon the attitude that the

70. See, for example, Ebner, *Elementary Education in Ancient Israel*, p. 34, and Drazin, *History of Jewish Education*, p. 130.

71. Eliezer Berkovits, *Jewish Women in Time and Torah* (Hoboken, NJ: Ktav, 1990), pp. 25–28.

72. Frankiel, *The Voice of Sarah*, pp. 42–43.

73. See Chaim Hisiger, "Roots and Legends," *Nishma* 5 (June 1989): 1.

74. See Rabbi Isaac Hutner, "Shiur be-Hilkhot Hinukh" (in Yiddish), in *Divrei Rabboteinu* (New York: Torah U'Mesorah, 1959), pp. 11–16.

75. Hisiger, "Roots and Legends," p. 1.

development of compulsory schooling was a step forward in the history of education. If this phenomenon was not viewed as such, as Rabbi Hutner has suggested, then other inferences may be drawn as to why *zwang-schule* was not instituted for girls. It may be that home education was working for girls, that the home was continuing to successfully provide the girl with all the instruction she needed to live a good and pious Jewish life. The same could not be said of the quality of boys' education within the home. Thus society was forced to institute compulsory schooling for boys while willing to allow home education for girls to continue. Whatever the reasons may be, it is apparent from mishnaic and midrashic sources, as we will subsequently see, that there was nothing surprising about women's studying Bible and Oral Traditions. Women certainly attended synagogue lectures, yet all of this was done on a voluntary basis.

It should be stated, however, that there existed, during the first century of the Christian era, one Jewish group in which women participated, more or less, on equal footing with men in the study of the Torah. They were the Therapeutae, a sect of Jewish ascetics, believed to have settled in the vicinity of Alexandria, Egypt. The sect, composed of both men and women, was characterized as being unusually severe in its discipline and mode of life. According to Philo, who gives the only original account of this community,[76] members of the sect devoted their entire time to contemplation, prayer, study, and spiritual exercise. They read the Holy Scriptures and sought wisdom from them by taking them as allegory as well as fact, because they believed that the words of the literal text were symbols of something whose hidden nature is revealed by studying the underlying meaning. For six days a week the Therapeutae lived apart and sought wisdom in solitude. On the Sabbath, men and women met in the common sanctuary—a double enclosure with one portion for men and the other for women, for women attended these services with the same ardor as the men, and they listened to a highly intellectual discourse by the eldest and most skilled in their doctrines:

> The eldest of them who has the most profound learning . . . speaks with steadfast look and with steadfast voice, with great powers of reasoning . . . investigating with great pains, and explaining with minute accuracy the precise meaning of the laws, which sits, not indeed at the tips of their ears, but penetrates through their hearing into the soul, and remains there lastingly; and all the rest listen in silence to the praises which he bestows upon the law, showing their assent only by nods of the head, or the eager look of the eyes. And this common holy place . . . is a twofold circuit, being separated partly into the apartment of the men, and partly into the chamber for the women, for women

---

76. See "On a Contemplative Life," in *The Essential Philo* (Philo Judaeus), ed. Nahum N. Glatzer (New York: Schocken, 1971), pp. 311–330.

also, in accordance with the usual fashion there, form a part of the audience, having the same feelings of admiration as the men, and having adopted the same sect with equal deliberation and decision. . . .[77]

THE MISHNAIC (OR TANNAITIC) PERIOD

With the destruction of the Second Temple in 70 C.E., religious institutions in Judea gradually changed. The period under discussion here includes the first two centuries of the Common Era, a span of time that is known in Jewish history as the mishnaic (or tannaitic) period. During these two hundred years the Jewish people, living at the crossroads of continents and civilizations, fought two desperate wars to maintain their national independence against the greatest empire on earth–imperial Rome–and failed. But during the same time they also fought for the right to live their own way of life, and in that struggle they prevailed. When the Temple was destroyed by the Romans, a serious vacuum was felt. To a large extent, that vacuum was filled by the activities surrounding the rabbinic academies. "They administered the law, they mended it when necessary, legislated when necessary, and continued ceaselessly to explore the hidden recesses of the Torah."[78] During those two centuries of political turmoil and spiritual depression, when the danger of the loss of traditional knowledge was grave, the scholars of these institutions, known as the *Tannaim* (the word *tanna* means literally "to hand down orally," "study," "teach"), appreciated the urgent need to collect the different strands of tradition and weave them into organized bodies of material. It was thus that the *Mishnah*–the literary production of halakhic tradition by an outstanding group of scholars who populated these academies–came into being and was completed by the year 200 C.E.

Historians speculate on the development of elementary education for boys.[79] For various reasons not all boys could take advantage of the available secondary schools, and those remained largely ignorant. Historians posit that in order to rectify this state of affairs, the High Priest, Joshua ben Gamla, in 64 C.E., established free elementary schools in every town and province where Jews resided in large numbers. Those who refused to heed this advice were ostracized.[80] Drazin maintains, "This is the first instance in recorded history that we find an institution of universal and compulsory elementary education

---

77. Ibid., p. 318.

78. Greenberg, "Jewish Educational Institutions," p. 938.

79. See Drazin, *History of Jewish Education*, pp. 44–49; Ebner, *Elementary Education in Ancient Israel*, pp. 47–50; and Morris, *The Jewish School*, pp. 18–19, for elaboration.

80. See, for example, *Bava Batra* 8a, *Bava Metzia* 85a, *Berakhot* 47b, *Kiddushin* 41a, *Sotah* 22a, and *Mishnah Avot* 2:5. Also see Aberbach, *Ha-Hinukh ha-Yehudi*, p. 21.

established."[81] This completed the organization of the Jewish school system with its three distinct levels of education (advanced, secondary, elementary, in order of development).[82]

From all that has been said, we can clearly appreciate how very vital and fundamental an institution the Jewish school became for boys. Whenever, in fact, these schools did develop, there is no indication from any source whatsoever that parallel educational opportunities existed for girls. Whether the reasons for this were social or functional, the trend had been marked for centuries to come.

That women were excluded from the educational processes comes as no surprise. In general, the exclusion of women within the public domain was taken for granted. In the private domain, women enjoyed a high degree of autonomy and were able to study individually. Unlike assertions by some feminist scholars that women in classical antiquity, including the Jewish world, were mere chattel of their patriarchal owners,[83] it would seem that within the mishnaic world, women were legal persons and had total control over all their activities, with possibly one exception. In her chapter "The Image and Status of Women in Classical Rabbinic Judaism,"[84] Judith Romney Wegner formulates the status of women as it appears in the *Mishnah*. She

---

81. Drazin, *History of Jewish Education*, p. 46.

82. Greenberg, "Jewish Educational Institutions," pp. 923–924, comments as follows: "The chief educational contribution of Jewish religious leaders of the Second Commonwealth was the principle that a basic elementary Jewish education must be provided by the community for every Jewish boy regardless of his social or economic status. The goal thus set was probably never fully attained, no more than any modern society with laws for universal compulsory elementary education has attained its goal. But it can be said without fear of serious contradiction that except for periods of communal disintegration or impoverishment following mass persecutions and plagues . . ., universal elementary education for boys was more fully attained among Jews up to the end of the 18th century than among any other contemporary group. The rabbis forbade a Jew to live in a community which had no elementary school teacher. Every community having at least 10 Jewish families could be compelled by law to maintain a teacher in its midst although not all of the 10 families may have had pupils for him. It was, moreover, a widespread practice during these centuries for a family living in isolation to invite a teacher to become a part of the household in order to teach the children. An authority of the 4th century suggests that only if a Jewish child were captured as an infant and raised among non-Jews could he grow up without an elementary Jewish education. (See *Shavuot* 5a.) This is most likely an exaggeration. . . . But none can gainsay the fact that the elementary Jewish school in which Jewish children learned how to read Hebrew and translate the Pentateuch has been the most widespread institution of the Jewish community for the past two thousand years."

83. See Simone de Beauvoir, *The Second Sex* (New York: Vintage, 1974), p. 93.

84. See Baskin, *Jewish Women in Historical Perspective*, pp. 68–93.

concludes that a woman always remain a person except, under certain circumstances, in respect to "ownership" of her sexuality (for example, if a woman is married, only her husband has access to her sexuality).[85] The aforesaid applies to the private domain; in the public domain, women are excluded from performance of time-contingent positive precepts and further-more excluded from leadership roles in synagogue, study house, and court-house. The *Mishnah* proscribes exclusive groups of women, slaves, and chil-dren for the purpose of celebrating the Passover sacrifice,[86] which surprisingly translates somehow, for Wegner, into precluding women from engaging together in Torah study. The net result, according to Wegner, is that women were excluded from all the "intellectual and spiritual forms and forums of mishnaic culture."[87]

However, there is indication in the *Mishnah* that girls may have received instruction in the reading of Scriptures from the hands of their parents as did the boys, both before and after the founding of elementary schools, as the following statement suggests: "But he may teach his [friend's] sons and daughters Bible."[88] The strongest evidence that women studied Scriptures and *Mishnah* on a regular basis can be found in *Tosefta, Berakhot* 2: 12: "[The *zav* and] the *zavah* and the *niddah* and the *yoledet* (women in various stages of impurity) are permitted to read all of Scriptures and to study *Mishnah, Midrash, Halakhot*, and *Aggadot*." The existence of this passage indicates that it was the prevailing custom of women to engage in such study; otherwise, the statement would have been superfluous. The particular problem that is addressed here is the issue of reciting Scriptures during states of impurity.

---

85. Ibid., pp. 70–76. Wegner defines a legal person as an entity possessing both entitlements and obligations, whereas a legal chattel is a piece of property having neither rights nor duties. She finds that the *Mishnah* links a woman's social identity to ownership of her sexuality; vis-à-vis her husband she is sexual chattel. Inasmuch as, obviously, this cannot mean that, regarding conjugal relations, a husband may do whatever he pleases with his wife, Wegner does present an interesting idea in that, for women, personal status is connected to sexuality. However, one may challenge Wegner's use of the term "chattel" as she defines it, for as she herself points out, sexual contact is primarily the wife's right and the husband's duty (*Ketubot* 5:6–7). In addition, a husband is barred from having sexual relations with his wife against her will.

86. See *Mishnah Pesahim* 8:7.

87. Ibid., p. 75.

88. *Mishnah Nedarim* 4:3. The specific context of this expression involves the issue of a person's having made a vow to the effect that his fellow may not derive any benefit from him. The *Mishnah* outlines the courtesies that the person may or may not perform for his friend as a result of having uttered the oath. One of the favors he is permitted to extend is to teach his friend's sons and daughters Scriptures. It should be noted that the citation "daughters" is lacking in some texts of early commentators and in some manuscripts.

Another indication that there were girls who studied the Torah is the fact that the *Mishnah* prohibits the employment of a woman as a schoolteacher.[89] Such a law was sensible only because there must have been women who had the proper educational background to serve as teachers.[90] One such woman might have been the "wise" woman we read of in both the Jerusalem and Babylonian Talmuds[91] who posed an erudite question of biblical interpretation to Rabbi Eliezer. The intricate nature of the question presupposes a woman who had substantial knowledge and a keen understanding of the biblical text. Though Rabbi Eliezer avoids the woman's question (not surprisingly, as it was the selfsame sage who objected to women's studying Torah), both Talmuds proceed to answer the woman's question, indicating that the Rabbis considered it well-founded and worthy of examination. Another learned woman may have been the daughter-in-law of the great second-century tannaitic leader Rabbi Akiva. In a marriage contract between the son of Rabbi Akiva and his bride, undoubtedly unusual, she guarantees "to feed and keep him and to teach him Torah."[92] It should be stated that Rabbi Moshe Margoliot, major expositor of the Jerusalem Talmud,[93] interprets this passage in the sense that the bride's undertaking to financially support her husband will enable him to devote his time to learning Torah, an action for which his wife gets the credit. On the other hand, Rabbi Adin Steinsaltz, a contemporary Talmudist, interprets the statement to mean that she actually taught him Torah.[94]

Because girls received their education solely from their parents, the scope of such education naturally varied in direct proportion to the knowledge possessed by the parents. As an example, Beruriah, daughter of an illustrious Torah scholar, herself became an outstanding Torah scholar. We can perhaps assume that it was for this reason that the Rabbis advised that a man should always endeavor to marry the daughter of a scholar, "for if he dies, or if he is exiled, he can rest assured that his children will be scholars."[95] On one hand, we can take this statement as an intimation that the daughter of a scholar was likely to be educated and to transmit that education to her children. On the other hand, we can deduce from this declaration that it meant merely to convey that the daughter of a scholar might have an appreciation for scholar

89. *Mishnah Kiddushin* 4:13. See *Kiddushin* 82a.

90. Aberbach, *Ha-Hinukh ha-Yehudi*, p. 49, suggests that there were women who worked as teachers; these women, however, were "exceptional."

91. *Sotah* 3:4; *Yoma* 66b.

92. *Ketubot* 5:2.

93. Moshe Margoliot (Lithuania, eighteenth century), commentary of *P'nei Moshe*, ad loc.

94. Adin Steinsaltz, *The Essential Talmud* (New York: Bantam, 1976), p. 138.

95. *Pesahim* 49a.

ship, which would lead her only to ensure that her sons received a high-quality religious education. Rabbi Steinsaltz is of the opinion that the more learned the family, the greater the likelihood that the girls would be educated, either through regular studies or by attending their brothers' lessons. He states, "The halakhic ruling that 'the wife of a *haver* [scholar] is as he'[96] reflects the degree of loyalty and of knowledge of *Halakhah* attributed to the women of scholarly families. The ruling was of considerable significance in that, as a result, the wives of the sages were treated with the same respect as their husbands and therefore enjoyed higher status than the common people."[97]

There is some evidence in the Talmud to suggest that women, upon bringing their children to school each day, would pose to their sons' teachers questions of law that they wished to have resolved.[98]

A number of knowledgeable women are mentioned in talmudic stories. It is instructive to read these stories as indicative of what was considered possible for women to achieve. Though it is difficult to determine how extensive a woman's religious education was in the period under discussion, at least one woman of this period was said to have possessed great knowledge in Torah.[99]

Beruriah: Torah Scholar par Excellence

Beruriah, who lived in Palestine during the second-century C.E., gained fame "as the only woman in talmudic literature whose views on halakhic matters are seriously reckoned with by scholars of her time."[100] According to the Babylonian Talmud,[101] she was the wife of Rabbi Meir, himself a man of stature and wisdom whose decisions were entered into the Talmud, and the daughter of the illustrious Rabbi Haninah ben Teradyon, who was martyred in the Bar Kokhba rebellion[102] of 135 B.C.E. She and her brother were brilliant students and while quite young were considered authorities on different questions of Jewish law. It is related in the *Tosefta*[103] that Rabbi Halafta questioned Simeon ben Hananiah on a particular point of law. Rabbi Simeon,

---

96. *Avodah Zarah* 39a; *Shavuot* 30b.

97. Steinsaltz, *The Essential Talmud*, p. 141.

98. See, for example, *Ta'anit* 2:13; *Megillah* 1:4. See also Aberbach, *Ha-Hinukh ha-Yehudi*, p. 89.

99. See Anne Goldfeld, "Women as Sources of Torah in the Rabbinic Tradition," *Judaism* 24 (Spring 1975): 245–256.

100. *Encyclopaedia Judaica*, vol. 4, p. 701.

101. *Avodah Zarah* 17b–18a.

102. The Bar Kokhba war was a Jewish insurrection led by Simeon Bar Kokhba against the Romans, which was ultimately suppressed. Many great rabbis were massacred by the Romans in this period.

103. *Tosefta Kelim (Baba Kamma)* 4:9.

in turn, queried the son and daughter[104] of Rabbi Haninah ben Teradyon for an answer. Beruriah's brother answered one way; Beruriah answered differently. When Judah ben Baba, another mishnaic scholar, heard these differing opinions, he remarked, "Haninah's daughter teaches better than his son."

Elsewhere in the *Tosefta*,[105] Beruriah is once again acknowledged as settling a question of Jewish law: "Beruriah says: 'A door bolt may be drawn off one door and hung on another on the Sabbath' " (without violating the stricture against work on the Sabbath). When this law was repeated before Rabbi Joshua, he commented, "Rightly did Beruriah say." Interestingly enough, the law was also incorporated into the *Mishnah*[106] under Rabbi Joshua's name. One wonders why the *Mishnah* credits Beruriah's ruling to someone else. Is it on account of her having been a woman?

Just how great Beruriah's learning was considered can be found in a passage from the Talmud that relates that Rabbi Simlai asked Rabbi Johanan to teach him the particularly intricate Book of Genealogies. Rabbi Johanan refused at first, but after repeated requests by Rabbi Simlai, he finally consented. Rabbi Simlai proposed that they learn it in three months, whereupon Rabbi Johanan became angry and said, "If Beruriah . . . who studied three hundred laws from three hundred teachers in one day could nevertheless not do her duty in three years, yet you propose [to do it] in three months?"[107]

It is interesting to note that this story is recorded for posterity in the Talmud. Beruriah, a woman, is held up as an example to an illustrious male rabbi, for the Rabbinic impression of Beruriah recorded in this passage is of "a remarkable, astute, and dedicated scholar with considerable motivation to learn."[108]

Beruriah's interpretive skills, sharp wit, and incisive quips are evident in a number of talmudic anecdotes. Beruriah is credited with the guiding principle and exegetical rule of "look to the end of the verse." This is expounded in two instances in the Talmud.[109] In one case it is related that a nonbeliever said to Beruriah, "It is written (Isaiah 54:1) 'Sing, O barren, thou didst not bear.' Because she did not bear children is she to sing?" Beruriah replied, "You fool! Look to the end of the verse, where it is written, 'For the children of the desolate shall be more than the children of the married wife, saith the Lord.' " Apparently the point is that at present she is barren, but in the future she shall

---

104. The *Tosefta* does not identify the siblings by name. Rabbi Haninah ben Teradyon had another daughter (*Avodah Zarah* 18b). I assume that the *Tosefta* is referring to Beruriah and not to her sister.

105. *Tosefta Kelim (Baba Metzia)* 1:3.

106. *Mishnah Kelim* 11:4.

107. *Pesahim* 62b.

108. Goldfeld, "Woman as Sources of Torah in the Rabbinic Tradition," p. 249.

109. *Berakhot* 10a.

have many children. Another point made by Beruriah was that by "the desolate," Isaiah was referring to Jerusalem, and "the married wife" was a simile for Rome, so that in the future Judea and Jerusalem will be more numerous than Rome.[110] Concluding her comments with a sharp retort to the nonbeliever, Beruriah queries, "But what then is the meaning of 'a barren woman that did not bear'?" And she answers, "Sing, O community of Israel, who resembles a barren woman for not having borne children like you for *Gehenna* [hell]."

Beruriah's high moral stature and her skill in biblical exegesis are illustrated by the following story in connection with her brilliant husband, Rabbi Meir. The Talmud relates[111] that there were once some highwaymen in the neighborhood where Rabbi Meir resided who caused him a great deal of trouble. Rabbi Meir accordingly prayed that they should die. His wife Beruriah said to him, "How do you make out [that such a prayer should be permitted]? Is it because the Psalmist (Psalms 104:35) says, 'Let *hatta'im* (sins) cease out of the earth?' Is it written '*hot'im*' (sinners)?[112] Further, look at the end of the verse: 'and let the wicked men be no more.' Since the sins will cease, there will be no more wicked men. Rather pray for them that they should repent, and there will be no more wicked." Rabbi Meir prayed for them, and they repented. When this episode was told to Rabbi Yehudah ben Baba, he said, "Our daughter has said better than our son."[113]

By her more astute exegesis Beruriah revealed the unseemliness of her husband's behavior. By careful examination of her line of reasoning, Beruriah showed him the fallacy of his thinking. Apparently highly respectful of her abilities, Rabbi Meir acceded to her interpretation and altered his course of action.

Even though women were exempt from teaching, as from studying,[114] it seems as if Beruriah guided students in their studies, as the following pericope from the Talmud suggests.[115] Beruriah once observed a student studying in an undertone. Rebuking him, she exclaimed, "Is it not written 'ordered in all things and sure' (2 Samuel 23:5)? If it [the Torah] is ordered in your 248 limbs it will be 'sure.' Otherwise it will not be 'sure.' " In other words, if you study without making audible sounds, you will forget what you learn, but if you make sounds, then you will remember. In this passage, Beruriah's skills in

---

110. See *Berakhot*, trans. and notes by Maurice Simon, ed. Isadore Epstein (London: Soncino Press, 1984), notes on *Berakhot* 10a.

111. *Berakhot* 10a.

112. In Hebrew, the two related words "sins" and "sinners" are expressed by using the same root in two different word forms.

113. *Tosefta Kelim* (*Baba Kamma*) 4:17.

114. *Kiddushin* 29a.

115. *Eruvin* 53b–54a.

biblical exegesis again manifest themselves. Taking a verse out of its literal context, she applies it to a living situation and derives a lesson from it to impart to the student. We have the impression here of a teacher who not only had a keen understanding of the biblical text but also was seriously concerned about the educational and spiritual welfare of the students. In her analysis of Beruriah, Anne Goldfeld notes that this passage, by way of inference, insinuates that Beruriah "felt a personal obligation to teach, despite the fact that as a woman she was exempt from such an obligation."[116]

In the same section of the Talmud, Beruriah displays concern for the moral welfare of an individual. Her ready wit is also discernible:

> Rabbi Jose the Galilean was once on a journey when he met Beruriah. "By what road," he asked her, "do we go to Lydda?" "Foolish Galilean," she replied, "did not the sages say thus: 'Engage not in much talk with women'? You should have asked: 'By which to Lydda?'"[117]

In refusing to exchange idle words with Rabbi Jose, Beruriah "lives the words of Torah and her actions conform to Rabbinic teachings."[118] The teacher in her is apparent as well, as she instructs Rabbi Jose in moral etiquette.

A number of contemporary thinkers have difficulty with this passage. Robert Gordis, a prominent twentieth-century conservative rabbi, suggests that this passage makes sense only on the assumption that Beruriah is speaking ironically. In his opinion, it contains an undertone of resentment on her part toward the Rabbinic dictum against much talk with women, and it reflects a sense of frustration regarding the restrictions placed on her sex.[119] However, Rabbi Samson Raphael Hirsch specifically points out that the term sichah, which is used in the sages' dictum "Engage not in much talk with women,"[120] refers merely to idle talk and gossip, not to serious conversation. He states, "A man who truly respects [a woman] will have more to offer her than just trivial talk and idle chatter for her amusement"[121] In this light, the parameters outlined by the traditional understanding of this passage may seem to be more suitable in analyzing Beruriah's remarks to Rabbi Jose.

The story by which Beruriah is best known is the one that shows her unusual courage, discipline, strength of character, total commitment to the

---

116. Goldfeld, "Women as Sources of Torah in the Rabbinic Tradition," p. 250.

117. Eruvin 53b.

118. Goldfeld, "Women as Sources of Torah in the Rabbinic Tradition," p. 251.

119. Robert Gordis, "Valeria Beruriah," Universal Jewish Encyclopedia, vol. 2 (New York: Universal Jewish Encyclopedia, Inc., 1940), p. 243.

120. Mishnah Avot 1:5.

121. Rabbi Samson Raphael Hirsch, Chapters of the Fathers: Translation and Commentary (Jerusalem and New York: Feldheim, 1972), commentary on Mishnah Avot 1:5.

will of God, and utilization of her considerable interpretive abilities to reinforce her convictions. It concerns the untimely passing of her two sons on the
Sabbath, which occurred while their father, Rabbi Meir, was at the house of
study.[122] When he returned at the conclusion of the Sabbath and asked for his
sons, his wife replied that they had gone to the house of study. When Rabbi
Meir said that he had looked for them there and had not seen them, his wife
handed him the cup of wine for the *Havdalah*[123] service. With the prayer
completed, Rabbi Meir again inquired after his sons. Beruriah told him that
they had gone out and would return soon, and she proceeded to serve Rabbi
Meir his evening meal. After dinner, she put a halakhic question to him:
"Rabbi, earlier today a man gave me a deposit and now he has come to claim
it. Must I return it?" Rabbi Meir, surprised that his wife should entertain such
doubt, replied, "Can there be any question about the return of property to its
owner?" "I did not care to let it go out of my possession without your
knowledge," responded Beruriah. She then proceeded to lead Rabbi Meir into
the room in which the bodies of their two sons lay on the bed. When she drew
back the covers, Rabbi Meir cried out in grief and despair over his two brilliant
sons, whose young lives were snuffed out so tragically. Beruriah reminded
him, "Did you not tell me yourself that one must return a deposit to its owner?
The Lord gave and the Lord hath taken away; blessed be the name of the
Lord." It is interesting to note that contrary to the talmudic assumption[124] that
women display "light-headedness" and emotionalism under pressure, it is
Rabbi Meir who is overwhelmed by grief and Beruriah who remains calm and
composed.

The end of Beruriah's life is shrouded in mystery. A passage in the
Talmud[125] relates how a warrant for Rabbi Meir's arrest was circulated by the
Romans throughout Palestine on account of his daring rescue of Beruriah's
sister from the clutches of the Romans. To avoid capture, Rabbi Meir escaped
to Babylonia, where he remained until the death of the emperor Hadrian.
Here the Talmud adds a cryptic phrase that has puzzled scholars and writers
for centuries: "Some say it was because of that incident [the story just related]
that he ran away to Babylonia; others say because of the incident about
Beruriah."[126] What incident is never discussed, mentioned, or hinted at in the
Talmud or in the *Midrash*. In a commentary of Rashi's on that talmudic
passage, he recounts a degrading story. He relates that one day Beruriah

---

122. *Midrash* on Proverbs 31:1. (This *Midrash* was composed in the years 640–900
C.E.)

123. The *Havadalah* service is a ceremony that marks the conclusion of the
Sabbath.

124. *Kiddushin* 80b; *Shabbat* 33b.

125. *Avodah Zarah* 18b.

126. Ibid.

ridiculed the Rabbinic dictum[127] that women are temperamentally light-headed and tend to succumb under intense pressure. Rabbi Meir, her husband, soon after ordered one of his students to test her virtue. After repeated urging on the part of the student, Beruriah yielded to his advances. The shame of what she had done drove her to commit suicide. Rabbi Meir, overcome with remorse, fled to Babylonia.

This story of Rashi's is not challenged by subsequent commentators. It presents, however, many halakhic and other difficulties. The behavior of Rabbi Meir in creating a test of Beruriah's virtue would, according to Rabbinic law, be in violation of the prohibition of *"lifnei iver lo titen mikhshal"* ("do not place a stumbling block in front of the blind").[128] This is understood by the rabbis as prohibiting one from assisting or serving as a causal link in another's transgression.[129] Even if one were to argue that Rabbi Meir never expected the matter to develop as it did, the very flirtatious behavior that the student would have initiated toward Beruriah, a married woman, would have been prohibited.[130] Given Beruriah's sensitivity to any infringement of a strict code of conduct between man and woman, as evidenced by her response to Rabbi Jose the Galilean on the road to Lydda, her allegedly blatant violation of one of the foundational laws of Judaism is extremely difficult to accept.

Based on such grounds, some modern Jewish writers, such as Greta Fink, question the accuracy of the story: "This story is wholly at variance with what is known of Beruriah's character and that of Rabbi Meir. It is almost inconceivable that Beruriah would engage in such an immoral act and even more unbelievable that Rabbi Meir would actively engage his own student to seduce a married woman, a cardinal sin for both."[131]

A more plausible explanation of the passage in question, in Fink's opinion, is that Beruriah, who was noted for her incisive wit and verbal barbs, not always under firm control, said something against the Roman occupiers so that Rabbi Meir was forced to seek refuge in Babylonia. Since no mention is made of Beruriah after this incident, it is presumed that she must have died about this time.[132] There is, however, no support in subsequent literature for Fink's understanding of what may have happened.

Wegner claims that the point of the legend of Beruriah's end was meant to show that women who deviate from the female norm will come to a bad

---

127. *Kiddushin* 80b; *Shabbat* 83b.

128. Leviticus 19:14.

129. See *Sefer ha-Hinukh, Mitzvah* 232, for the general statement of law. The application of this law in specific circumstances is very technical and beyond the scope of this work.

130. See *Shulhan Arukh, Even ha-Ezer* 21.

131. Greta Fink, *Great Jewish Women* (New York: Bloch, 1978), p. 17.

132. Ibid.

end.[133] In Wegner's view, this story teaches us about the negative views that for many centuries excluded women from participating in the greatest intellectual accomplishments of Rabbinic Judaism.[134] However, one may just as well draw another conclusion from the story. The "villain" of the piece, if there is one, would appear to be Rabbi Meir. If there is a lesson to be learned, it may seem to center on Rabbi Meir's behavior, namely, that one should refrain from acting like Rabbi Meir in testing another, rather than that women should be discouraged from the study of Torah. In any event, there is no doubt that Beruriah was fully accepted as a scholar and teacher in her time (mishnaic era) and in talmudic times as well.

If women such as Beruriah were able to attain remarkable heights in Torah scholarship, we might wonder if such women were the exception or the rule. At least, we might wonder whether women in this period possessed an elementary level of Torah knowledge similar to that of male youths. After all, great scholars abounded in those days, from whom their wives and daughters may have acquired Torah knowledge, such as Beruriah was fortunate to receive from her father and her husband. Indeed, even the maidservant of Rabbi Judah the Prince (c. 200 C.E.), the redactor of the *Mishnah*, is said to have helped the great scholar and his students to interpret difficult biblical passages and rare Hebrew words by muttering clues to their interpretations as she cleaned the room.[135] Her knowledge of Torah would have been acquired throughout her many hours of service to Rabbi Judah, during which she was fortunate to have been exposed to the scholarship of great minds.

In concluding this discussion of women's religious education in mishnaic times, I would be remiss if I were not to acknowledge a remarkable woman who, though she herself did not become a Torah scholar, is credited in the talmudic literature as being the impetus, the inspiration, and the driving force behind the ability of her husband to rise from illiteracy and ignorance to become one of the outstanding scholars of all time, the great Rabbi Akiva. Indeed, throughout the centuries many women were so imbued with a love for Torah that they encouraged their husbands to devote themselves for a number of years solely to Jewish education while they willingly shouldered the economic responsibility. Jewish tradition exalted woman's role and reward in this regard.[136] The classic example of a woman's deep devotion and appreciation for the study of Torah at the expense of forgoing her own needs is illustrated in the story of Rachel (second century C.E.), daughter of the

---

133. For such an interpretation, See Rabbi Jacob Moellin, *Responsa Maharil*, no. 199.

134. Judith Romney Wegner, "The Image and Status of Women in Classical Rabbinic Judaism," p. 76.

135. *Rosh Hashanah* 26b; *Megillah* 18a.

136. See, for example, *Berakhot* 17a.

wealthy Kalba Savua of Jerusalem, who was disowned by her father after marrying the ignorant shepherd Akiva. She saw in Akiva a man of modest and noble character who had the potential to achieve greatness. Encouraged by Rachel, he studied for twenty-four years at the academy in Jerusalem while she saw to the family income. In time he mastered the intricate texts and became teacher to thousands of disciples. The Talmud records that when this famous scholar returned home after all these years with twenty-four thousand disciples accompanying him, he publicly acknowledged in the presence of all his students the debt he owed to his wife with these frank words: "All that I am, and all that you are, is owing to her" (i.e., the credit for our achievements is hers).[137] And so, if women by law were exempt from Torah study, the tradition clearly respected and acknowledged their contributions in enabling their husbands to fulfill their legal obligations in this regard.

THE TALMUDIC (OR AMORAIC) PERIOD

In the centuries preceding and following the compilation of the *Mishnah* (completed c. 220 C.E.), the Jews in Palestine were crushed by Roman rule and oppression. The collapse in 135 C.E. of Bar Kokhba's insurrection sent many scholars from Palestine to Babylonia. The refugees helped raise the level of Jewish learning in the latter country. In both the Palestinian and Babylonian academies, the *Mishnah* became the basis for further study and analysis by a group of scholars known as the *amoraim* (the word *amora* means literally "sayer," "spokesman," "interpreter"). The debates and discussions in the academies were included in the *Gemara*, which amplified and clarified the *Mishnah*. Around the year 350 C.E., the Jerusalem *Gemara*, containing the accumulated legal documents and debates of the Palestinian schools, was completed. Conditions in Palestine did not encourage intensive intellectual activity, and it is therefore not surprising that the Babylonian *Gemara*, completed about a century and a half later (c. 500 C.E.) is superior to it. "The two compendia," writes Rudavsky, "demonstrate the difference in the life and conditions in these two respective countries; the Babylonian reveals the thriving Jewish life in that country in the early centuries of the present Era, while the Jerusalem *Gemara* attests to the progressive deterioration of the Jewish community in Palestine during the same period."[138] The *Mishnah* and *Gemara* together form the Talmud.

It is during this time that the debate about whether or not a girl should be obligated in the learning of Torah is settled conclusively. In the *Gemara*, in

---

137. *Ketubot* 62b–63a.

138. David Rudavsky, *Modern Jewish Religious Movements* (New York: Behrman House, 1967), p. 103.

tractate *Kiddushin,*[139] the sages expound the following three points: women have no obligation to teach others; women have no obligation to teach themselves; and others have no obligation to teach women. Women are thus effectively exempt from the studying and teaching of Torah.[140] (See Chapter Three for elaboration.)

One may question whether, in spite of this exemption, there were women who studied Torah in depth, beyond the laws that were necessary for them to know, which knowledge was acquired both in the home and by attendance at sermons in the synagogues. Leafing through the pages of the Talmud, one encounters women of stature, women of intelligence and wisdom, women whose opinions and advice were weighed by the rabbis and accepted. Examples of such women are Valeria the Proselyte (first century C.E.);[141] the clever and intelligent Ima Shalom (end of first century),[142] wife of the selfsame Rabbi Eliezer ben Hyrcanus, who opposed the education of girls; the daughters of Elisha ben Avuyah (second century C.E.);[143] the daughter of Rabbi Hisda, who was the wife of Rami Bar Hama and, later, the wife of Rava (third century C.E.);[144] the daughter of Rabbi Abahu (c. 300 C.E.);[145] the foster mother of Abaye (c. 300 C.E.);[146] the mother of Ravina (fifth century C.E.);[147] and the women of Schekhnitziv, Babylonia.[148] Proverbs and maxims, legends and folklore are attributed to some, wise opinions to others, and knowledge of Greek to Rabbi Abahu's daughter. Yet in none of these cases, with the possible exceptions of Valeria (who was proficient in the biblical text and would question apparently contradictory verses) and the mother of Abaye (whose opinions were accepted as *Halakhah*), can we say with any degree of certainty that their store of wisdom encompassed a thorough knowledge of Torah as well, although it is quite possible that these women were in fact learned. The most interesting anecdotes concerning a knowledgeable woman are found in the Talmud's portrayal of Yalta. She is purported to have lived in the fourth century C.E. and to have demonstrated erudition and wit in scholarly discussions with her husband and his colleagues.

---

139. *Kiddushin* 29b.

140. For an early discussion of education in the talmudic period, and especially for information concerning the education of girls, see T. Perlow, *L'Education et l'enseigment chez les Juifs a l'époque talmudique* (Paris, 1931), pp. 98–101.

141. *Rosh Hashanah* 17b.

142. *Shabbat* 116b; *Bava Metzia* 59a; *Sotah* 20a.

143. *Hagigah* 2:1.

144. *Hagigah* 5a.

145. *Pe'ah* 1:1; *Shabbat* 6:1.

146. *Gittin* 67b; *Ketubot* 39b and 50a; *Kiddushin* 31b; *Pesahim* 110a.

147. *Berakhot* 39b; *Menachot* 68b.

148. *Yevamot* 37b.

Yalta: Biblical Exegete and Defender of Women's Rights

Yalta was the wife of Rabbi Nahman and daughter of the *Resh Galuta* (exilarch).[149] Accounts of her in the Talmud,though sparse, portray a woman who was educated, intelligent, of strong will and character, and a defender of women's rights. Her husband held her in high esteem, and when he entertained prominent scholars he would ask them to send her their greetings. On one occasion he asked Rabbi Judah, a distinguished contemporary who was visiting him on a legal matter, to send Yalta his greetings. When Rabbi Judah demurred, quoting successive statements in the name of Samuel, another prominent *amora*, as to the impropriety of having any association with women, Yalta responded with this message to her husband: "Settle his case before he makes you appear like any ignoramus."[150] On another occasion, when her husband was entertaining Ulla, also a talmudic scholar, and the latter stubbornly refused to send her any wine of the cup over which he had recited a blessing, she broke four hundred jars of wine in her anger and sent Ulla this retort: "Gossip comes from peddlers and vermin from rags," or, What can you expect from a man like that?[151] But it is Yalta's skill in biblical exegesis that suggests her depth of comprehension of Torah might have been considerable, as the following astute observation by Yalta to her husband, quoted in the Talmud, implies:

> For everything that the Divine Law has forbidden it has permitted us an equivalent: It has forbidden us to eat blood, but permitted us to eat liver, which is all blood. . . . It has forbidden us the fat of cattle, whereas the fat of chicken and of certain types of species is allowed. It has forbidden us swine's flesh but it has permitted us the brain of the *shibbuta*.[152] It has forbidden us the *gerutha*[153] but it has permitted us the tongue of the fish [which has the taste of the *gerutha*]. It has forbidden us the married woman but it has permitted us the divorcée during the lifetime of her former husband. It has forbidden us the brother's wife but it has permitted us the levirate marriage. . . .[154]

The insightful point that Yalta was expounding is that the Torah has permitted something of similar enjoyment for everything it has forbidden. She thus concludes her remark with "I wish to eat meat in milk [Where is its equivalent?]," whereupon her husband told the butcher to give her roasted

---

149. *Kiddushin* 70a. The *Resh Galuta,* or exilarch, was considered the leader of the Jewish nation in exile.

150. *Kiddushin* 70a–b.

151. *Berakhot* 51b.

152. The *shibbuta* is a kind of fish, the brain of which has the same taste as swine's flesh. According to some it is the mullet, according to others the sturgeon.

153. The *gerutha* is a forbidden bird identified with the moor-hen.

154. *Hullin* 109b.

udder. The inclusion of these passages within the legal layers of the Talmud enlightens us as to the unabashed use of traditions in the names of women during this period. Important resources could not be dismissed.

The early twentieth-century Russian talmudic scholar Rabbi Barukh Epstein is of the opinion that even the ordinary, nameless women living in talmudic times were knowledgeable in Jewish law.[155] He deduces this from a passage in tractate *Kiddushin* (13a) in which Rabbi Ahai questions, "Do then *all* women know the law?" From the fact that the word *all* was inserted by Rabbi Ahai in his question, Rabbi Epstein concludes that "women, in general, knew the law, though not all women, just as not all men know the law."[156]

Some reflections of the reality of women's knowledge of Jewish tradition can be gleaned from the compositions and compilations known as *Midrashim*. Scholars are widely divided on the dating of the various components of this literature. Suffice it to say that the majority of *Midrashim* reached final form by the close of the talmudic period. In Wegner's opinion, the *Midrashim* were composed by men whose androcentric views are obvious in this literature.[157] While her assertion may be challenged, the possibility of such an opinion reinforces the notion that when we come across statements referring to women's knowledge, we must seriously consider that they reflect a reality that was not to be denied. The rabbis, closely reading the lines of the Hebrew biblical text, posited that girls were no less knowledgeable than boys in regard to complex laws of the Torah. It would seem most plausible that the rabbis of the *Midrash* placed their own conceptions of the "Torah state" in their exegesis.[158] They idealized the reign of Hezekiah (c. 727 B.C.E.) by regarding him as having been completely righteous[159] and devoted to the study and dissemination of Torah.[160] Through his efforts, knowledge of Torah was universal so that "they searched from Dan to Beersheba and no ignoramus was found; from Gabbah to Antipares and no boy, girl, man, or woman was found who was not thoroughly versed in the laws of purity and impurity."[161]

---

155. See *Mekor Barukh* (Vilna, 1928), pp. 1958–1959.

156. Ibid., p. 1959.

157. See Wegner, "The Image and Status of Women in Classical Rabbinic Judaism," p. 79.

158. For an understanding of how *Midrashim* are to be interpreted, whether in a literal or in an allegorical manner, see Rabbi Isaac Abohav, *Menorat ha-Ma'or* (Jerusalem: Eshkol, n.d.), Introduction. See English translation by Rabbi Yaakov Yosef Reinman, *Menoras Hamaor, the Light of Contentment* (Lakewood, NJ: Chinuch, 1982), pp. 245–246. See also Abraham Hassan and Moshe Kupetz, "The Use of Midrash in Adult Education," *The Jewish Observer* 26:4 (May 1993): 37–41.

159. *Sanhedrin* 94b.

160. *Song of Songs Rabbah* 4:8.

161. *Sanhedrin* 94b. In the first-century C.E. the historian Flavius Josephus made a similar contention. See *Against Apion* 2:20.

Here the rabbis emphasized their own conception of how the ideal Torah state should operate: "No boy, girl, man, or woman" should be uneducated in traditional laws."[162]

A tradition preserved in the *Targum* to the Prophets, best dated to the close of the second-century C.E. (although final redaction was likely in the seventh century), has no difficulty in envisioning a woman's studying in an academy. As 2 Kings 22:14 reads, "So Hilkiyahu the priest and Ahikam and Akhbor and Shafan and Asaya went to Huldah the prophetess. . . . Now she sat in Jerusalem in the *mishneh* and they spoke to her." Targum Jonathan translates "She sat in Jerusalem in the *mishneh*" to mean that she was "in the house of study." The rabbis of the *Midrash* took this a step further. They claimed that while Jeremiah admonished and preached repentance to the men, she did likewise to the women.[163] We see here that the rabbis were able to envision a society in which women could engage in both public learning and moral instruction. This vision continued into the Middle Ages, when some commentators understood that Huldah had taught the Oral Law to the elders of her generation.[164] Others concluded that she taught the entire Book of Deuteronomy in public so as to emphasize the punishments for those who transgressed against the secrets of the Torah.[165] This medieval commentary sees Huldah as a public mystic. Another medieval commentator remarks on the husband's words to the Shunamite woman in 2 Kings 4:23 – "Why are you going to him [Elisha, the prophet] today; it is neither the New Moon nor the Sabbath" – that it was customary for women (as well as for men) to go on special occasions and receive instructive practice from the great leaders of their day.[166]

Up to this point, our sources cannot be considered properly historical regarding the education of women in late antiquity. The Talmud, although valuable as a historical source, is not what can properly be called "history" by modern critical standards. The greatest works of Judaism have little interest in history. As the testimony of *Am Olam* (the eternal people), these writings have characteristically had little regard for the historical sense of time. "At their

---

162. Aberbach, *Ha-Hinukh-ha-Yehudi be-Tekufat ha-Mishnah veha-Talmud*, p. 31, suggests that this *Midrash* is to be regarded as an expression of longing on the part of the sages of the *Mishnah* for an ideal state of education, in which everyone would be thoroughly versed in the most difficult of Torah laws. This is the state of education the sages envisioned as having existed in the time of Hezekiah; Aberbach suggests that in all probability such an ideal state of education did not exist in early times.

163. *Pesikhta Rabbati* 26:129, trans. and intro. W. S. Braude (Jerusalem 1968) (a medieval *Midrash* on the festivals of the year).

164. See additions to the printed Rashi commentary on 2 Kings 22:14.

165. Ibid.

166. See commentary of Rabbi Levi ben Gershom (Ralbag, 1288–1344) on 2 Kings 4:23.

foundation they are profoundly ahistorical, expressing a relationship that stands outside of time: the relationship between the people of Israel and the Eternal."[167] Some rabbinical scholars have argued that the talmudic rabbis did not so much intend to communicate historical information as to slant historical materials tendentiously in the direction of religious and ethical notions.[168] Furthermore, these works traditionally disregard the Greco-Roman conventions of conveying information that have shaped all Western forms of education.[169] In addition, the prescriptive statements in rabbinic literature may not capture women's actual social religious status or experience.[170] Sources for the ensuing periods often meet the standards of modern historians inasmuch as they are primary evidence, based on the writings of these women or on the writings of people who knew these women.

---

167. See H. Abramson, "The Jew in History," *Nishma* 8 (1991).

168. See, for example, Azariah dei Rossi, *Me'or Eini'em* (Jerusalem: Makor, 1970), in particular, his treatment of historical *aggadot* (chap. 15 and 16). See also Rabbi Yaakov Abohav, *Menorat ha-Ma'or*, Introduction.

169. Abramson, "The Jew in History," provides the following example: Aristotle postulated that it was possible to learn by proceeding either from general principles to details or from details to general principles. The Talmud, by contrast, "does not proceed from the simple to the complex, or from the general to the particular" (Adin Steinsaltz, *The Talmud, the Steinsaltz Edition: A Reference Guide* [New York: Random House, 1989], p. 7), nor does it necessarily proceed from the particular to the general.

170. For example, from the aforementioned quoted statement from *Tosefta Berakhot* 2:12, that women in various stages of impurity *may* study Scriptures, *Mishnah*, etc., we cannot derive with absolute certainty that women, in fact, did engage in such study. We can, however, assume so.

5

A Historical Survey of Jewish
Education for Women:
Part II—The Hegemony of
Babylonian Authority and Its
Aftermath in the East and West

In this chapter we will examine the state of Jewish education for women in those areas that the Gaonate of Babylonia directly influenced. The countries of Iraq and Egypt contained communities that came under the Babylonian influence, and the coast of North Africa and Spain became centers spreading the culture of these communities. The legacy of this influence remains virtually intact in Yemen today, while those who were exiled from Spain in 1492 maintained their culture in Italy, Amsterdam, the Ottoman Empire, and England. Here we will look at the educational achievements of women in these locales.

GEONIC, POST-GEONIC, AND ISLAMIC PERIODS

Our knowledge of education for Jewish women in Islamic countries has been greatly enhanced by documents discovered in the Cairo *Genizah*. This storehouse of important letters, rabbinic responsa, ancient texts, and personal accounts was discovered at the close of the nineteenth century. To this date, however, only a fraction of the materials has been studied and published. Use of these documents enables scholars to gain new insight into the daily lives of Jews who lived from the ninth to the twelfth centuries.[1] Very little of what

---

1. For an overview of this period, see Judith Baskin, "Jewish Women in the Middle

has been found was written by women, so that the images that we have are primarily those of males. We know little of the thoughts and feelings of women who lived in the Middle Ages, and it is an impossible task to recover them.

However, the *Genizah* documents do indicate women's dedication to providing their children with a solid Jewish education. If a woman had more Jewish knowledge, she assisted her children in their studies. Expressions such as "she raised him and taught him Scriptures," or "she raised her children and taught them Torah," as was said of an Alexandrian woman,[2] may be taken to mean that if the woman herself did not teach her children, she invested effort to see that they would be taught properly. Similarly, we read of a woman separated from her husband, who moved from Alexandria to Cairo solely for the purpose of providing her son with a superior religious education.[3] Analogous stories of women's dedication to the education of their children, even occasionally against the father's wishes,[4] appear from time to time among the *Genizah* documents. These cases are just some examples of the value of the *Genizah* find.

We also possess responsa and legal codes written by the heads of academies in this period. Although these writings have been known for centuries, they can now be corrected and enlarged by the newfound documents. Our study of the Islamic world, for the most part, covers the period to the end of the twelfth century, at which point centers of Jewish life shift from Islamic countries to European lands. A sizable Jewish presence, however, continued to exist in North Africa and Middle Eastern countries up until relatively recent times. Within the Islamic world, we find several references, even in later centuries, to the presence of educated Jewish women in Arabic lands. Subsequent to this, the focus shifts almost solely to European countries.

General Background

By the end of the sixth century, the Babylonian Talmud was undergoing final redaction. The Jewish community in Babylonia had become the leading

---

Ages," in *Jewish Women in Historical Perspective*, ed. Judith Baskin (Detroit: Wayne State University Press, 1991), pp. 94–114, and Sondra Henry and Emily Taitz, *Writen out of History: Our Jewish Foremothers* (Sunnyside, NY: Biblio Press, 1988), pp. 71–82.

2. Solomon Dov Goitein, *A Mediterranean Society*, vol. 2 (Berkeley, CA: University of California Press, 1971), p. 71.

3. Ibid.

4. See Solomon Dov Goitein, *Sidrei Hinukh Bimay ha-Geonim u-Bet ha-Rambam* [Patterns of Education in the Geonic and Maimonidean Periods] (Jerusalem: Hebrew University Press, 1962), pp. 72–74, for the text of a letter written by a woman to the Jewish leader David the Second regarding her husband, who had become alienated from Judaism and was endangering the Jewish education of their children.

community and center of talmudic scholarship among the Diaspora, a position it was to maintain for another five hundred years.[5] The period between the sixth and eleventh centuries has been described by Louis Ginzberg, scholar of Talmud, *Midrash*, and *Aggadah*, as the "Middle Age of Jewish history or the dark age, dark in the sense of obscure. No period in the history of postexilic Israel is more momentous than this and none so obscure."[6] It was an era in which the Talmud became entrenched as a comprehensive guide of Jewish conduct in everyday life. Although knowledge of the period is scant, certain writings of the scholars of the time reveal a good deal about the spread of education, the general concern for education, and the high level of scholarship attained by the Babylonian community. Many synagogues had both a *Bet Sefer* for elementary and a *Bet Talmud* for advanced study. At the peak of this network of educational institutions were the two major academies of Sura and Pumbedita, which "contributed so richly to Jewish scholarship and through the interpretation of the *Halakhah*, set the pattern for Jewish religious life and the place of study in it."[7] These two academies were the recognized leaders of Jewish religious and cultural life throughout the world up until the turn of the millennium. Closed for a brief time in the sixth century, they were reopened in 589 C.E. under the supervision of the *Geonim* (heads of the academies). The *Geonim* were accepted as spiritual heads not only in Babylonia but also in the other lands of the dispersion. In the seventh century, Babylonia's influence was enhanced by the Arab conquests of many Mediterranean countries, extending as far as Spain, which united them with Babylonia by the bond of a common language, Arabic. This "facilitated personal contact and communication between the Jewries of the Geonic [and post-Geonic] period and helped establish and solidify a more or less uniform style of Jewish life."[8]

One of the dominant components of this style of life was the upbringing of

---

5. Information on the history of Jewish education in the Middle Ages was gleaned essentially from the following sources: Simhah Assaf, *Mekorot le-Toldot ha-Hinukh be-Yisrael* [Sources for the History of Jewish Education] (Tel Aviv: Dvir, vol. 1, 1930, 1954; vol. 2, 1931; vol. 3, 1936; vol. 4, 1947). This work contains excerpts from many primary sources pertaining to Jewish education from the Geonic period to the Enlightenment; Elijah Bortniker, *Encyclopaedia Judaica*, vol. 6, pp. 403–413; Goitein, *Sidrei Hinukh Bimay ha-Geonim u-Bet ha-Rambam*; Simon Greenberg, "Jewish Educational Institutions," in *The Jews: Their History, Culture and Religion*, ed. Louis Finkelstein (Philadelphia: Jewish Publication Society of America, 1949), pp. 916–949; Julius Maller, "The Role of Education in Jewish History," in *The Jews: Their History, Culture and Religion*, pp. 896–915; and Nathan Morris, *Toldot ha-Hinukh Shel Am Yisra'el*, book 2, vols. 1 and 2 (Jerusalem: Rubin Mass, 1977).

6. Quoted in Maller, "The Role of Education in Jewish History," p. 904.

7. Bortniker, *Encyclopaedia Judaica*, vol. 6, p. 403.

8. Ibid.

children. As in previous eras, children's education began at home, where at a
very early age they noted numerous observances, learned some of the benedictions, and began participating in many traditional practices, especially on
the Sabbaths and holidays, when they became acquainted with rituals and
celebrations. Beginning at the age of 6, a boy entered elementary school,
where, in the early stages of formal education, he would learn to read and
write the Hebrew alphabet and then proceed to diligent study of the Torah,
the books of the Prophets, and Hagiographia. A later tendency was to neglect
these works in favor of Talmud, which a boy would begin studying around
the age of ten, commencing with *Mishnah* and certain tractates in the *Gemara*.
In some schools the native language and arithmetic were also taught. Elementary education among Babylonian Jewry was apparently so effective that
Petahiah of Regensburg recorded in his travel diary (of 1180) that "there is no
one so ignorant in the whole of Babylonia, Assyria, Media and Persia, that he
does not know the 24 books [of the Hebrew Bible] with their punctuation and
grammar."[9] Undoubtedly exaggerated, it does reinforce information from
other sources indicating that basic instruction in the Islamic world of Sephardic Jewry was the privilege of nearly all boys during the centuries of the
Gaonite and for many generations to come.

The elementary schools were also preparatory institutions for more advanced studies in the *Bet ha-Midrash*. At the advanced level, the subject studied
was almost exclusively the Talmud. The stress on Talmud brought about a
nearly complete elimination of Bible and *Mishnah* from schools beyond the
elementary. It was believed that because older students were pressed for time,
having soon to embark on earning a living, the study of Talmud should be
paramount, because the Talmud contains much of the other works. This
same logic was to be applied to many Jewish educational systems throughout
the Diaspora during the course of subsequent centuries and eras.

A unique feature of the activities of the Babylonian academies was the
Kallah. Twice a year, large gatherings of students and scholars would assemble
at the academies and spend a month in study and discussion. Serving in the
manner of a popular university, it was able to reach out to various communities
of the Diaspora through the students who came to study, thereby influencing
the spiritual and intellectual life of Jews in the remotest communities.

This entire educational enterprise, however, was restricted to the male population. Girls, of course, learned a great deal at home and were taught those
observances that they were required to know. But institutionalized education,
as the boys received, was largely closed to girls in the Geonic period, as well as
in the many centuries of post-Geonic life in the Islamic countries of Eastern and

---

9. See "The Travels of Petahiah of Regensburg," in J. D. Eisenstein, *Otzar Masa'ot*
[A Compendium of Jewish Travels] (Tel Aviv, 1969), p. 49. Also quoted in Simhah
Assaf, *Mekorot le-Toldot ha-Hinukh be-Yisrael*, vol. 3, p. 1.

North Africa. According to Solomon Dov Goitein,[10] historiographer of Jews in Mediterranean countries, the girls were excluded from the schools because the school's purpose was to prepare students for participation in synagogue life, a function from which women were primarily excluded.[11] Additionally, Jewish society was to a substantial degree influenced by the surrounding Islamic culture, which vigorously excluded women from any kind of systematic education.[12] Furthermore, inasmuch as it was customary for a Jewish girl (as for an Arabic girl) to wed at a very early age, little time was available for her intellectual enlightenment.[13] A number of documents found in the *Genizah* in Cairo allude to the fact that a certain number of women may have been completely or partially illiterate.[14] Yet, other letters written by women show that in addition to performing household chores, some women were highly literate and held important positions outside the home.[15]

We may speculate that this state of affairs wherein women took the initiative to fulfill themselves beyond the confines of the home was due to two reasons: first, these women reaped some educational benefit from living in an environment in which academic learning and excellence of scholarship were so highly valued. Second, this was a period characterized by the rise of a bourgeois class and a flourishing free economy. It would appear that some Jewish women had broad privileges in the economy and possessed considerable independence in their position as married women.[16] If this were so, then it would follow that some women would be concerned to further their own and their daughters' access to education. In contrast to Yemen, where it was not permitted to teach women even prayer,[17] Babylonian and North African

---

10. See Goitein, *Sidrei Hinukh*, p. 63.

11. Though she was largely excluded from synagogue life, a woman had the right to appeal to the community for assistance during the transaction of public affairs in the synagogue, both during and after services. Public appeals were often made for food, clothing, money for the needy, education for poor children, and so on. Private persons also had the right to appeal to the community for aid in a wide variety of matters. For such appeals the appellant had to get permission of the synagogue authorities in advance. The request was put into writing and read to the assembled Jews in the petitioner's presence. If a woman petitioned, she would probably appear in the front of the women's gallery so that she could be seen by everyone. (See Solomon Goitein, "Jewish Women in the Middle Ages," *Hadassah* 55 [October 1973]: 14–15.)

12. S. D. Goitein, *Jews and Arabs: Their Contacts Through the Ages* (New York: Schocken, 1955), pp. 185–186.

13. Nathan Morris, *Toldot ha-Hinukh Shel Am Yisrael*, pp. 182–183.

14. Goitein, *Sidrei Hinukh*, p. 63.

15. Henry and Taitz, *Written out of History: Our Jewish Foremothers*, p. 75.

16. Goitein, *Sidrei Hinukh*, p. 63. See also Henry and Taitz, *Written out of History: Our Jewish Foremothers*, p. 75.

17. Goitein, *Sidrei Hinukh*, p. 63. See also Aharon Ben-Dod, *Ha-Hinukh ha-Yehudi*

Jewry were heedful of providing even orphan girls with at least the rudiments of religious education: knowledge of prayer.[18] Indeed, the synagogues contained a separate section for women who would regularly attend services though they did not participate fully in synagogue life.[19] The women's gallery was called *Bayt Al-Nisa'*, "the place for women."[20] For the sake of women who did not understand much Hebrew, the vernacular was occasionally introduced into the synagogue. Thus an Arabic translation of the twenty-fourth chapter of Genesis was sung in the East on the Sabbath after a wedding.[21] The minor tractate *Soferim* made it mandatory to translate, for the women, the weekly readings from the Pentateuch and the Prophets before the close of the service. The translation was not read verse by verse after the Hebrew, but as one continuous passage.[22] According to this same tractate, even "the little daughters of Israel were accustomed to go to the synagogue."[23]

---

be-Tzfon Taiman u-Shorshuv ba-Yahadut [Jewish Education in Northern Yemen and Its Roots in Judaism] (Jerusalem: Leket, 1980), pp. 73–75. Ben-Dod describes Jewish education for women in Yemen as being minimal. The vast majority of women could neither read nor write, though in the informal environment of the home they learned to recite certain blessings and very basic prayers (which they could memorize and did not need to read), as well as the fundamentals of faith and the laws they were required to know. Goitein, in *Jews and Arabs: Their Contacts Through the Ages*, hypothesizes that the illiteracy of the women of Yemen, in particular, was likely due to the considerable distance of the Yemenite community from other Jewish centers, making the Islamic influence on Jewish culture far greater, so that the strict exclusion of Moslem women from any kind of systematic education would have its parallel in the Yemenite Jewish culture as well (see pp. 185–186). However, Goitein states [*A Mediterranean Society*, vol. 2, p. 184] that it was customary practice among Yemenites who had no son to instruct a daughter in higher Jewish subjects. He questions whether this was for the benefit of the girl or to fulfill the commandment: "you shall teach your children."

18. Goitein, *Sidrei Hinukh*, pp. 68–69. See my subsequent text for elaboration of this point.

19. Ibid., p. 63. See Also S. D. Goitein, *A Mediterranean Society*, vol. 2, pp. 144 and 183.

20. Goitein, *A Mediterranean Society*, vol. 2, p. 144.

21. From the responsa of Jacob ben Israel of Morea (Venice, 1632), no. 82, cited in Israel Abrahams, *Jewish Life in the Middle Ages* (London: Edward Goldston, 1932), p. 369.

22. *Massekhet Soferim*, ed. Joel Mueller (Leipzig, 1878), chap. 18, para. 4–6, p. 35, and notes, p. 256. (One of fourteen uncanonical treatises, referred to as minor tractates, appended to the end of the fourth order of the Talmud. Some scholars attribute the minor tractates to the Geonic period; recent scholarship favors a much earlier date.) This custom of reading the translated passage as a whole was usual with the Byzantine Jews in the ninth century.

23. Ibid.

Education of Women

The level of women's knowledge of Torah in Babylonia and North Africa may be compared to that in Byzantium. In general, the position of women in the Byzantine Empire was somewhat higher than in Moslem countries, and there were noteworthy women in the eleventh and twelfth centuries.[24] A certain letter of unknown date and unknown place may be assigned to this time and place.[25] This letter, discovered among the Cairo *Genizah* documents, was written by one Lady Maliha in an elegant, poetic Hebrew. According to Franz Kobler, collector of Jewish wills and letters,[26] there is no reason to doubt that it was the composition of Maliha herself. Hence, an instance of woman's familiarity with the Holy Tongue is revealed. In addition, Maliha makes reference to "consulting a Torah scroll" regarding a decision to be made as to whether to undertake a dangerous journey. By opening the scroll and using as an omen the passage turned up, she "obtained a disappointing answer" and concluded that she should not set out on the impending voyage. Maliha's words convey the impression of a woman well accustomed to Bible study.

If girls in this period did not receive instruction in a formal school environment, some may have acquired private tutoring in their own home or in small group sessions, as the following excerpt from a poem ascribed to the *gaon* Rabbi Hai (Baghdad, ninth century) suggests: "If thou shalt bear sons and *daughters* [emphasis mine] . . . purchase for them books according to the best of your ability, and arrange to provide a teacher for them at a tender age. . . ."[27]

In one of Maimonides' responsa (twelfth century), there is a question from a blind teacher in Alexandria who taught young girls (evidently in a group setting) and vowed not to teach the daughters of a certain man who had displeased him. Having regretted his rash words, the teacher was concerned, for the girls refused to study with anyone except him (on account of the fact that the girls, who in Eastern countries were veiled, would not remove their veils in front of any but a blind teacher, and there were none other in the neighborhood besides him), and the women (who were usually the girls' teachers) did not teach them correctly. Maimonides allowed the man to teach the girl after rescinding his vow.[28] From the sentence "women did not teach

24. See Judith Herrin, "In Search of Byzantine Women: Three Avenues of Approach," in *Images of Women in Antiquity*, ed. Averil Cameron and Amelie Khurt (London and Canberra: Croom Helm, 1983), pp. 157–189.

25. Henry and Taitz, *Written out of History* p. 104.

26. The letter is included in Franz Kobler, *Letters of Jews Through the Ages*, vol. 1 (London: Ararat Publishing Society, 1953), pp. 147–148.

27. Quoted in Assaf, *Mekorot le-Toldot ha-Hinukh be-Yisrael*, vol. 2, p. 8.

28. This responsum is quoted in *Teshuvot ha-Rambam*, ed. Joshua Blau, vol. 2, resp. 276 (Jerusalem: Mekitse Nirdamim, 1957). Also quoted in Assaf, *Mekorot le-Toldot ha-Hinukh be-Yisrael*, vol. 3, p. 2. See also Goitein, *A Mediterranean Society*, vol. 2, p. 183.

them correctly" we can deduce that women's teaching of religious subjects was not a rare occurrence, though their level of expertise may have been questionable at various times and in differing places. We may also note Paul Johnson's claim that women, in certain places and times, had their own all-female classes, which may have been taught by blind teachers.[29]

It is conceivable that even so much as some type of coeducation might have existed. In one of the documents uncovered in the Cairo *Genizah* we read not only of two teachers, a male and a female, working side by side, but also of a little girl who visited the schoolhouse regularly with her brother. The letter from the male teacher contains a request for home assistance regarding a poorly behaved student:

> I am informing my master that I am unable to succeed in the education of this lad, and perhaps you can help me. When I strike him . . . the *Morah* [female teacher] immediately jumps up and removes him from my clutches. . . . From the moment that he enters, he does not cease to fight and curse . . . he *and his sister* [emphasis mine], and especially when I am not in the [school]house. . . .[30]

From the words "and especially when I am not in the house" it can be deduced that this teacher engaged in various enterprises, and a woman assisted him. Furthermore, from the reference to the boy's sister, we may infer that even if she had not accompanied him as an equal participant in formal study, her presence afforded her the opportunity to be exposed to the kind of learning that was her brother's prerogative to receive.

That education of daughters was considered of paramount importance to at least some parents is evident in the poignant testament (date uncertain, possibly early twelfth century) discovered among the *Genizah* documents: the final and sole request of a loving and devoted mother, addressed to her sister in Fostat, Egypt, with the future religious education of her young daughter uppermost in her mind:

> I am informing you, my sister . . . that I am very ill and my hour is near. . . . My sister, if God wills that I die, my prime directive to you is that you care for my younger daughter and make an effort to see that she should study. Indeed, I know that I place upon you a considerable burden, [asking of you] not only to support her but to educate her as well. But we have an example in our mother, our teacher, who was a "servant of God". . . .[31]

---

29. Paul Johnson, *A History of the Jews* (London: Weidenfeld and Nicolson, 1987), pp. 201–202.

30. This letter is included in Goitein, *Sidrei Hinukh*, p. 65.

31. The entire letter is included in Goitein, *Sidrei Hinukh*, p. 66.

In the dying woman's words it is evident that she recognized a fundamental principle in Judaism: in order to attain the level of a "servant of God," a woman too needs first to be an erudite person, such as was the educated and righteous mother of the writer and her sister. She therefore enjoined her sister to see that her daughter received a proper education, although she was well aware that the expenses for this would severely tax the family's strained finances.

A *Genizah* document contains this dirge of a father for his daughter who had died as a mature woman but whom he had taught while she was a girl: "When I remember how intelligent, how knowledgeable, how graceful of diction you had been. . . . Would I could listen to you again while I taught you the Bible or questioned you in its knowledge by heart, 'let me see your face, let me hear your voice' [Song of Solomon 2:14]."[32]

Even the education of orphan girls was considered. A letter found in the Cairo *Genizah* (date uncertain), addressed to the leader of the Jewish community in Egypt from a woman appointed guardian over two female orphans, is a case in point. In it she discusses the possibility of obtaining religious education for the two girls, particularly knowledge of prayer, from a woman teacher who lives nearby.[33]

Some women were teachers. Obviously, they had acquired sufficient proficiency in the religious subject matter to enable them to teach it. Indeed, there were to be considerable instances of women throughout the Middle Ages, both in the Arabic Jewish (Sephardic) world and in the Ashkenazic (north, central, and eastern European) world, who engaged in private teaching or were elementary, and even secondary, school teachers. In the Islamic Jewish world, the words for female teacher – *morah* or *mu'allima* – appear, from time to time, on fund allotment lists of community budget committees, found in the Cairo *Genizah*,[34] though these terms may also refer to teachers of needlework.

In a responsum of Maimonides,[35] we read of a young woman without means of sustenance who turned to the teaching of Bible to young children, together with her brother. Even when her brother departed and her eldest son assisted her with the teaching, she nonetheless remained the master teacher. She was apparently successful in her work, as she was able to employ first her older son and then also her younger son to assist her in her teaching. The woman, who lived in Egypt in the twelfth century, and who was obviously extremely poor, nevertheless had acquired sufficient knowledge and aptitude

---

32. Quoted in Goitein, *A Mediterranean Society*, vol. 2, p. 184.

33. The letter is included in Goitein, *Sidrei Hinukh*, pp. 68–69.

34. Goitein, *Sidrei Hinukh*, pp. 69–70. See also Goitein, *A Mediterranean Society*, vol. 2, p. 185. In most cases, though not all, the term *mu'allima* (woman teacher) may have designated a teacher of embroidery and other female arts (vol. 1, p. 128).

35. Maimonides, *Teshuvot ha-Rambam*, ed. Joshua Blau, vol. 1, resp. 34.

to become an elementary school teacher. This last fact is significant, because we can see that, though women from the rabbinic or wealthy classes may have had greater opportunities to receive an education, the possibility of poor girls' receiving an education existed as well.

Women Scholars

Up to this point we have considered the situation of elementary education for girls and have taken note of women teachers. We will now look at the evidence for women scholars in this period. In the more prominent homes of the wealthy or rabbinical classes, and especially in homes where there were no sons, parents were more punctilious in providing their daughters with a superior Jewish education,[36] which they may, in turn, have transmitted to others, in the capacity of teacher, and even scholar. The daughter of Rabbi Nissim ben Jacob of Kairouan (Tunisia, eleventh century) was a "scholar of Torah and a righteous woman."[37] When her husband was killed, she escaped to Lucena, where she was supported by the community with great honor until her death. The physician Samuel ben Yehudah the Maghrebi (twelfth century) writes of his mother, one of three daughters of Isaac of Basra, Iraq, all of whom were scholars of considerable ability, "They delved into the wisdom of the Torah and regularly wrote in Hebrew."[38] In Petahiah of Regensburg's travel diary (1180), he writes admiringly of the distinguished daughter of Rabbi Samuel ben Ali of Baghdad, an only child, who was "proficient in Bible and Talmud." She instructed young men in the Scriptures through a lattice, so that her male students could not see her.[39]

The tradition of women's scholarship in this region culminated in a most remarkable Torah scholar. Asenath, daughter of Rabbi Samuel Barazani of Kurdistan (sixteenth–seventeenth centuries), later the wife of Rabbi Jacob Mizrahi of Amadiyah in Northern Iraq, remains a unique figure of feminine scholastic prominence. A letter of this woman, currently in the possession of Hebrew Union College in Cincinnati, reveals a scholar of substantial ability who undertook the difficult task of lecturing at and maintaining a *yeshivah*.[40]

---

36. See E. Brauer, *Yehudei Kurdistan* [The Jews of Kurdistan] (Jerusalem: Israeli Institute for Folklore and Anthology, 1947), p. 148.

37. Abraham Zacuti, *Yuhasin ha-Shalem* [The Complete Book of Lineage], ed. A. Freiman (Frankfurt: M. A. Wahrmann Verlag, 1924), p. 212. See also Ben Zion Dinberg, *Yisrael ba-Golah* [Israel in the Diaspora], vol.2 (Tel Aviv: Dvir, 1926), p. 356.

38. Ben Zion Dinberg, *Yisrael ba-Golah*, vol. 2, p. 356. Also quoted in Assaf, *Mekorot le-Toldot ha-Hinukh be-Yisrael*, vol. 2, p. 28.

39. See "The Travels of Petahiah of Regensburg," in J. D. Eisenstein, *Otzar Masa'ot*, p. 49. Also quoted in Assaf, *Mekorot le-Toldot ha-Hinukh be-Yisrael*, vol. 3, p. 1.

40. See Jacob Mann, *Text and Studies in Jewish History and Literature* (Cincinnati:

Tanna'it Asenath (Barazani) Mizrahi: *"Rosh Yeshivah"*[41]

In her youth, Asenath had studied Bible and Talmud with her father, a renowned Talmud scholar and bibliophile and the acknowledged leader of Kurdistan Jewry. Her husband, Jacob, busy with his own research and duties as leader of the Jewish community in Mosul, left his wife to teach in the *yeshivah* he maintained there. In her letter to the Jewish community in Amadiya, Asenath describes her activities as teaching Judaism, instructing and preaching how to keep the laws of ritual ablution, Sabbath, family purity, prayer, and the like.[42]

After the early death of her husband, Asenath endeavored valiantly to preserve his school, continuing to do so even after the appointment of a new community rabbi. Many troubles beset her. Unpaid debts brought collection agents to her home to obtain possession of her house and confiscate all personal belongings. "They took everything," she writes. "They even took the books that were before me."[43] She thus appealed to the Jewish community of Amadiyah to come to her aid so that she could carry on her lectures without having to resort to collecting the funds personally, which, in her own words, "is not the style of a woman."[44] Her appeal, in poem and prose, does credit to her knowledge of Hebrew and biblical and Rabbinic literature, revealing the extent of her passion and commitment to raise disciples and preserve Judaism for future generations.

Asenath expressed her feelings about her life as follows:

I am in this difficult situation because I fell into debt and I have nothing to sell. And I don't have a grown son or messenger to solicit funds for us in the

---

Hebrew Union College Press, 1931), vol. 2, pp. 507–515. See also Cecil Roth's entry "Barazani, Asenath Bat Samuel," *Encyclopaedia Judaica*, vol. 4, p. 204. Henry and Teitz, in *Written out of History*, p. 108, consider Asenath and Rabbanit Mizrahi as two separate women. Abraham Ben-Yaacob, *Kurdistan Jewish Communities* (Jerusalem: Kiryath-Sepher, 1980), p. 37, informs us that they are one and the same. This information is based on stories related through the centuries about the woman known as Asenath bat Samuel Barazani Mizrahi. Meyer Benayahu, "Rabbi Samuel Barazani, Leader of Kurdistan Jewry," *Sefunot* 9 (1964): 27, refers to Asenath and identifies her as the daughter of Rabbi Samuel Barazani. His biographical information about her is consistent with what we know of *Tanna'it* Mizrahi, but he corrects Mann's identification of her husband as Jacob ben Judah, and reads instead Jacob ben Abraham.

41. *Rosh yeshivah* The title given to the head or dean of a secondary Jewish school. Her title, *tanna'it*, designates her as a master of the Oral Law.

42. See Mann, *Text and Studies in Jewish History and Literature*, vol. 2, p. 510.

43. Ibid., p. 510.

44. Ibid., p. 511.

community. And it is not the custom of a woman to solicit in the community. All glorious is the daughter of a king within; gold embroidery is her clothing. I, in my day, did not depart my house. I was the daughter of a king–Who are the kings? The rabbis. I was raised on the knees of scholars, I was the joy of my father. And no work did he teach me except the work of Heaven, to fulfill what was said, "And thou shall meditate upon it by day and by night." He had no sons but only daughters. And he also had my husband swear that he wouldn't make me do any work, and he did as he was commanded. At the beginning my husband was very busy with his own studies and did not have time to teach the students. Thus, I would teach them in his stead. I was his helpmate. And now, because of many sins,[45] he went to his rest and left me and the children to our sorrows. . . .[46]

In writing her letter, Asenath abbreviates her life: childhood, early adulthood, and widowhood. Of necessity, her feelings about herself are sharpened while she is able to assimilate these feelings to her purpose at hand: appealing for money to the Jewish community.

She discloses her plight as a woman who cannot personally solicit funds, noting that she has no grown son or messenger to act on her behalf. Her status as a woman in her society is made abundantly clear. She sums up that status with the traditional code words that justified a woman's maintaining a private and nonpublic posture: "All glorious is the daughter of the king within; gold embroidery is her clothing" (Psalms 45:14).

Accordingly, it is beyond her place to personally approach the community publicly, and instead she subtly expressed the tensions within her in writing to the community. For in her very next words she turns around this phrase "daughter of the king," which is associated with women's staying at home and engaging in family activities, and tells us that she is also the "daughter of the king" in a different sense. She quotes the talmudic statement, "Who are the kings? The rabbis" (*Gittin* 62a). As the daughter of a rabbi (who has no sons) she is trained to be a Torah scholar rather than a typical housewife. And this is her problem. As the daughter of a king she must remain private; as the daughter of a rabbi she needs funds to maintain her religious communal activities. This is her double bind.

We can gauge Asenath's personal feelings in that she looks at herself from her father's vantage point. Since her father had no sons, she was trained to be "the joy" of her father. She expresses nothing of any normal childhood activity. Then she describes her early adulthood. She tells us that her father had forced her husband to promise that she would be freed of all household

---

45. This expression is used as a formulaic justification for tragedy but is not meant to cast aspersion on her husband.

46. Translated from Ben-Yaacob, p. 36. Compare with Henry and Taitz, p. 113.

chores so that she could devote herself to her studies. What we see in the structure of her writing, and by what she tells us and does not tell us, is that she is an extension, perhaps by no choice of her own, of her father and her husband.

The result was that she assumed communal responsibility. After the deaths of her father and her husband she found herself needing to be either a private woman or a public scholar, yet she had no choice but to function as both. The picture that emerges is of a strong, courageous, and intelligent woman who is frustrated, under these trying circumstances, in her dual role. This double bind she accepts as destined from birth, and it is this picture that she presents to the community in her plea for funds. Her frustration may have been compounded by the realization that letter writing would not get her as far as personal solicitation, as her husband had occasionally resorted to letter writing to raise funds for his *yeshivah*, but with little success.

Understanding her unique position as a woman community teacher, Asenath is careful throughout her lengthy letter to never refer to the school as hers, or to herself as its head. She appeals in the names of her father and husband so that "their Torah and their names may not be extinguished from the community."[47]

Although her letter was not designed to reveal her inner emotions, she was not able to mask her deepest feelings about her situation as a communal woman.

The legacy of Asenath lives on in Kurdish folklore, where her name is considered as potent protection against evil to this day. A letter written to her by the poet Yitzhak Hariri mentions her by name. The letter has been used by its owners to place under the heads of sick people as a *segulah* (amulet) for health.[48]

Asenath Barazani Mizrahi demonstrated the ability to manage her home, to be a leading talmudic scholar, to look after the financial needs of her institution, and to gain fame as a poet and mystic. Letters from leading scholars and mystics were addressed to her and she became known by the title *Tana'it*, a term reserved for the greatest male teachers of the second century.

Erich Brauer refers to women teachers in Kurdistan from the seventeenth century onward:

The wife of Rabbi Simeon would teach children in Amadiyah approximately 300 years ago. One hundred fifty years ago the wife of Rabbi Asher was employed in the same work, also in Amadiyah. One hundred years ago the sister of Rabbi Eliyahu would assist him in teaching. . . . Not long ago there was

---

47. See Mann, *Text and Studies in Jewish History and Literature*, vol. 2, p. 510.
48. See Abraham Ben-Yaacob, *Kurdistan Jewish Communities*, p. 37 n. 49.

a young girl . . . who assisted her father in teaching. When her father died she also said the *Kaddish*[49] in synagogue.[50]

Brauer is of the opinion that educated women in Kurdistan, although rare, were generally the daughters of scholars and rabbis who had no sons and therefore instructed their daughters for practical purposes, so that they could assist their fathers (or husbands) in teaching. As many of the religious leaders in Kurdistan functioned not only as rabbis and teachers but also as ritual slaughterers and circumcisors, they were frequently called away on community business and required substitute teachers in their classrooms in their absence. Their daughters and wives performed in that capacity.[51]

To conclude our discussion of women scholars in this region, we will cite from the book of responsa *Rav Pe'alim*, written by the early nineteenth-century Baghdad rabbi Joseph Hayim ben Elijah Al-Hakam. Here we come across an interesting responsum[52] concerning the obligation of women ("who are proficient in Bible and pray daily") to participate in a particular aspect of prayer ritual. Rabbi Joseph Hayim's response is instructive, as it conveys a picture of the considerable involvement of some women in the study of Torah and in prayer in latter-day Baghdad:

> Truthfully, it is not known for women to participate in *Tikkun Hazot*[53] even though they are intelligent and scholarly women, whose custom is to study Psalms and to have fixed periods of study each day. . . . And yet, there is a custom in our household that women awake prior to sunrise, and though they do not recite *Tikkun Hazot* they are engaged [in other religious] study. My grandmother [for instance] would study 18 chapters of *Mishnah*. . . . Also during

---

49. This is a memorial prayer that a son is obliged to say for a period of eleven months during public service in synagogue following the death of a parent. A daughter is not obligated to do so. Whether a woman *may* do so is subject to varying opinions. For elaboration, see Getsel Ellinson, *Serving the Creator*, vol. 1, pp. 117–118 and n. 12; Judah H. Henkin, "Amirat Kaddish Al Yidei Eshash," *Hadarom* 54 (Sivan 5745/1985): 34–48; Joel B. Wolowelsky, "Modern Orthodoxy and Women's Changing Self-Perception," *Tradition* 22:1 (Spring 1986): 65–81; and Joel B. Wolowelsky, "Letter to the Editor," *Hadarom* 57 (Ellul 5748/1988): 157–158.

50. Brauer, *Yehudei Kurdistan*, p. 149.

51. Ibid., p. 148.

52. For the full text, see Joseph Hayim ben Elijah, *Rav Pe'alim*, Kuntrus "Sod Yesharim," para. 9. For excerpts, see Assaf, *Mekorot le-Toldot ha-Hinukh be-Yisrael*, vol. 3, p. 84, or Solomon Ashkenazi, *Ha-Ishah ba'Aspaklariah ha-Yehudit* [The Woman in the Jewish Perspective] (Tel Aviv: Yizra'el, 1955), vol. 1, p. 52.

53. Prayers recited at midnight in memory of the destruction of the Temple and for the restoration of the Land of Israel. The author of *Rav Pe'alim* offers mystical explanations as to why women are exempt from this particular prayer ritual.

the night of *Hoshanna Rabbah*[54] the women would remain awake and would study *Mishneh Torah* [the Book of Deuteronomy] and Psalms, and the prayers of *Kortei ha-Brit.* . . .[55]

This excerpt portrays a picture of at least some women engaged in the study of Bible, Psalms, *Mishnah,* and prayer. It appears as if they devoted "fixed periods of study each day" to the pursuit of learning and to prayer, even remaining awake all night during one holiday to study and pray. Girls in general in nineteenth-century Iraq were literate, according to Yehezkel Yiftah,[56] having learned to read and write Hebrew in a *heder.*[57]

Having noted the existence of women students and scholars, we now turn our attention to women scribes. When I speak of women scribes, I am not referring to a scribe in the sense of the halakhically defined "*sofer,*" a professional expert in the writing of Torah scrolls, *tefillin,* and *mezuzot* used for religious ritual. Rather I mean women who copied religious texts for use by the general community in the days before the advent of the printing press, when every Jewish work had to be transcribed by hand. There are on record a number of women who copied with understanding and meticulousness the biblical text as well as highly intricate talmudic treatises, in both the Sephardic and the Ashkenazic worlds. This activity furnished women with an excellent means of acquiring a not inconsiderable education. A Pentateuch of the Late Middle Ages, discovered in Yemen and written in precise and beautiful style, is inscribed with the following inscription: "Please do not fault me if you find herein a mistake, as I am a nursing woman, Miriam the daughter of Benayah the Scribe."[58]

At first, it seems surprising that this manuscript was found in Yemen, considering that women in Yemen were, by and large, illiterate.[59] Noting, however, that Miriam's father was a scribe, one can understand how she was more likely to be literate as well as educated. If she happened to have been an

---

54. The seventh and final day of the festival of Sukkot (Tabernacles), when it is the custom of some men to study Torah all night.

55. Special prayers said by Sephardic women, especially on the eve of a circumcision.

56. Yehezkel Yiftah, *Ha-Hinukh ha-Yehudi be-Iraq be-Dorot ha-Ahronim* [Jewish Education in Iraq in Recent Generations] (Nahalal: Hotsa'at Yad-Eli'ezer, 1983), p. 38.

57. *"Heder"* is the common name for the old-fashioned elementary school for the teaching of Judaism. As distinct from the *Talmud Torah,* which was a communal institution maintained by the community for children whose parents were too poor to pay tuition fees, the *heder* was a privately owned institution, the teacher receiving the fees from the parents. It was generally housed in a room (*heder,* in Hebrew) in the private house of the teacher.

58. Goitein, *Sidrei Hinukh,* p. 64.

59. Aharon Ben-Dod, *Ha-Hinukh ha-Yehudi be-Tz'fon Taimon,* p. 73.

only child, it would also explain her level of education, since it was common practice among Yemenites who had no son to instruct a daughter, as did their brethren in Kurdistan, in higher Jewish subjects, even including the laws and practice of ritual slaughtering.[60] There is also indirect mention of another female scribe in the *Genizah* documents: we are told that the Jewish community of Daquq (today called Tawuq), Iraq, was headed by Azarya, "son of the female copyist." He was praised by the Hebrew poet Judah al-Harizi for his noble descent and character as well as his munificence.[61]

In summation, our sources show us that in various periods in the Eastern lands and North Africa—the world of Sephardic Jewry—women were excluded from most of the educational functions of the synagogue. Nevertheless, there are some references to tutorial help offered to girls, to scholarly women and scribes, and to women teachers. Even though an extensive Jewish education was not a viable option for the majority of Jewish women residing in Arabic lands, the opportunity for women to acquire at least a rudimentary education and, in exceptional cases (especially when a woman was a daughter of a rabbi, scribe, poet, etc.), a superior education, did exist in an informal if not an institutional context.

THE SEPHARDIC CENTERS OF SPAIN, PROVENCE, ITALY, AND ELSEWHERE

The general culture of the Sephardic areas did not offer women much outlet for their talents, but the milieu of the Golden Age of Spain imbued Jewish communities there with a higher level of tolerance and greater opportunities. Although from the end of the eleventh century this Golden Age declined, eventually disappearing with the onset of the Inquisition, nevertheless the inheritance of this era remained strong up to modern times. It is to these communities that we now turn.

Spain

General Background

Simha Assaf, in his anthology of sources relating to Jewish education, states that relative to the rich literary legacy that was bequeathed to Jewry by Spanish Jewish scholars, sources regarding educational patterns in Spain are

---

60. Goitein, *Jews and Arabs: Their Contacts Through the Ages*, p. 186. There is even mention of a Yemenite woman poet. Goitein refers to *Sham'ah*, the daughter of the greatest of Yemenite poets, Shalom Shabazi (seventeenth century), who was herself a poet; some of her Hebrew compositions are still known. See *Jews and Arabs*, p. 186.

61. Goitein, *A Mediterranean Society*, vol. 2, p. 184.

not plentiful, although but they are by no means nonexistent.[62] Indeed, during the period of the Middle Ages, there appeared for the first time in Jewish literature treatises on education, mostly chapters in various books, testaments, or commentaries, some of which are quite informative about the educational practices of the time.[63] For example, a school curriculum was fully outlined by Joseph ibn Aknin, who lived mostly in North African lands but whose opinions represent typical Spanish views. Besides Torah, *Mishnah*, and Talmud, he advocated the study of grammar, poetry, logic, mathematics, astronomy, music, physical science, and metaphysics.[64] Such Spanish curricula, however, were not universal; indeed the issue of advanced "extraneous" studies stirred Jewish communities repeatedly in both Spain and southern France.[65] There were those who feared that broad general education would lead to a weakening of the faith, a fear not without foundation in reality. Spanish Jewry of the twelfth and thirteenth centuries experienced a weakening of the faith in some of its best educated circles. This resulted in a countertendency on the part of leaders troubled by the phenomenon. With the arrival from Germany in 1305 of Asher ben Jehiel, who became rabbi in Toledo, talmudic study gained greatly because of his efforts and influence.[66] As a result, Jewish education in Spain took a turn away from the trend during the two or three previous centuries, restricting itself mainly to Torah and Talmud. In certain groups, particularly those in the higher economic and social strata, the practice of engaging in secular studies persisted.[67]

As for elementary education, though the Spanish Jewish communities of the thirteenth century gave some measure of attention to it, the need was still far from satisfactorily met.[68] The talmudic academies, presided over by distinguished scholars, were of course not intended to provide a broad popular education. Very little is heard during this period about the appointment of teachers for all the children of a community. The children of the upper classes

---

62. S. Assaf, *Mekorot le-Toldot ha-Hinunkh be-Yisrael*, vol. 2, p. 4. See further, F. Talmage, *David Kimhi: The Man and the Commentaries* (Cambridge, MA: Harvard University Press, 1975), pp. 10–11.

63. For elaboration, see Bortniker, *Encyclopaedia Judaica*, vol. 6, pp. 406–407.

64. For excerpts of Aknin's curriculum, see Assaf, *Mekorot*, vol. 2, pp. 36–40. For elaboration on the educational curriculum of Spanish Jewry, see also Abrahams, *Jewish Life in the Middle Ages*, pp. 388–391.

65. See Bortniker, *Encyclopaedia Judaica*, vol. 6, p. 407. For elaboration on this subject, see Yitzhak Baer, *A History of the Jews in Christian Spain* (Philadelphia: Jewish Publication Society of America, 1966), vol. 1, pp. 292–305; vol. 2, pp. 235–237.

66. Baer, ibid., vol. 1, pp. 297f.

67. Ibid., vol. 2, p. 72.

68. See Baer, ibid., vol. 1, p. 236. In earlier centuries, elementary education had been fairly widespread, but apparently had dwindled over time.

received their broad and versatile education at the hands of private tutors, and the more refined families of the middle class also had to provide out of their own means for the private tuition of their children, which was, for the most part, limited to elementary subjects. It is Yitzhak Baer's assumption that talmudic training in Spain did not at this time attain the high standard existing in Germany.[69] There were many Jews of the middle and lower estates who did not know how to read or write. Among all classes laxity in religious observance was prevalent, out of both neglect and ignorance, as well as out of deliberate heresy. The spiritual leadership of the day centered a great deal of attention on the maintenance of sound family life.[70] In the fifteenth century, communal statutes were drawn up regarding public funding of instruction in Torah. Every community of fifteen families was enjoined to engage a good children's teacher. In localities with forty or more Jewish families, the communities were to make every possible effort to maintain a teacher of Torah, who would impart instruction in "Talmud, *halakhot*, and *aggadot.*"[71] Thus, the state of religious education improved somewhat for the Jewish communities of that era.

Views of Spanish Rabbis Concerning Women and Torah Study

If sources relating to the education of the male sex are not abundant, references to Jewish education and women are indeed very few. In a thirteenth-century work by Jonah ben Abraham Gherondi, Spanish rabbi, author, and novelist, considerable thought is devoted by the author to the role and contribution of the woman in the Jewish education of both the child and the adult.[72] Though Rabbi Jonah's views express nothing new or daring, the "uniqueness" of Rabbi Jonah, in Morris's opinion,[73] is "in his approach and emphasis, in his sympathetic and understanding attitude regarding the woman's position in society and the education of children, and perhaps more so, in his style of writing, abounding in tenderness, gentleness and transparent sincerity."[74] Rabbi Jonah accepts unhesitantly the nonobligation of women in Torah education as outlined in the Talmud and regards their role in a manner reminiscent of the talmudic rabbi Rav, who stated, "Whereby do women earn

---

69. Ibid.

70. Ibid.

71. See Baer, *History of the Jews*, vol. 2, p. 261.

72. Excerpts of Jonah Gherondi's work *Iggeret ha-Teshuvah* ("Epistle of Repentance") appear in Simha Assaf, *Mekorot*, vol. 2, pp. 46–47, and Nathan Morris, *Toldot ha-Hinukh Shel Am Yisrael*, vol. 2, pp. 28–29. Subsequent quotes are from these pages.

73. Morris, *Toldot ha-Hinukh*, vol. 2, p. 33.

74. Ibid.

merit? By making their children go to synagogue to learn Scripture and their husbands to the house of study to learn *Mishnah*."[75] Yet Rabbi Jonah elaborates on Rav's words and formulates a "new and honorable" role for women in the education of their sons and of their daughters, the role of guide and natural instructor of their children in Torah and *mitzvot*. He regards the woman's function in the education of her children as paralleling and complementing that of the schoolteacher, for formal instruction, in and of itself, is liable to lead to a situation in which learning, but no real education in Torah values and life, takes place. In reading Rabbi Jonah's words, one receives the impression that he speaks not merely in idealistic, theoretical, or apologetic terms, but according to what he perceives the reality to be, based on his observations of the activities of contemporary women in the education of their children (and husbands). Here are Jonah Gherondi's views on the subject:

> "So shall you say to the House of Jacob and state to the Children of Israel" (Exodus 19:3) – When the Torah was given, Moses was commanded to speak first to the House of Jacob, and they are the women. . . . Why was he commanded to speak to the women first? Because they send their children to learn Torah, and have compassion for them when they return from school, and draw their hearts [to Torah] with kind words, and watch over them that they not remain idle from Torah study, and instill in them fear of God in their childhood. . . .

Thus far, Rabbi Jonah is echoing the words of the Talmud. Now he elaborates:

> We can derive from these words that women are the reason [that] study of Torah and fear of God [exist]. . . . These modest women [by their encouragement] help their husbands to escape the burden of their work, which causes them at times to forget to devote time to Torah study. It is the obligation of the women to remind their husbands to study Torah, and not to indulge in idle activity. . . . The woman should be mindful of praying morning, noon, and night. At the end of her prayers, her main supplications should be for her sons and daughters, that they should be observant Jews, and that her sons should be successful in Torah study, because the main merit of the woman in the World to Come is when her children worship God. And when she has passed on, and her children are observant in Torah and possess the fear of God, it is considered as if she is alive, and she is on the highest rungs in the World to Come.

That Rabbi Jonah reminded women to be heedful of praying three times a day may indicate that women in Spain possessed elementary literacy or, at the very least, were able to recite Hebrew prayers verbatim. That he expected the

---

75. *Berakhot* 17a.

mothers to educate their daughters to be observant Jews demonstrates that girls received a practical education in Jewish law and ritual. Though Rabbi Jonah unquestionably saw the role of woman as enabler, the importance he ascribed to the woman in her task is clearly evident in his placing her on the pinnacle of Jewish attainment: a share at the highest levels in the World to Come.

Jonah Gherondi's confidence in the Jewish woman as "keeper of the faith" was shared by another Spanish scholar, Rabbi Joseph Yavetz, among the Jews expelled from Spain in 1492. In his writings he bitterly denounces the "educated people" who threw off the "yoke of Torah and *mitzvot*" and converted to Christianity in order to escape their bitter fate. He has high praise, however, for the ordinary and poorly educated people and for women who "gave their money and lives in sanctification of God's Name. . . . The woman who is careful to observe all of God's laws and to give up her life for the sake of Torah . . . is regarded much more highly by her Creator than those who consider themselves educated. . . . It is these Spanish women who came and brought their husbands to die in sanctification of God's Name."[76] Rabbi Joseph Yavetz is implying that though the "educated people" may have had more book knowledge, both in religious and secular fields, it was without real foundation in faith. The common people and the women, on the other hand, may not have had the best of formal educations; nevertheless they had a practical education deeply rooted in Jewish religious tradition and values, enabling them to withstand the severe trials the Inquisition was to inflict upon them.

Confidence in women's ability to ensure the transmission of the religious heritage was not shared uniformly by all Spanish scholars. In a responsum of thirteenth- and fourteenth-century rabbi Asher ben Jehiel (known by his acronym, Rosh), we read of a woman who wishes to leave her husband, who is heavily involved in gambling with dice. She has a young son, whom she wishes to remain with her, whereas her husband desires that the lad remain with him. One would have expected Rabbi Asher to recommend that the boy remain with his mother. After all, the suitability of a father who spends his days in gambling to educate his child in Torah and religious law is highly questionable. Nevertheless, Rabbi Asher rules that the boy remain with his father: "Just as a girl should remain with her mother, since her mother spends more time with her and can educate her in piety and laws pertaining to women, so should a boy, whose father is obligated to educate him in Torah

---

76. Quoted in Morris, *Toldot ha-Hinukh*, vol. 2, p. 34. Joseph Yavetz's reference to the "educated people" implies those who received the benefits of a broad general education, including both religious and secular studies, and not to those who received only a religious education.

and *mitzvot*, remain with his father."[77] Conspicuous in this responsum is the differing emphasis on the respective education of girls and boys: girls are to be educated in piety and in matters pertaining to women by the mother, who spends time with her daughter in the home and is more capable than the father of rendering such an education. Boys are to be educated in Torah and *mitzvot*, which men, who are obligated in the fulfillment of all precepts, are more qualified to impart. A similar responsum exists of thirteenth-century Spanish scholar Rabbi Solomon ben Adret (Rashaba).[78]

Assaf relates a responsum of twelfth-century Spanish scholar Rabbi Joseph ibn Migash regarding the question of whether a girl should remain with her mother or spend the days with her brothers.[79] What is interesting is not so much the responsum but Assaf's interpretation of it. In the responsum, Rabbi Joseph replies, "Because the mother generally watches over her more than the father, and she teaches her and guides her in what is necessary for girls to learn and become accustomed to, such as spinning and supervision of household affairs, and she instructs her in the ways and customs pertaining to women . . . and all this is not of the work of man or of his nature. . . ."[80] In the introduction to his quotation of the responsum, Assaf states, "From the responsum we can have some idea regarding the state of education of girls in that period of time in Spain. However, we should not conclude that the education of girls was limited to household work. His [Joseph ibn Migash's] intention was merely to point out the advantages of a girl's remaining with her mother, for as far as formal instruction is concerned, the father, as the mother, could engage a tutor (*melamed*) for her."[81] Unfortunately, Assaf does not supply us with other sources to buttress his contention that girls may have been tutored privately in formal instruction. Perhaps Assaf's intention was that his readers were not to draw from ibn Migash's responsum definite conclusions with regard to the state of women's education in Spain, of which almost nothing is mentioned in the sources he has been able to examine.

Evidence for Education of Women

That some girls may have received some form of private tutoring is a distinct probability. After all, Spain (Arabic Spain to a greater degree than Christian

---

77. Asher ben Jehiel, *Responsa* (Vilna, 1881), sec. 82, para. 2. Also quoted in Morris, *Toldot ha-Hinukh*, vol. 2, p. 182.

78. Solomon ibn Adret, in the Book of Responsa falsely attributed to Nahmanides (Warsaw, 1883), para. 38. See also Morris, *Toldot ha-Hinukh*, p. 181.

79. The responsum is quoted in Assaf, *Mekorot*, vol. 2, p. 22.

80. Ibid.

81. Ibid.

Spain) in the Middle Ages was a major center of Jewish learning and productivity, known for its progressive views on education, views that may have had a spillover effect on the education of some women. Indeed, we may hypothesize that, considering the educational picture in Italy (where many Spanish Jews fled after their expulsion in 1492) resembled that in Spain and there is considerable documentation regarding Italian Jewish women's having acquired some type of formal education, albeit in later centuries, a similar situation may have existed in Spain. Furthermore, considering that many children of the upper and middle classes in Spain received private tutoring, a number of parents may have extended such tutoring to their daughters as well.

Undoubtedly, exceptionally learned women existed in Spain, as they did throughout the Jewish world. Ezra Fleischer, Hebrew University's expert on medieval Jewish poetry, has recently discovered poems by the wife of Dunash ibn Labrat (mid tenth century). Dunash was the most famous of the Spanish Jewish grammarians and formulated the intricate rules for Spanish Jewish poetry. He was absent from Spain over many years, and his wife corresponded with him in beautiful Hebrew poetry. She clearly had mastered meter, rhyme, and Hebrew literary sources.[82] Arabic poetry has been found written by a woman, Qasmuna, who has been identified as the daughter of Samuel ha-Nagid, the prolific poet, eminent talmudic scholar, and leader of Spanish Jewry in the eleventh century. Scholars have speculated that Samuel ha-Nagid may have taught his daughter Hebrew poetry as well.[83] The wife of the twelfth-century Hebrew poet and philosopher Judah Halevi is mentioned in *Shalshelet ha-Kabbalah* ("Chain of Tradition") of sixteenth-century Italian historiographer Gedaliah Ibn Yahya, as being a learned woman.[84] His daughter, Hulda, was learned as well as being a poetess in her own right. She wrote an acrostic entitled *"Bat Halevi"* ("Daughter of Halevi"), which appears in the *divan* of Rabbi Judah Halevi.[85]

Women teachers may have also existed in this part of the Jewish world. We read of a silk weaver, one Juan de Sevilla, who confessed before the Inquisition. Among other things, he stated that he had "given his son to a Jewish woman for purposes of religious instruction."[86] Among the lower

---

82. See Goitein, *A Mediterranean Society*, vol. 5, 1988, pp. 468–469, and E. Fleischer, "On Dunash ibn Labrat, His Wife and His Son: New Light on the Beginnings of the Hebrew-Spanish School," in *Jerusalem Studies in Hebrew Literature*, vol. 5, 1984, pp. 189–202. The letters are found in the Cairo Genizah Collection at Cambridge, Taylor-Schechter NS 143.46; VIII.202, and VIII.387.

83. Goitein, *A Mediterranean Society*, vol. 5, pp. 469–470.

84. G. Ibn Yahya, *Shalshelet ha-Kabbalah* (Warsaw, 1928), p. 19.

85. M. Kayserling, *Die Juedischen Frauen in der Geschichte, Literatur und Kunst* (Leipzig, 1879), p. 136.

86. Yitzhak Baer, *Toldot ha-Yehudim bi-Sepharad ha-Notsrit* (Tel Aviv: Am Oved,

classes of Jews, where the level of education during certain periods was poor even for the male population, girls certainly received no extra educational benefits, other than what their mothers may have been able to transmit to them.

In the fourteenth and fifteenth centuries, the climate of Spanish Jewry was brutally altered when a Christian reaction toward Judaism made itself felt. Especially in the fifteenth century, a considerable number of Jews were forcibly converted. Many of these *Conversos* (also referred to as *Marranos*) became ostensibly Christian, but remained secretly Jewish. In the new living conditions of the Jewish underground, educational restrictions against women lost their significance, and many had the opportunity to become both student and teacher; they were also active participants in synagogue ritual.[87] In a list of *Converso* worshipers appear twenty names: twelve are of women and eight are of men.[88] Furthermore, we read of a Passover seder celebration, presided over by one María Díaz, la Cerrera, who excelled in her erudition and in her righteousness.[89] She is mentioned in various Inquisition trials both as a dynamic personality among both the *Conversos* of Ciudad Real and the refugees from that town in Palma and as one who did much to promote the Jewish way of life.[90] A complete picture of María Díaz's Jewish character forms from the statements made by various witnesses, but more particularly from the deposition of Fernando de Trujillo, who, when still a Jew, served as rabbi to a group of *Conversos*. In his testimony he relates how María celebrated the Passover seder according to all the rules, kept the festival of Sukkot (Tabernacles) as well as other Jewish holidays, and was in general so observant and so erudite that she was thoroughly knowledgeable in the Mosaic

1965), p. 425. This work is the Hebrew original version of Baer's *History of the Jews in Christian Spain*. Interestingly, in relating the testimony of Juan de Sevilla, the two versions are identical except for the omission of one (crucial, for our purposes) sentence from the English translation (vol. 2, pp. 354–356), which appears in the original Hebrew. The sentence in Hebrew is: *"Et b'no she-nolad lo mosar le-ishah yehudit le- hinukh"* (p. 425, Hebrew version; "The son that was born to him he gave over to a Jewish woman for educational instruction").

87. For an excellent portrayal of the active role that women among the *Conversos* undertook in the underground Jewish life of the community, see Hayim Beinart, *Conversos on Trial* (Jerusalem: Magnes Press, 1981). See especially the section entitled "The Women," pp. 226–232, and chap. 7, "The Jewish Life of the Conversos," pp. 237f.

88. Ibid., p. 253. See also n. 58 on that page. Given the secret circumstances under which the *Conversos* had to worship, places reserved for assembly were generally obscure rooms in private homes. Naturally, under these conditions there could be no female gallery, so the men and women sat apart (Ibid., pp. 249–250).

89. Ibid., pp. 226, 271.

90. Ibid., p. 226.

Laws and precepts. It was de Trujillo who said that María had a Jewish name and was called by it (although he did not remember it); that is to say, in this too she surpassed all the other *Conversos*, returning to her people and identifying herself completely with her Jewish brethren.[91] It is thus not surprising that she was called to trial on heresy charges; however, she fled town a fortnight before the arrival of the Inquisition. Haim Beinart rightfully comments on her, "She can be justly called a righteous woman whose entire life in Judaism was for Judaism's sake. She stood the test of her Jewish belief when she took up the wanderer's staff and left for an unknown destination."[92] The list of *Converso* women who were tried by the Inquisition is long, and one can go on describing their Jewish way of life as they observed *mitzvot* themselves and were partners to their husband's Jewish life.[93] Many were the women who risked or relinquished their life in sanctification of God's Name during the years of persecution by the Inquisition, both in Spain and in other countries where the long arm of the Inquisition extended. Where they were deficient in formal knowledge they made up for it in heights of spirituality, which is perhaps the true measure of "education" in Judaism – education being defined here as the transmission of Jewish religious ideals, values, and practices.[94]

Provence

The Jewish settlements in Provence, in southern France, resembled those of Spain in their educational and cultural development.[95] The fortuitous geographical circumstance by which Provence was situated between three great intellectual centers – Spain, Italy, and Franco-Germany – had a decisive effect on the development of Provence as a major center for Jewish learning and literature.[96] Many towns had important academies and scholars.[97] In such a

91. Ibid., p. 227.

92. Ibid.

93. For elaboration, see Beinart, *Conversos on Trial*, pp. 226–232. See also Baer, "The Inquisition," *A History of the Jews in Christian Spain*, chap. 14, pp. 324f.

94. See further, Joel L. Kramer, "Spanish Women in the Cairo Genizah," *Mediterranean Historical Review* 6:2 (December 1991): 236–267. Unfortunately, the article was not readily available in Toronto.

95. Sources regarding Jewish life in Provence in the Middle Ages are not plentiful. Two sources I have been able to obtain deal primarily with the political, cultural, and religious life of the Jews and their relations with their non-Jewish neighbors, and not with education per se. They are Armand Lunel, *Juifs du Languedoc de la Provence et des états français du Pape* (Paris: Albin Michel, 1975), and L. Mouan, *Quelques Recherches sur l'état des Juifs en Provence au Moyen-Age* (Paris, 1879). See further, Talmage, *David Kimhi*, pp. 10–11.

96. See also Alexander Shapiro, *Encyclopaedia Judaica*, vol. 13, p. 1263.

climate, girls may have benefited in acquiring some formal education. In the sixteenth century, the French Protestant scholar and philologist Joseph Justus Scaliger expressed his amazement at the excellent state of education among the Jewish women of Avignon (in southeastern France, formerly part of Provence), indicating that few of them were unable to read.[98]

Italy

General Background

After the expulsion of the Jews from Spain and Portugal, Italian Jewry became the major Jewish community of the Mediterranean lands. Here, too, education was the hallmark of the Jew. From the thirteenth century on, Italian Jews had been active in the study of Hebrew poetry, Bible, and Talmud, but in all of these pursuits Italian Jewry more or less followed paths paved in Spain and southern France.[99] An important feature of Jewish education in Renaissance Italy (fourteenth–sixteenth centuries) was the inclusion of general subjects into the program. Following an educational trend that had its origins in the western Mediterranean European lands, Jewish education aimed at training individuals to be at ease in Italian life and society as well as faithful Jews, rather than to be talmudic scholars.[100] Public efforts on behalf of Torah study were expressed in a form that was typical of the weak organizational structure of the Jewish communities during the Renaissance.[101] Among the manifold duties of the rabbi, who received his salary from communal coffers, was instruction of the young, especially the children of the poor, in the *Talmud Torah* schools, set up for this purpose.[102] Even a leading head of a *yeshivah* like Rabbi Judah Minz of Padua (fifteenth century) was obliged to perform this

---

97. See also E. Bortniker, *Encyclopaedia Judaica*, vol. 6, pp. 407–408.

98. See Cecil Roth, "Outstanding Jewish Women in Western Europe," in *The Jewish Library: Women*, ed. L. Jung (London and New York: Soncino Press, 1970), pp. 152, 247–268.

99. For elaboration on the educational curriculum of the Jews of Italy, see Abrahams, *Jewish Life in the Middle Ages*, pp. 388f.

100. For a thorough picture of Jewish life in Renaissance and post-Renaissance Italy, the following works are recommended: Cecil Roth, *The History of the Jews of Italy* (Philadelphia: Jewish Publication Society of America, 1946); Cecil Roth, *The Jews in the Renaissance* (Philadelphia: Jewish Publication Society of America, 1959); and Moses A. Shulvass, *The Jews in the World of the Renaissance* (Chicago: E. J. Brill, 1973).

101. Shulvass, *The Jews in the World of the Renaissance*, pp. 169, 270.

102. Ibid.

duty.[103] Rabbi David ibn Yahya mentioned that among his multiple tasks as chief rabbi of the Jews in Naples, he had to be "a tutor of small children."[104] Well-to-do people would send their children to a private school or would keep a private teacher in their home. But the Renaissance's most characteristic educational feature was the employment of the private tutor. There were two principal reasons for this: the aspiration for a well-rounded education for the children, and the fact that there were many towns with only one Jewish family. Nearly all the *condotta* (contractual agreements) drawn up with Jewish loan bankers allowing them to conduct business in towns where no other Jews resided included permission to have a teacher brought by the family in order to instruct their children.[105] Eventually, as the Talmud Torahs, originally established for the benefit of the poor, became well organized, they were generally placed into the service of all the members of the community, both rich and poor.[106] Higher Jewish learning was provided in the *yeshivot*, which were established in the larger Jewish communities. Jewish students also attended general higher schools, mainly medical colleges.

Most scholars have claimed that the Renaissance in Italy produced a type of woman who, like the man, strove to achieve fulfillment in all of life's aspects. Jacob Burckhardt, the great historian of the movement, considers the women to have been on a footing of social equality with men.[107] It was inevitable, then, that this structure of society should be reflected in Jewish life as well. Women in the Jewish community, too, attained a more prominent position. Some Jewish women were capable financiers, managing pawnshops, concluding *condotta* with an acumen identical with that of men, providing cloth for the Pope's troops, and venturing unescorted into fairs to engage in trade.[108] Jewish female physicians drew even more attention.[109] A few outstanding Jewish women played a prominent role in public life. Notable among them were Bienvenida Abrabanel, wife of Don Samuel, who, like her husband, had access to royal courts;[110] the educated women of the Da Pisa family, who

103. Ibid.

104. Ibid.

105. Ibid., p. 169.

106. We will return to a discussion of these *Talmud Torah* schools when we speak of education of women in Italy.

107. See Roth, *The Jews in the Renaissance*, p. 49. See, however, Howard Adelman, "Rabbis and Reality: Public Activities of Jewish Women in Italy During the Renaissance and Catholic Restoration," in *Jewish History* 5 (Spring 1991): 27–28.

108. Roth, *The Jews in the Renaissance*, p. 49. See also Roth, *The History of the Jews of Italy*, p. 214, and Shulvass, *The Jews in the World of the Renaissance*, pp. 166–167.

109. Roth, *The History of the Jews of Italy*, pp. 214, 240; Roth, *The Jews in the Renaissance*, p. 50; and Shulvass, *The Jews in the World of the Renaissance*, p. 167.

110. See Judith Harari, *Ishah ve-Em be-Yisrael* (Tel Aviv: Massada, 1959), pp. 95–97;

entertained princes and people of high repute;[111] Doña Gracia Mendes, head of the banking house of Mendes;[112] and the mother of the rabbi and scholar Leon da Modena.[113] These women were noted for their religious enthusiasm, for their public and charitable spirit, for their knowledge of affairs, and as patronesses of learning and advocates of their people in times of crisis. The new situation of women in the Renaissance found expression in a literary debate on the role and character of the woman, a debate in which authors, rabbis, and mystics participated, at times positively, sometimes cynically, often uninhibitedly, but always seriously.[114] A representative opinion of that generation's scholars on the Jewish woman is reflected in a statement by Rabbi Jacob da Fano in *Shilte Hagibborim* (Ferrara, 1556): "I know that many daughters have done valiantly in contemporary times."[115]

On the other hand, Howard Adelman, writing about the public activities of Jewish women in Italy during the Renaissance, disputes the contention that the Renaissance had a liberating effect on Jewish women.[116] He argues that the rich materials preserved from this period give a mistaken impression. An investigation of Jewish law and its interpreters will show that women's activity was restricted to their home and their family, for the most part. Adelman considers the correspondence of the time, Jewish communal record books, archives, magistracies, courts, autobiographies, and other Renaissance literature to portray his picture of the Italian Jewish woman.

Evidence for Torah Study by Women

One cannot ascertain the degree of knowledge of Torah attained among Jewish women of this time. Considering women's general position in Renaissance society, it may be assumed, according to historian Moses Shulvass, that

---

Roth, *The History of the Jews of Italy*, p. 215; and Shulvass, *The Jews in the World of the Renaissance*, p. 166. See also Cecil Roth, "Outstanding Jewish Women in Western Europe," in *The Jewish Library: Women*, ed. L. Jung, pp. 154–155.

111. Shulvass, *The Jews in the World of the Renaissance*, p. 166.

112. See Harari, *Ishah ve-Em be-Yisrael*, pp. 98–102; Roth, *The History of the Jews of Italy*, pp. 215, 301, 308; and Trude Weiss-Rosmarin, *Jewish Women Through the Ages* (New York: Jewish Book Club, 1940), pp. 68f. See also Roth, "Outstanding Jewish Women in Western Europe," pp. 155–156.

113. Shulvass, *The Jews in the World of the Renaissance*, p. 167.

114. For elaboration on the unique debate that the "enemies of women" and the "defenders of women" carried on with intense heat in the Renaissance, see Israel Zinberg, *A History of Jewish Literature*, vol. 4 (Cleveland: Press of the Case Western Reserve University, 1974), pp. 97–99.

115. Quoted in Shulvass, *The Jews in the World of the Renaissance*, p. 166.

116. See Adelman, "Rabbis and Reality," pp. 27–40.

they possessed a fair degree of Jewish knowledge.[117] Cecil Roth, another historian of Renaissance Jewry, believes that education given to women in Italy at this period was to some extent modeled on that received by men.[118] Although instruction in the Talmud was considered a superfluity for the woman (although, as we shall see, there were exceptions), the humanistic element in education was enjoyed by both sexes. Jewish women of the upper class at least were initiated into elementary Hebrew studies in the same way as their brothers[119] under the auspices of the private tutor, which was so characteristic an educational feature in Renaissance Italy. Hezekiah Rieti, dedicating his Judeo-Italian translation of Proverbs (Venice, 1617) to Isaiah Massarani of Mantua, told how his esteem for the family dated back to the time when he had been entrusted with the task of *"educating in good letters"* his patron's daughter-in-law, Sorellina Saraval.[120] A teacher in Piedmont, at this time, specialized in the instruction of girls.[121] But the instructors might be women: David Reuveni, the adventurer who aroused messianic hopes in the first half of the sixteenth century, mentions in his diary a woman teacher who taught Bible to the daughter of a Roman Jew, whom he considered to have made remarkable progress in her studies.[122] The fact that Hebrew poems and other literature were often written in honor of, or for the benefit of, women obviously implied that some were able to read and understand them.[123]

Women in the Synagogue

In the fifteenth and sixteenth centuries, prayer services were translated into Judeo-Italian, using Hebrew characters. Some translations were dedicated to women. In 1596 the Pope banned these translations. We thus learn that women could read Hebrew characters, but many of them did not understand the language. This may be compared to women in Salonika who prayed in the vernacular. Some Italian men also prayed in the vernacular because they could not pray in Hebrew. Other women, particularly among rabbinic families, were fluent in Hebrew, recited their deathbed confessionals in Hebrew, wore *tefillin* during prayers, and led other women in prayer. The best known of women precentors was Anna d'Arpino. Women made and dedicated

---

117. Shulvass, *The Jews in the World of the Renaissance*, p. 281.

118. Roth, *The Jews in the Renaissance*, p. 50.

119. Ibid.

120. Ibid.

121. Ibid., pp. 50–51.

122. Ibid., p. 51.

123. Ibid. See also Shulvass, *The Jews in the World of the Renaissance*, pp. 167–168. An example is the works of Abraham Jaghel Gallichi: *Eyshet Hayil* and *Ge Hizzayon*, in which he sets down his ideas regarding a woman's role.

decorations for the Torah scrolls, and the Italian *mahzor* praises women for this labor.[124]

Women Scholars and Functionaries

As in other parts of the Jewish world, Italy also had its share of exceptionally educated women, in both Renaissance and post-Renaissance times. David Reuveni noted that the women of the Da Pisa and Abudarham families knew all twenty-four books of the Bible.[125] Women of the Modena family were reputed to be talmudic scholars. Pomona da Modena, of Ferrera (end of fifteenth century), was said to be as well versed in Talmud as any man and was honored by Rabbi David of Imola with a detailed responsum on Jewish law pertaining to *kashrut*, which only a seasoned scholar could have understood. Her son, Abraham ben Yehiel Modena, celebrated her piety in over a thousand liturgical poems, composed between 1536 and 1552.[126] Another member of this family, Fioretta (or Batsheba) da Modena–wife of Rabbi Solomon da Modena, mother of the physician and scholar Mordekhai da Modena, and ancestress of a whole line of distinguished scholars–was even more remarkable. Her grandson, the kabbalist Aaron Berekhiah da Modena, writes of her that she was steadily engaged in the study of Scriptures, *Mishnah*, and the codes of law; had a close acquaintance with the writings of Maimonides; was a student of the kabbalistic work, the *Zohar*; mapped out for herself a regular sequence of advanced study week by week; and was considered to be largely responsible for the love of Jewish lore that distinguished her learned family. In her old age she emigrated to Safed in the Holy Land, where she died.[127]

Learned women of post-Renaissance (seventeenth-century) Italy include Miriam Luria, daughter of David Hayim Luria of Padua and member of a large and prominent family of scholars,[128] and Benvenida Ghirondi, wife of Mordekhai Ghirondi, also of Padua. Benvenida conducted talmudic disputa-

---

124. See Adelman, "Rabbis and Reality," pp. 30–32.

125. For excerpts from David Reuveni's diary, see Assaf, *Mekorot*, vol. 2, pp. 112–113. See also Shulvass, *The Jews in the World of the Renaissance*, p. 281.

126. Roth, *The Jews in the Renaissance*, p. 51. See also Kayserling, *Die Juedischen Frauen*, pp. 140–141.

127. See Aaron Berakhiah de Modena, *Ma'avar Yabbok* (Vilna, 1927), Introduction. Excerpted in Assaf, *Mekorot*, vol. 4, p. 54. See also Roth, *The Jews in the Renaissance*, pp. 51–52; Kayserling, *Die Juedischen Frauen*, p. 141; and Shulvass, *The Jews in the World of the Renaissance*, p. 282.

128. Kayserling, *Die Juedischen Frauen*, p. 180. Miriam's parents are included in the lineage of the Luria family in Abraham Epstein, *Kitvei Abraham Epstein*, ed. A. Habermann, vol. 1 (Jerusalem: Mossad Harav Kook, 1950), p. 328.

tions with distinguished scholars of her time, who were profuse in their admiration of her erudition and her wisdom.[129] She was proficient in Talmud and *Midrash* and instructed her son in Bible, Hebrew grammar, Talmud with the commentary of Rashi, and the writings of Maimonides. She also instructed other young people. Her annotations to enigmatic liturgical poems and difficult passages of the Bible were numerous.[130]

Some women in Italy had mastered the codes to such an extent that they were formally authorized to act as *shohet* (ritual slaughterer).[131] Traditionally, women have been discouraged from the practice of *shehitah* (ritual slaughter), although if they perform the *shehitah* properly, their slaughter is ritually valid.[132] In contemporary times, a license to practice *shehitah* is not generally issued to women, but in former times we do find women engaged in this occupation. It is recorded that in 1556, Rabbi Isaac Immanuel de Lattes of Mantua issued diplomas to two young women in Mantua to practice *shehitah*, after each "was tested on the laws of ritual slaughter and was found to be fluent in all the myriad details."[133] In 1614 and 1626, licenses were issued to a woman, one Izota, daughter of Elhanan da Fano, to practice ritual slaughter and vein removing.[134] Another woman was known to have studied the laws of ritual slaughter in Rabbi Jacob Weil's *Shehitot u-Bedikot*, a popular handbook for ritual slaughterers.[135]

Women scribes and printers existed in Italy as well. The earliest known is Paola de Mansi of Rome (thirteenth century),[136] whose beautifully written

---

129. Benvenida's grandson, the Italian scholar and biographer Mordekhai Samuel Ghirondi, testified to her learnedness in his *Toldot Gedolei Yisrael* (Trieste, 1853), a biographical dictionary of Jewish scholars and rabbis. For excerpts of his testimony regarding his grandmother and father, see Assaf, *Mekorot*, vol. 2, p. 237. See also Kayserling, *Die Juedischen Frauen*, p. 180.

130. Kayserling, *Die Juedischen Frauen*, p. 180.

131. Assaf, *Mekorot*, vol. 2, p. 239; Roth, *The Jews in the Renaissance*, p. 52; and Shulvass, *The Jews in the World of the Renaissance*, p. 280. See also Rabbi Hayim David Azulai (Hida), *Birkei Yosef* (Vienna, 1860, glosses to the *Shulhan Arukh*), *Yoreh De'ah* 1:4, where the author mentions the existence of women *shohatim* in Italy.

132. *Hullin* 2a, b; Maimonides, *Mishneh Torah*, Laws of *Shehitah* 4:4; *Shulhah Arukh*, *Yoreh De'ah* 1:2.

133. See responsa of Rabbi Isaac de Lattes (Vienna: Friedlander, 1860), para. 139, for full text of the licenses. Photostats of the licenses issued by Rabbi Isaac appear also in Solomon Ashkenazi, *Dor Dor u-Minhagav* (Tel Aviv: Don, 1977), pp. 255–256. See also Assaf, *Mekorot*, vol. 2, p. 239.

134. Assaf, Ibid.

135. Shulvass, *The Jews in the World of the Renaissance*, p. 282. For a more nuanced analysis see Adelman, "Rabbis and Reality," pp. 32–34.

136. See Abraham Berliner, *Geschichte der Juden in Rom von der Altesten Zeit bis zur Gegenwart* (Frankfurt am Main: J. Kauffmann, 1893), vol. 2, pp. 39–40; 116–118. Cecil

manuscripts and elaborate colophons have been preserved. They attest to her considerable competence in both scribal art and knowledge of Hebrew. In 1288, she copied two large volumes of commentaries to the Bible. Upon completion, she stated, "May it be God's will that I merit to study and meditate upon [the words of the Torah], I and my children, and my children's children to the end of time, and may I be worthy of seeing the fulfillment of the verse 'And a redeemer shall come to Zion. . .' " (Isaiah 59:20).[137] At the request of a relative, she later (1293) transcribed a compendium of laws written by Rabbi Isaiah de Trani (1180–1260).[138] In 1306, she copied a prayer book for her son Solomon, to which she added her own explanations.[139]

Two centuries later, the physician Abraham Conat of Mantua, one of the earliest Hebrew printers, active at Mantua in 1476–1480, was assisted in his work by his wife, Estellina Conat, known as the first woman printer of the Hebrew language. She set up the type for at least one of the books that was printed in the Conat printing house and attributed to her, although she undoubtedly aided her husband in the publication of other works published in their firm.[140] The widow of Meshullam Cuzi, founder, in 1475, of the primitive press at Piove de Sacco near Padua, was responsible for carrying on his work after his death. Similarly, the daughter of Joseph Gunzenhausen directed her father's press for a time in Naples, following his demise in 1490.[141] Reyna, duchess of Naxos, daughter of the noted humanitarian and patroness of learning, Doña Gracia Mendes,[142] established her own printing press at Belvedere, near Constantinople, with the money remaining after the confiscation of most of her fortune following the death of her husband. The printing press was subsequently transferred to Kuru Chesme, on the Bosporus. Her many works, now of utmost rarity, were published due to the "enthusiasm for Jewish studies of a pious Jewish lady, brought up as a Christian, who was at one time one of the most famous beauties in Europe

---

Roth refers to her as Paola dei Piatelli (Anau) in *The Jews in the Renaissance*, p. 52. Kayserling refers to her as Paola dei Mansi in *Die Juedischen Frauen*, p. 137. Harari refers to her as Paula from the family of Anau in *Ishah ve-Em be-Yisrael*, p. 80.

137. Berliner, *Geschichte der Jueden in Rom*, p. 117.

138. Ibid.

139. Ibid., pp. 117–118.

140. Abraham Habermann, *Nashim Ivriyot be-Tor Madpisot, Mesadrot, Motsiot le-Or, ve-Tomkhot be-Mehabrim* (Berlin: R. Mass, 1933), p. 7. See also Roth, *The Jews in the Renaissance*, p. 52.

141. Roth, *The Jews in the Renaissance*, p. 52.

142. They were members of the ancient Jewish family of Beneviniste, which had been among the victims of the forced conversion in Portugal in 1497. After residing in Italy for a time, mother and daughter moved on to Constantinople, where they returned to the religion of their ancestors.

and who, if she so desired, might have been a leader of Spanish or Flemish aristocracy."[143]

Religious Literature for Italian Jewish Women

The love of the book evoked by the Renaissance and the invention of the art of printing created multifarious literature among the Jews of Italy. Though our attention is fixed here on the Sephardic communities in Italy, we should not ignore the Ashkenazic contributions. Books were printed in Italy in every language spoken by the composite Italo-Jewish community – Hebrew, Italian, Yiddish, and Judeo-Italian – and incorporated many old and new literary genres. The existence of a large Ashkenazic population in northern Italy during the Renaissance led to the emergence of a body of literature written in Yiddish. Whereas Italian Yiddish literature included secular works, most Yiddish works belonged in the various literary categories that served religious needs, especially those of the Jewish woman.[144] It became customary to prepare for the women handwritten volumes containing a mélange of religious and secular works.[145] The core of the Yiddish religious literature consisted of translations and paraphrases of various scriptural books whose purpose was to serve the needs of women, as well as the pupils in the northern Italian Ashkenazic schools who were taught to interpret the Scriptures in Yiddish.[146] During the sixteenth century, seven Yiddish editions of biblical books appeared in Italy.[147] These books included a translation of the Pentateuch (Cremona, 1560) and the Psalms by Elijah Bahur (Venice, 1545). About this time the *Shemuel Buch*, an excellent paraphrase of the biblical Book of Samuel, was published in Mantua. In 1548, Yiddish translations of several Apocryphal books appeared in Venice. In addition to biblical books, Italian Ashkenazic Jewish women had at their disposal a variety of manuals and treatises that served to guide the daily religious life, such as *Mitzvot Nashim* ("Laws of Women"), or *Frauen Buechlein*. The prayer book, the Passover *Haggadah*, and *Pirkei Avot* (The Sayings of the Fathers) were also available in Yiddish translations.[148]

Italian Jewish women also had their own literature in Italian and the Judeo-Italian dialects. The literature in Judeo-Italian consisted mostly of trans-

---

143. Roth, "Outstanding Jewish Women," pp. 156–157. See also Habermann, *Nashim Ivriyot*, pp. 10–11.

144. Shulvass, *The Jews in the World of the Renaissance*, p. 226.

145. Ibid., p. 224.

146. Ibid., p. 226.

147. Ibid.

148. Ibid., pp. 226–227. See Chapter 7 for elaboration on Yiddish literature.

lations of the Scriptures and the prayer book. In addition, it also contained original works offering religious direction, especially to women. In the Hebrew introduction to the Italian guide *Hokhmat Nashim* ("The Wisdom of Women"; 1565), the author, Jehiel Manoscrivi, explicitly stated that he wrote in Italian because many women did not understand Hebrew.[149] *Mitzvot Nashim* was translated into Italian (Venice, 1606) by Jacob Heilbronn, a writer who lived toward the end of the Renaissance.[150] In the early part of the Renaissance, Bible translations were generally written in various dialects that were spoken in central and southern Italy. They began to approximate literary Italian only at the close of the period. An example of one such reputedly remarkable Italian Bible translation is the Psalms by Leone da Sommi. We also find in this time period an Italian translation of *Sayings of the Fathers*.[151] Quite prolific was the Judeo-Italian liturgical literature, the *"volgare* prayers."* At least twelve translations of the prayer book were made in the fifteenth and sixteenth centuries. Some of the prayer books that are extant in manuscript were explicitly prepared for women, and most copies of the printed prayer books were probably owned by women.[152] Shulvass states that it was characteristic of the period that translations of prayers by a woman were recited in the synagogue.[153] Sermons were preached in the synagogue mostly in Italian, although generally published in Hebrew.

One woman who had the distinction of having her liturgical translations incorporated into the prayer books of many communities was the gifted poet Deborah Ascarelli (early seventeenth century).[154] Little is known of her personal life, except that her husband, Joseph Ascarelli, was president of the Catalan synagogue in Rome. Her reputation as a poet was considerable. She was one of the first persons in modern Europe to whom came the inspiration of translating Hebrew liturgical hymns into vernacular, poetical versions. Her greatest enterprise in this direction was her translation of a poem, *Meon Hashoalim* ("The Abode of the Suppliants") by Moses Rieti (the Hebrew Dante of the fifteenth century), which was published, together with the Hebrew original, in Venice in 1602. Because of its lofty style it was regarded as akin to religious poetry and was recited in the synagogue. Deborah also translated important parts of the prayer book, such as the "Reproof" of Rabbi Bahya, the

---

149. Ibid., p. 228.

150. Ibid., p. 229.

151. Ibid., p. 228.

152. Ibid., pp. 228–229.

153. Ibid., p. 229.

154. See A. Berliner, *Geschichte der Jueden in Rom*, p. 194; Kayserling, *Die Juedischen Frauen*, p. 159; Nahida Remy, *Das Juedische Weib* (Leipzig, 1892), p. 170; Roth, "Outstanding Jewish Women in Western Europe," p. 159; Roth, *The Jews in the Renaissance*, pp. 56–57; Shulvass, *The Jews in the World of the Renaissance*, p. 229.

"Great Confession" of Rabbenu Nisim, and the Sephardic *Avodah* of Yom Kippur. A poet who dedicated to her one of his works addressed her thus: "Deborah, if others in triumph rejoice,/But for Israel's glory thou raiseth thy voice."[155]

Perhaps the most interesting of writers and poets among Italian Jewish women was Sara Copia Sullam, a contemporary of Deborah Ascarelli. She possessed a passionate love for her people, was a vigorous defender of her faith, and shed luster on the Jewish community of Venice in the first half of the seventeenth century. She is a personality who calls for elaboration.[156]

Sara Copia Sullam: Poet and Vindicator of her Faith

Born in Venice in 1592, daughter of Simon and Rebekah Copia, Sara was given by her father a liberal education, as was usual among the well-to-do Italian Jewish families of that day. She acquired an excellent knowledge of Hebrew, Greek, Latin, Spanish, and Italian, and above all so developed her literary talents that she soon ranked among the foremost Italian poets. She also excelled as a singer and performer on the lute and harpsichord and possessed a personality of rare charm. The history of her people evoked her deepest sympathy. The towering forms of the prophets roused her admiration and enthusiasm. She was deeply moved by the vast difference between the glorious past of her people and their present humiliation. She combined her profound attachment to the Jewish faith with a great love for Greek philosophy. When in 1614 she married Jacob Sullam, a wealthy and cultivated Venetian Jew, her home became a meeting place of distinguished Jews and Christians, poets and scholars, Venetians and foreign visitors, many of whom were attracted to Sara's home by dint of her intellectual attainments, gifted poetry, and spirited personality. But soon after her marriage a crisis occurred in Sara's life, when she became involved almost simultaneously in two dramatic conflicts, both of which originated in her deep devotion to Judaism. It is through sonnets, letters, and a manifesto written in connection to these conflicts that she became best known. Unfortunately, with the exception of a few poems and the manifesto, all her writings have been lost.

The first of these episodes was caused by the Genoese poet and monk Ansaldo Ceba, who published an epic poem in 1618, dealing with the story of

---

155. Remy, *Das Juedische Weib*, p. 170.

156. Information regarding Sara Sullam was compiled from the following sources: Judith Harari, *Ishah ve-Em be-Yisrael*, pp. 93–94; Franz Kobler, *Letters of the Jews Through the Ages*, vol. 2, pp. 436–447; Helen Leneman, "Sara Coppio Sullam, 17th-Century Jewish Poet in the Ghetto of Venice," *Response* 15:3 [51] (1987): 13–22; Remy, *Das Juedische Weib*, chap. 10, pp. 166f; Roth, "Outstanding Jewish Women," pp. 157–159; and Roth, *The Jews in the Renaissance*, pp. 57–58.

Esther. The work made a deep impression on Sara, who considered it an exaltation of the Jewish faith. Sara wrote the author an enthusiastic letter, assuring him that she slept with the poem under her pillow and congratulating him on choosing the tragic figure of Esther as a literary theme, rather than a conventional motif drawn from classic Greek and Roman sources. The letter had, however, a disconcerting effect, as the flattered priest immediately sensed an opportunity for winning over a tender and sympathetic soul for the church. This intention became the main subject of the correspondence, conducted at a remarkably high literary level, which was to follow between the two writers for the next four years, in which they exchanged sonnets, letters, and gifts. Ansaldo's desire to win Sara for the faith that he regarded as indispensable for her salvation was stimulated by a serious illness, from which he never recovered. This desire thus became "the deepest and last passion of his life."[157] He succeeded in persuading Sara to read the New Testament, Plato, and even the writings of San Luis de Granada, the Spanish preacher. But all this served only to confirm her faith, and when Ceba died, five years after making her acquaintance, he despairingly commended her to the prayers of his friends. His letters to her were published posthumously in 1623, but letters written to Ceba by Sara were omitted from that publication and subsequently lost.[158]

The second episode occurred in 1621, when the priest Baldassar Bonifaccio, who later became bishop of Capo d'Istria attacked Sara in a pamphlet, claiming that the poet had denied the immortality of the soul, a belief shared by Jews and Christians alike. In Venice of those days, where the Inquisition, established since 1454, was still powerful, such a charge exposed Sara to serious danger. Although Sara was ill at the time, her strong spirit proved equal to the occasion. Within two days she composed a public reply to Bonifaccio in which she ably defended herself against the allegation and refuted the opinion denying immortality of the soul, attributed to her by Signor Bonifaccio. The manifesto, the almost only extant work of Sara, is notable for the mordant wit it displays, as well as for its inexorable logic. It also shows Sara's profound erudition. With subtle wit, Sara dedicated the manifesto to the memory of her father, movingly addressing the soul of the departed—convincing testimony of her belief in the immortality of the human soul.[159] Bonifaccio replied to Sara's manifesto. But his answer was nothing but a futile attempt to cover a retreat. After Sara's brilliant defense, nobody took his accusation seriously.

---

157. Kobler, *Letters of the Jews Through the Ages*, p. 436.

158. Ceba's publication is entitled *53 Lettere di Ansaldo Ceba, scritte a Sara Copia Sullam e dedicate a Marc Antonio Doria* (Genoa, 1623). Two of the letters are printed in Kobler, *Letters of the Jews Through the Ages*, pp. 438–441.

159. The manifesto is included in Kobler, *Letters of the Jews Through the Ages*, pp. 442–447.

Sara died in 1641, but her epitaph, discovered in a Hebrew manuscript, apparently a composition by Leon da Modena, is proof that she preserved her greatness of spirit until her death:

> The implacable angel struck with his arrow swept away
> and did to death the virtuous Sara,
> the sage among women, the crown of the poor,
> who made herself a companion of all sufferers.[160]

A subsequent writer, Bartolomeo Gamba, wrote in 1832 about Sara Copia Sullam that she was "extraordinarily lettered, a perfect musician, poetess without peer and worthy of admiration for her letter-writing style. She needed rare spirit and indomitable energy to keep her head, never weakening, with the obsessive proselytes assailing her. She will always be admired for her unyielding attachment to the faith of her ancestors."[161]

Communal Education in the Seventeenth and Eighteenth Centuries

In the post-Renaissance era of the seventeenth and eighteenth centuries – the Ghetto period of Italian Jewry – *Talmud Torah* schools, originally established for the benefit of the poor, became well organized and were placed in the service of all members of the community. The management of the schools was left to *Talmud Torah* societies that operated them according to carefully formulated regulations.[162] All expenses were defrayed by way of voluntary contributions, nothing being accepted from parents. Education was broad: the elements of the vernacular were taught as were those of Hebrew. While the schools may have been primarily for boys, girls in Italy learned a great deal at home through private instruction and excelled in their general and Jewish knowledge, because Italian Jewish parents were concerned, to a considerable degree, with the education of their daughters.[163] Yet there is evidence to suggest that a number of girls, at least in their early years, attended the *Talmud Torah* schools as well. Roth describes a typical arrangement for the eighteenth century, in a community of less than a thousand people, as one in which "a free school for boys and girls alike was set up, attendance at which was universal."[164] Indeed, so great an emphasis was placed on education, in both the religious and the secular fields, for adults as well as for children, that, in

---

160. Printed in Kobler, *Letters of the Jews Through the Ages*, p. 447.

161. Quoted in Helen Leneman, "Sara Coppio Sullam," op. cit., p. 18.

162. See Assaf, *Mekorot*, vol. 2, p. v (Introduction); vol. 4, p. 10 (Introduction); Roth, *History of the Jews of Italy*, pp. 363–364.

163. Assaf, *Mekorot*, vol. 2, p. v.

164. Roth *History of the Jews of Italy*, p. 363.

Roth's words, "At a period when illiteracy was generally rampant, in the Ghetto it was exceptional."[165]

Evidence that girls participated in instruction in the *Talmud Torah* schools derives from a variety of sources. In a manuscript found in the *Talmud Torah* in Livourne, a teacher, one Rabbi Isaiah of Montaniena, writes as follows:

> Today, on the 22nd of Elul, 5353 (1593) I began a program of study for the daughter of Emmanuel Lattes . . . Dulce, "Above women in the tent shall she be blessed." [Judges 5:24]
>
> Let this day be remembered for good, the 11th of February [the Hebrew year] 5356 (1596) . . . on which I made an agreement with Abraham Segre . . . that he will send his daughter Ricca to study with me. . . . "Above women in the tent shall she be blessed. . . ."[166]

In the regulations of the benevolent society of Bologna, reference is made to a number of women teachers who taught young children, "both boys and girls."[167]

In Rome a special *Talmud Torah* for girls was established in 1745,[168] apparently with the intention of educating girls from poor homes who were unable to receive private instruction. Assaf prints a document written on April 24, 1745, which describes the motivation underlying the establishment of the school:

> "One who saves a single soul of Israel, it is as if one has saved an entire world" [*Bava Batra* 11a] . . . Praised are those individuals who recognized this fact and drew a good lesson from it. . . . For when they saw the indigent people who bore daughters, who from the age of three should have been educated in religious rituals and practices. . . . And yet their mothers were unable to educate them even in basics, such as blessings, prayers, and at the least, knowledge of the obligation of prayer on girls as it is not a time-bound law. . . . And their fathers have the great burden of eking out a meager existence, and do not have the opportunity [to educate them]. . . . Consequently, the girls grow up unrefined and ignorant [and the cycle continues]. . . . Thus, those whom God has called banded together to rectify this state of affairs, to prepare the young girl in school, providing funding to men and women teachers, so that "the daughter of the king" should not veer away [from the path of Torah].[169]

---

165. Ibid., p. 364.

166. Quoted by Assaf, *Mekorot*, vol. 2, p. 121, from Carlo Bernheimer, *Catalogue des manuscrits ets livres rares de la Bibliothèque du Talmud-Torah de Livourne* (1914).

167. See Assaf, *Mekorot*, vol. 2, pp. 197–199.

168. Ibid., p. v (Introduction) and pp. 203–204. See also Roth, *History of the Jews of Italy*, p. 364. In Roth's *The Jews in the Renaissance*, p. 50, the date is incorrectly attributed as 1475. This Talmud Torah school in Rome is the earliest evidence I have found of formal schooling for girls.

169. Assaf, *Mekorot*, vol. 2, pp. 203–204.

Characteristic of Italian Jewry was the fact that elementary teaching was mainly in the care of "Dames' Schools" conducted by women.[170] Indeed, the noted Italian talmudic scholar Rabbi Jacob Pardo states in his halakhic work *Appe Zutre* (Venice, 1797), "The custom has become widespread that women teach the young children, both boys and girls. Widows especially engage in this occupation as they do not have the burden of housework as much, and can therefore properly attend to the children."[171] The functions and salary of the woman teacher, referred to as the *"melamedet,"* are set down in some of the *Talmud Torah* societies' regulations. For example, the ordinances of the *Talmud Torah* in Modena stated that the school was to have at least three teachers— two men and one woman teacher—"who were to be present at all times to disseminate Torah to all who came to study."[172] The woman teacher was to instruct the young children, aged three and older, in learning of the Hebrew alphabet and reading of Hebrew until they could fluently read biblical verses, with the proper intonation. When the students attained the level of being able to accurately address (i.e., read) any verse in Torah, the Prophets, and the Hagiographia on their own, they were to graduate to the next level, at which point instructional duties were to be taken over by the male teacher. The female teacher was to teach the elementary-school-age children in her own home.[173] Both the woman and the men teachers were to keep account of all books given to them by the *Talmud Torah* societies.[174] Hours of instruction for both the women and men teachers are stipulated.[175] The woman teacher's home and the *Talmud Torah* schoolrooms were to be subjected to regular inspection by a supervisor.[176] Similar functions are described for the women teachers in regulations of the *Talmud Torah* society of Ferrera.[177]

In the records of the benevolent society of Bologna, praise is lavished on nineteen women, listed by name, for their dedicated work in instructing children in knowledge of Torah and Judaism. Indeed, the list includes a number of widows.[178]

The noted Italian Jewish Hebraist, Elijah Morpurgo (1740–1830), in a

---

170. See Assaf, *Mekorot*, vol. 2, p. v (Introduction), as well as citations of subsequent sources; Roth, *History of the Jews of Italy*, p. 364.

171. Quoted in Assaf, *Mekorot*, vol. 4, p. 246.

172. Quoted in Assaf, *Mekorot*, vol. 2, p. 174. The entire regulations are printed on pp. 169–182.

173. Ibid., pp. 171 and 175.

174. Ibid., p. 177.

175. Ibid., pp. 176–177.

176. Ibid., p. 178.

177. Ibid., pp. 209–210. The entire regulations are printed on pp. 206–213.

178. This list from the files of the benevolent society of Bologna is included in Assaf, *Mekorot*, vol. 2, pp. 195–197.

letter penned to the Jewish Educational Society in Berlin in 1784 describing patterns of Jewish education in Italy, explains the reasoning behind the employment of women to teach the young in Italy: "Truthfully, women are more tender-hearted and teach with patience, educating each child according to his pace."[179]

In conclusion, according to most historians of Italian Jewry, Jewish women in Italy attained a level of religious education superior to their counterparts in other regions of the Jewish world during the Renaissance and Ghetto periods. This was due to the influence of the Renaissance, which produced a type of person who strove to achieve fulfillment in all of life's aspects. The positive and encouraging attitudes on the part of rabbinical scholars, such as Rabbi Isaiah de Trani (the Younger, "Riaz"; thirteenth century) and Rabbi Samuel Archivolti (sixteenth century) (see Chapter Three) may have also set the tone for participation by women in various aspects of Jewish education in Italy, though naturally, not to the full extent that was the prerogative of the Jewish male population.

OTHER NON-ASHKENAZIC CENTERS

Other non-Ashkenazic communities, founded by Jews who had been forced to leave Spain and Portugal because of the Inquisition or expulsions, also seem to have taken women's education more seriously. In Safed, Palestine of the sixteenth century, special teachers were appointed to instruct women and children in reciting the prayers and blessings.[180] In eighteenth-century Amsterdam, the teacher Moses Cohen Belinfante included girls in the *Talmud Torah* school, which had originally been established by *Marranos* in 1616 for boys of the Spanish-Portuguese community. The program of study included the Books of the Bible, Hebrew language and grammar, and Hebrew poetry as well as general studies.[181] In London, where Jews had been readmitted in the seventeenth century under the patronage of Oliver Cromwell, girls were visited at their home by a private Hebrew tutor.[182] In 1730 the Villareal Girls'

---

179. Quoted in Assaf, *Mekorot*, vol. 2, p. 228. The entire letter appears on pp. 222–233.

180. Solomon Schechter, *Studies in Judaism* (Philadelphia: Jewish Theological Seminary of America, 1908), p. 242. For Hebrew original source see p. 298, para. 17. Mention is made of a woman teacher who taught in Hebron in 1654 in J. D. Eisenstein, *Otzar Masa'ot* [A Compendium of Jewish Travels], p. 210.

181. See Rachel Elboim-Dror, *Ha-Hinukh ha-Ivri be-Eretz Yisra'el*, vol. 1 (Jerusalem: Isaac ben Tzvi, 1986), p. 12.

182. See Assaf, *Mekorot*, vol. 1, p. 184, where a work by Johanan ben Isaac of Holleschau (seventeenth century) is excerpted, entitled *"Ma'aseh Rav."* It is a criticism of

School was founded in London to provide training in Judaism, languages, and domestic science for poor girls. The Portuguese *Marrano* Isaac da Costa Villareal, who died in 1729, had made provisions in his will for the education and sustenance of poor girls in gratitude for his deliverance from the hands of the Inquisition and his successful escape to England. The Jewish curriculum was rather meager, consisting mainly of instruction in elementary Hebrew and in prayer.[183]

---

a London rabbi in regard to his decision on a divorce and excommunication and appears in *Teshuvot ha-Geonim* (Amsterdam, 1707). In this work, reference is made to girls' studying with private tutors.

183. For a detailed description of the school curriculum and regulations, see Albert M. Hyamson, *The Sephardim of England* (London: Methuen, 1951), p. 85, and R. D. Barnett, "Anglo-Jewry in the Eighteenth Century," in *Three Centuries of Anglo-Jewish History*, ed. V. D. Lipman (Cambridge: Jewish Historical Society of England, 1961), pp. 53–54.

6

A Historical Survey of Jewish Education for Women: Part III—Christian Europe in the Twelfth to Fifteenth Centuries

The sources from which the present study proceeds can be categorized: responsa, wills, diaries, writings of women, autobiographies, eulogies, and letters. Each of these documents presents its own set of problems to unearth issues of fact, issues of generalities, and issues of interpretation. Even problems concerning the reliability of true readings and variants occur. Nevertheless, historians can put together cohesive pictures of women's activities in the Middle Ages from the extant sources.

TWELFTH AND THIRTEENTH CENTURIES

General Background

The twelfth and thirteenth centuries represented times of upheaval for the Jews of France and Germany. By the beginning of the thirteenth century, papal decrees placed Jews in ghettos, removed many of their rights, and provided the impetus for attacks against Jewish books. The rise of the monastic movements and the fury of the Crusaders combined to create an environment of fear and instability within the Jewish communities. Nevertheless, Jewish women enjoyed a relatively high status in those times. It is in connection with Passover that we find a general statement regarding men's estimate of women during those centuries. By law, a Jewish woman was not obligated to "recline at table," unless she were a woman of esteem. "Nowadays, however," states a thirteenth-century authority, Rabbi Mordekhai ben Hillel of Nuremburg, "all Jewesses are women of status (nashim hashuvot)."[1] The esteem in which women of the time were held is best summed up in the statement made by one of the Tosafists, Rabbi Isaac of Corbeil (thirteenth century), about his countrywomen: "If they are not prophetesses they are the daughters of prophetesses, and one may rely on their accepted custom."[2]

Women ran businesses or conducted their family life from positions of authority.[3] Indeed the involvement of women in business became so commonplace that the talmudic premise "Whatever a wife acquires is [automatically] acquired by her husband,"[4] became no longer relevant.[5] Many responsa of the period on problems involving women include statements such as these: ". . . and certainly in these times that women are trustees [of estates], storekeepers, businesswomen, lenders and borrowers, and take and receive deposits. . . ."[6] and "Nowadays, it is commonplace for women to engage in business."[7]

If we can brush aside the political problems besetting the Jews at this time, we will see that Jewish women, albeit excluded from roles in feudal society, maintained their pride and levels of education. They needed basic skills in reading, writing, and arithmetic to engage in the mercantile endeavors that were open to them in that period. Because Jews were prohibited from working within guilds and from working the land, they were, in effect, forced to lend money. The church had, for a period, stopped Christians from lending money at interest. With the rise of capitalism spurred on by new markets in the East, which had resulted from the travels of the Crusaders, money was needed. Since canon law did not affect Jews, Jews were able to lend money at interest. Jewish women engaged in these transactions. When we consider the

---

1. Rabbi Mordekhai ben Hillel, *Piskei ha-Mordekhai, Pesahim* 108.

2. Quoted by Rabbi Baruch haLevi Epstein in *Mekor Barukh* (Vilna: Rom, 1928), p. 1975, from Isaac of Corbeil's *Sefer Mitzvot Katan*.

3. See, for example, Cheryl Tallan, "Medieval Jewish Widows: Their Control of Resources," in *Jewish History* 5 (Spring 1991): 63. See her reference note 3 to Avraham Grossman, "The Historical Background for the Ordinances on Family Affairs Attributed to Rabbenu Gershom Me'or ha-Golah," in *Jewish History: Essays in Honour of Chimen Abramsky*, ed. A. Rapoport-Albert and S. Zipperstein (London: Halban, 1988), p. 14.

4. *Gittin* 77a.

5. See, for example, Rabbi Eliezer ben Nathan (Mainz, twelfth century), *Sefer Raban*, S. Albeck, ed. (Warsaw, 1905), para. 115.

6. Ibid.

7. Rabbi Meir of Rothenburg, *Responsa of Maharam*, R. N. Rabinowitz, ed. (Lemberg, 1860), sec. 57.

basic literacy skills gained by non-Jewish women, we see that Jewish women shared these skills as well.[8] Jewish girls, although they spoke their local vernacular, would have also been familiar with the Hebrew alphabet. Their major concentration was on acquiring domestic skills and religious domestic knowledge. The issue of teaching women intellectual subjects was no less problematic in the wider society than it was in Jewish society. Nevertheless, we would be wrong to think that women, Jewish or Christian, were deprived of all education in those times.[9]

A medieval backdrop to which the educational and social status of Jewish women can be compared may be gleaned from didactic works addressed to Christian women from the thirteenth century onward. Generally speaking, the education of women in the Gentile world meant inculcating manners, house crafts, and religious sensibilities. We hear very little about intellectual development. Women in the upper classes would be expected to be fashionable and to be adept at chess, music, reading, and writing. All education aimed at training women to be good wives. The upper classes enjoyed formal instruction in expensive schools or nunneries. Less privileged girls could learn trades by apprenticeship or attend elementary schools in the towns. In the fourteenth and fifteenth centuries in Germany, elementary schools for girls were widespread. The result was that many women were able to read and write, and some possessed libraries. The majority of peasant women, however, had no education at all.[10]

Misogynist preachings by some Christian clergymen discouraged women from any reading, or at least from reading anything but Scriptures. The view of women throughout this period was somewhat inconsistent. On one hand, women were "the gates of hell," but on the other, they were modeled after Mary as "the queen of heaven." Women were able to achieve prominence through being either mystics or learned nuns. When the code of chivalry that had elevated women declined, the status of women became more narrow and uniform.[11]

Synagogue as a Means of Education

Apart from acquiring basic skills for business, Jewish women managed to absorb an attachment to their tradition and its teachings through the institu-

---

8. See Judith Baskin, "Jewish Women in the Middle Ages," in *Jewish Women in Historical Perspective*, ed. Judith Baskin (Detroit: Wayne State University Press, 1991), p. 104.

9. See Judith Baskin, "Some Parallels in the Education of Medieval Jewish and Christian Women," *Jewish History* 5 (Spring 1991): 41–47.

10. Eileen Powers, *Medieval Women* (London: Cambridge University Press, 1975), chap. 4.

11. Ibid., chap. 1.

tion of the synagogue. Women had long attended synagogue on the Sabbaths, and the practice continued into these centuries. The minor talmudic tractate *Soferim*[12] had advocated translating for women the weekly readings from the Pentateuch and Prophets before the close of the service.[13] Indeed, states Solomon Schechter in *Studies in Judaism,* the virtues that constituted the claim of women in the Middle Ages to religious distinction, noted of hundreds of women in the memorial books of the time, were modesty, charity, and daily attendance at the synagogue morning and evening.[14] That women attended *daily* synagogue services is indeed surprising, considering the difficulty women had in extracting themselves from familial responsibilities. Even attendance by young Jewish girls at synagogue services was customary, as is remarked upon by the thirteenth-century halakhist Rabbi Isaac of Vienna: "It is the custom of the little daughters of Israel to attend synagogue services regularly in order to give reward to those who bring them [the parents] and they [the girls] to receive their reward, and also, owing to little ones' attending synagogue services, fear of God enters their heart."[15] Women were also present at the rabbinic sermons delivered on the Sabbath.[16] The synagogue, by its very existence, played an influential role in women's religious and educational activities.[17]

By the end of the thirteenth century, and perhaps even earlier, Jewish women had their own prayer meetings in rooms at the side of and a little above the men's synagogue; communication between the rooms was by means of a small window or balcony. Or if the women had no separate apartments, they sat at the back or side of the men's synagogue in reserved places, screened by curtains.[18] In their own prayer meetings the women were led by female precentors, some of whom acquired considerable reputation. The epitaph of one of them, Urania of Worms, belonging to the thirteenth century, reads as follows:

> This headstone commemorates the eminent and excellent lady Urania, the daughter of Rabbi Abraham, who was the chief of the synagogue singers. His

---

12. Soferim, chap. 18, para. 4–6.

13. *Massekhet Soferim,* ed. Joel Mueller (Leipzig, 1878), chap. 18, paras. 4–6, p. 35, and n., p. 256. Cf. Abraham Berliner, *Hayei ha-Yehudim be-Ashkenaz bi-Yemei ha-Benayim* (Tel Aviv: Tsiyon, 1968), p. 8.

14. Solomon Schechter, *Studies in Judaism* (Philadelphia: Jewish Publication Society of America, 1917), p. 325. See also below, *The Testament of Eleazar of Mayence.*

15. Rabbi Isaac of Vienna, *Or Zarua,* vol. 2, para. 48.

16. Rabbi Mordekhai ben Hillel, *Piskei ha-Mordekhai, Shabbat* 311.

17. See Emily Taitz, "Kol Ishah – The Voice of Women: Where Was It Heard in Medieval Europe?" *Conservative Judaism* 38 (1986): 46–61.

18. Abrahams, *Jewish Life in the Middle Ages,* pp. 39–40. See also I. M. Elbogen, *Ha-Tefillah be-Yisrael,* p. 351, and Mordekhai ben Hillel, *Piskei ha-Mordekhai, Shabbat* 311.

prayer for his people rose up unto glory. And as to her, she, too, with sweet tunefulness, officiated before the female worshipers, to whom she sang the hymnal portions. In devout service her memory shall be preserved.[19]

Appearing on the list of martyrs from the city of Nuremburg, killed by Rindfleish in the thirteenth century, is Rechenza, another female precentor "who prayed for the women."[20] Dulce of Worms is said to have been a "singer of hymns and prayers, and a speaker of supplications."[21] It is related of Guta, daughter of Nathan (d. 1308), that "she prayed for the women in her lovely prayer."[22]

In addition to women precentors, the institutions of the *firzogerin* (woman reader) and the *woilkennivdicke* ("the well-knowing one") became established in many synagogues throughout the Middle Ages and early modern period in Europe.[23] It was the duty of such a woman to read aloud (or sing if she were also a precentor) and translate the prayer into the vernacular for the benefit of her less learned sisters.

Women's conscientious attendance at synagogue services is evinced in a responsum of Rabbi Meir of Rothenburg,[24] in which we read of an ordinary, anonymous widow who, embroiled in a dispute with another widow, contemplates departing the city. She argues, however, "that it is not worth her while leaving her city of residence, abandoning her relatives, her home, and her place of prayer in a *minyan*."[25] Obviously, this woman was devoted to her prayer service, which was a small place, or possibly a rented room where the congregation gathered, but was as dear to her as if it were her own home.

---

19. Quoted in Israel Abrahams, *Jewish Life in the Middle Ages* (London: Edward Goldston, 1932), p. 40. Also referred to in Berliner, *Hayei ha-Yehudim be-Ashkenaz*, p. 9.

20. Simon Bernfeld, *Sefer ha-Dema'ot*, vol. 2 (Berlin: Eshkol, 1924), p. 40. See also Berliner, *Hayei ha-Yehudim be-Ashkenaz*, p. 9.

21. From the eulogy of Rabbi Eleazar of Worms for his wife, Dulce, found in Assaf, *Mekorot le-Toldot ha-Hinukh be-Yisrael*, vol. 4, p. 3. The eulogy is also included in I. Kamelhar, *Rabeinu Eleazar mi-Germiza: ha-Rokeah* (Rzeszow, 1930), pp. 17–20.

22. Israel Zinberg, *A History of Jewish Literature*, vol. 7 (New York: Ktav, 1975), p. 23 n. 68.

23. Schechter, *Studies in Judaism*, p. 324. See also Israel Zinberg, *A History of Jewish Literature*, vol. 7, pp. 23–24, 251, and Isaac Levitats, *The Jewish Community in Russia, 1772–1844* (New York: Octagon Books, 1970), p. 169.

24. *Teshuvot Maharam*, ed. Yitzhak Cahana, vol. 2 (Jerusalem: Mossad Harav Kook, 1957), para. 71.

25. A *minyan* is the designation for the quorum of ten male adults necessary for public prayer service. (See Chapter two for elaboration.) Since women cannot be counted toward a *minyan* of ten, we must assume that the woman's usage of the term *minyan* is figurative rather than literal; that is, she prayed alongside a *minyan* of ten men on a regular basis.

Indeed, women have always manifested a strong devotion to the houses of prayer and study. Many were those who provided funding for the construction and adornment of synagogues and houses of study. These edifices were often named after their benefactresses.[26]

Exclusion of Women from Formal Education Enjoyed by Males

Because women were more generally educated in the home and somewhat in the synagogue, they did not participate in the curriculum that was studied by many males. This curriculum was somewhat different from the one current in Spain. Jews in Christian Europe had not been exposed to the philosophic and literary legacy of Islam, and therefore their education was more focused on religious studies than was the case in Spain, Provence, and Italy. In those countries, the curriculum of studies in Jewish homes and schools at various times and among various groups included, in addition to the Bible and Talmud, the study of Hebrew language and grammar and of contemporary Hebrew poetry, as well as such secular subjects as philosophy, mathematics, medicine, poetry, and music. The scholastic tradition, often antiphilosophical in Germany and other central European countries, had its counterpart among the Jews. The Jews, for the most part, confined their studies to more narrow religious matters. Education was based exclusively on the Bible and the Talmud. The elementary Judaic program[27] remained much the same as in earlier centuries, the primary addition to the course of study being the Bible commentary of Rashi, the explicator par excellence whose commentaries helped young boys.[28] At the advanced levels[29] many new books were

---

26. Solomon Ashkenazi, in *Dor Dor u-Minhagav* (Tel Aviv: Don Publishing House, 1977), pp. 227–240, lists the names of over twenty women who contributed to this cause during the Middle Ages and early modern period. Simha Assaf, in *Mekorot le-Toldot ha-Hinukh be-Yisrael*, vol. 1, p. 149, has an excerpt from the *Worms Memorbuch*, containing the names of many women, as well as men, who did likewise.

27. In the western Mediterranean countries of Spain, southern France, and Italy, the elementary school was known as the *Midrash Katan* (a term probably taken from the French *petite école*). In northern France, Germany and central and eastern Europe, the elementary school was known as the *heder* (the word meaning "room") or the *Talmud Torah*. The *heder* was a privately run institution, generally held in a room in the teacher's private home or in the synagogue, the teacher receiving his fees from the parents. The *Talmud Torah* was a community-supported institution for poor boys, whose parents were unable to pay tuition fees.

28. See Baskin, "Education of Medieval Jewish and Christian Women," p. 110, n. 5, for bibliography.

29. Secondary schooling, which began at approximately age twelve or thirteen, was referred to as the *Midrash Gadol* (grande école) in western Mediterranean lands and as the *Yeshivah* in northern, central, and eastern Europe.

introduced, including the works of the great medieval Bible and Talmud commentators and eventually including the works of codifiers.

Informal Education and the Existence of Women Scholars

In the European lands, Jewish girls, by and large, received no formal education. Like their counterparts in the Arabic world, Jewish women in Europe were wed at a young age; hence, little time could be devoted to the education and intellectual enlightenment of girls.[30] Yet the cultural stature of women should not be judged by what is known of their formal education. Despite the lack of institutionalized study, the facts remain that there are Hebrew codices on abstruse subjects copied by medieval Jewish women, that a considerable number of learned women were cited as authorities due to their competency in *Halakhah*, and that a number of women conducted public lessons.[31] Yet, even among the population at large, great care was devoted to the inculcation of what Naomi Cohen, professor of Jewish thought at Haifa University, refers to as "the basic level of acculturation,"[32] that is, that level of knowledge necessary to be a functioning member of the community. For girls this was conceived to consist of the basic laws of Shabbat (the Sabbath), *Kashrut* (kosher food), appropriate sexual behavior, and the major prayers and blessings. Though often done informally in the home, it was nevertheless done.

However, women were able, in spite of all, to become knowledgeable in Jewish subjects. Illuminating is testimony from the non-Jewish world. In

---

30. Two noted sages of the Tosafists speak in apologetic terms of this practice. Rabbi Eliezer of Toques (c. 1280) rationalizes that the custom of betrothing young girls was forced on fathers by the repressive nature of the Diaspora, which fostered the fear that money set aside for a dowry today might be gone tomorrow. To keep a young girl from spinsterhood, her father was urged to betroth her at a young age, in case he could not afford it later. Rabbi Peretz ben Elijah of Corbeille (d. c. 1295), commenting on the rabbinical decree that urged allowing a daughter to mature and choose her own mate (Tosafot, *Kiddushin* 41a), emphasizes that this decree was relevant in a time when Jewish men were plentiful. During this time, however, when Jews were a minority, the youngest daughters ought to be betrothed lest they be taken away by a Gentile, which was a serious consideration in the insecure times of the Crusades, when Jews feared for the future. Early marriages, therefore, comments Breyer, who cites the observations of the two sages (*The Jewish Woman in Rabbinic Literature*, vol. 2, p. 98), contributed to family stability and communal cohesiveness.

31. Naomi G. Cohen, "Women and the Study of Talmud," *Tradition*, 24:1 (Fall 1988): 28.

32. Indeed, a medieval rabbi asserts that many Jewish women in Germany were, in the beginning of the fifteenth century, noted for their knowledge of the laws. See Rabbi Jacob ben Moses Moellin, *Responsa Maharil* (Cracow, 1881), no. 199.

contrasting the Jewish norm concerning education with that customary among Christian society in his day, a pupil of the Christian scholastic Abelard, of twelfth-century Paris, writes as follows:

> If the Christians educate their sons, they do so not for God, but for gain, in order that the one brother, if he be a cleric, may help his father and mother, and his other brothers. . . . But the Jews, out of zeal for God and love of the law, put as many sons as they have to letters, that each may understand God's law. . . . A Jew, however poor, if he had ten sons would put them all to letters, not for gain, as the Christians do, but for the understanding of God's law, *and not only his sons, but his daughters* [emphasis mine].[33]

Though the anonymous pupil of Abelard may have been exaggerating for effect, his words certainly suggest that Jewish women did not desist from religious studies. However, we shall now note that the descendants of Rashi, the great commentator on the Bible and Talmud in the eleventh century, began a tradition of educating their daughters. And even after that period, many illustrious families in most countries in Europe continued the tradition of education. However, the state of education for these elite families remained constant. What did shift as the centuries progressed was the emphasis on more education for women of less renowned families as male attitudes incorporated greater awareness of women's abilities and women's need for outlets for their religious sensitivities.

Women of the House of Rashi and Their Contemporaries: Continuing the Tradition

Among the outstanding Jewish women scholars of the Middle Ages, the women of the family of the illustrious Bible and Talmud commentator Rabbi Solomon ben Isaac, known as Rashi (northern France, eleventh century), rank prominently. Rashi had no sons, only daughters, and from their early days of childhood, they were immersed in an environment of learning and Torah. They acquired considerable knowledge from their father and his students, and they married prominent scholars.[34] When Rashi was ill and at the end of his life, he made use of one of his daughters as amanuensis for the purpose of his literary writings and correspondence. She wrote halakhic codices and re-

---

33. Quoted in Beryl Smalley, *The Study of the Bible in the Middle Ages* (Oxford: Basil Blackwell, 1952), p. 78. She quotes from the anonymous pupil's work, *Commentarius Cantabrigiensis in Epistolas Pauli e Schola Petri Abalardi* ii. 434, ed. A. Landgraf (South Bend, In: Notre Dame University, 1937).

34. See E. M. Lipschuetz, "Rashi," in *Sefer Rashi*, ed. Y. L. Maimon (Jerusalem: Mossad Harav Kook, 1956), pp. 175–176. See, also, Solomon Ashkenazi, "Nashim Lamdaniyot be-Mishpahat Rashi," in *Dor Dor u-Minhagav*, p. 211; Judith Harari, *Ishah*

sponsa in her father's name, as he recorded in one place: "My strength is weakened, my hands useless to do anything. I cannot pen my thoughts; therefore, my daughter, I have called you."[35] The oldest daughter, Jochebed, married Rabbi Meir ben Samuel, who had attended the Mainz academy with Rashi. Four sons were born to Jochebed and Meir, and they all became famous scholars: Isaac, Samuel (Rashbam), Solomon, and the youngest but greatest of them, Jacob, popularly known as Rabeinu Tam. They all belonged to the outstanding group of French scholars of the subsequent generation, who founded the school of *tosafot*.[36] Another daughter, Miriam, was married to the talmudic commentator Judah ben Nathan (Rivan). They had a learned son, Yom Tov. A third daughter, whose name may have been Rachel, was married to (and divorced from) a Rabbi Eliezer and the mother of the noted scholar Shemaiah. Jochebed and Miriam each had a daughter of their own, Hannah and Alwina, respectively, who continued the family tradition of learning and were well versed in rabbinics. Hannah applied her knowledge to familiarize the women of the community with the commandments entrusted to them.[37] Alwina informed Rabbi Isaac ben Samuel (known as the Ri, 1120–1200), a contemporary Tosafist, in the ritual practices traditional in the house of Rashi, referring to her mother, Miriam, as her authority.[38] Jochebed's daughter-in-law, Miriam, the wife of Rabeinu Tam, was also a well-educated woman who at times decided questions that arose in her town and may have been in close, continuous contact with various rabbis to advise them of her questions and answers.[39]

---

ve-Em be-Yisrael (Tel Aviv: Masada, 1959), pp. 78–79; and Menachem Keddari, *Encyclopaedia Judaica*, vol. 13, p. 1559.

35. Quoted in Rabbi Zedekiah ha-Rofei (Italy, thirteenth century), *Shibolei ha-Leket* (Vilna, 1887), vol. 2, p. 53. Also quoted in Barukh Epstein, *Mekor Barukh* (Vilna, 1928), p. 1955.

36. Tosafot expanded on Rashi's commentary to the Babylonian Talmud, including divergent interpretations, queries and responsa, and halakhic rulings.

37. In correspondence between the nineteenth-century scholars S. D. Luzzatto and Leopold Zunz, Hannah is mentioned with regard to educating the women in her community to make the blessing on the Shabbat candles *after* having lit them. (Generally, one makes a blessing on a *mitzvah* prior to performing the act; in this case, if one were to make the blessing before lighting the candles, the blessing itself would usher in the Sabbath, and one would not be able to light the candles, it being considered a prohibited act on the Shabbat proper.) See *Otzar Nehmad*, ed. I. Blumenfeld (Vienna, 1856), p. 10. Regarding Hannah, see also Solomon Ashkenazi, *Dor Dor u-Minhagav*, p. 212.

38. Berliner, *Hayei ha-Yehudim be-Ashkenaz*, p. 8. He mistakenly refers to Alwina as the wife of, rather than the daughter of, Rabbi Judah ben Nathan.

39. Ashkenazi, *Dor Dor u-Minhagav*, p. 213. See also E. Urbach, *Ba'alei ha-Tosafot* (Jerusalem: Bialik Institute, 1980), p. 61. Also see *Teshuvot Maimoniyot*, "Hilkhot

A contemporary of the daughters of Rashi, Bella, sister of the French scholar Rabbi Isaac ben Menahem the Great (eleventh century), was a scholar in her own right. She educated the women of her town in points of law,[40] and many scholars accepted as authoritative the example of her religious practices.[41]

The wife[42] of the French Tosafist Rabbi Samuel ben Natronai (known as Rashbat; twelfth century) was considered so knowledgeable in Torah law that Rabbi Eliezer ben Joel ha-Levi (Ravyah), one of the outstanding Talmudists and decisors of that generation, cites her customs as proof in one of his halakhic rulings.[43] A thirteenth-century responsum of one of the Tosafists mentions her, as well as another Miriam who was a granddaughter of Rashi's (the author does not mention the name of her mother—could it have been Jochebed or perhaps Rachel? It may have even been his *daughter* Miriam, but due to a transcribing error she is mentioned as his granddaughter), in reference to a question on the ritual purging of utensils. He states, "Such was the custom in . . . the house of Miriam, the granddaughter of Shlomo (Rashi) . . . but Miriam, the wife of . . . Rabeinu Tam was more stringent," and concludes, "We can rely on the testimony of the daughters of the leaders of the generation."[44]

The question as to how these women gained their knowledge is best answered by surmising that, as girls, they studied at home with their fathers and brothers or with tutors. Evidence of girls' having studied privately can be found in the twelfth- or thirteenth-century work *Sefer Hasidim*, a collection of halakhic rulings, customs, and moral and mystical statements by Rabbi Judah he-Hasid. In advising as to who should teach Torah to girls, he permits the hiring of a teacher, albeit not a bachelor. The best recourse, suggests the author, is for "the father to teach his daughter or his wife."[45] Elsewhere, Rabbi Judah mentions the scriptural adeptness of "women in the land of Canaan [the

Ma'akhalot Asurot," para. 5, printed in modern editions of Maimonides' *Mishneh Torah*.

40. See, for example, the correspondence between S. D. Luzzatto and Leopold Zunz in *Otzar Nehmad*, ed. I. Blumenfeld, p. 10. See also Berliner, *Hayei a-Yehudim be-Ashkenaz*, p. 8.

41. See, for example, Rabbi Simha of Vitry (twelfth century), *Mahzor Vitry* (Berlin, 1889), para. 610, 635, and Rabbi Isaac of Vienna (twelfth–thirteenth centuries), *Or Zarua*, vol. 1, para. 363.

42. It is unfortunate, but a fact, that a number of women of the time are referred to as "the wife, daughter, or sister of" rather than by their given name.

43. Berliner, *Hayei ha-Yehudim be-Ashkenaz*, p. 8.

44. "Teshuvot Maimoniyot, Hilkhot Ma'akhalot Asurot," para. 5, in modern editions of Maimonides' *Mishneh Torah*.

45. Rabbi Judah he-Hasid, *Sefer Hasidim*, ed. R. Margolius (Jerusalem: Mossad Harav Kook, 1957), para. 313.

Slavic countries and Bohemia] who could recite all the consolations of Isaiah, *b'girsa* (by heart)."[46]

Testimony to young girls' and women's involvement in religious education comes to us also by means of a poignant eulogy delivered by the distinguished scholar Rabbi Eleazar ben Judah Rokeah of Worms (c. 1165–1230) for his wife, Dulce, and his two daughters following their brutal murders at the hands of the Crusaders in 1215. In it, he praises his wife for having taught the women prayers and for delivering lectures to them.[47] Of his thirteen-year-old daughter, Bellette, he says, "She learned all the prayers and psaltery from her mother . . . she sat to hear Torah from my mouth."[48] He bemoans the loss of his younger daughter, Hannah, who at the age of six "read the *Shema* each day, the first paragraph. . . ."[49] Let us proceed to examine the life of Dulce in greater detail.

Dulce: *Eyshet Hayil* (Woman of Valor), par Excellence

An interesting movement of this period is that of the *Hasidei Ashkenaz*, a pietistic group in Germany. One woman of this fascinating group in late twelfth and early thirteenth century was noted for her learning as well as her piety. Dulce (d. 1214), wife of the distinguished rabbi Eleazar Rokeah of Worms, together with her daughters, died a martyr's death at the time of the fourth Crusade. Memorialized in a touching eulogy by her husband (in which he paraphrases The Woman of Valor in Proverbs 31),[50] she presents as a diligent and dynamic woman who not only supported her husband and family but was also active in the rich religious and cultural life of the community, led the women in prayer, and may have given public discourses to women on the Sabbath.[51] In what may have been an introduction to the

---

46. Judah, he-Hasid, *Sefer Hasidim*, ed. J. Wistinezki (Frankfurt am Main: Wahrmann, 1924), para. 212. In the Margolius edition of *Sefer Hasidim*, this sentence is omitted.

47. Assaf, *Mekorot le- Toldot ha-Hinukh be-Yisrael*, vol. 4, p. 3.

48. Ibid., p. 4.

49. Ibid.

50. The eulogy was published in its entirety in the periodical *Shomer Zion ha-Ne'eman*, ed. J. Ettlinger (1849), p. 158b. It was subsequently reprinted in I. Kamelhar, *Rabbenu El'azar mi-Germiza: haRokeah* (Rzeszow, 1930), pp. 17–20. Excerpts are included in Assaf, *Mekorot le- Toldot ha-Hinukh be-Yisrael*, vol. 4, pp. 3–4. Excerpts also appear in L. Landshuth, *Amudei ha-Avodah* (Berlin, 1857), p. 25, in a slightly different version. This version is Moritz Steinschneider's, taken from the Oppenheim collection of manuscripts at Oxford.

51. See Abrahams, *Jewish Life in the Middle Ages*, p. 368; Solomon Ashkenazi, *Ha-Ishah ba-Asplakariah ha-Yehudit*, p. 132; Barukh haLevi Epstein, *Mekor Barukh*, p.

eulogy, Rabbi Eleazer writes, "Prior to the ghastly cataclysm, which left me utterly devastated, my wife had supported the family, making it possible for me to devote myself to my studies."[52] He also refers to her having bought parchment to write books.[53] In the eulogy, he proceeds to cite her myriad accomplishments:

> She was like the merchants' ships [allegory from Proverbs 31] to feed her husband, enabling him to study . . . she spun wool for *tzitzit* and parchment for *tefillin* and Torah scrolls. . . . She sewed 40 Torah scrolls . . . her hands mended the garments of the students and the torn books . . . her hands were outstretched to the poor . . . she engaged tutors for her children from her earnings. . . .[54]

Of her scholarship and dedication to religious study, Rabbi Eleazar writes:

> She purchased books with her earnings. . . .
> She sings psaltery and prayer, mouthing supplications,
> Reciting daily confession on behalf of all living souls.
> She recites the compounding of the *qetoret* (holy incense)[55]
>   and the Ten Commandments
> In all places she taught women [to] sing the praises.
> She organizes the regular services, morning and evening,
> Coming early to synagogue and staying the last. . . .
> She stands on her feet all day on Yom Kippur and prays. . . .
> She opens her mouth in wisdom and is knowledgeable in
>   all the prohibited and permitted.
> She sits on the Sabbath day and listens to her husband's lecture . . . (or
>   alternatively: On the Sabbath day she sits and expounds)[56]

1955; Nahida Remy, *Das Juedische Weib*, p. 140; and Roth, "Outstanding Jewish Women in Western Europe," op.cit., p. 152, all of whom state that Dulce gave public lectures on the Sabbath, although it is not stated explicitly in the text of the eulogy published by Ettlinger and Kamelhar. In the slightly different version of Steinschneider, it appears to be stated. See below.

52. Kamelhar, *Rabbenu El'azar mi-Germiza*, pp. 17–18. Also quoted in Bernfeld, *Sefer ha-Dema'ot*, vol. 3, p. 328.

53. Ibid. See also Landshuth, *Amudei ha-Avodah*, p. 25. Throughout the Middle Ages the practice of retaining a scribe to write scholarly works for scholars or the masses was widespread. The Jewish woman was known throughout the generations as a zealous supporter of this practice. We can assume from the statement "She bought parchment to write books" Dulce did similarly, but did not actually write the books.

54. Ibid., pp. 18–19. See also Assaf, *Mekorot le-Toldot ha-Hinukh*, vol. 4, pp. 3–4.

55. A prayer commemorating the sacrificial service in the Temple in Jerusalem.

56. Landshuth, p. 25, cites Steinschneider's version of the eulogy, copied from the Oppenheimer manuscripts at Oxford (ms. opp. 572, 8), and reads it as follows: "On the Sabbath day she sits and expounds [learned dissertations]. . . ." The popular printed

> Modest and wise . . . she performs every *mitzvah* with alacrity . . .
> She engaged tutors for her children from her earnings.
> She is knowledgeable and learned [in Torah] and serves her Creator
>   with happiness. . . .[57]

The eulogy portrays a woman whose love for Judaism and for learning propelled her to acquire books with her earnings, to participate in the manufacture of religious objects, to spend many hours in devotional service, and to lead the women of her community in prayer, aiding those who could not understand the Hebrew words. An expert in law, she shared her extensive knowledge with the women of her community.

Indirectly, too, Jewish women have contributed to the furtherance of Jewish learning by dispensing of their means to support scholars and enable them to write books. As just noted, Dulce may have been one such patroness of Jewish learning. In *Sefer Hasidim*,[58] we read of a generous husband who had presented his wife with a monetary gift to do with as she pleased. Her sole request was to purchase a religious book or to retain a scribe for the purpose of writing one, so that she could then lend it to scholars. Jewish women were reputed throughout the generations as staunch supporters of that cause.

Passing References to the Testimony of Women Concerning Jewish Law

Rabbis tell us of traditions passed down by women in that period. Rabbi Samuel of Falaise (d. 1280), teacher of Rabbi Meir (Maharam) of Rothenburg, decided a point of law according to the testimony of his mother-in-law, wife of Rabbi Abraham ben Hayim.[59] Similarly, Rabbi Hayim ben Isaac of Vienna, son of the author of the halakhic compendium *Or Zarua*, accepted his wife's customs as evidence of their permissibility.[60] We noted occurrences of this phenomenon among the female descendants of Rashi as well.

---

version (of Ettlinger, Kamelhar and Assaf) states somewhat differently, "On the Sabbath day she sits and listens to the lectures of her husband." We can assume that all those writers who speak of Dulce as having given lectures on the Sabbath, without citing their source, are relying on Landshuth's version of the Oxford manuscript, as copied by Steinschneider. On text-critical grounds one might argue that the version that has Dulce preaching on the Sabbath is the original one. It would seem that a scribe haphazardly copied this as if the rabbi himself were preaching, since he might have automatically assumed that a woman could not possibly be teaching Torah.

57. "Shomer Zion ha-Ne'eman," p. 158b; Kamelhar, *Rabbenu El'azar mi-Germiza*, p. 19; Assaf, *Mekorot le-Toldot ha-Hinukh*, vol. 4, p. 34.

58. Rabbi Judah he-Hasid, *Sefer Hasidim*, ed. Margolius, para. 874.

59. See Rabbi Isaac of Vienna, *Or Zarua*, vol. 2, para. 256.

60. Berliner, *Hayei ha-Yehudim be-Ashkenaz*, p. 8; cf. *The Responsa of Rabbi Hayim ben*

We can surmise that Jewish scholars in France and Germany in the twelfth and thirteenth centuries shared knowledge openly with their wives and daughters. The women were not part of the academies of their fathers or husbands but they were not kept in ignorance. We know of these women only through the writings of scholars; the average person did not write books. Nevertheless, we may surmise that women of the elite families in those centuries might have been conversant with the Hebrew language and important traditional texts.

FOURTEENTH AND FIFTEENTH CENTURIES

Prominent Women

The tradition of women from elite families who learned and even mastered talmudic texts reached a high point in the fourteenth century. The mother of Rabbi Mattityahu Treves who was the Rabbi of the Paris community in the years 1360–1385 and a descendent of Miriam, daughter of Rashi, was as learned "as a rabbi," in the opinion of the nineteenth-century scholar Leopold Zunz.[61] She could explain intricate passages in the Talmud and interpret difficult problems posed by the Tosafists.[62] The fourteenth-and fifteenth-century Spanish halakhist and Bible exegete Rabbi Simeon ben Tsedek Duran respected her opinion and quoted her in his responsa: "I have heard from my father . . . who recounted in the name of the *Rabbanit*, wife of Rabbi Joseph ben Johanan and mother of Rabbi Mattityahu. . . ."[63]

Another case of women from elite families in this period draws our attention. Rabbi Jacob ben Moses Moellin (known as Maharil, 1360–1427), the foremost Talmudist of his generation and head of the Jewish communities of Germany, Austria, and Bohemia, had two learned sisters, Bunlin and Simha, upon whose customs and opinions he relied, at times, when making halakhic decisions.[64] Redel, the daughter-in-law of Rabbi Israel Isserlin, pre-eminent rabbi of Germany in the fifteenth century and author of the book of

---

Isaac, para. 101, 146. A fellow countrywoman, Palora, wife of the late thirteenth–early fourteenth-century halakhist Rabbi Isaac of Duren, author of a code of dietary laws entitled *Sha'arei Dura* (Soslov, 1907), was known to have been very knowledgeable in talmudic studies. (See Ashkenazi, *Ha-Ishah ba-Asplakaria ha-Yehudit*, vol. 1, p. 128.)

61. Cited in Ashkenazi, *Dor Dor u'Minhagav*, p. 214. Zunz wrote a biography of Rashi in *Zeitschrift fuer die Wissenschaft des Judentums* (Berlin, 1825), which he edited.

62. See also Barukh Epstein, *Mekor Barukh*, p. 1955.

63. *Responsa of Shimon ben Tsedek Duran (Tashbetz)*, vol. 3 (Lemberg, 1891), para. 78.

64. See Jacob ben Moses Moellin, *Responsa of Maharil* (Cracow, 1881), no. 57 and 58, for example.

responsa *Terumot ha-Deshen* (Venice, 1519), was known to have studied Torah with as much diligence as men. In a book of responsa written by Rabbi Isserlin's disciple, there is mention of an elderly man by the name of Yudel Sofer as being her teacher.[65] Redel studied "in an area frequented by most members of the household, and this particular elder was married." Apparently she was very modest and took care not to remain alone with her tutor. Furthermore, she followed Rabbi Judah ha-Hasid's proscription that a woman should not be taught by an unmarried man.

And again we find another example of learned women from rabbinic families. A contemporary of Redel, Hendelin Cohen of Breslau, conducted a learned correspondence with Rabbi Israel Isserlin, following the death of her husband, concerning the talmudic laws of inheritance.[66] Hendelin's remarks to Rabbi Isserlin so impressed the Talmudist that he began his second responsum to her with the verse from Judges (5:24), "Above women in the tent shall she be blessed."[67]

What we see is a constant tradition in which women of elite families are schooled, albeit privately, in higher Jewish learning. In the latter part of the fifteenth century, many people turned to the learned wife of Rabbi Phinehas of Prague (distinguished disciple of Rabbi Israel Isserlin) for advice and instruction. In one of the responsa manuscripts located in the National Library in Jerusalem, we read as follows:

> Rabbi Pinhas of Prague had a wife of his youth who was as learned as she was pious, and he [Rabbi Phinehas] and many [others] solicited her frequently [for advice] because of her knowledge and good deeds. When she saw that she could not bear children, she induced him to divorce her, for the sake of Heaven, and marry another woman. And she herself raised the children of another woman. And almost every day the rabbi [Rabbi Phinehas] would go to the doorway of her home to consult with her and to take advice from her regarding the concerns of individuals and the community. And it was known that only because of the ban of Rabbi Gershom [forbidding polygamy] did he divorce her.[68]

Reminiscent of the daughter of Samuel ben Eli in Baghdad and of Asenath in Kurdistan is the following woman scholar. The great-granddaughter of Rabbi Mattityahu and ancestor of the scholarly Luria family, Miriam Spira Luria (Germany, fifteenth century) was undoubtedly the most outstanding of

---

65. Joseph ben Moses, *Leket Yosher*, ed. J. Friemann (Berlin, 1903), *Yoreh De'ah*, p. 37.

66. See Israel Isserlin, *Terumat ha-Deshen* (Venice, 1519), resp. 260, 261.

67. Ibid., resp. 261.

68. Quoted in Ashkenazi, *Ha-Ishah be-Asplakaria ha-Yehudit*, p. 121.

Torah scholars among Rashi's female descendants.[69] It was said of her that
she gave public lectures and expounded the Talmud and halakhic codes in a
yeshivah, before a company of distinguished students. Her modesty was such
that during her lectures she remained hidden from the eyes of her students by
a curtain, so that only her voice could be heard.[70] Rabbi Joseph Cohen Tzedek
writes in his *Dor Yesharim* about Miriam, "And the daughter of our Rav,
Shlomo Spira, the *rabbanit*, as learned as a man, her strength was in her Torah."
Rabbi Joseph Joselmann (fifteenth–sixteenth centuries), the greatest of Jewish
lobbyists of the Middle Ages, writes about her a number of times in his *Sefer
ha-Mikna*, telling how she taught Talmud and Jewish law for many years to
outstanding students.[71]

We also hear of women who were very accomplished but did not come
from elite families. Some were trained only by their father, and of others we
do not know how they received their knowledge. Two cases from the
fifteenth century are illustrative. Noted as a copyist was Frummet of Ahrweiler (a small town near Bonn). She transcribed the abbreviated code of the
Mordekhai[72] in the year 1430. This manuscript, which is still extant, is housed
in the National Library in Paris and reputedly demonstrates meticulous
accuracy and beauty of penmanship.[73] We also find that the first Christian
Hebraist to produce a Hebrew grammar, Conrad Pelliken (1478–1556), wrote
in his memoirs of his great love for the Hebrew language. He attributed his
motivation to study this language to an account that he heard, in 1489, while
still a lad, of a Jewish woman who easily won a debate with a professor of
religion by way of her masterful replies.[74]

The fourteenth and fifteenth centuries show us examples of women from
elite families but also indicate that others were able to achieve high levels of
education as well. It would not be fair to attribute all anonymous cases to elite
families without due warrant. That we hear of women apart from elite lineage
indicates that such women were probably self-educated. Although much of

---

69. See Abraham Epstein, *Kitvei Abraham Epstein*, ed. A. Habermann, vol. 1, pp.
312, 314, 315, 318, where Miriam's genealogy is outlined and we are informed of her
erudition.

70. Ibid., pp. 312, 313. See also Solomon Luria, *Responsa of Maharshal* (Lvov, 1859),
no. 30, and Kayserling, *Die Juedischen Frauen*, p. 138.

71. In private communication, Prof. Robert Werman of Hebrew University informed me of the citations in Tzedek and Joselmann's works.

72. A halakhic compendium written by Rabbi Mordekhai ben Hillel (thirteenth
century), following the tractates of the Talmud.

73. See Berliner, *Hayei ha-Yehudim be-Ashkenaz*, p. 9. See also M. Kayserling, *Die
Juedischen Frauen* p. 139.

74. See David Kaufman, *Ba-Meh Narim et Ruah ha-Dat be-Kerev Nasheinu u-Venoteinu?*
(Zhitomir, 1909), p. 9.

our evidence is found in the sources written by the elite, we cannot ignore the situation of the more ordinary woman.

Education and the Average Woman

If girls did not receive instruction in a formal school environment, there is evidence to indicate that a considerable number of girls were given at least a basic elementary religious education in their own home or in a group setting. Many Jews of the Middle Ages and post–Middle Ages were in the habit of writing wills, in Hebrew, in which they imparted instruction of an ethical and religious nature to their children and their descendants. Some of these wills are valuable for our purposes in that they portray parents who considered the religious education of their daughters a value of paramount importance, not to be trifled with. The *Testament of Eleazar of Mayence* is a case in point.[75] It is the work of the "simple and frank"[76] German Jew Eleazar ben Samuel of Mayence, who died in his native city on the first day of the Jewish New Year of 5117 (1357). One of the most significant features of this testament is the author's concern for the studies and occupations of his daughters. In fact, the author throughout insistently includes his daughters in his admonition to his children. Instructive are the following excerpts:

> These are the things which my sons and daughters shall do at my request. They shall go to the house of prayer morning and evening, and shall pay special regard to the *tefillah* [the "Eighteen Benedictions"] and the *Shema* [Deuteronomy 6:4]. So soon as the service is over, they shall occupy themselves a little with the Torah [the Pentateuch], the Psalms, or with works of charity. Their business must be conducted honestly, in their dealings with both Jew and Gentile. They must be gentle in their manners and prompt to accede to every honorable request. They must not talk more than is necessary; by this they will be saved from slander, falsehood, and frivolity. They shall give an exact tithe of all their possessions; they shall never turn away a poor man empty-handed. . . . My daughters must obey scrupulously the laws applying to women. . . . If they can by any means contrive it, my sons and daughters should live in communities, and not isolated from other Jews, so that their sons and daughters may learn the ways of Judaism. Even if compelled to solicit from others the money to pay a teacher, they must not let the young *of both sexes* [emphasis mine] go without instruction in Torah.[77]

---

75. This testament is included in Israel Abrahams, *Hebrew Ethical Wills*, vol. 2 (Philadelphia: Jewish Publication Society of America, 1926), pp. 207–218. Also quoted in part in Jacob Marcus, *The Jew in the Medieval World* (New York: Atheneum, 1975), pp. 314–316.

76. These are the words Marcus uses to describe the author of this testament. Abrahams describes him as an "average Jew."

77. Abrahams, *Hebrew Ethical Wills*, vol. 2, pp. 208–210.

Significantly, when the author had separate instructions for his sons or his daughters, he prefaced his remarks by stating to whom they are addressed. The following paragraph is included in a section he prefaced with "my sons and daughters" and not with "my sons," as we might have expected: "Every one of these good qualities becomes habitual with the one who studies the Torah. . . . For this gracious toil fix daily times, of long or short duration . . . week by week read at least the set portion with the commentary of Rashi."[78]

Eleazar of Mayence paints a vivid picture of girls immersed in the religious and educational life of the community: Daily attendance at synagogue, fixed periods of study, payment of teachers for religious instruction for both sons and daughters, scrupulous adherence to the laws pertaining to women and to correct ethical conduct on both personal and professional levels—all of which require knowledge of Jewish law—and residing in Jewish communities are goals that Eleazar hopes to be continually fostered in his daughters as well as his sons, so that "their sons and daughters [in turn] may learn the ways of Judaism." Most compelling is the fact that this is the testimony of an average Jew, which demonstrates that even ordinary girls, and not just exceptional ones, were given a basic Jewish education, albeit in a less formal manner than boys.

---

78. Ibid., p. 214.

7

A Historical Survey of Jewish Education for Women: Part IV— Christian Europe in the Sixteenth to Eighteenth Centuries

SIXTEENTH CENTURY

The Ascendancy of Eastern Europe

In the centuries following the Middle Ages, many Jews migrated from western to eastern Europe. In Poland, Lithuania, and Russia and in neighboring countries, where the vast majority of Jews settled, education continued to be the preoccupying interest of the Jewish communities. The educational institutions that grew up in eastern European countries were similar to those in other countries from which Jews came. At the beginning of the sixteenth century there was a huge wave of immigration from Bohemia and Germany into Poland, and the Jews who came from those countries brought with them their language—which developed into Yiddish—as well as their cultural and communal organizations.[1]

---

1. See, for example, S. M. Dubnow, *History of the Jews in Russia and Poland*, trans. I. Friedlaender (New York: Ktav, 1975), pp. 65f, 114f; Julius B. Maller, "The Role of Education in Jewish History," in *The Jews: Their History, Culture and Religion*, ed. Louis Finkelstein (Philadelphia: Jewish Publication Society of America, 1949), pp. 911–912; and Bernard D. Weinryb, *The Jews of Poland: A Social and Economic History of the Jewish Community in Poland from 1100 to 1800* (Philadelphia: Jewish Publication Society of America, 1973), pp. 32, 107f.

In the autonomous Jewish communities of eastern Europe, elementary and secondary education were centered in the *hadarim*, while higher education was fostered in the *yeshivot*. Attendance at the *heder* was compulsory for all children from six to thirteen years of age. The subjects of instruction at these schools were the Bible in the original, accompanied by a translation into the Judeo-German vernacular, and the easier treatises of the Talmud with commentaries. Secular education, with the exception of basic arithmetic, was generally not taught. The establishment of these *hadarim* was left to private initiative, every Jewish elementary-level teacher (*melamed*) being allowed to open a *heder* for boys and to receive from their parents compensation for his labors. Only the *hadarim* for poor children or for orphans, the so-called *Talmud Torahs*, were maintained by the community from public funds. Both the *heder* and the *Talmud Torah* were under the supervision of the community authorities (the *Kahal*), who regulated the policies and curricula of the schools. The higher talmudic school or college—the *yeshivah*—under the care of the *Kahal* and the rabbis, provided a complete religious and juridical education based on the Talmud and the rabbinical codes of law, developing both the lay scholar and the learned rabbi.[2] "To the extent that the Pentateuch, *Mishnah*, and, especially, Talmud and the codes were the means of regulating the life of the Jewish people," states Maller, "their study had functional value, preparing its students for life in the Jewish community."[3] Indeed, the value placed on Jewish education was so high that the seventeenth-century Polish Jewish chronicler Nathan Hannover wrote: "In no country was the study of the Torah so widespread among the Jews as in the Kingdom of Poland. . . . Every Jewish community supported college students. . . . There was scarcely a house in the whole of Poland where the Torah was not studied, or where [at least one member of the family] was not an expert in Jewish learning. . . ."[4]

---

2. See Dubnow, *History of the Jews in Russia and Poland*, pp. 114–115, and Maller, "The Role of Education in Jewish History," pp. 911–912.

3. Maller, "The Role of Education in Jewish History," p. 912.

4. Nathan Hannover, *Yeven Metzula* (1653), toward the end. Hannover's panegyric to Polish-Jewish school life appears also in Simha Assaf, *Mekorot le-Toldot ha-Hinukh be-Yisrael*, vol. 1 (Tel Aviv: Dvir, 1930), pp. 110–112; appears in English in Dubnow, *The Jews in Russia and Poland*, pp. 116–119. The interested reader may wish to read the rest of Hannover's description for elaboration. Not all were laudatory of prevailing educational patterns in Poland. Rabbi Yehuda Loew of Prague (Maharal, 1525–1609) severely criticized the elementary and *yeshivah* programs and methods of study (see Assaf, *Mekorot*, vol. 1, pp. 45f, for excerpts of Rabbi Loew's writings on the subject). Hannover's contemporary, Solomon Ephraim of Lenchitza, also disparaged the methods of instruction then in vogue at the *yeshivot*, in his work *Amudei Shesh* (ed. Lemberg, 1865), pp. 18b, 61b. For elaboration on the state of education in eastern Europe in the sixteenth–eighteenth centuries, see also Jacob Katz, *Tradition and Crisis* (New York: Schocken, 1971), pp. 183–198; Nisson E. Shulman, *Authority and Commu-*

Though the seventeenth century saw a decline of Jewish schools and of Jewish learning, owing to persecutions, the importance of learning remained undiminished in Jewish life in the cities and villages of eastern Europe.[5]

Education of girls remained very limited in eastern Europe, as in other geographical locals and periods. Socially, eastern European women of this period (as their counterparts in other regions) were emerging from the restricted circle of home life.[6] Women shared the burden of making a living and in some cases were the main bearers of this burden. They were also officially regarded as partners in property ownership. In Silesia and Poland, we find Jewish women as heads of households or businesses and as owners of houses.[7] The Polish halakhic authority, Joseph ben Mordekhai Gershon ha-Kohen Katz (1510–1591), in his book of responsa, reports an instance of a woman's buying a house in her own name.[8] He also mentions the case of a young man's liquidating his own business to join in partnership with his betrothed. When the engagement was canceled he claimed compensation from her for the loss sustained by him through the venture.[9] Business undertakings often necessitated traveling the country, which, for women especially, was fraught with danger. The responsa of the period refer to women who were taken captive by Tartars.[10] Frequent mention of such cases justifies the assumption that these journeys were undertaken by women in connection with commerce and trade.[11]

Some Jewish women – wives as well as widows of tax collectors, a physician, and businessmen – had connections in the king's court, from which they

nity: *Polish Jewry in the Sixteenth Century* (Hoboken, NJ: Ktav, 1986), pp. 82–90; and Moses A. Shulvass, *Jewish Culture in Eastern Europe* (New York: Ktav, 1975). For elaboration on Jewish education in Russia following the years of the partition of Poland (1772), when many Jewish communities were transferred from Polish to Russian rule, see Isaac Levitats, *The Jewish Community in Russia, 1772–1844* (New York: Octagon, 1970), pp. 188–197.

5. For elaboration, see Shulvass, *Jewish Culture in Eastern Europe*, pp. 174–176.

6. See, for example, Myer S. Lew, *The Jews of Poland* (London: Edward Goldston, 1944), pp. 121–124; Nisson Shulman, *Authority and Community*, pp. 22–25; and B. Weinryb, *The Jews of Poland*, pp. 98–99. See also Charlotte Baum, "What Made Yetta Work? The Economic Role of Eastern European Jewish Women in the Family," *Response* 7:2 (Summer 1973):32–38.

7. See Shulman, *Authority and Community*, p. 23, and Weinryb, *The Jews of Poland*, p. 99.

8. Joseph Katz, *She'erit Yosef* (Cracow, 1893), resp. 75. Cf. Lew, *The Jews of Poland*, p. 122.

9. Katz, *She'erit Yosef*, resp. 16.

10. Ibid., resp. 72, 77. Cf. Lew, *The Jews of Poland*, p. 123, and Shulman, *Authority and Community*, pp. 22–23.

11. See Lew, *The Jews of Poland*, p. 123, and Shulman, *Authority and Community*, p. 22.

received various privileges and exemptions from taxes.[12] Poor women, too, were active as street vendors or as producers of various articles of clothing. Rabbi Solomon Luria (Maharshal), the sixteenth-century halakhic decisor and Talmudist, sums up the status of women of his time: "Our women now conduct business in the house [and] represent the husband."[13]

In the charitable work of the Polish Jewish communities, women took a share in the life of the community and greatly assisted the communal leaders. The Statute of the Jewish community of Cracow reads, "Thus shall the pious women act: they shall collect money for charitable purposes, for dowering the bride, for poor women in confinement, etc."[14]

That the high standards of religious life were shared and fostered by women the sources amply attest.[15] From Luria we learn that it was due to the Jewish women in Poland that the custom of abstaining from meat during the first nine days of the Hebrew month of Ab (in commemoration of the destruction of the Temple in Jerusalem) was extended to the whole three weeks of national mourning. Rabbi Luria tells us that he did not approve of this; nevertheless it is testimony to the religious fervor of the women.[16] Rabbi Benjamin Aaron Ben Abraham Slonik, sixteenth- and early seventeenth-century Polish rabbi, tells of communities where, as a precautionary measure, women had acted more strictly than the law requires.[17] Indeed, Rabbi Slonik greatly encouraged women's desire for pious expression, particularly in the performance of time-bound laws from which women are exempt, inasmuch as it was indicative "of the acceptance of the yoke of the kingdom of heaven [on the part of the women], and [because] it gives spiritual satisfaction to them."[18] There were isolated cases of infidelity, however,[19] and slander seems to have been a common failing among women.[20]

---

12. Weinryb, *The Jews of Poland*, p. 99. An example of one such court Jewess was Rachel (or Rashka, fifteenth century), mother-in-law of Rabbi Jacob Polak, a pioneer of rabbinic learning in Poland. She was granted an honorary position at the king's court and was the only Jewish person to receive the right to own a house in Cracow after the expulsion of Jews in 1495. For elaboration of her activities, see Weinryb, p. 99.

13. Solomon Luria, *Responsa of Maharshal*, para. 99.

14. Quoted in Lew, *The Jews of Poland*, p. 122. Cf. Shealtiel Isaac Graeber, *Otzar ha-Sifrut*, vol. 4 (Cracow, from 1887), p. 588.

15. See, for example, Rabbi Moses Isserles, *Responsa of Rema* (Warsaw, 1883), resp. 2. Cf. Lew, *The Jews of Poland*, p. 121. Also see Shulman, *Authority and Community*, pp. 23–24, for elaboration.

16. Solomon Luria, *Responsa of Maharshal*, resp. 54.

17. Benjamin Slonik, *Responsa* (Vilna, 1894), resp. 5. Cf. Shulman, *Authority and Community*, pp. 23–24, 105–106.

18. Benjamin Slonik, *Responsa*, no. 62. Cf. Shulman, *Authority and Community*, pp. 24–25, 147–148, for the full text of Rabbi Slonik's responsum.

19. Moses Isserles, *Responsa of Rema*, no. 12; Luria, *Responsa*, no. 33.

20. Isserles, *Responsa*, no. 45; Luria, *Responsa*, nos. 12, 28, 101.

The towering value placed on education in the Jewish communities of eastern Europe did not extend itself to the formal religious education of women. Girls remained outside the school, their instruction not being considered obligatory according to Jewish law. According to Solomon Dubnow, historian of Russian and Polish Jewish life, no *hadarim* for girls are mentioned in any of the documents of the time,[21] although private instruction was given to girls in some affluent families.[22] The girls were taught at home to read the prayers in Hebrew,[23] but they were seldom instructed in the Hebrew language, so that the majority of women had but an imperfect notion of the meaning of the prayers, in the original. Consequently, the women began in the sixteenth and seventeenth centuries to use the translations of the prayers in the Jewish vernacular, the so-called Judisch-Deutsch.[24] No doubt, some girls, not tutored formally, managed on their own to acquire reading skill at home, where book learning was highly regarded and assiduously practiced.

Prominent Jewish Women in the Sixteenth Century

As in previous centuries, women of elite rabbinic families demonstrate levels of learning that would have exceeded those of many men. That women of distinction were then to be found in eastern and central Europe indicates that the rabbinic families that were now established there continued the tradition of raising knowledgeable daughters. There are a number of well-known cases of such women in the sixteenth century. This section spans the careers of those women.

Pearl Reich Loew was the wife of the renowned Talmudist, moralist, and mathematician Rabbi Judah ben Bezalel Loew (Maharal, 1512–1609) of Prague. Hers is the story of a woman who was determined to prove that the intensive Torah education of a woman could only but enhance the relationship between husband and wife and add a dimension of mutual respect and support in the marriage.[25]

Pearl Loew: Torah Partner in Marriage

When Pearl Reich was but a child of six, she became affianced to a brilliant young lad of ten, Judah ben Bezalel Loew. Realizing his great genius, she

21. Dubnow, *The Jews in Russia and Poland*, p. 121.

22. E. Bortinker, *Encyclopaedia Judaica*, vol. 6, p. 414.

23. Shulman, *Authority and Community*, p. 22.

24. Ibid., p. 121. See also Lew, *The Jews of Poland*, p. 121.

25. Information on Pearl Loew was gleaned from Yosef Yitzhak Schneerson, *Lubavitcher Rabbi's Memoirs*, trans. N. Mindel, vol. 2 (Brooklyn: Kehot Publication Society, 1956), pp. 180f.

decided to study assiduously, so that he would never have cause to be ashamed of her. She studied in secret until the age of fourteen, when Judah returned from studying at the *yeshivah*. He was so amazed and delighted to discover the depth of his fiancée's Torah scholarship that he prepared a special curriculum for her to study during the next four or five years, during which he studied at another *yeshivah*.[26]

Due to economic and other factors, the couple did not marry until Judah was thirty-two and Pearl was twenty-eight. Judah was astonished to discover the extent of Pearl's progress in Torah study during the twelve years since he had last met with her. She had become an accomplished Torah scholar. After a period of economic hardship, during which Pearl was the breadwinner in order to allow her husband the opportunity to study undisturbed, their livelihood improved, and Pearl could feel free to sit and study. Every day she had a lesson with her husband, who considered her his equal in scholarship. They studied Talmud together, as well as ethics and metaphysics. Pearl used to say that since she was eight years old, never a day passed when she did not spend at least five hours studying Torah. When Rabbi Judah became renowned and would receive halakhic queries from many communities, Pearl would read these letters to him and write out his replies. She arranged and redacted all twenty-four of her husband's literary works. It is told that in no fewer than eight places, she found errors in her husband's writings, where he had misquoted the talmudic sages, Rashi, or the Tosafists. As a result, the Maharal held his wife in high esteem, applying to her the verse from Proverbs 31:30: "Many women have done valiantly, but you have surpassed them all."[27]

Let us now proceed to consider the achievements of another learned woman, Bella Falk, wife of the Polish *yeshivah* head and halakhist Rabbi Joshua Falk (c. 1555–1614).

Bella Falk: "The Splendor, Glory, and Crown of Her Generation"

A biographical vignette of Bella Falk's life is vividly etched by her son, Rabbi Joseph Yuzpa, in the introduction he wrote to his father's work *Derishah*,[28] one part of a commentary on the comprehensive halakhic code, *Tur*. Bella Falk was the only daughter of Israel Edels, a wealthy philanthropist and the communal leader of Lemberg. Her father would have secured the gratification of his daughter's every whim, but Bella rejected worldly pleasures, preferring

---

26. Ibid., p. 183.

27. Ibid., pp. 192–194.

28. See the introduction to *Derishah* on *Tur, Yoreh De'ah*, part 2. All subsequent quotations are from this source.

instead to immerse herself in prayer and study. She was a vegetarian all her life and ate simply and sparingly, merely tasting the delicacies she prepared in honor of the Sabbath before distributing them to the poor. Each day she rose hours before sunrise to pour out her heart in prayer before God. She had in her possession the key to the synagogue's women's gallery, for she was always the first to enter and the last to leave. After completing her prayers, she would study the biblical portion of the week along with the commentary of Rashi as well as the other commentaries. Her son writes of the gratification experienced by the many students of Rabbi Falk who had the opportunity of sharing a dinner with the learned couple and who would witness Bella's engaging in learned discussions with her husband during the meal. Her original commentaries were, in her son's words, "sweeter than honey," and her knowledge of laws pertaining to women was equal to that of the great rabbis of her generation.

Bella also rendered decisions on Jewish law. One of her most noteworthy contributions to *Halakhah* concerned the ritual kindling of candles on holiday evenings. She pointed out that when the candles are lit on festivals, the benediction should be recited before the candles are lit, a procedure that is reversed on the Sabbath, when it is forbidden to light the candles after the blessing has been uttered. (Her contemporaries were mistakenly accustomed to light festival candles in much the same manner as they did the Sabbath candles.) Furthermore, she noted that on the eve of the second festival day, it is forbidden to light the candles until the stars appear, for one may not begin preparations for the second day while it is still the first day; however, on the eve of the first day of the holidays, candles should be lit punctually just as on the Sabbath (again, a practice in which Jewish women were [and still are] deficient). Two centuries later, the distinguished halakhic authority Rabbi Ezekiel Landau of Prague (known as the *Noda be-Yehudah*) was to uphold Bella Falk's decision on this matter, referring to her as one whose "heart was full of wisdom."[29] This is just one example, wrote her son, of Bella's deep sincerity and dedication to comprehending fully the ways and means of the Torah.

When she was not occupied with prayers or studies, Bella visited the sick and comforted the mourners. She worked late into the evening weaving fringes and affixing them to prayer shawls, and preparing the parchments on which Torah scrolls would be written. She devoted herself to the spiritual and material upbringing of her children and grandchildren. After her husband's death, she journeyed to and throughout the Holy Land, settling in Jerusalem.

---

29. M. Kayserling, *Die Juedischen Frauen in der Geschichte, Literatur, und Kunst* (Leipzig, 1879), pp. 177–178. See also Batya Bromberg's article on Bella Falk, "Nashim Mehadshot Dinim ba-Halakhah," *Sinai* 59 (1966): 248–250; for Rabbi Landau's comment, see p. 249.

She passed away at the age of fifty-eight and was buried with great honor in Jerusalem. Her son acclaimed her as "the splendor, glory, and crown of all the people of her generation, a model of splendor for all daughters of Israel."

A fellow countrywoman of Bella Falk was Rebecca Sirkes, daughter of a prominent talmudic scholar of Poland, Rabbi Joel Sirkes (1561–1640). Rebecca was an accomplished scholar in Bible who astounded her elders, even while yet a youngster, with her erudition and brilliance.[30] Dinah Wahl, her contemporary, was so familiar with the Talmud that she could quote certain passages verbatim, when necessary, for example, as she did when she proposed to her future husband, the Polish rabbi Joshua Hoeschel of Cracow (1578–1648), using a play on words on a talmudic dictum.[31]

Our study of prominent women throughout the centuries is based on information caught by happenstance in the writings of others. We might well assume that the more of these women we know about, the more there were.

Religious Literature for Women

General Background

If intensive scholarship was not part of the popular culture for women, spiritual and devotional works were nonetheless reaching the larger masses. The late Middle Ages witnessed the development of a new literary language in the form of a mixture of German and Hebrew and other languages, ultimately known as Yiddish.[32] In the course of time, Yiddish became not

---

30. It is related that once, at a Sabbath meal, during which Rabbi Sirkes and a choice group of students were engaged in a discussion of Torah matters, one of the students posed a question regarding Maimonides' instructions to a scribe when printing a ten-or-more-letter word in a Torah scroll (Maimonides, *Mishneh Torah*, Laws of a Torah Scroll 7:6). Where did the Torah contain a ten-letter word? mused the student. Rabbi Sirkes, aware of his young daughter's thorough knowledge of Scriptures, challenged the 12-year-old Rebecca to think of a word containing ten letters or more that appears in the Torah (the Five Books of Moses). Rebecca responded with the assertion that the Torah contained no such word but that the Prophets contained a ten-letter word, citing the source and word (see Joshua 12:21). She reflected for a moment and then gave an example of an eleven-letter word contained in the Book of Esther (9:3) to the astonishment of the assembly of learned gentlemen. See *Arim ve-Immahot be-Yisrael*, ed. J. L. Fishman, vol. 1 (Jerusalem: Mossad Harav Kook, 1948), p. 18.

31. For elaboration, see Kayserling, *Die Juedischen Frauen*, pp. 139–140. Also see Aryeh L. Lifschitz, *Avot Atarah la-Banim* (Warsaw, 1927), p. 156, and Barukh Epstein, *Mekor Barukh*, p. 1956.

32. See *Encyclopaedia Judaica*, vol. 11, p. 356, and Israel Zinberg, *A History of Jewish Literature*, vol. 7, chap. 5 (Cleveland: Press of the Case Western Reserve University,

only the lingua franca of northern and eastern European Jewry but also the language in which a great and creative literature, which mirrored the folk spirit, was written. Emerging sometime during the thirteenth century, literary Yiddish was at first the medium of a secular literature that brought German popular romances, songs, and entertainment forms to the Jewish community. Subsequently acquiring Jewish character and themes, Yiddish literature was designed initially for women and less-educated men whose Hebrew was poor. Nevertheless, the language became a medium for everyone and, in consequence, not only was a religious and pietistic literature produced but, in the modern era, a major secular literature as well. Inasmuch as Yiddish has always been written in Hebrew characters, its connection with the Hebrew language was maintained, and as the pronunciation of words taken from German became modified, the original connection with German became more remote.

One salient fact about early Yiddish literature is that it was written principally for women, and, frequently, under their direct patronage. Accordingly, Yiddish works centered on subjects that were amusing or instructive for women. Most of the material was translated from Hebrew or the European languages and was modified to suit the taste of the feminine audience. Yiddish writing, therefore, usually took the form of tales or romances, and in the religious field, of translations of the Bible (some translations appeared in German proper), the prayer book, petitional prayers entitled *tehinnot*, Apocryphal books, and ethical and moralistic literature. Special books emphasizing women's religious duties and status were written or compiled.[33] Legal and philosophical literature were generally not translated.

Often changed to fit the "feminine temperament," Yiddish translations of the *tehinnot*, for example, portray God as a loving father rather than as a stern judge, emphasize the merit of the matriarchs rather than that of the patriarchs, and define rewards in terms of pious and virtuous children. It is significant to note that the ranks of the authors of works of this kind included a considerable number of women – some of whom will be noted herewith and in subsequent sections – a phenomenon rare in Hebrew writing. Zinberg is of the opinion that the cradle of the *tehinnot* stood at the *firzogerins* who used to read or sing prayers and supplications in the vernacular before the women in the synagogue.[34] In the view of Chava Weissler, contemporary scholar of Yiddish devotional literature, the *tehinnot* literature reveals an intensely religious life and a richly imagined spiritual world. Her survey of the many occasions on

---

1972–1978), from which much of the following information is excerpted.

33. For elaboration, see Zinberg, *A History of Jewish Literature*, vol. 7, chap. 5, who discusses women's literature and folk literature. See also Arthur Posner, "Literature for Jewish Women in Medieval and Later Times," *The Jewish Library: Women*, ed. Leo Jung (London and New York: Soncino Press, 1970), pp. 63–83.

34. Zinberg, *A History of Jewish Literature*, vol. 7, p. 251.

which women recited *tehinnot* indicates the important religious events of women's lives and, in comparison with the occasions for Hebrew prayers, how men's and women's spiritual concerns differed. Furthermore, her analysis of the content of the *tehinnot* affords us with a picture of how women understood their religious activity.[35]

The Writings of Rebecca Tiktiner: Educator of Women

Beginning with the sixteenth century, women applied their knowledge to educating their own sex by making available to them in the vernacular the important books and tracts on Jewish religious and ethical practice. Rebecca Tiktiner achieved prominence as a scholar, preacher, and lyricist throughout Judeo-German society.[36] Known as a leading educator in her native city of Prague, which had a large Jewish community of German origin, she instructed young women in talmudic and midrashic literature, as well as in rituals and Jewish ethics, and gained special distinction by her writings for women. She translated into Yiddish-Deutsch the eleventh-century ethical-philosophical classic *Hovot ha-Levavot* (*The Duties of the Heart*), by Rabbi Bahya ibn Pakuda. Her poetic attempts included a lyrical epic of a philosophical nature for the festival of Simhat Torah (entitled *Simhat Torah Lied*, Prague, n.d.),[37] as well as a liturgical poem in Hebrew as an introduction to a book. Her major work, *Maineket Rivkah* (*The Nurse of Rebecca*, Prague, 1609; Cracow, 1618), published in the Yiddish-Deutsch dialect, is an engrossing contribution to ethics and *Halakhah*.[38] It contains her Sabbath discourses, poems in Hebrew and Yiddish, and her own responsa related to women's halakhic problems.

The printer mentions in the introduction that the book proves "that a woman can also compose a work of ethics and offer good interpretations as well as many a man."[39] He praises Tiktiner's exegetical prowess, noting that such enterprises were unheard-of for women in his time.

The book is divided into seven "gates," the largest of which is the fifth,

---

35. For a survey and analysis of *tehinnot* literature, see Chava Weissler, "The Traditional Piety of Ashkenazic Women," in *Jewish Spirituality*, ed. Arthur Green, vol. 2 (London: Routledge & Kegan Paul, 1987), pp. 245–275. See also her article, "For Women and for Men Who Are Like Women: The Construction of Gender in Yiddish Devotional Literature," *Journal of Feminist Studies in Religion* 5:2 (Fall 1989): 7–24.

36. See Assaf, *Mekorot*, vol. 4, pp. 45–46. See also Ashkenazi, *Dor Dor u-Minhagav*, pp. 217–218.

37. For excerpts, see Zinberg, *A History of Jewish Literature*, vol. 7, p. 285. Also see Henry and Taitz, *Written out of History*, p. 100, for the English translation.

38. This work is included among the booklists in Halperin's *Seder ha-Dorot* (Warsaw, 1881), "She'mot ha-Sefarim," p. 69.

39. See Henry and Taitz, *Written out of History*, p. 94.

devoted entirely to the upbringing and education of children. Rebecca Tiktiner's comments on the education of boys and girls and the contribution of the mother to their education are instructive. Regarding boys' education, she writes:

> If she [the mother] has growing sons, she should sit in the home and attend to their prayers and benedictions, and not rely on the *Rebbe* [the teacher of boys]. Also the lessons which a mother studies with her son are far more successful than what he acquires from another, as we see from the verse [Proverbs 1:8] "Hearken, my child, to the discipline of your father, and do not forsake the Torah teachings of your mother." The Gemara questions: "Why does it state the Torah teachings of your mother, and the discipline of your father?" It is because the father is occupied with his business and is seldom at home, and if he sees his son misbehaving he rebukes and disciplines him. But the mother, who is generally at home, can supervise her children and can do much benefit. She can learn [Torah] with them and can scrutinize their every action and word, as the Torah states [Deuteronomy 6:7]: "Teach them [the words of Torah] diligently to your children and speak of them while you sit in your home, etc." . . . that is to say, that you shall sit near your sons and you shall speak with them words of Torah and not idle chatter. . . . [The verse concludes] "and you shall speak of them when you retire . . ." that is to say, when your children lie down to sleep you tell them stories from the Torah and from the *Gemara*. . . .[40]

It is interesting to note Rebecca Tiktiner's total confidence in the ability of a Jewish woman to transmit the teachings of Torah to her sons. Moreover, her faith in the mother supersedes her confidence in the capability of both the *Rebbe* as well as the father to do a satisfactory job in this regard. She takes the verse in Deuteronomy, which has clearly been halakhically interpreted as being the obligation of the father, and sees it as having personal relevance to women. She regards the verse in Proverbs as an obvious indication of where the educational duties of the woman lie. Finally, her remarks clearly imply the expectation of a moderate level of religious education on the part of women of her time. This can be taken as another indication that if women were not instructed formally, they acquired in some informal way, through either parents, tutors, or lecturers such as she, the rudiments of Jewish knowledge.

Regarding the education of girls, interestingly, although she herself was a very learned woman, she does not make formal study the main objective for girls. Rather, she echoes the refrain of all the generations that regarded the inculcation of ethics and morality as being the principal goal in girls' education: to teach them good character traits and modest behavior. Industriousness is also encouraged by her. She uses as models the assiduous activity of the biblical Rebecca, who despite her wealth, drew water and fed all the camels

---

40. Quoted in Assaf, *Mekorot*, vol. 4, pp. 45–46.

personally, as well as the Woman of Valor portrayed by King Solomon. Tiktiner applies an original interpretation to the rabbinic adage "A daughter born first is a good sign for the sons"[41]: "This is because she can help the mother in the education of the children that will come afterward; therefore every woman should make an effort to educate her daughter in ethical behavior."[42] The role of the mother and daughter as enabler is one that Rebecca Tiktiner espoused without reservation.

Rebecca Tiktiner's activities as author, lyricist, translator, and lecturer so inspired the famed Christian Hebraist Johann Christophe Wagenseil (1633–1705) that he commended her highly in his Latin translation of the mishnaic tractate *Sotah* (Altdorf, 1675).[43] In 1719, George Zeltner, a German professor and missionary, wrote a special Latin essay on this remarkable sixteenth-century woman. He describes her as "a rather rare example of learned women in the Jewish nation."[44]

Translations and Other Works Used by Women

The foregoing examples of sixteenth-century learned women from elite families can now be placed within the larger framework of devotional and traditional works to which women had access. For the most part, women did not understand Hebrew, the language of literary, scholarly discourse. Translations of traditional books helped open the door for them to the world of Jewish learning.

The first printed Yiddish translation of the Pentateuch and *Haftarot* (readings from the Prophets) was by a convert to Christianity, Michael Adam, in 1544. In 1560, Judah Leib Bresch appended an abbreviated version of the Rashi commentary to the Adam translation. Several editions of the *Teutsch-Humash* (translated Pentateuch) appeared in the subsequent centuries in which aggadic and interpretive embellishments were mixed with the text. Yiddish translations of biblical books other than the Pentateuch also appeared, including a translation of the Psalms (1545); of Proverbs (1582); and of Isaiah, together with an abridged version of David Kimhi (Radak)'s commentary (1586). Similarly, German translations of biblical books made their appearances, the first in 1625. The avowed purpose of these translations was to provide both entertainment and enrichment for women and for men who could not under-

---

41. *Bava Batra* 141a.

42. Quoted in Assaf, *Mekorot*, vol. 4, p. 46.

43. Zinberg, *A History of Jewish Literature*, vol. 7, p. 241. Already in Wagenseil's time, Rebecca Tiktiner's book *Meineket Rivkah* had become extremely rare (see Zinberg, p. 242). A burnt copy is in the Rare Book Room of the Jewish Theological Seminary in New York City.

44. Ibid. Also see Henry and Taitz, *Written out of History*, p. 95.

stand Hebrew and to wean them away from reading German romances and from card playing. Thus, for example, Judah Leib Bresch, in the introduction to his Yiddish translation of the Pentateuch *Haftarot* and the Scrolls (Basle, 1583), stated that he wanted women to be able to appreciate the true meaning of the text so they would no longer be moved to turn to "silly, useless German tales."[45] Similarly, Rabbi Yonah Landsofer of Prague (1678–1712) wrote in his will that the reading of biblical works published in German be encouraged. "It is necessary for them [the women] to read the text in translation in order to comprehend the meanings and truths contained therein."[46]

During the approach of the seventeenth century and into that century, another type of literature designed for use by women appeared, which was devoted to ethical instruction. In 1577, Benjamin ben Aaron's *Frauen Buechlein* (*Ladies' Book*) first appeared and was translated into Yiddish in 1610. Other popular ethical works, either original or translated from the Hebrew, that appeared were the classic *Maase-Buch* by Asher Anshel (1602), consisting of tales from aggadic literature; the thirteenth-century work *Sefer Hasidim*; and *Brantspiegel*, by Moses Henochs of Prague (1602).[47] Another such work was Rabbi Benjamin Slonik's *Seder Mitzvot Nashim, Eyn Schoen Frauenbuechlein*, a very popular Yiddish book printed three times during the author's lifetime (Cracow, 1577, 1585; Basle, 1602) and subsequently translated into Italian by Jacob Heilbronn. The ostensible purpose of that work was to teach the laws specifically applicable to women, but it included much more, being a complete, moralistic work that addressed itself to the lifetime of a woman and her relationships to God, her family, her community, her possessions. It discusses manners and morals; the ritual laws pertaining to food; modesty; rearing children; the love between husband and wife; happiness in marriage; and the role of woman in society. It has a section addressed to the husband as well. The book contains many inspirational passages, including a vision of messianic times and how women can bring about the ultimate redemption.[48]

At the end of the seventeenth century and continuing well into the eighteenth century, the following works were produced: *Lev Tov*, by Isaac ben Eliakim of Posen (Amsterdam, 1670); *Kav ha-Yashar* (*The Straight Line*), by

---

45. See Breyer, *The Jewish Woman in Rabbinic Literature*, vol. 2, p. 115. See also Isadore Fishman, *The History of Jewish Education in Central Europe (16th to 18th Centuries)* (London: Edward Goldston, 1944), p. 119. For an excerpt from Bresch's introduction, see Zinberg, *A History of Jewish Literature*, vol. 7, pp. 120–121, and Assaf, *Mekorot*, vol. 1, p. 40. Bresch's work was also written for men who were not proficient in Hebrew, as he states in his introduction.

46. Quoted by Assaf in *Mekorot le-Toldot ha-Hinukh be-Israel*, vol. 1, p. 180. See also Fishman, *The History of Jewish Education in Central Europe*, p. 120.

47. For excerpts, see Assaf, *Mekorot*, vol. 1, pp. 54–60.

48. See Shulman, *Authority and Community*, p. 191.

Rabbi Zvi Hirsch Kaidenover of Frankfurt (1705); *Sefer ha-Midot* (*The Book of Good Deeds*), dedicated to a Frau Murada of Gunsberg (eighteenth century); and the translation of the classic fourteenth-century ethical work *Menorat ha-Maor* (*The Luminous Candlestick*), by Rabbi Isaac Abohab. The ethical works all note in their prefaces that they were intended for use by young girls and women.[49] We can now see that the spread of popular works that were accessible to women gave impetus for them to become acquainted with the classics of Jewish literature. In later centuries, this line can be followed in greater detail.

The work that had strongest impact on women in the seventeenth century was the *Ze'enah u-Re'enah*, by Jacob Ashkenazi (1620).[50] This work contained biblical and later stories; aggadic and midrashic homilies; and comments on Jewish life, customs, and morals, as told by a remarkable raconteur. The following section examines more closely the development of this literature.

SEVENTEENTH CENTURY

Women Scholars

The seventeenth century witnessed the proliferation of women who achieved proficiency in their Jewish learning. A woman who attained a height of scholarship beyond that of many men and close to the level of the most learned men of her generation was a descendant of Pearl Loew – Hava Bacharach of Prague – who became an authority on the Bible and *Midrash*. Her level of erudition attests to the abilities of women to excel in learning, if given the opportunities to do so. Hava was fortunate to have received such opportunities, growing up in a rich intellectual environment that encouraged her academic achievements in the field of Torah.

Hava Bacharach: "A Crown of Glory"

Hava Bacharach (Prague, c. 1585; d. Sophia, 1652) was the daughter of Rabbi Isaac ben Simeon Katz and the granddaughter of Rabbi Judah Loew, the Maharal of Prague.[51] Having been born into an academic milieu of scholarship

---

49. See Breyer, *The Jewish Woman in Rabbinic Literature*, vol. 2, pp. 117–118, and Arthur Posner, "Literature for Jewish Women in Medieval and Later Times," pp. 63–83. See also Fishman, *The History of Jewish Education in Central Europe*, p. 120, and "The Ethical Will of Shabbtai Hurwitz," in Assaf, *Mekorot*, vol. 1, p. 69.

50. See Harvey Minkoff and Evelyn B. Melamed, "Was the First Feminist Bible in Yiddish?" *Moment* 16:3 (June 1991): 28–33 and 52.

51. See Jair Hayim Bacharach, *Havot Ya'ir* (Lemberg, 1869), introduction, p. 3b.

and raised by a scholarly mother, Faiga, who provided her daughter with an excellent Jewish education,[52] Hava became exceptionally well versed in rabbinical and biblical writings. She mastered the Hebrew language so completely that even scholars in her milieu asked her opinion regarding obscure passages or ambiguous expressions.[53] She would often engage her father's students in debates over correct Halakhic rulings.[54] Her expertise extended to thorough knowledge of the Bible, the *Midrash*, responsa literature, halakhic codes, penitential prayers, and the biblical translations (*Targum*) of Onkelus and Jonathan ben Uziel.[55]

Hava's grandson, Rabbi Jair Hayim Bacharach, one of the foremost respondents of the seventeenth century and author of an epoch-making work, *Havot Ya'ir*, writes in the introduction to his book that his grandmother would study the *Midrash Rabbah*[56] without commentaries and jot down her own interpretations. Her scholarly abilities were such that her own explanations usually coincided with the foremost commentaries on the *Midrash*. In certain instances, when Hava's explanation differed from the prevailing interpretation, she was able to demonstrate that her rendition was superior. Her father drew on her expertise in compiling his commentary, *Matanot Kehunah*, on the *Midrash*. In addition, she was said to have suggested new interpretations of the festival prayer book, penitential prayers, Rashi, the Bible, and the *Targumim*.

At the age of fifteen, Hava married a prominent scholar of rabbinics and rabbi of Pohorelice, Moravia–Abraham Samuel Bacharach.[57] By various

---

I. T. Eisenstadt, in his book of genealogy, *Da'at Kedoshim* (St. Petersburg, 1897–1898), p. 217, cites Hava as being the *daughter* of the Maharal. We must assume that this is a printing error, especially as he cites an excerpt from *Havot Yair*, which clearly states that Hava was the granddaughter of the Maharal.

52. Ashkenazi, *Ha-Ishah ba-Asplakaria ha-Yehudit*, p. 122. See also Nahida Remy, *Das Juedische Weib*, p. 207, and M. Kayserling, *Die Juedischen Frauen in der Geschichte*, p. 176. From the various sources I consulted, I was unable to determine precisely how Hava acquired her schooling. I assume it was partly from her mother, who was herself a learned woman, partly from tutors, and perhaps mostly from attending her father's discourses that he delivered to his students.

53. See Bacharach, *Havot Ya'ir*, introduction.

54. Ashkenazi, *Ha-Ishah*, p. 123.

55. See Bacharach, *Havot Ya'ir*, introduction. Also see Kayserling, *Die Judischen Frauen*, p. 176.

56. "The Large Midrash," so designated because of its length. It consists of *midrashim* to each of the books of the Torah and to each of the five Scrolls (Lamentations, Esther, Ruth, etc.).

57. See Judith Harari, *Ishah ve-Em be-Yisrael* (Tel Aviv: Massada, 1959), p. 82. Also see "Bacharach, Moses Samson Ben Abraham Samuel," in *Encyclopaedia Judaica*, vol. 4, p. 49.

misfortunes and by expulsions from their home, the family lost everything, but Hava's most difficult trial was the loss of her husband when she was only thirty years old.[58] She returned with her son, Moses Samson, then age fifteen,[59] to her parents' home in Prague and remained faithful to her husband, even in death, declining all offers of marriage. Her grandson relates that Rabbi Isaiah Horowitz, a renowned contemporary spiritual leader and author of the monumental ethical work *Shnei Luhot ha-Brit* (Amsterdam, 1649), wished to marry the young widow. When Hava refused his proposal, Rabbi Horowitz is reported to have said, "My sins were responsible for my not having been privileged to marry so holy a person as she."[60]

When her son, Rabbi Samson, received the post of rabbi of Worms (1650), Hava accompanied him. She assisted him in rendering halakhic decisions and was said to have lectured at the synagogue.[61] In the year 1652, she set out for a much-longed-for pilgrimage to the Holy Land. Her grandson recounts that wherever she stopped on her way to Palestine, people treated her as their honored guest, "for her reputation preceded her."[62] Unfortunately, she was never to fulfill her desire to settle in the Holy Land, for she died en route, in Sofia, Bulgaria, where she was buried with great honor. Her name was immortalized by her grandson in his magnum opus, *Havot Ya'ir* (1699). The title comes from Deuteronomy 3:14 and means "the tent-villages of Jair," implying that his decisions were but modest expressions of his opinions, in contrast to former respondents, whose works were like fortified towns. In the German pronunciation, the title becomes "Haves Yair," meaning also "the Jair of Hava," or, as Hava's grandson states, "Ya'ir attributed to the pious woman Hava,"[63] thus constituting a tribute to his erudite grandmother and female founder of the Bacharach house, lauded by her grandson as "singular in her generation as a Torah scholar, a pious woman, and a Crown of Glory."[64] She

---

58. See Harari, *Ishah ve-Em be-Yisrael*, p. 82; Kayserling, *Die Juedischen Frauen*, p. 176; and Remy, *Das Juedische Weib*, p. 207. See also Bacharach, *Havot Ya'ir*, introduction.

59. See Harari, *Ishah ve-Em be-Yisrael*, p. 82.

60. Quoted in *Havot Ya'ir*, introduction.

61. Ashkenazi, *Ha-Ishah*, p. 123.

62. Bacharach, *Havot Ya'ir*, introduction.

63. Bacharach, *Havot Ya'ir*, introduction. Rabbi Bacharach and his work, as well as the reference in the title to his grandmother, are also mentioned by Solomon Freehoff, *The Responsa Literature and a Treasury of Responsa* (New York: Ktav, 1973), p. 85.

64. Rabbi Bacharach explains that though he was descended from an outstanding family of scholars, each of whom he could have memorialized in his work, he chose to memorialize his grandmother. His reasoning was that the memories of each of the male scholars will live on in their own published works, and through their children who are called after their fathers' names, "which is generally not the case with women."

is acclaimed in the *Worms Memorbuch* for her extraordinary scholarship and piety.[65]

Also listed in the *Worms Memorbuch* are another three exemplary women:

Eva, daughter of Isaac Leipnitz, wife of Abraham Samuel, rabbi of Worms. Her name shall be remembered because she was profoundly learned, and because she was conversant in the Bible and all its commentaries and in the *Midrash*. There was no woman before her so deeply learned.

Remembered, the aged Rebecca, daughter of Jeremiah Neustadt, because she regularly attended synagogue morning and evening, devoting all her life to benevolence.

Remembered, the pious and esteemed Miriam Sinzheim, of Vienna, who went morning and evening to the synagogue, praying with devotion and giving all her life to benevolence. She supported students of the Bible [Torah] in various congregations, especially in ours of Worms. She built the synagogue of the great rabbi Rashi, establishing free seminaries and stipending students.[66]

Hava Bacharach's contemporary, Sprintza Kempner, a native of Braunschweig, Germany, and wife of Rabbi Mordekhai Kempner, may have surpassed even Hava as a student of the philological intricacies of the biblical text.[67] She was also credited with having known the *Mishnah* by heart. Her grandson, Rabbi Moses Konitz, testified that her expertise in *Gemara* was such that many quoted her verbatim.[68] Somewhat later in the century, Esther of Cracow, daughter-in-law of Rabbi Joshua Heschel, engaged in spirited and skillful verbal exchange with the scholars of her time, utilizing biblical phrases in the place of mundane conversation to express a viewpoint. She was respectfully addressed as "Esther from the Bible."[69]

Another remarkable woman of seventeenth-century Belorussia was Deborah, daughter of Samuel Nachum of Minsk. Not only was she an accomplished, learned woman of exceptional courage, but she also almost single-handedly transformed a spiritually decadent town into a center of Torah learning and charity. To fully appreciate the extraordinary character of this woman, one must read her biography in its entirety; suffice it here to highlight

---

65. See Ashkenazi, *Ha-Ishah*, p. 123, for the quotation from the memorial book.

66. Quoted by Ray Frank, "Women in the Synagogue," *Papers of the Jewish Women's Congress, 1893* (Philadelphia: Jewish Publication Society of America, 1894), p. 60.

67. See Kayserling, *Die Juedischen Frauen*, p. 178; Remy, *Das Juedische Weib*, p. 208; and Trude, Weiss-Rosmarin, *Jewish Women Through the Ages* (New York: Jewish Book Club, 1940), p. 64.

68. Kayserling, *Die Juedischen Frauen*, p. 178.

69. See Ashkenazi, *Ha-Ishah*, p. 124.

some of the significant aspects of her life and direct the reader to further inquiry.[70]

Deborah, Daughter of Samuel Nahum: Builder of a Torah Community

Deborah, the sole surviving child of a family of which several sons and daughters had died in infancy, was exceedingly cherished by her parents. Her father, a Torah scholar and astute businessman, entrusted none but himself with her education. By the time she was ten years old, she had a thorough knowledge of the Pentateuch and the Prophets and began to learn *Mishnah* and the *Shulhan Arukh*. In addition, her father taught her mathematics as well as to read and write the Polish language. At age fifteen, Deborah was studying Talmud with the commentary of Rashi.[71]

When Deborah was eighteen years old, she married a fine, young, successful businessman and proceeded to bear two daughters and a son. Tragedy then entered the life of the happily married woman when, within a span of four years, she lost her husband and all three children to a series of epidemics. Deborah returned to her childhood home, determined to hide her grief from her parents and to find new meaning in her life that would justify her existence.[72]

It should be said that Minsk, the city of Deborah's childhood and early married life, was noted for the advanced education of the Jewish women there. It was taken for granted that all the women could read and pray in Hebrew, but in addition there were many who could study Torah, including Bible, *Gemara*, and Rashi, on a par with men.[73] Deborah had two childhood friends who, though less brilliant than she, had studied the same as she. Now the three of them, grown women, gathered together on a regular basis and studied Torah together. They established study circles among the young Jewish women of Minsk, where Deborah lectured frequently, impressing all with her oratorical skills and lucid expositions, as well as with her enthusiasm, courage, and compassion for others.[74]

Several years after her family tragedy Deborah remarried, this time to a reclusive but kindhearted and scholarly man named Nahum Tevel of Vitebsk, who was happy to leave his business concerns in Deborah's capable and willing hands while he led a saintly existence of prayer and study. Deborah quickly proved to be an able businesswoman with a compassionate understanding of her employees. Within a few months she had established herself

---

70. See Schneerson, *Lubavitcher Rabbi's Memoirs*, vol. 1, chap. 12, pp. 185f.
71. Ibid., pp. 185–186.
72. Ibid., pp. 186–187.
73. Ibid., p. 184.
74. Ibid., pp. 187–188.

as head of her husband's business, but apart from that she had made a name for herself in the sphere of Jewish education among the men as well as the women. Long accustomed to the educated women of Minsk, she was shocked by the appalling ignorance displayed by the Vitebsk women. Deborah determined to change this undesirable state of affairs and set about arranging study circles for Vitebsk women in the same way as she had done in Minsk. She also called attention to the lack of institutions for looking after the sick and needy, and gave a lead in their establishment and support. Noting the lack of Torah institutions and the spiritual deprivation among the men as well, she embarked upon an ambitious ten-year plan, with her husband's unconditional financial support and approval, to transform Vitebsk into a center of Torah learning. She did this by sending off five or six promising students from the local *yeshivah* to be educated at the best eastern European *yeshivot*. They would remain there at her and her husband's expense until their education was of a sufficiently high level to enable them to return to Vitebsk and give the Vitebsk community the benefit of their higher education and learning. But as this would obviously take some years, Deborah and her husband, in the meantime, imported suitable teachers from the foremost *yeshivot* of Poland and Lithuania, who were willing to come with their wives and families to settle in Vitebsk. She undertook the cost of all expenses, including the maintenance of the teachers and their families while they were in Vitebsk. Very soon it became a matter of course that people of all ages flocked to hear "a word of Torah." Deborah's dream of making Vitebsk a center for Torah had become a living reality.[75]

These were indeed happy and productive years for Nahum and Deborah, but their happiness was marred by the absence of children. Deborah spent much of her spare time browsing among her husband's superior collection of books on a wide variety of subjects.[76] She studied Talmud daily and was already reviewing the six volumes of *Mishnah* for the second time.[77] After many years of marriage, they were finally blessed with a daughter, but tragically Nahum passed away shortly before her birth.[78] Deborah named her baby Nehamah, after her husband, Nahum (the name Nehamah also means "comfort"). Deborah brought up her daughter in a fashion similar to her own upbringing, providing her with private teachers so that she too should eventually become a Torah scholar. At Nehamah's *Bat Mitzvah*, a sealed letter from Nahum, which was to be opened only at that occasion and not earlier, directed Deborah to establish a *yeshivah* in the name of their child. The cost and

---

75. Ibid., pp. 188–195.

76. Ibid., p. 192.

77. Ibid., p. 191.

78. For an account of the fascinating circumstances surrounding the birth of the baby girl, see Schneerson, *Lubavitcher Rabbi's Memoirs*, vol. 1, pp. 195–199.

maintenance of the institution would be provided for from the funds of the
child's inheritance. Thus it was that in the year 1697, a *yeshivah* was established in Vitebsk that was called after a woman. The men generally referred to
it as "Nehamah, Rabbi Nahum Tevel's *Yeshivah*," while the women called it
"Nehamah, Deborah's *Yeshivah*," in recognition of the widow Deborah's
well-earned popularity.[79]

Many of the learned women discussed here are known to us by way of
references in the works of their husbands or others. I would presume that a
considerable number of educated women did not find their way into scholars'
works, remaining unacknowledged or unidentified by name. The following
example is illustrative: An anonymous writer traveled through the towns and
cities of seventeenth-century Bohemia and Moravia, painting a vivid picture of
life in those communities, including the educational patterns of the time. He
writes in his diary about a teacher who had "a pious and learned wife, intelligent and knowledgeable . . . and he taught us *Halakhah* and also the explanation of *Tosafot* . . . and she instructed us in fear of God and ethical conduct."[80]
The nameless traveler evidently attributed the contributions of *both* the man
and the woman to his intellectual and religious growth and development.

It is worth noting that nowhere in the sources is the opinion expressed about
these learned women that they had no need for such learning or that their
knowledge was too extensive and unnecessary. Nowhere are these women
regarded with anything other than the highest admiration. Though women
were exempt from the *mitzvah* of *Talmud Torah* (study of Torah), it appears that
a girl who wished to study further could do so by means of private instruction.
It is even conceivable that no limits were placed on the extent of instruction of
the motivated *individual* woman who wished to pursue learning on her own,
as is the case among some of the women we have explored, who appeared to
have acquired familiarity with talmudic content as well.[81]

Literature for Women and the Attitude toward Knowledge for Women

The most notable and influential Yiddish work to become a major source of
Jewish knowledge for women was the *Ze'enah u-Re'enah* (lit. *Come and See;* Yid.

79. Ibid., pp. 198–199.

80. Excerpts from the diary appear in Assaf, *Mekorot,* vol. 4, pp. 66–71. See p. 71 for
reference to the teacher's wife.

81. Information regarding these women is fairly scant, so I was unable to determine precisely how extensive was the talmudic knowledge of such women. Were
they equally knowledgeable in the halakhic and midrashic aspects of Talmud? Had
these women left writings of their own, rather than having their comments incorporated sporadically into the works of their menfolk, we would be able to draw more
definite conclusions.

pronunciation *Tsenerene*; title taken from Song of Songs 3:11), an exegetical Yiddish rendering of the Pentateuch, the *Hafarot*, and the Five Scrolls. Composed at the end of the sixteenth century by Jacob ben Isaac Ashkenazi, this work, notwithstanding the feminine form of its name, was intended "to enable [both] men and women . . . to understand the word of God in simple language,"[82] an indication that there may have been many men, as well, who had difficulty in comprehending the text of the Bible in its original form.[83] Nevertheless it became a book used primarily by women as reading matter on the Sabbath. The work consists of discourses on selected topics and passages from the weekly portion of the Pentateuch, the *Haftarot*, and the Scrolls, the method used being a combination of *peshat* (literal exegesis) and *derash* (free interpretation), interwoven with legends from the *Midrash* and other sources, stories, and topical comments on moral behavior. The author used numerous sources, of which some are cited by name, including Rashi, Bahya ben Asher, and Nahmanides. Ashkenazi complemented this work with *Ha-Maggid*, a similar interpretation of the rest of the Bible.[84] Israel Zinberg, in *A History of Jewish Literature*, describes the *Ze'enah u-Re'enah* and its impact on generations of European Jewish women as follows:

> Old-Yiddish literature is not . . . a special "women's literature" but a genuine "folk-literature," which addresses itself to the broad strata of the people. On the other hand, there is very clearly discernible in the style and character of this literature the tender and womanly . . . in which feeling and the emotive mood obtain dominance over the logically intellectual and aridly abstract. And this amiable, intimate "feminine style" finds its clearest expression in Jacob Ashkenazi's *Ze'enah u-Re'enah*. Not without reason did this work become the most beloved book among Jewish women. The tender tone, the unique rhythm which breathes the harmonious integrity of the deeply believing soul, endowed the book with a special grace. Hence, it is not surprising that *Ze'enah u-Re'enah* became the "women's Torah," the guide of the Jewish mother and wife, her spiritual and intellectual mentor. For many generations *Ze'enah u-Re'enah* was not missing from any Jewish home. . . .[85]

---

82. From the frontispiece on the oldest extant edition. See Chava Turniansky, *Encyclopaedia Judaica*, vol. 16, p. 967.

83. Indeed, Jacob Ashkenazi further confirms this by his declaration on the title page of his other work, *Sefer ha-Maggid*: "So that all the people of the land, both small and great, might themselves know and understand how to read all of the twenty-four books [of the Bible], since previously only one from a city and two from a family had a name and a memorial [i.e., a book] out of which to exposit . . . [Henceforth] a person will not have to seek an expositor or interpreter . . . and can study them himself." (Quoted in Zinberg, *A History of Jewish Literature*, vol. 7, pp. 130–131.)

84. Ibid. See also *Encyclopaedia Judaica*, vol. 11, p. 357, and Zinberg, *A History of Jewish Literature*, vol. 7, pp. 130–131.

85. Zinberg, *A History of Jewish Literature*, vol. 7, pp. 132–133. For actual excerpts

By the seventeenth century this work was well-known and very popular, and scholars were interested in having their daughters study it or other such works. Rabbi Sheftel Horowitz (Frankfurt, seventeenth century), in his ethical will,[86] adjures his daughters and daughters-in-law to study Bible with German translation, as well as the book *Lev Tov*, an ethical and religious work written in Yiddish by the seventeenth-century Yiddish moralist and author Isaac ben Eliakim of Posen. Unlike some other Yiddish ethical works, *Lev Tov* was addressed to both men and women. It counseled the men to honor their wives because a wife educates the children to keep a Jewish home, and it stressed that men and women have equal rights.[87] Rabbi Horowitz was following the example of his grandfather's will, which was entitled *Yesh Nohalin*. The author was Rabbi Abraham ben Shabtai ha-Levi Horowitz (Prague, sixteenth century), a scholar of note and author of several legal, philosophical, and ethical works.[88] He wrote: "Caution your sons and daughters regarding prayer, reciting Grace After Meals, as well as the rest of the commandments and ethical behavior."[89] His grandson was more interested to see that the women study as well. The tone that stresses education fits a mood that we can identify as having roots in the earlier will.

That ordinary girls were given a measure of religious education is clearly demonstrated in the remarkable memoirs of a seventeenth-century auto-biographer, Gluckel of Hameln (1645–1724),[90] who has been styled the German-Jewish Pepys of her time.[91] Though not noted as a scholar or teacher, she deserves mention in the context of this work for the impression her memoirs convey of a seventeenth-century Jewish woman, possibly representative of a good many of her contemporaries or predecessors, who received at least the rudiments of Jewish religious and other necessary knowledge.

---

from the *Ze'enah u-Re'enah*, see pp. 133–135. See also Shulvass, *Jewish Culture in Eastern Europe*, pp. 130–132. The *Ze'enah u-Re'enah* has been translated into English by Art Scroll (1983).

86. For an excerpt see Assaf, *Mekorot*, vol. 1, p. 69.

87. *Encyclopaedia Judaica*, vol. 9, p. 18.

88. Rabbi Abraham Horowitz was also the father of Rabbi Isaiah Horowitz (known as the *Shelah ha-Kodesh*), author of the well-known halakhic, ethical, and mystical work *Shnei Luhot ha-Brit*.

89. Assaf, *Mekorot*, vol. 1, p. 64.

90. Gluckel's memoirs appear in English in *The Life of Gluckel of Hameln*, trans. from the original Yiddish and ed. Beth-Zion Abrahams (New York: Thomas Yoseloff, 1963).

91. Described as such by Cecil Roth in "The European Age: The Success of the Medieval Jewish Ideal," in *Great Ages and Ideas of the Jewish People*, ed. Leo Schwarz (New York: Random House, 1956), p. 295. Pepys was a contemporary popular English chronicler.

Gluckel of Hameln: Yiddish Memoirist

The first autobiography we know of that was written by a Jewish woman—the life story of Gluckel of Hameln—is written in Judeo-German, with astonishing candor and precision. Gluckel describes a life spent in the ghettos of the seventeenth and part of the eighteenth century: Hamburg, Gluckel's birthplace; the legendary little Hameln; and, lastly, Metz, where she passed away in her seventy-ninth year. Her work is replete with moralistic injunctions at every possible opportunity. Apart from frequent admonitions and religious reflections, Gluckel, in the most charming manner, inserts into her narrative numerous parables and fables gathered from her extensive reading of religious literature. She wants to imbue her children with her own faith in God's mercy and in the immortality of the soul, and, above all, to influence their conduct. Indeed, her book starts out with detailed instructions to her children on how they might best serve the Creator of the world.

Gluckel's memoirs embody a vast amount of rabbinic legend, talmudic lore, and ethical teaching. She quotes frequently from Scriptures. It has been pointed out that in the original Judeo-Deutsch (Yiddish) in which her book is written, one-third of the total vocabulary is Hebrew.[92] Insofar as it is assumed most women did not know Hebrew—the language of Jewish scholarship—this comes as somewhat of a surprise. Her memoirs inform us whence this knowledge was gleaned. Of her father she relates, "He had his daughters taught religious and worldly things."[93] She makes reference to "having been in *heder* [the traditional, privately supported Jewish elementary school] all day,"[94] and while it did not take her as far as the Talmud and rabbinics, she was certainly taught Hebrew reading and writing and may have acquired knowledge in Scripture and other necessary knowledge as well. Some scholars doubt that Gluckel studied the text of the Bible and the Hebrew morality books in the original. They think her learning was probably drawn chiefly from the folk literature that Gluckel was familiar with through her extensive reading.[95] Nevertheless, her wide knowledge of the current and Judeo-Deutsch literature is evidenced by her references to works of the period and the way she utilizes some of the current moralistic tales then so popular. Of the stories she recounted she would make statements such as: "This story I found in a book written by a certain worthy man from Prague."[96] She was pro-

---

92. See Roth, "The European Age: The Success of the Medieval Jewish Ideal," op. cit., p. 295.

93. *The Life of Gluckel of Hameln*, ed. Beth-Zion Abrahams, p. 13.

94. Ibid., p. 14.

95. See Zinberg, *A History of Jewish Literature*, vol. 6 (New York: Ktav), p. 244.

96. Ibid., p. 31.

foundlyinfluenced by *tehinnot* and often echoed them in her meditations. Gluckel respected and honored Jewish scholarship and learning, and she lived her own life according to the teachings of the "rabbinical sages of blessed memory."

Evidence for Education of Women

Gluckel's autobiography is important for the history of education for women. Gluckel's reference to having attended *heder* is surprising, yet it appears that in seventeenth-century Germany and Moravia, boys and girls may have attended *heder* together.[97] Isidore Fishman relates, for example, how in Nicholsburg (Moravia) it was quite common that girls attended the Jewish school side by side with boys, although the number of girls was limited.[98] Instruction of girls was, however, confined to reading and prayer book, any more advanced learning being denied to them. In 1691, a Nicholsburg statute forbade teachers to give instruction in *Humash* (the Pentateuch) to boy pupils if there were as many as five girls in the class.[99] Fishman points out that there was generally but one classroom in which instruction was given to several grades. The edict may have therefore been made in order to prevent inadequate instruction of pupils. It would appear from this that the teacher could give instruction in prayer book only to both sexes if there were more than five girls present, but if there were fewer in the class he could give the boys instruction in *Humash* as well. Hence, if girls, such as Gluckel of Hameln, were in a classroom with fewer than five girls, they could have indirectly benefited from the boys' instruction in *Humash*. Several years later a further enactment forbade a girl to be present in a teacher's house where Talmud was being taught, unless she came there merely to learn needlework from the teacher's wife. Even then such instruction had to take place in a room on a story other than the one on which the class met.[100] Furthermore, if there were any boys present learning *Humash*, no more than four girls of the age of 7 or older could be admitted, including those taught needlework by the teacher's wife, unless such instruction were, again, given on a different story.[101] Here, too, it appears, says

---

97. Since elementary education was offered in schools to non-Jewish girls in Germany at the time (as mentioned in Chapter Six), we may speculate that this had some influence on the education of Jewish girls as well.

98. Fishman, *The History of Jewish Education in Central Europe*, p. 118.

99. Ibid., pp. 118–119. The statute is printed in its original Hebrew-Yiddish in Moritz Guedemann, *Quellenschriften zur Geschichte des Unterrichts und der Erziehung bei den Deutschen Jueden* (Amsterdam: Philo Press, 1968), p. 260, para. 19.

100. Ibid., p. 119. For the original Hebrew-Yiddish text of the statute, see Guedemann, *Quellenschriften*, p. 276, para. 3.

101. Ibid. See also Guedemann, p. 276, para. 4.

Fishman, that the teacher could admit more than this number of girls provided they were younger than 7.

Sometimes girls were taught Hebrew grammar. The Jewish bibliographer Shabbtai Bass, in his preface to the second edition of Be'er Moshe,[102] published in 1682, complained that teachers in general paid no attention to Hebrew grammar, and especially teachers of boys and girls and older students. He therefore added a few grammatical rules for their guidance.[103]

Devotional Prayers for Women

With the growth of translated works for women, the seventeenth century continued the interest shown at the end of the sixteenth century in devotional works designed for women. We have already noted their effect on Gluckel of Hameln, who recites parts of them in her account of her life. Several women were active in translating the Hebrew prayers into the vernacular and/or composing new prayers and poetry especially suited to the religious feelings of women.

Among those women who thus enriched Jewish liturgy in the sixteenth and seventeenth centuries were Litte of Regensburg (sixteenth century), who wrote a liturgical poem on the Book of Samuel, entitled the History of David[104]; Roizl Fishels of Cracow, who in 1586 published Moses Stendal's translation of the Psalms and, along with it, wrote a lengthy preface in verse, emphasizing the indispensability of oft-repeated Psalms[105]; and Hannah Katz (Prague and Amsterdam, seventeenth century), who composed lyrical prayers in Yiddish, the material for which was taken, according to her testimony, from midrashic and talmudic sources. They include "A Prayer to Moses," "A Prayer for the Sabbath," and "A Prayer for the [Hebrew] month of Elul."[106]

Women Printers

The printing of books was a highly skilled art. A printer had to know the fine points of the texts in order to ensure that the quality of the work would not be

---

102. This work is an interlinear (Yiddish) translation to the Pentateuch and Five Scrolls, by Moses Saertels of Prague.

103. Fishman, Jewish Education in Central Europe, p. 119.

104. Abrahams, Jewish Life in the Middle Ages, p. 386; Ashkenazi, Dor Dor u-Minhagav, p. 218; and Kayserling, Die Juedischen Frauen, p. 150.

105. See Ashkenazi, Dor Dor u-Minhagav, p. 218; Abraham Habermann, Nashim Ivriyot be-Tor Madpisot, Mesadrot, Motsi'ot le-Or ve-Tomkhot be-Mehabrim (Berlin, 1933), pp. 8–10; and Zinberg, A History of Jewish Literature, vol. 7, p. 242.

106. See Ashkenazi, Dor Dor u-Minhagav, p. 219. See also Remy, Das Juedische Weib, p. 271.

amiss. In some places, Jews were not allowed to print books. Quite often authors would oversee the printing of their works personally to guarantee high quality. Printers worked from handwritten manuscripts and had to be adept in setting Hebrew type accurately. Readers insisted on fine work, since a mistake could result in a break of the tradition. Mistakes always occurred, but the trust given a printer was necessary, and when non-Jews did the printing, Jews still supervised. Jewish women printers actually set the type for some of the first printed Hebrew books. Jewish printers were among the first to take advantage of Gutenberg's invention, and the history of Jewish typography preserves the names of a number of women who either worked at typesetting or owned printing shops. In his book on the subject, Abraham Habermann lists approximately sixty women of both western and eastern Europe who were active as printers, publishers, and patronesses of learning.[107] One may assume that these women printers and publishers acquired a fair degree of knowledge in the course of printing or publishing a wide variety of works related to Bible, Talmud, *Halakhah, Midrash,* prayer, Hebrew grammar, ethics, and the like. As examples of women involved in this endeavor in the Ashkenazic centers of the seventeenth and eighteenth centuries, the following are representative: Tcharna Meisels of Cracow set the print for a number of scholarly works, including *Yam Shel Shlomo* (Cracow, 1633–1635), the talmudic commentary of the sixteenth-century halakhic decisor Solomon Luria (Maharshal).[108] Eidel, daughter of Isaiah Menahem Mendel of Prague, financed the publication of the Penitential Prayers (Cracow, 1665) from her own means. At the conclusion of the book, the following accolade is inscribed: "Remembered for good is the learned woman, the lecturer, the patroness and the pious woman Eidel . . . who funded, for the benefit of many, the publication of Penitential Prayers. . . . May her merit prevail for us and all of Israel."[109]

Ella and Gela, daughters of the proselyte Moses ben Abraham of Nicholsburg and Prague, were industrious printers in the printing houses set up by their father in Dessau and then Halle. In the introduction to a work printed in Dessau in 1696, Ella states that she set the type herself, and as she is only nine years old, she asks that any printer's errors be overlooked.[110] She assisted her brother in printing an edition of the Talmud in Frankfurt in 1697–1699. At the end of tractate *Niddah* (1699) of that edition, the following is inscribed: "Printed by his sister, the young girl Ella, daughter of Moses ben Abraham."[111] Ella also printed the Holiday Prayer Book (1700) in conjunc-

---

107. Habermann, *Nashim Ivriyot.*
108. Habermann, *Nashim Ivriyot,* p. 12.
109. Ibid., p. 12.
110. Ibid., p. 13. See also Remy, *Das Juedische Weib,* p. 148.
111. Habermann, *Nashim Ivriyot,* p. 14.

tion with her brother. There she states: "All this was my handiwork, Ella, daughter of Moses, and the handiwork of my brother, Israel. . . ."[112] The second daughter, Gela, when yet in her early teens, printed, among other works, a whole prayer book by herself (Halle, 1710) and penned the following naive and touching verse on the final page: "One year does vanish, another one is near,/still of a redemption we nothing did hear."[113]

Fiola Shlenker Hirsch, born in Bavaria, lived at the same time; she was wedded in second marriage to a printer by the name of Jacob Hirsch. In the year 1727, she and her husband jointly set and printed the great work of Rabbi Jacob ben Asher, *Arba'ah Turim*, the most exhaustive codex of Jewish law. Her husband writes in the introduction the following dedication to his wife: "I cannot refrain from extending praise to God for providing me with a help-meet in second marriage, my modest and pious wife, Fiola, who assisted me equally in this great work. . . ."[114]

Judith Rosanes, wife of Polish rabbi Zevi Hirsch Rosanes (eighteenth century), managed a printing works in Lvov (Lemberg), in which she published the works of many contemporary scholars.[115]

EIGHTEENTH CENTURY

Women Scholars

In the eighteenth century the continuing tradition of women scholars from illustrious rabbinic families is no less than in past centuries, and indeed we find a proliferation of such women. Let us now turn to those women who continued the momentum of the past in building an outlook to enhance the creative impulses of women. This age eventually culminated in the emancipation of Jews from the confines of the ghetto. Women in future centuries, who would, as a whole, assume greater communal responsibility, could not have achieved what they did without the examples of the past – the bridges to modernity.

Krendel Steinhardt of Germany[116] was a descendant of a family of rabbis and married the renowned halakhic authority Rabbi Joseph ben Menahem

---

112. Ibid.

113. Ibid., p. 15. See also Remy, *Das Juedische Weib*, p. 148.

114. Habermann, *Nashim Ivriyot*, p. 16. See also Remy, *Das Juedische Weib*, p. 149, and Kayserling, *Die Juedischen Frauen*, p. 149.

115. Habermann, *Nashim Ivriyot*, p. 19. Habermann includes a list of works that Judith printed.

116. See Kayserling. *Die Juedischen Frauen*, pp. 178–179; I. L. Maimon, *Sarei ha-*

Steinhardt (1720–1776). She herself was called *Die Rebbecin* by her admirers.[117] In his work, Steinhardt quotes comments and novellas by his learned wife.[118] She also urged her husband to publish his work.[119] Krendel was so well versed in Hebrew studies that even the rabbis abided by her decision in explanation of obscure and difficult passages.[120] Krendel's husband lauded her erudition and wisdom in the introduction to his book of responsa, *Zikhron Yosef.* Her brother, Rabbi Isaiah Berlin, testified in the introduction to his unpublished work *Yesh Seder la-Mishnah* that his sister was "famous throughout the land" for her scholarship.[121] Krendel's sister, Marla Katznellenbogen, wife of Rabbi Hirsh Katznellenbogen, was also reputed to be "pious, gracious, and learned."[122]

Rabbi Hayim Joseph David Azulai of Jerusalem (known by his Hebrew acronym, Hida), a leading halakhist, mystic, emissary, and bibliographer of the eighteenth century, spent most of his active years traveling abroad as an emissary of the communities of Palestine for the collection of funds for the upkeep of academies and scholars. In his encounters with Jews in various communities, he met a number of women for whose scholarship he had high praise. One was Krendel Steinhardt.[123] An anecdote is related by Rabbi Azulai, who once had occasion to lodge at the Steinhardts' home in Feurth. His point was to show her wit and erudition.[124]

Me'ah, vol. 1 (Jerusalem: Ahiasaf, 1961), pp. 247–248; Remy, *Das Juedische Weib*, pp. 208–209; T. Weiss-Rosmarin, *Jewish Women*, p. 64; and Isaac Weiss, *Avnei Bet ha-Yotser* (Paks, Hungary, 1900), pp. 30–31. See also Yehosua Horowitz, "Joseph ben Menahem Steinhardt," in *Encyclopaedia Judaica*, vol. 15, p. 368.

117. Remy, *Das Juedische Weib*, p. 208.

118. See, for example, Joseph Steinhardt, *Zikhron Yosef* (Fuerth, 1773), p. 17a, sec. 13. See also "Hiddushim ve-Drashot," published in *Zikhron Yosef*, p. 99b.

119. Steinhardt, *Zikhron Yosef*, introduction.

120. One example of such casuistry is cited by her husband: In the *Midrash* the following passage is found: "Ten years were taken from Joseph's life, on account of his allowing his brothers, the sons of Jacob, to say the words 'Thy servant, our father,' ten times," disregarding the reverence due to parents. The difficulty in the passage is that in reality the brothers uttered these words only five times. Krendel explained the difficulty accordingly: Joseph, pretending that he did not understand Hebrew, the language of his brothers, had their words repeated to him by the interpreter and thus actually listened to them ten times (Zikhron Yosef, p. 96b).

121. Weiss, *Avnei Bet ha-Yotser*, p. 31.

122. Ibid.

123. See the bibliographical work of H. J. D. Azulai, *Shem ha-Gedolim*, vol. 1 (Vilna, 1853), in section entitled "Rabbanit" (p. 159 in the Ortsel, 1954, reprinted edition).

124. J. L. Maimon recounts this story in *Sarei ha-Me'ah*, pp. 247–248: Eager to lavish hospitality on her distinguished guest, Krendel planned an especially festive Sabbath meal. It happened that just that week there was a scarcity of fish in town, and Krendel had difficulty in finding one to serve in honor of the Sabbath and her illustrious guest. After much hardship, she succeeded in locating a fish, spending a great deal of

Another woman Hida admired was Gittele, wife of Rabbi Yeosha of Worms. Rabbi Azulai tells how he was granted hospitality by the couple and in the course of a lavish meal replete with *divrei Torah* (words of Torah), his hostess made an astute observation, indicative of her breadth of knowledge in Torah. When her guest acknowledged the validity and profundity of her statement, her husband commented in jest, "I am pleased that one thing has delighted you!"[125] Hida also had words of praise for Dina Segal, daughter of Rabbi Aryeh Leib of Amsterdam and wife of Rabbi Saul ben Isaac Segal of The Hague.[126] She was known as a prolific writer of Hebrew poetry.[127]

Gittele Eger, living in the latter part of the eighteenth century, was acknowledged as a learned woman. She was the only daughter of the German rabbi and author Akiva ben Simha Bunim (known as Rabbi Akiva Eger "the Elder") and the mother of the scholar and exemplary humanitarian Akiva Eger ("the Younger") of Posen. Her brother, Wolf Eger, rabbi of Leipnick, testified that "she was as learned as a man."[128] Her son, Akiva, so admired his mother for her erudition and piety that he assumed her maiden name, Eger, rather

---

money in its purchase. When Rabbi Azulai heard that it was on his account that she had paid so exorbitant a price for a fish, he stated that in his opinion it was "a profanation of God's name." On the Sabbath day, many distinguished members of the community came to pay their respects to the great Jerusalemite. Krendel circulated among her guests, serving delicacies she had concocted from the fish purchased at great expense the previous day, deliberating bypassing Rabbi Azulai in the process of serving. When the rabbi commented on her omission, stating, "Were not all these preparations done in my honor? Why will the *Rabbanit* not give me a taste of these delicacies?" Krendel sagaciously responded with a passage from the Talmud: "Wherever a profanation of God's name is involved, one does not pay respect to a rabbi" (*Berakhot* 18b). For other anecdotes regarding Krendel Steinhardt's life, as well as comments she expressed that are evidence of her breadth in Torah knowledge, see Maimon's work.

125. H. J. D. Azulai, *Ma'agal Tov ha-Shalem*, ed. A. Friemann (Jerusalem: Mekitzei Nirdamim, 1934), p. 24. See also n. 2 on that page.

126. Ibid., p. 153. See also n. 6 on that page.

127. In a verse she once penned, she switched the Hebrew letter *het* for an identical sounding letter, *khaf*. Her brother reproved her for her "mistake," to which she shrewdly responded with a verse from Isaiah (40:31): *"Ve-kovei Hashem yahlifu koah,"* meaning, "But those who put their hope in the Lord shall exchange (renew) [their] strength." In Hebrew the word for "strength" is *koah*, spelled with the two selfsame letters she interchanged in her verse. She used a play on words as if to say, "Those of faith may exchange a *het* for a *khaf*." Her response is testimony to her sharp-wittedness as well as her familiarity and ease with the biblical text. (Ibid. For reasons I am unable to determine, J. L. Maimon, *Sarei ha-Me'ah*, vol. 1, p. 249, attributes this story to Krendel Steinhardt.)

128. Rabbi Wolf testifies thusly in the *Responsa of Rabbi Akiva Eger*, vol. 1 (Vienna, 1889), "Pesakhim," resp. 29. See I. Weiss, *Avnei Bet ha-Yotser*, p. 37a.

than his father's name, Ginz.[129] Akiva Eger's biographer, Saul Blum, writes of
Gittele that if not for her encouragement, Akiva would not have undertaken
the yoke of the rabbinate. "As a person asks of the Word of God, so did he
consult with and heed her advice. . . . She guided him from afar with her sage
counsel."[130] Many were the erudite conversations Gittele engaged in with her
husband and her son, quoting talmudic and other scholarly sources that
demonstrated the scope of her knowledge of Torah.[131] Sarah Oser (Belbirsk,
Poland, and Vilna, Lithuania; eighteenth century) was erudite in Bible, the
Midrash, and Talmud, as well as an expert in Hebrew grammar. She was often
called upon by scholars to assist them in elucidating difficult passages in the
aforementioned sources, and she published Hebrew poetry.[132] Her contemporary, Tcharna Rosenthal, a Hungarian Jew, was similarly fluent in Bible
and acquainted with many talmudic sources, which she cited accurately and
fluently. She carried on a spirited correspondence with Moses Mendelssohn,
philosopher of the German Enlightenment.[133]

That women from rabbinic families were often highly knowledgeable
themselves is attested to in a fascinating account contained in the memoirs of
Dov Ber Birkenthal of the Galician village of Bolechow (1723–1805).[134] He
writes that as a young boy, he would visit on the Sabbath the home of the
local rabbi, Mordecai (Segal) Horowitz, to receive instruction in Talmud from
the spiritual leader:

> Sitting next to [the rabbi] was his modest sister, Leah, a learned woman of
> repute. . . . The rabbi would assign to me a passage in Talmud to study, and
> would then lie down for a nap following the meal, as he was a sickly man. His
> sister, Leah, would sit and observe the difficulty I had in comprehending the
> passage, as well as *Rashi's* commentary on the topic, and would say to me:
> "Why do you puzzle so? Recite for me the Talmudic passage upon which you
> are snagged." I would begin reciting the passage, or the *Rashi*, and then she
> would continue to recite the passage or the commentary verbatim in a clear
> tongue. She would explain the topic to me thoroughly and incisively, and I
> gleaned much knowledge from her teachings. When the rabbi would awake, I
> knew how to elucidate the topic in the Talmud accurately.[135]

129. I. Weiss, *Avnei Bet ha-Yotser*, p. 37a.

130. Saul Blum, *Gedolei Yisrael: Hayei Rabbenu Akiva Eger* (Warsaw, 1938), p. 49.

131. The interested reader may wish to read about the content of some such
conversations in J. L. Maimon's *Sarei ha-Me'ah*, vol. 1, pp. 268–269.

132. Kayserling, *Die Juedischen Frauen*, p. 180.

133. Ibid., pp. 180–181.

134. Excerpts from *The Diary of Dov of Bolekhov* (Berlin, 1922) appear in Assaf,
Mekorot, vol. 4, pp. 110–111. For general elaboration on Dov Ber Birkenthal and his
memoirs, which are a significant contribution to Jewish history of the eighteenth
century, see Zinberg, *A History of Jewish Literature*, vol. 8, pp. 169–173.

135. Assaf, *Mekorot*, vol. 4, p. 111.

Devotional Literature

This century again saw a continuation of the process whereby women created liturgical recitations for their sisters. Many were composed and compiled in Germany, but eastern Europe produced a number of talented women who engaged in this creative enterprise: Ellush, daughter of Mordecai Michals of Slutzk, achieved recognition with her Yiddish translation of Aaron Berekhiah of Modena's *Ma'avar Yabbok* (1704), a special collection of prayers for the sick and dying. Ellush also translated the morning prayers (Frankfurt an der/Oder, 1704).[136] Bella Hurwitz Chasan's (Prague, early eighteenth century) writings include a *tehinnah* for the Ten Days of Repentance.[137] Rachel Sofer, of Pinczow (Poland), wrote *tehinnot* (Frankfurt am/Main, 1723).[138] Serel Segal Rappaport, daughter of Rabbi Jacob Halevi Segal of Dubno and wife of Rabbi Mordecai Katz Rappaport of Olesnica (Silesia) and Uman (Ukraine), authored the very popular *"Tehinnah* of the Matriarchs for Rosh Hodesh Elul [a Jewish month]" (Lvov, 1784), in which she appeals to the matriarchs of the Jewish people – Sarah, Rebecca, Rachel, and Leah – requesting them to protect their children, with their great merit, in the latter's deep distress.[139]

The most outstanding example of the feelings of a woman in this period of explosion of women's liturgical poems is found in another *"Tehinnah* of the Matriarchs." This poem was composed by a woman who bore the name of all four of the matriarchs, as indicated in the subtitle of the *tehinnah*: "This *tehinnah* is arranged by the scholarly woman Sarah Rebecca Rachel Leah, daughter of the rabbi . . . Yokil Segal Horowitz . . . of Glogau (Poland) and wife of . . . Rabbi Shabbetai . . . of Krasny (Ukraine)."[140]

Sarah Rebecca Rachel Leah Horowitz: Woman Activist

Chava Weissler, in a well-researched article on this remarkable woman, notes that she was an accomplished talmudic scholar who defended her rights to rabbinic learning.[141] Her one surviving poem is written in Hebrew, Aramaic,

---

136. See Ashkenazi, *Dor Dor u-Minhagav*, p. 219, and Zinberg, *A History of Jewish Literature*, vol. 7, p. 242.

137. Remy, *Das Juedische Weib*, p. 270. See also Ashkenazi, *Dor Dor u-Minhagav*, p. 219, and Trude Weiss-Rosmarin, *Jewish Women Through the Ages* (New York: Jewish Book Club, 1990), p. 65.

138. Ashkenazi, *Ha-Isha ba-Asplakaria ha-Yehudit*, p. 129.

139. For excerpts of Serel's *tehinnah*, see Zinberg, *A History of Jewish Literature*, vol. 7, pp. 257–258. See also I. T. Eisenstadt, *Da'at Kedoshim* (St. Petersburg, 1893), pp. 160–165.

140. Quoted in Zinberg, *A History of Jewish Literature*, vol. 7, p. 258.

141. Chava Weissler, "Prayers in Yiddish and the Religious World of Ashkenazic Women," in *Jewish Women in Historical Perspective*, pp. 159–177. See especially pp. 170–173.

and Yiddish and was to be recited in the synagogue on the Sabbath preceding the New Moon. In her two-page Hebrew introduction to the poem, she discusses the significance of women's prayer, the proper way for women to pray, and, above all, when women are, and are not, to listen to their husband. Men ignored her. Women could not read her. The Hebrew introduction was soon dropped: "Although you may say that a woman is not competent in reasoned argument, nonetheless,'the crown of Torah is left [for the generations],' and in my view, I am bringing merit to the many. . . . Whoever wishes to undertake to toil in the Torah may do so."[142]

Horowitz's phrasing is replete with citations from rabbinic and mystical literature to demonstrate that women have greater religious importance than is generally accepted. She bolsters all her arguments and then remarks, "I have many other proofs. . . . This matter has certainly not escaped the discerning eye, and I will not speak in the ears of a fool."[143] In Horowitz's view, women should attend synagogue twice daily, not for idle gossip but for true devotional prayer. Only this way can Redemption occur. She remarks that when the Talmud stipulates that women acquire merit by sending their sons to learn and their husbands to study, it means that women are to be obeyed in these instances over the wishes of their husband. It does not mean that women do not acquire merit through their own active performance of commandments. But regarding matters of the World to Come, such as Torah study, women must protect their family from neglect. She does not say that this precludes women's own study of Torah.

Of the many *tehinnot* written for women, the considerably larger part are anonymous, but a few names of composers of such prayers have been preserved, as we have seen. Of all the known authors, the most popular among them was Sarah Bas-Tovim (c. late seventeenth or early eighteenth century). This name was so beloved and well-known in the Jewish world that it became something of a legend. Indeed, Sarah's fame led to the publication of later *tehinnot* under her name by others, including a number of nineteenth-century *Haskalah* (Jewish Enlightenment) writers.[144]

Sarah Bas-Tovim: *Tehinnot* Writer Nonpareil

The surname Bas-Tovim ("daughter of good people"), likely a pen name, is an indication that the composer of the *tehinnot* was descended from distinguished ancestry.[145] Indeed, her *tehinnot* record that she came from a quite prestigious

142. Ibid., p. 171.
143. Ibid., p. 172.
144. See Zinberg, *A History of Jewish Literature*, vol. 7, pp. 252–253, for elaboration.
145. See Chava Weissler, "Woman as High Priest: A Kabbalistic Prayer in Yiddish

family. Her father, Mordecai, was a great scholar, son of the rabbi of Satanov (Ukraine) and grandson of the rabbi of Brest-Litovsk, Russia. She was born in the Ukraine and grew up in a wealthy home.Impoverished in her adulthood, she wandered from place to place. Zinberg believes that she may have been a *firzogerin*, a precentress in the women's synagogues, "pouring out her embittered and grieved heart in elegiac petitions, lyrically tender *tehinnot*."[146] Two collections of *tehinnot* by Sarah Bas-Tovim containing ethical laws and commandments in rhymed verse have been preserved. The first, *Sheker ha-Cheyn*, was written with the intention of serving as "a remedy for the soul in this world and in the World to Come."[147] The second collection, *Shloyshe She'orim* (*Three Portals*), includes three types of supplications: the first deals with the three main *mitzvot* prescribed for women,[148] the second is a *tehinnah* to be prayed when the new moon is blessed, and the third is a prayer for the Days of Awe.

The boldest assertion in Bas-Tovim's *Shloyshe She'orim* is that women study Torah in the World to Come. Weissler observes that if women were excluded from studying Torah on earth, at least they would engage in this study in Paradise. Since such a sentiment must have been revolutionary, it was expunged from some later editions of the text. In Sarah Bas-Tovim's depictions, women could imagine themselves in radically different situations from that in which they lived–surrounded by myriads of righteous women, devoting themselves to studying Torah, and praising God.[149]

This image may have its precedent in an earlier portrayal of the Divine Chamber that righteous women occupy in the World to Come. According to a midrashic text printed in a compilation of medieval manuscripts, the Divine Academy in the Future World will be eighteen million parasangs by eighteen million parasangs. Here the righteous women who labored to have their children taught Torah receive their reward. Their faces are illuminated with the Divine Splendor as they hear "a renewed Torah" from the Divine Mouth. And each word is translated and explained by an attendant.[150]

---

for Lighting Sabbath Candles," *Jewish History* 5 (Spring 1991): 24 n. 19. Weissler discusses the historicity of Sarah.

146. Zinberg, *A History of Jewish Literature*, vol. 7, p. 254.

147. Ibid. For excerpts of her introduction to this work, see p. 254–255.

148. They include *hallah*–separating a small portion of the dough in memory of the priestly tithes; *niddah*–marital separation during menstruation and ritual immersion following menstruation; and *hadlakah*–lighting candles on the eve of Sabbath and festivals.

149. See Weissler, "Prayers in Yiddish and the Religious world of Ashkenazic Women," p. 176.

150. Found in Adolph Jellinek, *Beit ha-Midrash*, vol. 6 (Liepzig, 1878), p. 151. Also found in *Otzar Midrashim*, ed. J. D. Eisenstein, vol. 1 (New York, 1915), p. 89.

In the introduction to *Shloyshe She'orim,* Sarah incidentally presents certain details of her life, writing, "May God have mercy on me . . . so that I may not have to be a wanderer long. . . . [May] my being a wanderer be an atonement for my sins. And may God forgive me for the fact that in my youth I chattered in the synagogue during prayers." In her conclusion, she urges her readers to have pity on widows and orphans and those wrongly imprisoned, and she warns of the evils resulting from jealousy and pride.[151] Little is known of Sarah's later life.

Another composer of *tehinnot* lived in the city of Brody at the end of the eighteenth century. Her work, *Imrei Shifra,* is unique in its use of Yiddish translations of the *Zohar,* the mystical canon of Judaism.[152]

Shifra bas Joseph: Woman Mystic

Shifra bas Joseph is described as a learned woman, wife of the Torah scholar Rabbi Ephraim Segal, judge of Poznan. The introduction to her work mentions her piety and her plan to travel to the Holy Land with her husband. Chava Weissler questions the accuracy of the information in the introduction, but the fact remains that the *tehinnah* emphasizes repentance, judgment, and punishment after death. The work stresses the importance of Sabbath observance for women, and it weaves kabbalistic themes around the motif of lighting Sabbath candles. Weissler ponders whether the mystical movements of the time stimulated Shifra's interest in these themes. What is interesting is that the *tehinnah* rejects the midrashic association of lighting Sabbath candles as a rectification for Eve's sin and instead relates the ritual to the active role of the male High Priest as his image is portrayed in the *Zohar.* Weissler expresses some doubt that the liturgy was composed by a woman but notes that it was recited by women.

Other writings by women, of a nonliturgical nature, which were known in Europe in the seventeenth and eighteenth centuries, are an abridged Yiddish version of the tenth-century historical classic *Josippon*[153] (Cracow, 1670), by

---

151. See Zinberg, *A History of Jewish Literature,* vol. 7, pp. 255–256, for excerpts of Bas-Tovim's preface and conclusion to this collection of *tehinnot.* Also see Weissler, "The Traditional Piety of Ashkenazic Women," pp. 253–256.

152. See Weissler, "Woman as High Priest," pp. 9–26. All the information regarding Shifra is gleaned from her article.

153. *Jossipon* is a medieval version of Josephus's history, written in Hebrew, of anonymous authorship, describing the period of the Second Temple, and authored in southern Italy. A lengthy work, its translator would have to have been substantially knowledgeable in Hebrew, as well as talented in the art of condensing a considerable amount of material.

Eidel Mendels, first of Frankfurt am/Main, then of Cracow,[154] and a Yiddish translation of the Book of Esther (Berlin, 1717) by Penina, daughter of Wolfe.[155] Bella Hurwitz Chasan (Prague, early eighteenth century) wrote books in Yiddish entitled *A History of the House of David* (Prague, 1705) and *The Tale of Isaac ben Eleazar* (Prague, n.d.); she collaborated with Rachel Reidnitz Fargis in writing *A History of the First Jewish Settlements in Prague*, a work that, in the words of Nahida Remy, gave evidence of a remarkable knowledge of historical facts of the period.[156]

A woman scribe of note in the early eighteenth century was Sarah Oppenheim, of Prague and Breslau, daughter of the manuscript collector and chief rabbi of Moravia, David Oppenheim. In 1709 she copied in meticulous manner *Megillat Esther* (the Book of Esther). Some rabbis sanctioned its usage for the public reading of Esther on the festival of Purim.[157]

Forms of Education

That girls may have received some form of private instruction or may have engaged in individual study in Poland in the eighteenth century is attested to by Rabbi Ephraim Hayyot, who embarked from his native Galicia to Palestine via Italy in 1724 but was forced, owing to political circumstances, to return to his home in Galicia. In one of his works, he cautions against a teacher's instructing boys and girls together, stating, "In all the lands of Franconia (Germany), Italy, and Poland it is customary that there be a teacher (*melamed*) just for girls [separate from boys], and that is the proper manner in the eyes of God."[158] We can now note that girls were tutored, at times alongside boys. One suspects that the rabbi was not addressing the elite families of rabbinic

154. Ashkenazi, *Ha-Ishah ba-Asplakaria ha-Yehudit*, vol. 1, p. 128. See also Weiss-Rosmarin, *Jewish Women Through the Ages*, p. 65.

155. Ashkenazi, *Ha-Ishah*, p. 129. Ashkenazi does not state her native city. I am assuming that she may have lived in Germany, inasmuch as her work was published there.

156. *Das Juedische Weib*, p. 270. See also Ashkenazi, *Dor Dor u-Minhagav*, p. 219, and Weiss-Rosmarin, *Jewish Women Through the Ages*, p. 65.

157. Kayserling, *Die Juedischen Frauen*, p. 178. The acceptability of a *Megillat* (scroll) *Esther* written by a woman to fulfill the commandment of reading and listening to the *megillah* on Purim is a matter of halakhic dispute. (See Rabbi Y. M. Epstein, *Arukh ha-Shulhan, Orah Hayim* 691:3.) That some rabbis sanctioned the use of Sarah Oppenheim's *megillah* indicates that they shared the view that it was halakhically permissible to use a scroll written by a woman for public recitation and that furthermore, they trusted her qualifications as a *sofer*.

158. Quoted in Assaf, *Mekorot* vol. 4, p. 152, from Ephraim Hayyot's work, *Mikra'ei Kodesh* (Ortakoy, Turkey, 1729).

scholarship in his adjuration, for either they did not tutor their sons or daughters together or, if they did, they would hardly pay heed to criticism. The criticism would seem to be aimed at the lay level of Jewish society. Also, Rabbi Jacob Emden (1697–1776), one of the outstanding scholars of his generation, who resided in Emden, Germany, pointed out the impropriety of sending girls to the house of a teacher who was a bachelor, echoing the words of the thirteenth-century rabbi Judah ha-Hasid. Rabbi Emden advised that the girls should rather be sent to an expert woman teacher or, better still, be taught in their own home, so as not to be harassed by young boys on their way to school.[159]

Though parents may not have been as attentive to their daughters' formal religious education, they were concerned with their daughters' ethical and moral tutelage, as is evident in the instructions imparted by rabbis to their wives and daughters in a number of ethical wills. In the testament of a Rabbi Moses Isaac, head of the rabbinical court of the Polish city of Krotoszyn (d. 1797), he instructs his daughters as follows: "And you, my daughters, walk in an upright path, and be modest in your deeds. . . . If God will grant you riches and you shall have servants and maids, it is your obligation to engage in some type of work, as idleness leads to boredom. Be scrupulous in daily prayer, and read every Sabbath from the translated Bible. . . ."[160]

Thus we see that the religious education of girls was not entirely neglected, and that, indeed, many women could be rightly considered knowledgeable and even learned. And yet it should be stated that not all were happy with the situation as it existed. Here and there a lone voice could be heard decrying the lack of *institutionalized* education for girls and criticizing the quality of knowledge obtained by girls through the vehicle of works translated into the native languages of the various countries in which Jewish women resided. One vocal critic was Isaac Wetzler of Celle, Germany, who in 1749 aired his views in *Leibes Briev*, a chronicle of some import, documenting the economic and socioreligious state of the Jews in Germany in the eighteenth century.[161] The author is perplexed that girls are not taught the Pentateuch, Prophets, and Hagiographia directly from the source, thereby acquiring sufficient fluency in the Hebrew language, which in turn would enable them to pray with better understanding. He cites the talmudic passage that submits that he who teaches his daughter Torah is as if he teaches her *tiflut*, and he states that in his opinion it refers primarily to study of the Oral Law. He inveighs against the ironic situation in which the daughters of Israel are more conversant in foreign

---

159. Jacob Emden, *Migdal Oz* (Warsaw, 1882), p. 16a, no. 12.

160. Quoted in Assaf, *Mekorot*, vol. 1, p. 271. The will has been published in *Da'at Kedoshim* (St. Petersburg, 1897).

161. Excerpts from *Liebes Briev* are included in Assaf, *Mekorot*, vol. 4, pp. 111–119. See especially pp. 117–118 for Wetzler's critique of girls' education.

languages, such as Italian and French, than they are in Hebrew and sees no reason why reforms cannot be introduced that would have capable Jewish tutors instruct the girls in Bible and in Hebrew language. Wetzler cites the support of Rabbi Jacob Emden, who also bemoans this situation in his acclaimed Prayer Book. Wetzler criticizes the naive assumption of women that everything they read in the *Ze'enah u-Re'enah* and in the *Teutsch-Humash* is the "law of Moses," despite the fact that these works may contain aggadic tales whose veracity is suspect. He tells of one woman who claimed, based on her reading of the *Teutsch-Humash*, that the prophet Jeremiah was the son of a harlot. Had it not been the Sabbath, claims Wetzler, he would have consigned the book to the flames. He recommends to women that they read instead Jekuthiel ben Isaac Blitz's Yiddish translation of the Bible (1676–1679), which he considered to be a superior work to others of the time.[162]

An anonymous work, published in London in 1771, also advocates "educating girls just as we educate the boys," though the unidentified writer agrees that some subjects, such as *Gemara*, need not be taught.[163] Here we have the call for a more egalitarian form of education. However, the established authorities harbored no such ideas. The time for such education would have to wait. In the meantime, the leading sages of the century were concerned with moral attitudes. The Lithuanian rabbi Elijah Gaon (the "Vilna Gaon," 1720–1797), one of the greatest spiritual and intellectual leaders of Jewry in modern times, addressed a letter, a kind of spiritual testament, to his family when he set out for Palestine (which he never reached), in which he gives instructions for the spiritual education of his daughters. Addressing his wife, he states:

I beseech you that you guide your daughters to refrain from taking oaths, cursing, deceit, or quarreling. They should conduct themselves only with love, affection, and gentleness. Among the books I possess are various ethical works written in German . . . let them read them constantly, especially on the Sabbath. Always guide them in correct ethical and moral behavior. . . .[164]

In the eighteenth century, at the dawn of modernity, we see that strides are being made toward actual education of girls, and voices are being heard to bring these hopes to fruition. The proliferation of women's literature and liturgical pieces leads to the sentiment that more must be done if women are to remain within the fold while the call of the greater, modern world beckons from without.

---

162. Ibid., pp. 117–118.

163. See Assaf, *Mekorot*, vol. 1, p. 224, which contains excerpts from this anonymous pamphlet, written in German, entitled "On the Rearing of Children."

164. From the ethical will of the Gaon of Vilna, *Iggeret ha-Gra*, printed partially in Assaf, *Mekorot*, vol. 4, p. 144.

8

A Historical Survey of Jewish Education for Women: Part V— The Late-Eighteenth- and Nineteenth-Century Jewish World

We have now arrived at the threshold of the modern era. Before we go on to discuss the achievements of exceptional women from elite rabbinic and other families in this period, let us first briefly examine some critical historical developments in the Jewish world, with the emergence of Jewry into the era of emancipation. The accompanying changes in the internal organization of Jewish life, unprecedented in the annals of Jewish history, had profound effects on Jewish education, effects that would eventually lead to the establishment of universal Jewish education for women.[1]

GENERAL BACKGROUND

Traditional Jewish society in the late Middle Ages (sixteenth–eighteenth centuries) in western, central, and eastern Europe was characterized by almost complete seclusion from its surrounding milieu by virtue of being confined within ghetto walls. The intellectual life of the surrounding society in this era subserved the Christian theology, and thus by its very nature excluded the

---

1. For a comprehensive overview of the history and development of Jewish education in modern times, the monumental five-volume work of the noted educator Zevi Scharfstein is recommended: *Toldot ha-Hinukh be-Yisrael ba-Dorot ha-Aharonim* (Jerusalem: Rubin Mass, 1960–1966).

Jew. Deprived of citizenship and political rights and oppressed religiously, socially, and economically, Jews were left to cultivate their own tradition within the confines of their own community. There existed so wide a gulf between Jews and Gentiles that there could be no question of a divided identity. Jews identified fully with their own group and its religious and intellectual aspirations. Their intellectual horizons were limited to the Talmud; linguistically, too, their Yiddish dialect isolated them from their neighbors.

In the aftermath of the French Revolution and its call for equality and freedom, Jews in the nineteenth century achieved a measure of political freedom in Europe. Napoleon was willing to grant Jews the status of citizen but in return was determined to control Judaism and to assimilate Jews into Christian society. With the call for independence on the part of many states in midcentury, Jews indeed were allowed to become citizens in many countries. The ghetto walls were breached in western Europe, and Jews faced a grave threat to their traditional survival. All of subsequent Jewish history may be seen to be a reaction of some type to this event. Loss of the power of rabbinic authority in control of the people signaled power struggles that have not as yet subsided. Anti-Semitism did not abate but took on new forms in this period. Theological hatred was transformed into the wish for political disenfranchisement of Jews. But the benefits were considered by some to be enormous in the social, educational, and economic areas. In western Europe, Jews were emancipated from the Middle Ages.

The Jewish Enlightenment movement (*Haskalah*) of the late-eighteenth and nineteenth centuries was an aspect of the general Enlightenment in western Europe. The new scientific approach that had been gaining currency in Europe, the emphasis on reason as the arbiter of human thought and activity, the humanist movement and the new universal spirit that made the exclusion of the Jew "a gross anomaly,"[2] and the economic, social, and religious revolutions all combined to create a climate of liberal opinion and religious tolerance, that is, a belief in the innate right of man to life, liberty, and equality of opportunity. "While such advocates of religious freedom and toleration as Count Mirabeau and Montesquieu breached the walls from without, a group led by the German Jewish philosopher Moses Mendlessohn battered them from within."[3] They endeavored to prepare their fellow Jews in the ghetto for the era of emancipation and believed that secular enlightenment, that is, worldly learning, would demonstrate the Jews' worth and virtue

---

2. Term used by Michael A. Meyer in *The Origins of the Modern Jew: Jewish Identity and European Culture in Germany, 1749–1824* (Detroit: Wayne State University Press, 1967), p. 15.

3. David Rudavsky, *Modern Jewish Religious Movements* (New York: Behrman House, 1967, 1979), p. 18.

to the Christian world. It was thus on formulating a new educational program for their Jewish brethren, which would combine secular learning with a modernized Jewish religious studies program, that Mendelssohn and his group invested their efforts and pinned their hopes for the future of their people.[4] Meanwhile, there were those who sought to adjust their views and the laws and customs of Judaism to the spirit and standards of the new age. The Reformers in Germany instituted changes in traditional Jewish practice and observance, thus redefining Jewish theology. Other attempts to adapt Judaism to the changed conditions gave rise to additional alignments in religious Judaism: the neo-Orthodox as the extreme opposite to Reform and the Historical School (a forerunner of the American Conservative movement) in the center.[5]

While the struggle between the traditionalists and Reformers was being waged in the nineteenth century in Germany and central Europe, another religious contest, of ultimately far less consequence, engulfed the Jews of eastern Europe in the form of the clash between two Orthodox groups – the *Hasidim* and their opponents, the so-called *Mitnagdim*. Hasidism was a religious movement, born in the Ukraine in the latter part of the eighteenth century, partly in response to the difficult circumstances created by the breakup of Poland-Lithuania in the eighteenth century, partly as a response to religious persecution, and partly in reaction to the excessive Talmudism pervading the intellectual circles, which neglected the general populace, leaving them in a spiritual vacuum. Hasidism emphasized piety rather than scholarship, as well as the service of God in joy rather than ascetic self-denial. Ecstasy, mass enthusiasm, close-knit group cohesion, and charismatic leadership focused on the person of a *rebbe* ("leader") or *zaddik* ("righteous person") were to become the distinguishing socioreligious marks of Hasidism.[6]

---

4. For a comparative analysis of traditional Jewish education in the High Middle Ages with the educational program of the *Haskalah* as formulated by the German Enlightener Naphtali Herz Wessely and by his Russian counterpart Isaac Ber Levinsohn, see my unpublished paper (Jerusalem: Hebrew University, 1987) on the subject. See also Wessely's work, *Divrei Shalom ve-Emet* (Berlin, 1882), and Levinsohn's *Te'udah be-Yisrael*, ed. Emanuel Etkes (Jerusalem: Mercaz Zalman Shazar, 1977). See also Alexander Altmann, *Moses Mendelsohn* (Philadelphia: Jewish Publication Society of America, 1973), and I. Zinberg, *A History of Jewish Literature*, vol. 8, *The Berlin Haskalah*, and vol. 11, *The Haskalah Movement in Russia*.

5. For an excellent account of emancipation and adjustment within Jewry and the rise of modern Jewish religious movements, see Rudavsky, *Modern Jewish Religious Movements*; and Jacob Katz, *Out of the Ghetto* (Cambridge, MA: Harvard University Press, 1973).

6. For elaboration on the subject of Hasidism, see Samuel Aba Horodezky, *Ha-Hasidut ve-ha-Hasidim*, 4 vols. (Berlin, 1919–1922); Jacob S. Minkin, *The Romance of Hasidism* (New York: Macmillan, 1935); and Harry M. Rabinowicz, *The World of*

Although initially there was much friction and conflict between the *Hasidim* and their intellectually oriented opponents, the *Mitnagdim*, the schism was partially healed in the mid-nineteenth century, when both found themselves threatened by a new intellectual trend, the *Haskalah*, which portended to breach the walls of the ghetto and rend asunder the cohesiveness of the Jewish people and their immunity from assimilation. The *Haskalah*, or Jewish Enlightenment, penetrated eastern Europe from German lands. The Enlightenment, which mocked Hasidism, attempted to infuse into Jewish life modern philosophy and modern thought and to relieve education from the "chains" of theology and begin the teaching of secular subjects. The *Hasidim* and their opponents put up a united stand, which was to prove an effective hindrance to the spread of Enlightenment among the majority of eastern European Jews (although it certainly made inroads and was to create a secular brand of Jew). The leaders of the Jewish communities in eastern Europe resisted such schemes on the grounds that even a partially secularized education would deprive Jewish youth of traditional ways of life and, at the same time, not even enable them to find a place in the Gentile workplace. The rabbis were speaking to a reality. The reality was that unlike western Europe, where the Enlightenment was accompanied by emancipation of the Jews, in eastern Europe, emancipation did not take place. In fact, the political and economic situation of the Russian Jews as well as the Polish Jews, who had become the subjects of the Russian crown, sadly deteriorated in the nineteenth century.

The effects of the *Haskalah* on the educational and cultural spheres differed in the various European lands, depending upon the local culture and politics and on the numerical strength and the social and economic status of the Jewish population.[7] Whereas the traditional *hadarim*, *Talmud Torah* schools, and *yeshivot* continued to exist in almost all lands of Jewish residence, certain more liberal Jewish schools were established.[8] One result of both the spirit of enlightenment and the introduction, in various countries, of compulsory education and/or the establishment of government schools in the middle to late nineteenth century, was that the formal religious education of Jewish girls was more widely, though far from universally, considered and reckoned with, especially in liberal circles. These circles were often not concerned with halakhic parameters, and therefore the issue of the halakhic distinction between the sexes in formal religious education was generally not grappled with. The advancement in women's education as such was paralleled by a

---

Hasidism (London: Valentine, Mitchell, 1970), rev. and published as *Hasidism: The Movement and Its Masters* (Northvale, NJ: Jason Aronson, 1988).

7. See E. Bortniker, *Encyclopaedia Judaica*, vol. 6, p. 420.

8. See the five volumes of Z. Scharfstein, *Toldot ha-Hinukh be-Yisrael be-Dorot ha-Aharonim* (Jerusalem: Reuven Mass, 1960–1966).

decline in the overall quality of Jewish education within these circles. However, these trends did have their effects on those groups committed to a traditional Jewish way of life, as we shall see. Let us now examine some trends in Jewish education, country by country, during the period under discussion, highlighting the state of affairs in girls' religious education.

JEWISH EDUCATION

France

In France, the small French Jewry of the nineteenth century, formally organized as a consistory, opened schools in Paris – one for boys (1819),[9] and one for girls (1821)[10] – which were shortly afterward taken over by the municipality. Besides the general secular subjects, the schools offered a very limited program of Jewish studies. Additional schools of the same type, for boys and girls each, came into being as the Jewish population increased in Paris and in several other cities, particularly in southern France.[11] After midcentury, however, most Jewish families began sending their children to the government schools. Supplementary religious instruction was at a minimum. The Consistoire offered religious classes twice a week to the Jewish children in the public schools. Girls aged twelve and boys aged thirteen celebrated "Confirmation" on the holiday of Shavuot (Pentecost) in the synagogues.[12] In Alsace and Lorraine, Jewish education was more intensive,[13] but here too it became mainly supplementary by the beginning of the twentieth century.[14]

Italy

Even more precipitous was the decline of Jewish education in Italy,[15] where for centuries prior to the French Revolution there operated a well-organized system of both elementary and advanced Jewish schools, as we have seen. About sixteen hundred pupils, only 20 percent of the Jewish child population, including both boys and girls, attended Jewish schools at the close of the ninteenth century. These were mainly four-year elementary schools (some

9. Scharfstein, *Toldot ha-Hinukh*, vol. 1 (1960), p. 58.
10. Ibid., p. 59.
11. Ibid., see pp. 60–64.
12. Ibid., p. 62.
13. Ibid., p. 65.
14. Ibid., pp. 66–67.
15. Ibid., pp. 192f.

with two-year kindergartens), accepted by government authorities as fulfilling the legal requirements of elementary education. Jewish instruction was given in these schools for about one hour daily and consisted of reading, prayers, and selections from the Torah. Older children received "religious instruction" and limited knowledge of Jewish history.[16] The rabbinical seminaries in France and Italy were similarly weak.[17]

England

In England, prior to the introduction of compulsory education (1870), Jews maintained schools of their own.[18] By the beginning of the ninteenth century, English had replaced Portuguese and Yiddish as the language of instruction in Jewish congregational schools, which were reorganized and broadened. The one girls' school already in existence since 1730, the Villareal school, was amalgamated with a National and Infant School in 1839.[19] When a huge influx of Jewish immigrants arrived from eastern Europe in the nineteenth century, philanthropists established Jewish Free Schools for them in several cities. These Free Schools were able to devote as large a part of their curriculum to Jewish studies as they wished, prior to the Education Act of 1870. Consequently they had twelve hours of Jewish studies to eighteen hours of secular ones.[20] Though these schools were originally established for boys, as a result of a pastoral letter issued by Chief Rabbi of Britain Dr. Nathan Marcus Adler, a parallel institution for girls was opened in London in 1846, which merged with the Western Boys' Free School to form the Westminster Jews' Free School in 1853.[21] In about 1850, the West Metropolitan Jewish Schools in London were also founded, which were eventually transformed into the High School for Girls, intended to give a "good middle-class education to Jewish girls."[22] Charlotte von Rothschild established a girls' school for the

---

16. Ibid., pp. 195–196.

17. Ibid., see pp. 63–66 and 197–199, respectively.

18. For Jewish education in nineteenth-century England, see the following works: Chaim Bermant, *Troubled Eden* (New York: Basic Books, 1969), pp. 126–128; V. D. Lipman, *Social History of the Jews of England, 1850–1950* (London: Watts, 1954), pp. 45–49, 150–155; V. D. Lipman, *Three Centuries of Anglo-Jewish History* (Cambridge: Jewish Historical Society of England, 1961), pp. 86–88; Cecil Roth, *Essays and Portraits in Anglo-Jewish History* (Philadelphia: Jewish Publication Society of America, 1962), pp. 219f; and Scharfstein, *Toldot ha-Hinukh*, vol. 3 (1962), pp. 277f.

19. Albert Hyamson, *The Sephardim of England* (London: Methuen, 1951), p. 94.

20. See, for example, Bermant, *Troubled Eden*, p. 126, and Scharfstein, *Toldot ha-Hinukh*, vol. 3, p. 278.

21. Lipman, *Social History of the Jews in England*, p. 48.

22. Ibid., quoted on p. 48.

education of poor girls in Bell Lane, London (c.1860), where she herself lectured on religious topics on the Sabbaths and holidays.[23] By 1850, some two thousand Jewish children attended Free Schools in Britain, representing a remarkably high proportion of the total Jewish school-age population at a time when the Jews of Britain numbered no more than about thirty-five thousand.[24]

The Free Schools did not, however, enjoy a complete monopoly of Jewish education at this period. Some children attended Jewish fee-paying schools, oftentimes boarding schools, run by private individuals, and these were frequently of vastly differing educational standards. Though most of these schools were established for boys, at least one for girls came into being in this period. It was run by a woman writer, Miriam Mendes Belisaro, and her sisters in Hackney and was attended by most of the daughters of the wealthier families of Anglo Jewry.[25]

Another type of school, a trade school, was established by a group of philanthropists in London in 1807 in an effort to reform the Jewish poor. Called the Jews' Hospital, it was established for both boys and girls and was as much concerned with forming the character of its wards as it was with preparing them for a useful trade. To that end the children were provided with instruction in Jewish ethics and morals. When Amelia Solomon visited the school in July 1812, she noted with pleasure that the girls had learned Maimonides' Thirteen Articles of Faith. The Hebrew instruction of the children was nevertheless meager, consisting of nothing more advanced than the reading of the prayer book and selections from the Bible. In 1818, "A Daughter of Israel" (as she termed herself) published in London a small work entitled "The Jewish Preceptress, or Elementary Lessons, written chiefly for the use of female children educated at the Jews' Hospital."[26]

Following the Education Act of 1870, which established free primary schooling for children in Great Britain, no new Jewish Free Schools came into being, and the private, fee-paying establishments suffered a sharp decline. The level of Jewish education in the existing Free Schools drastically declined, as the schools were forced to change the ratio of Jewish to secular studies to $7\frac{1}{2}$ and 22 hours, respectively.[27] The majority of Jewish children attended the local public schools, where the boys and girls received limited religious instruction on the school premises after school hours, offered by the Society

---

23. Naheda Remy, *Das Juedische Weib* (Leipzig, 1892), p. 215.

24. Lipman, *Three Centuries of Anglo-Jewish History*, p. 86.

25. Hyamson, *The Sephardim of England*, p. 262.

26. See Todd Endelman, *The Jews of Georgian England, 1714–1830* (Philadelphia: Jewish Publication Society of America, 1979), pp. 236–240. Also see Cecil Roth, *Essays and Portraits in Anglo-Jewish History*, p. 231.

27. See Bermant, *Troubled Eden*, p. 126. Also see Sharfstein, vol. 3, pp. 279–280.

for the Diffusion of Religious Knowledge (1860) and its successor, the Jewish Religious Education Board (1893).[28] Such an allocation of religious instruction (for their boys, if not for their girls) was not sufficient for the newcomers, who poured into the country from eastern Europe after 1880, and to the horror of the old established communities in London and the provinces, which had been taking particular pride in the growth and achievements of the day schools, dozens of Yiddish-speaking *hadarim* and *Talmud Torah* schools were set up for boys (who would often meet as many as three times daily in-between school hours) throughout the country, which provided a far deeper basic training in Judaism.[29] Though girls were barred from these traditional educational institutions, many continued to receive supplementary after-school religious instruction or to attend the Free Schools. Thus, for example, by the turn of the century, the Jews' Free School in London's East End consisted of thirty-five hundred students, including both boys and girls, making it the largest school in Britain and reputedly the biggest Jewish teaching center in Europe, if not in the whole world.[30] Anglo-Jewish historian V. D. Lipman comments, "It may not be unsafe to say that in the first decade of this [the twentieth] century virtually all the boys and a fairly large proportion of the girls received Jewish instruction at some time between seven and fourteen years of age."[31] Though the quality and quantity of the formal Jewish education of girls (and of many boys, as well) left much to be desired, it was a beginning.

Germany

The German lands present a more complex picture. In Germany and Austria, emancipation and the Enlightenment brought about major changes in the Jewish style of living and in education. Unlike in the past, we now find strong assimilationist tendencies, especially in the large cities such as Berlin, where the Jewish communities were comparatively new and unencumbered by age-old local tradition and custom. Here we see considerable conversion, which at the beginning of the nineteenth century assumed the dimensions of a mass movement. The adherents of *Haskalah* shared the rationalist belief in the boundless efficacy of a rational education. They therefore turned to a change in the curriculum and methods of teaching as the main means of shaping a new mode of Jewish life. The old-style *hadarim* were replaced by modern Jewish schools for those who did not wish to send their children to the general

28. See Lipman, *Social History of the Jews in England*, pp. 151–155; Lipman, *Three Centuries of Anglo-Jewish History*, p. 86; and Scharfstein, *Toldot ha-Hinukh*, vol. 3, p. 279.

29. Bermant, *Troubled Eden*, pp. 126–127.

30. Scharfstein, *Toldot ha-Hinukh*, vol. 3, p. 278.

31. Lipman, *Social History of the Jews in England*, p. 155.

schools, where an anti-Jewish attitude often prevailed. They were established by funds provided by wealthy Jews and were attended mostly by children of the poor, as the wealthy classes were educated privately.[32] The curriculum stressed secular and vocational training, but some time was apportioned to religious studies as well. The Jewish program was meager, consisting of reading of prayers, some portions of the Bible translated into German (using Mendelssohn's translation), bits of Jewish history—mostly biblical—and religion and ethics. The traditional study of *Mishnah* and Talmud was abandoned even in the secondary schools.[33] These schools had a revolutionary effect on Jewish education, for they heralded the transfer of the center of gravity from Jewish studies to general subjects. Confirmation ceremonies, in imitation of the Christian custom, were introduced in these schools as well.[34]

Haskalah brought considerable change in the education of girls as well, reflecting the theories propagated by Rousseau in *Émile*, Book 5, in this regard.[35] The daughters of the upper classes generally studied under private tutors, because their parents desired to provide them with a humanistic education that would enable them to integrate into the cultural and social life of the surrounding society. The "enlighteners" soon realized the direction such education took, whereby "the daughters of Israel do not understand any of the prayers or other Hebrew studies assigned to them. Instead of devoting themselves on Sabbath and festivals to the Word of the Living God, they read nonsensical literature in foreign languages which corrupt their souls."[36] Indeed, many of these women were in the front lines of the numerous conversions taking place in Germany during this period. The "enlighteners" made efforts to remedy this state of affairs by organizing schools for girls based on the educational ideals of the *Haskalah*. They were attended mostly by children of the poor. The first such school for girls was the *Schulund Arbeitsanstalt*, established in 1798 in Hamburg, followed by the *Industrieschule*, founded in Breslau in 1801. Other girls' schools were instituted in Dessau (1799), Frank-

---

32. For an excellent account of the changes in education in Germany brought about by the *Haskalah*, see Mordechai Eliav, *Ha-Hinukh ha-Yehudi be-Germanyah b'Ymei ha-Haskalah ve-ha-Emanzipazia* [Jewish Education in Germany in the period of Enlightenment and Emancipation] (Jerusalem: The Jewish Agency, 1960). See also Katz, *Out of the Ghetto*, pp. 124f, and Scharfstein, *Toldot ha-Hinukh*, vol. 1, pp. 79f.

33. For a critique of these schools, see the writings of Rabbi Tzvi Hirsh Horowitz (1811), head of the rabbinical court of Frankfurt am Main, quoted in Scharfstein, *Toldot ha-Hinukh*, vol. 1, p. 105. For sample curricula of two of these schools, see Scharfstein, *Toldot ha-Hinukh*, vol. 1, pp. 109–111.

34. See Eliav, *Ha-Hinukh ha-Yehudi be-Germanyah*, pp. 257–270. Also see Scharfstein, *Toldot ha-Hinukh*, vol. 1, p. 101.

35. See Eliav, *Ha-Hinukh ha-Yehudi be-Germanyah*, p. 271.

36. The words of a foremost "enlightener," the principal of the school in Seesen, quoted in Eliav, *Ha-Hinukh ha-Yehudi be-Germanyah*, p. 273.

furt (1809), Berlin (1809 and 1818), Koenigsburg (1820s), and Posen (1833). The curricula of these schools stressed vocational training and handiwork but also included, in varying degrees, some Hebrew, Yiddish, German, the fundamentals of religion and ethics, biblical history, arithmetic, art, and music.[37] Some schools established by the "enlighteners" were coeducational.[38]

After midcentury, when larger numbers of children began to enroll in the general educational institutions of the government, supplementary schools for boys and girls came into being, from which students usually withdrew after the age of thirteen. Some religious instruction was also given in the general schools to Jewish students.[39] This limited religious instruction was of so dismal a nature that it prompted the scholar and historiographer Simon Bernfeld (1860–1940) to declare: "It is indeed a miracle if a young boy graduates from school with a slight knowledge of Hebrew, or if a young girl does not speak in a derogatory manner of Judaism."[40] Of the general state of Jewish education in ninteenth-century Germany, Bernfeld remarked, "One should not wonder at the many conversions taking place, but rather that Judaism continues to exist in Germany at all. This existence is not a credit to our generation but to prior generations. The national spirit has still not been extinguished but it will be, if there will be no great change in Jewish education."[41]

There was, however, a movement in Germany that countered these tendencies. Termed "Neo-Orthodoxy," it, like Orthodoxy, underscored faith and tradition; upheld supernatural revelation as the source and sanction of Jewish law, both Scriptural and Oral; accepted the validity of the customs and practices of the past; and was meticulous in Jewish observance and practice. It also, however, espoused the aim of integration with modern society and the liberation of Judaism from its intellectual isolation.[42] In essence, the movement is connected with Rabbi Samson Raphael Hirsch (1808–1888), chief exponent of Neo-Orthodoxy in Germany, and his doctrine of *Torah im derekh eretz* ("Torah together with the conduct of life," meaning in this context secular culture). Hirsch attributed a large measure of the defection of Jewish

---

37. For a detailed description of these schools and their curricula, see Eliav, *Ha-Hinukh ha-Yehudi be-Germanyah*, pp. 273–278.

38. Ibid., p. 278.

39. See Scharfstein, *Toldot ha-Hinukh*, vol. 1, pp. 116–125.

40. Quoted in Scharfstein, *Toldot ha-Hinukh*, vol. 1, p. 124.

41. Ibid., p. 125.

42. For elaboration on the principles of Neo-Orthodoxy as expressed in the writings of Rabbi Samson Raphael Hirsch, see Dayan I. Grunfeld's introduction to Hirsch's *Horeb: A Philosophy of Jewish Laws and Observances* (New York, London, and Jerusalem: Soncino Press, 1962), pp. xix–cliii. See also David Rudavsky, *Modern Jewish Religious Movements*, pp. 218–270.

youth to Reform or to Christianity to the ghetto's exclusion of modern secular culture from Jewish life. He believed in the employment of secular learning as a means of supporting and strengthening religious education. He maintained that the "estrangement between Judaism and general culture was not necessarily characteristic of Judaism, but was only the product of the ghetto and the forced segregation of the Jew."[43] Toward this end Hirsch adopted some of the features of the *Haskalah* program in educational matters, including the formal education of women.

Hirsch was a gifted educational theoretician as well as a practiced administrator, who translated his pedagogical ideas into reality in the elementary and secondary day schools he established in Frankfurt. Both elements – religious education and secular studies – were combined into a harmonious whole, though Hirsch did not regard the two areas of study as being on a par. Hirsch considered the religious instruction as primary and the secular as secondary, in contrast to the leaders of the Enlightenment. "The core of all knowledge for every Jew is Torah," he declared,[44] and therefore endeavored to provide his students with a high-quality Jewish education.[45] Girls were to be the recipients of such instruction as well.

Hirsch regarded the education of girls as being of selfsame value to the education of boys, and of equal necessity at this critical juncture in German-Jewish history. (For his views on the subject, see Chapter Three.) With the exception of the study of Talmud, no differences were to be made in the religious instruction of girls and boys. A radical innovation in traditional Jewish education was his idea of coeducation in all Jewish subjects, except Talmud, at the elementary level, which in his school consisted of three grades (his secondary school, consisting of six grades, was segregated).[46]

Hirsch established a coeducational elementary school in Frankfurt in 1853,[47] comprising 55 boys and 29 girls,[48] which expanded to a segregated

---

43. Rudavsky, *Modern Jewish Religious Movements*, p. 234. For elaboration, see Dayan I. Grunfeld, "The Torah and Humanism – A Jewish Theory of Knowledge," in *Horeb*, pp. 1xxxix–xcvii. See especially p. xcv.

44. Phrasing Hirsch in *Horeb*, p. 408.

45. One is tempted to elaborate on Hirsch's pedagogical principles; however, they are beyond the scope of this study. The interested reader may wish to read the following: the essays on Jewish education in Samson R. Hirsch, *Judaism Eternal*, trans. I. Grunfeld, 2 vols. (London: Soncino Press, 1956); Hirsch, *Horeb*, pp. 406–416; Rudavsky *Modern Jewish Religous Movements*, pp. 240–248; and Eliav, *Ha-Hinukh ha-Yehudi be-Germanyah*, pp. 227–231.

46. See Eliav, *Ha-Hinukh ha-Yehudi be-Germanyah*, p. 231; and Scharfstein, *Toldot ha-Hinukh*, vol. 1, p. 128.

47. There is a descrepancy in the date between Eliav and Scharfstein. Eliav places it at April 4, 1853 (see p. 231), and Scharfstein at 1855 (see vol. 1, p. 128).

48. See Eliav, *Ha-Hinukh ha-Yehudi be-Germanyah*, p. 231.

secondary school (comprising a total of nine grades) within a decade. In 1863 his students numbered 156 boys and 103 girls. In 1871, Hirsch established a separate girls' secondary school.[49] At the turn of the century, the boys' and girls' secondary schools consisted of 600 students.[50] His schools offered a substantial program of Jewish studies including Hebrew language, Bible with the commentary of Rashi, Jewish history, *Mishnah* and some Talmud with commentaries (for boys only), Jewish law and custom, and Hebrew literature and poetry. The general studies were programmed after the pattern of the government or private German schools. Girls also received instruction in handicrafts at the elementary level. In the elementary school, fifteen hours per week were allotted to religious studies; in the secondary schools, up to eighteen hours.[51] It may be safe to say that for the first time in Jewish history, girls were privy to a superior formal religious education.

Hirsch properly regarded Jewish education as the main artery of Jewish life. He made an original contribution in this area that had a lasting, though not universal, impact on Jewish educational theory and practice in both Germany and other countries until this day.

Eastern Europe

Insofar as religious education in nineteenth-century eastern Europe is concerned, as mentioned earlier, Western ideas began penetrating into the Polish-Russian domain after a lag of some decades. In Poland, contiguous to Germany, the Enlightenment first reached those in the more prosperous and worldly Jewish circles who believed that the educational system maintained by the Jewish communities was backward and that the cure for these ills was a school program incorporating many aspects of the Polish schools. The government, too, was interested in this educational issue, its aim being Polonization.[52] A similar situation obtained somewhat later in Russia when the government attempted a Russification of the Jewish schools and tried to destroy the *heder* and the *yeshivah*.[53] Many Jewish assimilationists in both

49. Ibid.

50. Ibid., p. 232.

51. For discussion of curriculum content, see Scharfstein, *Toldot ha-Hinukh*, p. 128; and Eliav, *Ha-Hinukh ha-Yehudi be-Germanyah*, p. 232.

52. For elaboration, see Scharfstein, *Toldot ha-Hinukh*, vol. 1, pp. 260–264, 275–278. See also Simon Greenberg, "Jewish Educational Institutions," in *The Jews: Their History, Culture and Religion*, ed. Louis Finkelstein (Philadelphia: Jewish Publication Society of America, 1949), p. 926.

53. For a full account of the government's attempts to russify the Jewish school system, see Michael Stanislawski, *Tsar Nicholas I and the Jews* (Philadelphia: Jewish Publication Society of America, 1983), and Scharfstein, *Toldot ha-Hinukh*, vol. 1, pp. 255f. Also see Isaac Levitats, *The Jewish Community in Russia, 1844–1917* (Jerusalem:

Poland and Russia supported the governments' efforts. Even some of the nonassimilationist *maskilim* ("enlighteners"), such as Isaac Baer Levinsohn,[54] cooperated with government, often not realizing its ulterior motives. The Polonization/Russification and proselytizing aspects of these schools were so pronounced, however, that the majority of Polish and Russian Jews resisted the governments' attempt to convert the *heder* into a school and remained faithful to their traditional style of schooling.

Nevertheless, some attempts were made by proponents of the *Haskalah* to offer Jewish girls formal religious training "that would prepare [them] to be the enlightened first teacher[s] of the child at home."[55] Special Hebrew schools for girls were established in Tchernigov (1862), Kishinev (1864), Minsk (1864), and other cities, where, in addition to secular subjects, the Hebrew language, Jewish history, interpretation of books of ethical value, and aspects of the Jewish religion formed part of the curriculum.[56]

Until the last quarter of the nineteenth century, all efforts to effect change in the Jewish educational system, whether sponsored by Jews themselves or by Gentiles, were inspired primarily by the desire to assimilate the Jew into the general population. By about 1885, there was a discernible change in attitude among the ranks of Jewish intellectuals when they realized that complete civil and social emancipation were not to be a consequence of secularization and modernization of Jewish life. At the same time, a renewed spirit of self-respect was awakened within the ranks of those Westernized or modernized Jews who were deeply attached to Judaism and to the Hebrew language and literature. Zionism and modern Hebrew made remarkable headway among all classes of the Jewish community. Yiddish language and literature simultaneously experienced unprecedented development. All this inner cultural revival was bound to be reflected in the community's educational activities. A new modern Jewish school appeared: the *heder metukan*, the "improved," progressive *heder*.[57] Unlike the *heder* and *Talmud Torah*, the language of instruction was Hebrew. There was less emphasis on religious piety and on rabbinic literature, but there was a positive attitude toward the Jewish religion and toward all the spiritual and cultural treasures of the Jewish people. New pedagogical methods and techniques were instituted. The uniqueness of

---

Posner and Sons, 1981), p. 118, and Simon Greenberg, "Jewish Educational Institutions," p. 926.

54. See note 4. See also Scharfstein, *Toldot ha-Hinukh*, vol. 1, pp. 271–275.

55. Emanuel Gamoran, *Changing Conceptions in Jewish Education* (New York: Macmillan, 1924), pp. 193–194.

56. Ibid.

57. See Scharfstein, *Toldot Ha-Hinukh*, vol. 1, pp. 389–410. See also Levitats, *The Jewish Community in Russia, 1844–1917*, p. 124, and Greenberg, "Jewish Educational Institutions," p. 927.

this new, "improved" *heder* consisted in that "once and for all [it] proclaimed the right of girls to a full Jewish education."[58] Some of the "improved" *hadarim* were coeducational, but new schools for girls also made their appearance, following the examples of two girls' schools that had gained considerable repute. These were the *Yehudiah* school in Vilna, whose students numbered in the hundreds and to which "people from far and wide came in order to view it,"[59] and the "First Hebrew School" of Puah Rakowski in Warsaw. Of Rakowski's school M. J. Fried wrote in his memoirs, "Rakowski conducted her school successfully for many years, producing a generation of Hebrew daughters in the full sense of the word, who even after they married, remained faithful to the Hebrew language and literature, and influenced positively the education of their children."[60]

Though these new schools for boys and for girls increased in number and flourished, they never replaced the *heder* and *Talmud Torah*, which remained predominant within eastern European Jewry until 1914. These new schools did not meet the religious standards of the Orthodox communities.

An interesting educational phenomenon during the nineteenth century, which was to have repercussions for the subsequent establishment of universal Jewish education for girls, was the remarkable development of the *yeshivah*. This, in spite of government interference and of the indifference to them of the modern, so-called enlightened Jewish groups. Many of the leaders of Russian Jewry during this period were products of the *yeshivot*, in which "high scholarship and originality raised the repute of talmudic studies and added dignity to those engaged in them."[61] The community of the small country of Lithuania pioneered in this respect when the Volozhin *yeshivah* was established in 1803 and from the very start introduced innovations in the method of study, offered considerable freedom for students in the choice of tractates to be covered, and later provided some general subjects as well, such as history and mathematics.[62] *Yeshivot* were founded in the ensuing decades in many other towns in Lithuania and Russia. A number of these were centers of distinctive Jewish philosophies, where, for example, ethics were stressed or hasidic ideology imparted.[63] Modern-type *yeshivot* also made their appearance;

---

58. Levitats, *The Jewish Community in Russia, 1844–1917*, p. 124.

59. Scharfstein, *Toldot ha-Hinukh*, vol. 1, p. 396.

60. M. J. Fried, *Yamim ve-Shanim* (Tel Aviv, 1939), vol. 2, p. 165. Quoted in Scharfstein *Toldot ha-Hinukh*, vol. 1, p. 396.

61. E. Bortniker, *Encyclopaedia Judaica*, vol. 6, p. 425.

62. Ibid. On the Volozhin Yeshivah, see Scharfstein, *Toldot ha-Hinukh*, vol. 1, pp. 339–345.

63. Ibid. For a description of the various other *yeshivot* that were established, see pp. 355–384. See also Levitats, *The Jewish Community in Russia*, p. 123.

these included general studies as an integral part of the program.[64] On the eve of World War I the enrollment in some thirty *yeshivot* in Russia, which at the time included the Baltic states, much of Poland, and Bessarabia, was about ten thousand students.[65]

The Balkans, Islamic States, and Other Countries Influenced by the Alliance Israélite Universelle

In the Balkans, and in the Moslem lands of the eastern Mediterranean and North Africa, an important factor in the modernization of Jewish education appeared in the second half of the nineteenth century, in the form of the Alliance Israélite Universelle (AIU).[66] This organization was an expression of the Jewish group-consciousness of French Jews, who, having achieved emancipation and assimilation in their own country, felt the responsibility incumbent upon them to help their coreligionists wherever they were suffering for, or discriminated against because of, their religion. The AIU began its activities in the political field but after about 1860 concentrated mainly on education. It was instrumental in westernizing to a great extent some of the Oriental-style *Talmud Torahs* of the old Turkish empire and the Maghreb countries, as well as those in Persia and the Balkans. Its first schools were established in Tetuan, Morocco, in 1862; in Tangiers in 1864; and in Damascus and Baghdad in 1865.[67] Soon a large network of schools, numbering more than a hundred on the eve of World War I, came into being.[68] The Alliance schools regarded the education of girls as acceptable practice and established either coeducational schools or separate schools for girls in the many cities of Bulgaria, Turkey, India, Syria, Lebanon, Palestine, Iraq, Persia, Libya, Egypt, Tunisia, and Algeria.[69] In Baghdad, the Alliance school for girls opened in 1893 with 788 students.[70] To train teachers for these schools, the AIU founded the École Normale Israélite Orientale in Paris (1867). Students were recruited from the AIU schools in the various countries, and their study in Paris was subsidized.

---

64. See Scharfstein, *Toldot ha-Hinukh*, vol. 1, pp. 384–389. Also see Levitats, ibid., p. 123.

65. Bortniker, *Encyclopaedia Judaica*, vol. 6, p. 426.

66. See Scharfstein, *Toldot ha-Hinukh*, vol. 5.

67. Ibid., pp. 13–14.

68. Ibid. See pp. 16–19 for a detailing of the many schools, including number of boy and girl students, established in all the countries of the Balkans and Moslem lands.

69. Ibid. See, for example, pp. 13, 16–19, 24–25, 32, 35–37, 52, 57, 67, 83, 92–94, 102, 115–117, 122, 125, and 127. See also Yehezkel Yiftah, *Ha-Hinukh ha-Yehudi be-Iraq be-Dorot ha-Aharonim* (Nahalal: Hotsa'at Yad Eli'ezer, 1983), p. 38.

70. Scharfstein, *Toldot ha-Hinukh*, vol. 5, p. 36.

A separate department for women teachers was also established.[71] The AIU educational institutions stressed French language and culture, but Hebrew, Bible, and other Jewish subjects were taught in them as well.[72] The work of the Alliance encountered difficulties when certain communities viewed the propagation of French culture in the schools as a danger to the traditional framework of Jewish life. In addition, the schools often came under criticism for their relatively meager Jewish content.[73] Interestingly, in certain locales such as Tetuan, Morocco, the number of girls in Alliance schools exceeded that of boys. Because girls did not have a religious obligation to study Torah, parents were not as concerned if the Jewish instruction of their daughters was not very extensive.[74]

Other Jewish schools in the communities where the AIU operated were influenced by their educational enterprises. Old *hadarim* underwent considerable modernization. School societies came into being in many cities of the Moslem or Eastern lands, which established schools for boys, and often for girls as well. Indeed, a non-Alliance girls' school was established in Mogador, Morocco, as early as 1840.[75]

Some women who were trained as teachers rose to the rank of principal, such as Cambridge-trained Rebecca Reuven, who, in the early part of the twentieth century, elevated to a superior level the standard of education in the Jewish school established by the B'nai Israel Benevolent Society for Promoting Education, in Bombay, India.[76]

Thus we see that in eastern and Islamic lands, the religious education of girls had become a reality toward the end of the nineteenth century, though the quality of the education offered to them in those early years (as well as to boys who attended the Alliance's schools and other school societies' institutions) was variable. Religious content was often meager, though occasionally satisfactory.

Palestine

In Palestine, education in the small *yishuv* (Jewish settlement), of which there were twenty-five thousand in 1880, largely resembled the traditional types

---

71. Ibid., p. 15.

72. Ibid. See, for example, p. 25 for a description of the Jewish content in the schools of the Alliance.

73. Ibid. See, for example, pp. 20, 25, 105, 111, and 136.

74. Ibid., see p. 115.

75. Bortniker, *Encyclopaedia Judaica*, p. 427. For a description of other Jewish school societies, see Scharfstein, *Toldot ha-Hinukh*, vol. 5.

76. Scharfstein, ibid. See pp. 74–75 for a comparison, in Rebecca Reuven's words, of the educational standards prevailing in her school prior to and after her assumption of her post.

prevailing in Jewish communities elsewhere.[77] The Jews of eastern European origin maintained the traditional *heder, Talmud Torah,* and *yeshivah,* where Yiddish was the language of instruction; the Sephardic and Oriental Jews sent their boys to the *kutub,* where they studied in Ladino or Arabic. Few girls, if any, attended the schools. Several attempts to establish modern schools were made in the second half of the nineteenth century. One such venture included a girls' school, the Evelina de Rothschild School, established in Jerusalem in 1864; in the 1870s it was transferred to the ownership of the Anglo-Jewish Association, changing its medium of instruction from French to English. For seventeen years it was ably administered by Fortuna Becher.[78] The historian Heinrich Graetz visited the school in 1872 and described its student body as comprising 187 girls – a quarter of the population of Jewish girls in Jerusalem – and its curriculum as consisting of Hebrew, religion, basic subjects, and handiwork. Undoubtedly, the level of religious education was not very high, but the school did attract girls from as far away as Morocco, England, Germany, and Persia in the 1870s and 1880s.[79]

United States of America

Across the oceans, a new country was making its appearance on the Jewish scene – the United States of America. Jewish education witnessed widespread and diverse development in America only with the advent of a huge influx of eastern European immigrants in the latter third of the nineteenth century and during various periods of the first half of the twentieth century. Indeed, the elaborate system of religious education in contemporary America is very much a product of recent times, though with roots in the past. As Alexander Dushkin and Uriah Engleman comment in *Jewish Education in the United States,* "As the Jewish population increased and flourished, Jewish schools proliferated rapidly in numbers and variety, forming today a complex and variegated pattern of educational organization."[80]

The nineteenth century, however, witnessed rudimentary efforts on the part of Jewish communities to provide their children with at least the basic elements of a religious education: knowledge of prayer, Bible, preparations for *Bar Mitzvah,* and elements of Hebrew language and grammar. In the period

---

77. For the state of education in Palestine in the nineteenth century, see Rachel Elbaum-Dror, *Ha-Hinukh ha-Ivri be-Eretz Israel* (Jerusalem: Yitzhak ben Tzvi, 1986), vol. 1, pp. 11–206.

78. See Judith Harari, *Ishah ve-Em be-Yisrael* (Tel Aviv: Massada, 1959), p. 270.

79. Ibid., pp. 88, 92, and 111.

80. *Jewish Education in the United States* (New York: American Association of Jewish Education, 1959), p. 1.

1840–1855, education was the responsibility of the synagogues, for the public school system was not well established, and in any case Jews feared the teaching of Christianity in schools conducted by Christians.[81] The aim of the congregational schools was "to give an elementary English education and formal instruction in Hebrew and religion."[82] Though education was limited largely to boys, some congregations did establish schools for girls. One of the schools established by a New York congregation, *B'nai Jeshurun*, was a self-supporting school for young ladies. The school was opened in December 1852 and the curriculum included "Hebrew studies: reading, writing, grammar, translation, prayers, Scriptures, and Bible history," as well as a program of secular studies and languages.[83] During this period, the practice of the "confirmation" of Jewish children began in the United States. It was introduced by Dr. Max Lilienthal, a German Jewish educator, at the *Anshei Chesed* Congregation, in 1846: "Every boy of twelve and every girl of eleven is to receive religious instruction from the Chief Rabbi himself from *Hanukkah* (Feast of Lights) to *Shavuot* (Pentecost). The instruction is to be religion in general, Jewish creed and revelation, immortality of the soul and the Thirteen Creeds [of Maimonides]. On Shavuot the children are to be publicly examined."[84] Generally, the instruction in the congregational day schools was of an elementary nature.[85]

Besides the congregational day schools, there also arose in this period a number of private Jewish boarding schools, mostly for boys. One, however, was called School for Young Ladies, run by the Misses Pallaches, established as early as 1841, and patronized by the Portuguese congregation *Shearith Israel* in New York. The religious educational curriculum was preparatory.[86] Frequently recurring advertisements by private Jewish teachers indicate that among both the Portuguese and the German Jewish communities, home instruction was usual.[87] Conceivably, girls benefited from private tutelage as well.

By the mid 1850s, with the rise of the religiously neutral public schools, the congregational schools collapsed. Most Jewish education was conducted thereafter in Sunday schools,[88] the first of which was founded in 1838 in

81. Nathan Glazer, *American Judaism* (Chicago: University of Chicago Press, 1972), p. 34. See also Scharfstein, *Toldot ha-Hinukh*, vol. 3, pp. 11f.

82. Alexander Dushkin, *Jewish Education in New York City* (New York: Bureau of Jewish Education, 1918), p. 46.

83. Ibid., p. 47.

84. Quoted in Dushkin, *Jewish Education in New York City*, p. 47.

85. Ibid.

86. Ibid., p. 50.

87. Ibid.

88. See Dushkin, *Jewish Education in New York City*, p. 52; Glazer, *American Judaism*,

Philadelphia by Rebecca Gratz[89] for "free instruction in Jewish history and related subjects to the Jewish children of Philadelphia."[90] These schools were opened to both boys and girls, who were instructed by volunteers, mostly women.[91] They flourished mainly because of the lessened significance of Hebrew in Reform Judaism (which was taking root in America in the second half of the nineteenth century) and due to the example of the nationwide Protestant Sunday schools.[92] The level of religious instruction was not high.

For the great influx of eastern European immigrants who arrived on America's shores from 1880 to 1920, the established American Jewish community offered no model for Jewish education. Hence they transplanted to the United States the traditional educational institutions of their native lands – the *heder, Talmud Torah,* and *yeshivah* – but changed their character in such a manner as to fit them into the new conditions. All of these institutions underwent profound modifications in the United States. The *heder* degenerated from the normal self-respecting school of the eastern European Jew to the level of the worst, unorganized, poorly taught, and unsanitary one-room country schools and practically disappeared. The *Talmud Torah* was transformed from a charitable institution for the education of poor children to a democratic communal institution, largely in the tradition of the *heder metukan,* for the after-school religious education of all Jewish children. Although highly successful, it failed to make proper provision for the study of Talmud. The *yeshivah* kept the original idea of a higher talmudical academy, but it also began to be applied to elementary Jewish parochial schools. These were to be all-day rather than supplementary schools with a high-quality religious studies program including intensive talmudic studies, in addition to a program of secular studies.[93] All these institutions, established from the 1880s onward, were at first restricted almost wholly to boys.[94] This was not surprising, considering that the eastern European immigrants merely transplanted their inbred educational tradition to the shores of America. It was not until 1910 that serious

---

p. 34; and Scharfstein, *Toldot ha-Hinukh,* vol. 3, pp. 24–27.

89. For elaboration on the life and work of Rebecca Gratz, see Greta Fink, *Great Jewish Women* (New York: Bloch, 1978), pp. 49–55.

90. Quoted by Judah Pilch in *Encyclopaedia Judaica,* vol. 6, p. 438. See also Scharfstein, *Toldot ha-Hinukh,* vol. 3, pp. 12, 22, and 116–120; Dushkin, *Jewish Education in New York City,* p. 52; and Glazer, *American Judaism,* p. 34.

91. See Dushkin, ibid., p. 52.

92. Ibid., p. 51.

93. For elaboration on the establishment of traditional educational institutions by the Eastern European immigrants in America, see Dushkin, *Jewish Education in New York City,* pp. 68f; Glazer, *American Judaism,* pp. 72–73; Greenberg, "Jewish Educational Institutions," pp. 929f; and Scharfstein, *Toldot ha-Hinukh,* vol. 3, pp. 30f.

94. Dushkin, *Jewish Education in New York City,* p. 134.

thought was entertained to providing American girls with a satisfactory formal Jewish education, when the first experimental schools – the Hebrew Preparatory Schools – of the newly formed Board of Jewish Education in New York were established. At first the schools were intended for both boys and girls, but "owing to the traditional neglect of the education of Jewish girls, it was considered of particular importance to emphasize their education now."[95] Talmud Torah schools as well opened their doors to girls in the first decades of the twentieth century.[96] It must be emphasized, however, that in 1908, when there were almost two million Jews in the United States, of whom probably three-quarters were eastern European immigrants and their children, only about 28 percent of the Jewish children of school age were receiving any form of religious education, and a quarter of these were in the almost useless Sunday schools.[97]

The schools of formal education we have looked at so far in this chapter reflect the curriculum of nontraditional, although not necessarily antitraditional, movements of the post-Enlightenment period. The brilliant exception to this was the program of Rabbi Samson Raphael Hirsch, whose ideas were shaped totally by concerns to preserve traditional study. The spread of these other schools raised anxieties among many traditional rabbis. It was clear that an Orthodox response had to be forthcoming to the threat of the success of the *Haskalah*-type schools. Hence, the founding of the Beth Jacob movement cannot be considered the initial stage of formal religious education for girls, but it can be considered the initial movement that won popular support and succeeded in widespread Orthodox Jewish education for women.

WOMEN SCHOLARS

As in previous centuries, there were individual women of prominent and other families in the nineteenth century who were noted for their erudition in Torah and their knowledge of Judaism. Many of these women illustrate that Jewish society has changed as a result of the Enlightenment. The women, including Orthodox women, assumed a more dynamic role within their milieu – they wrote, they preached, they gave spiritual advice. As Jews entered the mainstream of the societies in which they lived, their traditional social structures gave way to new perceptions. Jews could now see themselves and their tradition as forward thinking and universal. The tensions of (1) tradition versus secularism, (2) nationalism versus imperialism, and (3) enfranchising of

---

95. Ibid., p. 107.

96. See Greenberg, "Jewish Educational Institutions," p. 929.

97. Glazer, *American Judaism*, pp. 72–73.

women versus the status quo are part and parcel of the Jewish world as well as the wider one. These tensions affected all and may account for the new spirit that enveloped accomplished women in this period and subsequently.

Hasidic Women

Prominent among the accomplished women were ones from hasidic circles. Indeed, according to three historians of the movement—Samuel Aba Horodezky, Jacob Minkin, and Harry Rabinowicz—Hasidism can be credited for having "emancipated" the Jewish woman.[98] Though that assertion may be highly questionable, indeed exaggerated, in truth not a few women played quite an important part in the hasidic sect, both as followers and as leaders. As Minkin states, "Hasidism assigned to her a place and importance almost equal to that of her male partner."[99] Whereas women rarely came into contact with the traditional rabbi unless they went to consult him concerning the ritual affairs of their household, the *rebbe* or *zaddik* (the hasidic leader) encouraged the coming of women to him and made them welcome at the court. "As the husband is called a *hasid*, so the wife is called a *hasidah*."[100] The *hasidah*, states Rabinowicz, "occupied an honored position in the hasidic world."[101] According to Horodezky and Minkin, women often accompanied their husbands on their annual visit to the *zaddik* and sometimes went alone. "No door in his court that was open to men was closed to women. Like the male *hasid*, she wrote the prayer note and was ushered into the august presence of the saint with the same courtesy and ceremony [extended to] her husband."[102] States Horodezky, "Hasidism awoke faith and religious feeling in the heart of the Jewish woman. She returned home from the *zaddik* full of spiritual happiness and strong faith, which increased in intensity after every visit to the *zaddik*. In the spirit of this firm faith she managed her household affairs, educated her children, and exerted an influence for good on her husband, who had to struggle for his daily bread, [a struggle which] hardened his heart and enfeebled his intellect."[103] Many women among the *hasidim* were knowledgeable in Torah—at times, writes Horodezky, to a greater degree than their

98. See Samuel A. Horodezky, "The Jewish Woman in the Hasidic Movement," in *Ha-Hasidut ve-ha-Hasidim*, vol. 4 (Berlin, 1922), pp. 67–71; Jacob S. Minkin, *The Romance of Hasidism* (New York: Macmillan, 1935), pp. 345–347; Harry Rabinowicz, *Hasidism: The Movement and Its Masters* (Northvale, NJ: Jason Aronson, 1988), pp. 341f.

99. Minkin, *The Romance of Hasidism*, p. 345.

100. Ibid.

101. Rabinowicz, *Hasidism: The Movement and Its Masters*, p. 341.

102. Minkin, *The Romance of Hasidism*, p. 346.

103. Horodezky, *Ha-Hasidut ve-ha-Hasidim*, vol. 4, p. 68.

husband: "The *hasid,* burdened all week with worries of supporting his family, would on the Sabbath, weary and fatigued . . . take a hasidic book and skim through it half-heartedly. [On the other hand] his wife, the *hasidah,* the manager of the household, would generally find some leisure time to contemplate and read the writings of the *zaddikim;* she had sufficient time to broaden her knowledge and as a result, to influence her husband as well."[104]

Hasidism also accorded the right to the woman to rise to the rank of a *zaddik* (a phenomenon no longer witnessed in contemporary times; indeed, today many hasidic women would be considered the least "emancipated" of all traditional Jewish women, and the Hasidism of most sects very much a male stronghold, though women do continue to visit and consult with the *rebbe*[105]). "If she were worthy," writes Horodezky, "nothing could stand in her way. Indeed, there were several *hasidic* women who reached a position of which few men were worthy."[106]

The ability of women to have their own voice in Hasidism can be traced to the stories that circulated about Edel,[107] daughter of the founder of Hasidism, Rabbi Israel Ba'al Shem Tov (1700–1760). Edel enjoyed a reputation and influence in Hasidism in her own right. Her father is reported to have said of his daughter that she was taken from the treasury of most holy souls. It was said that she often accompanied her father on his many journeys and that he applied to her the verse in Deuteronomy 33:2, "At his right hand was a fiery Law unto them," for the first letters of the Hebrew words *eish dat lamo* ("a fiery law unto them,") make up the name Edel. It was told that she was learned in Torah and "fulfilled an important role" in disseminating to the people the hasidic thought and philosophy she had acquired from her father, the content of which was essentially the Oral Law.[108] She far surpassed her brother, the only son of Rabbi Israel, in Hasidism, and many were those who sought her council and wisdom. Edel's daughter, Feige,[109] also achieved fame in the

---

104. Ibid., pp. 68–69.

105. One exception might be the Lubavitcher sect of *Habad* Hasidism, whose leaders had strong family traditions of providing their daughters with a thorough Torah education. As a result, their wives and daughters through all seven generations of *Habad* Hasidism have played a highly influential role in the development of the movement and have been greatly respected among the *hasidim.* This subject deserves special treatment on its own.

106. Ibid., p. 69. See also Fink, *Great Jewish Women,* p. 68.

107. See Ashkenazi, *Dor Dor u-Minhagav* (Tel Aviv: Dan, 1977), p. 244; Horodezky, *Ha-Hasidut,* vol. 4, p. 69; Minkin, *The Romance of Hasidism,* p. 345, and Rabinowicz, *Hasidism: The Movement and Its Masters,* pp. 341–342. For elaboration on Edel, see Judith Harari, *Ishah ve-Em be-Yisrael* (Tel Aviv, Massada, 1959), pp. 109–110.

108. Harari, *Ishah ve-Em be-Yisrael,* p. 109.

109. See Ashkenazi, *Dor Dor u-Minhagav,* p. 244; Horodezky, *Ha-Hasidut,* vol. 4, p. 69; Harari, *Ishah ve-Em be-Yisrael,* p. 109; Minkin, *The Romance of Hasidism,* p. 345; and

world of Hasidism as a *zaddikah*, of whom it was said that the Holy Spirit rested upon her. She was the mother of the illustrious *zaddik* Rabbi Nahman of Bratzlav (1772–1811), whose gifts she helped to develop more than her husband's, who was quite an ordinary and mediocre man.

Though these women were not hasidic leaders, the fact that stories would circulate in which they had roles did much to enhance the position of women in the mystical world of hasidic thought. Thus the nineteenth century produced a number of learned women among the prominent hasidic families. This was so even though scholarship did not rank as high in the hasidic view of merit as did prayer and devotion. As a quasi-leader, Merish,[110] daughter of Rabbi Elimelekh of Lyzhansk (1717–1787), was renowned for her scholarship. *Hasidim* would go to hear her learned discourses and to receive her blessings. Frieda,[111] eldest daughter of Rabbi Shneur Zalman of Lyadi (1745–1830), is honored by *Habad hasidim* for her collection of her father's aphorisms. She wrote a number of remarkable manuscripts on a variety of subjects. Rachel Ashkenazi,[112] daughter of the *zaddik* of Opatow, Rabbi Abraham Joshua Heschel (1745–1825), was renowned in hasidic circles for her erudition in Torah and hasidic thought. It is reported that her father, an ardent believer in her powers, declared, "She has a holy spark." Her influence on the *hasidim* might have been considerable. Hannah Haya Twersky,[113] daughter of the *zaddik* Rabbi Mordekhai Twersky of Chernobyl (1770–1837), was acclaimed for her righteousness and generous spirit. Her brothers, *zaddikim* as well, proclaimed her a *zaddikah* capable of giving advice in spiritual matters, by stating there was no difference between them and her. Her aphorisms and parables spread her fame throughout Poland. She dealt tirelessly with the women who flocked to her for guidance, and she emphasized the importance of correct and careful education. Eidel, daughter of the *zaddik* Shalom Rokeah of Belz (1779–1855), contended with her brother for the mantle of their father. She succeeded somewhat in attracting her own court.[114]

Ashkenazi, Lenowitz,[115] and Rabinowicz list a number of other

Rabinowicz, *Hasidism: The Movement and Its Masters*, p. 343.

110. Rabinowicz, ibid., p. 343.

111. Ibid.

112. See Harari, *Ishah ve-Em be-Yisrael*, p. 110; Horodezky, *Ha-Hasidut*, vol. 4, p. 69; and Rabinowicz, ibid., p. 344.

113. See Harari, ibid., p. 110; Horodezky, ibid., vol. 4, p. 69; and Rabinowicz, ibid., p. 345.

114. See Yoram Bilu, "The Woman Who Wanted to Be Her Father: A Case Analysis of Dybbuk Possession in a Hasidic Community," *Journal of Psychoanalytic Anthropology* 8 (1985): 11–27.

115. Harris Lenowitz, "Women Saints in Early Hasidism," *Explorations: Journal for Adventurous Thought* 3:3 (1985): 27–34.

eighteenth- and nineteenth-century women who attained the heights of a *zaddikah*, celebrated for their intellect and erudition, their piety, and their righteousness. Some wore *tzitzit* (ritual fringes), put on *tefillin* (phylacteries), fasted on Mondays and Thursdays, and held court for the many *hasidim* who flocked to them for spiritual guidance and advice.[116]

With few exceptions, most women who succeeded in attaining the rank of a *zaddikah* were wives and daughters of *zaddikim* whose repute and personal approval generally guaranteed these women public recognition for their noteworthy sagacity and piety. One exception, and the most notable of all women hasidic leaders, daughter of a layman, was Hannah Rachel Werbermacher, popularly known as the "Maid of Ludomir," a personage worthy of further elaboration in this context.

Hannah Rachel Werbermacher: "Maid of Ludomir" – Hasidic Leader

Hannah Rachel was born in 1805 in Ludomir, a town in the Ukraine, daughter of Monesh Werbermacher, a well-to-do merchant of some learning.[117] An only child, she received the attention usually reserved for an eldest son, including a considerable education. She especially excelled in the study of *Midrash*, *Aggadah*, history from the Talmud, hasidic thought,[118] and the books of *Mussar*, which concerned moral discipline. She prayed with ecstatic emotion, which occasioned considerable astonishment. As soon as Hannah Rachel reached adolescence, her father's position drew many matchmakers, who negotiated excellent matches. Her father, however, refused all their efforts and betrothed her to a young man whom Hannah Rachel had known and loved from her earliest childhood. At about this time, Hannah Rachel's mother died, causing Hannah to become withdrawn and solitary and fall prey to moods of prolonged melancholy. Once, during a fit of depression and illness, she experienced a vision in which she received a "new and sublime soul."[119] Subsequently, she began to observe the religious duties of males, wearing *tzitzit*, and donning *tallit* (prayer shawl) and *tefillin* when she prayed. When her father died

116. See Ashkenazi, *Dor Dor u-Minhagav*, pp. 241f; and Rabinowicz, *Hasidism: The Movement and Its Masters*, pp. 341f.

117. For elaboration on the life of the "Maid of Ludomir" see Horodezky, *Ha-Hasidut*, vol. 4, pp. 70–71; Harari, *Ishah ve-Em be-Yisrael*, pp. 110–112; Rabinowicz, *Hasidism*, pp. 345–347; and Fink, *Great Jewish Women*, pp. 67–71. Also see Ada Rapoport-Albert, "On Women in Hasidism: S. A. Horodezky and the Maid of Ludmir Tradition," in *Jewish History: Essays in Honor of C. Abramsky*, ed. A. Rapoport-Albert and Steven J. Zipperstein (London: Halban, 1988), pp. 495–525.

118. See Ada Rapoport-Albert, "The Maid of Ludmir," *Kabbalah: A Newsletter of Current Research in Jewish Mysticism* 2:2 (Spring/Summer 1987): 1–3.

119. See Horodezky, *Ha-Hasidut*, vol. 4, p. 70, and Rabinowicz, *Hasidim*, p. 346.

shortly after, she also recited *Kaddish* for him. In addition, she spent the entire day studying Torah and praying. Her betrothal was annulled.

Hannah Rachel's father had left her a considerable fortune, with which she built a new *Bet ha-Midrash* (prayer and study house) with an adjoining apartment for her living quarters. The entire week she would sit in her quarters praying and studying the Torah. Every Sabbath at *Shalosh Seudot* (the third meal usually near the conclusion of the Sabbath), the door of the apartment would be opened, and the unseen "Maid of Ludomir" would deliver erudite and hasidic discourses, which were eagerly and appreciatively listened to by scholars and rabbis as well as by unlearned, pious people. Her fame spread far and wide, and she became known as a wonder-worker. Thousands of men and women made pilgrimages to her *Bet ha-Midrash* to attend her lectures or seek her curative powers. Gradually, a special group of *hasidim* was formed, which became known as the *"Hasidim* of the Maid of Ludomir."

Although the Maid of Ludomir was admired, she was clearly something of a maverick in traditional Jewish society. Even though most people did not wish to stop her from teaching, many felt it would be preferable if she were to be married. Prominent *zaddikim* attempted to persuade her to do so.[120] Finally, at the age of 40 she succumbed to the persuasive tongue of Rabbi Mordekhai of Chernobyl and wed a scholar whom the *zaddik* of Chernobyl highly recommended.[121] For whatever the reason, her popularity waned after her marriage. The marriage was short-lived and terminated by divorce. Hannah Rachel emigrated to Palestine, where she continued her mystical studies and engaged in rituals designed to hasten the appearance of the Messiah. Of the Maid of Ludomir, Greta Fink comments:

> To us it may seem that the Maid of Ludomir was a slightly eccentric nonconformist. However, she was part of the mainstream of mysticism, the basis of Hasidism, no different from the sainted *Ba'al Shem Tov* and other famous *rebbes*. Erudite, a mystic who possessed considerable charisma, she was able to overcome the strict and confining limitation which the ghetto imposed on women [and] become a famous *hasidic* leader. Had she been able to resolve the problem of marriage and spinsterhood, she might have become one of the greatest of the rebbes. As it is, she can lay claim to being a most noteworthy *hasidic* leader, one of the most original, and the first to settle in the Holy Land. She not only dreamt of hastening the end of the Jewish exile, but actually attempted to accomplish it.[122]

---

120. See Fink, *Great Jewish Women*, p. 70, for elaboration.

121. In the English account (S. A. Horodezky, *Leaders of Hasidism*, trans. Maria Horodezky-Magasanik [London, 1928]), Rabbi Mordekhai is said to have married Hannah himself, though this is not confirmed elsewhere.

122. Ibid., p. 71. See also Gershon Winkler, *Maiden of Ludmir* (New York: Judaica Press, 1990).

Tamar Frankiel, in *The Voice of Sarah*, demonstrates that the greatness of biblical women lay in their ability to work out their spirituality in contact with their world, in relation to people. They were able to balance their insight of a higher consciousness and the work of everyday life. In this light, the Maid of Ludomir is both a positive and negative model. On one hand, she exemplified the "deep unconscious connection with God that brings forth inspiration." On the other hand, in Frankiel's view, it is no accident that her unhappy marriage coincided with the decline of her powers and set her on an ultimately fruitless path. "Hannah had become a vessel for pure Torah and for inspired teaching, and she incorporated in her later life the great yearning for redemption, for the Messiah, for return to Jerusalem, and for the perfection of the world. But she apparently came to believe that redemption could be accomplished through the power of mind and spirit alone. She had not learned the lessons of the Mothers, that [women] must work out [their] spirituality in contact with the world, in relation to people."[123]

While on the subject of Hasidism, it should be noted that when Sarah Schenirer established the Beth Jacob network of girls' schools in Poland in the early twentieth century, thereby universalizing religious education for Jewish women, she was greatly supported in her endeavor by the approving attitude of a number of hasidic *rebbes*. The story is told about the hasidic *rebbe* Israel of Czortkov (1854–1934), who was approached by the leaders of several Jewish communities in Galicia, Poland, requesting the establishment of *yeshivot* for the hasidically oriented young men after the Lithuanian model. After consulting the famous hasidic rabbinic authorities of his time–Rabbi Yekele Rimanover and Rabbi Meir Arak–the *rebbe* of Czortkov replied as follows: "Let us first establish educational institutions for girls. Only by better educating the girls will they be able to appreciate the value of Torah and thus build traditional families and Torah-inspired homes."[124]

Lithuanian and Russian Women Scholars

Nineteenth-century eastern European women of nonhasidic circles also included their share of learned women. Feigel Zakheim (d. 1818), wife of Rabbi Joseph Zakheim of Vilna, was proficient in Bible, the *Midrash*, and ethical literature. Her righteousness was legendary as well.[125]

123. Tamar Frankiel, *The Voice of Sarah: Feminine Spirituality and Traditional Judaism* (San Francisco: Harper Collins, 1990), p. 49.

124. Menachem Breyer, *The Jewish Woman in Rabbinic Literature: A Psychosocial Perspective* (Hoboken, NJ: Ktav, 1986), vol. 2, p. 128, citing personal communication by Rabbi Abraham Kelman, quoting Rabbi Samuel Alter, author of *Likutei Bosar Likutei*.

125. For example, when Napoleon's troops invaded Vilna in the early part of the century, many women hid with their children in bunkers. Feigel deposited her only

Reyna Basya Berlin (daughter of Rabbi Isaac ben Hayim of Volozhin and wife of the man who transformed the *yeshivah* in Volozhin [Lithuania] into the spiritual center for all Russian Jewry during the nineteenth century – Rabbi Naphtali Tzvi Yehudah Berlin) was a learned woman who was accustomed to sit by the oven in the kitchen, even in the summertime, next to a table piled high with religious literature. These included the Bible, the *Mishnah*, various midrashic and ethical works, and the text of *Ein Yaakov* (a sixteenth-century work containing talmudic *aggadot* and commentaries). Her nephew, Rabbi Barukh Epstein, author of the *Torah Temimah*, a commentary on the Pentateuch, attests to the fact that her acumen in running a household was meager, as most of her time was devoted to religious study.[126] He also wrote that his aunt often lamented the exemption of women from certain precepts and was particularly grieved that women were not commanded to devote themselves to the study of Torah. Reyna Basya and her nephew Barukh recurrently discussed this sad state of affairs, engaging in learned repartee as they cited various interpretations on the subject.[127] She was hopeful, however, about the future of religious education for women, quoting Psalms (119:96) "I have seen an end to every endeavor," expressing the wish that a solution to this problem would arise as well.[128] Reyna Basya was particularly fond of citing great women of past generations who were known for their scholarship, and she was proud to be able to follow in their illustrious footsteps.[129]

Leah Lipkin of Latvia and Lithuania, mother of the nineteenth-century moralist Rabbi Israel (Lipkin) Salanter, was acclaimed for her erudition and scholarship. Her grandson, Rabbi Isaac Lipkin, wrote of her that she was "outstanding and sharp-witted in the study of Talmud." Many stories abounded regarding her mastery of Torah learning.[130] Tsertel Horowitz Schwartz of Shklov (Belorussia) was adept in Bible, Talmud, the codes, and *Midrash*. Her responsa and innovative Torah writings appeared in two publications of the late-nineteenth century – *Ha-Karmel* (Vilna, 1860–1879) and *Ha-Sharon* (Cracow, 1893), under the acronym of her name, Tsertel, daughter of Joshua Ho-

---

child with her husband for safekeeping and opened her home to the many orphans of war, concealing and supporting these children until after the siege, stating, "For my only son I will not worry, secure in the knowledge that his father will guard him with his life. As for these poor orphans, bereft of both mother and father, who will guard them, if not I?" She died prematurely, soon after the war, possibly as a result of her exertions on behalf of many refugees. (See I. S. Eisenstadt, *Da'at Kedoshim* [St. Petersburg, 1897–1898], pp. 186–187. See also Harari, *Ishah ve-Em be-Yisrael*, p. 86.)

126. See Epstein, *Mekor Barukh* (Vilna, 1928), pp. 1949–1950.

127. Ibid., pp. 1950f.

128. Ibid., p. 1976.

129. Ibid., pp. 1952–1953.

130. See Levi Ovchinski, *Toledot ha-Yehudim be-Kurland* (1908), p. 55.

rowitz. The aforementioned Rabbi Barukh Epstein stood in great admiration
of this woman, with whom he exchanged letters on a number of occasions.[131]
Rebecca Rabinowitz of Lithuania, sister of Rabbi Elijah David Rabinowitz-
Teomim (1842–1905; chief rabbi of the Ashkenazic community in Jerusalem
at the turn of the century), had no difficulty in interpreting difficult talmudic
passages that had been troubling many of her learned male contemporaries.
One of her responses to a perplexing question was published in the rabbinical
journal *Yagdil Torah* (Odessa, Russia, 1879–1885).[132]

A more liberal woman scholar of the time was Zionist leader Puah
Rakowski of Warsaw.[133] A precocious Hebrew student, she was reading
modern Hebrew literature at fifteen and even studying *Gemara*. She translated
from Russian into Hebrew and also wrote for the periodical *Ha-Tsefirah*. At
seventeen she was married, but after five years she left her husband, taking her
two small children with her. She then completed her education and became a
teacher-principal of a girls' Hebrew school in Lomza and then of the *Yehudiah*
girls' Hebrew school in Warsaw. She eventually set up a seven-grade girls'
school under her own auspices, known as "Puah Rakowski's First Hebrew
School," where she battled tirelessly to revive "the old national language" in
the hearts and minds of the girls. As she wrote, "Hebrew is a difficult
language, but a necessary one. It is not used at home or on the street, yet do not
our fathers and brothers have to study it for years in *hadarim* and *yeshivot* to
master it properly? [Why not girls?]"[134] Puah was instrumental in establishing the first women's Zionist federation in Poland. "As teacher, school
administrator, writer, and Zionist leader, she was an innovator, making a
place for the modern woman in Jewish communal life."[135]

A fellow Zionist activist was Lithuanian Esther Rubinstein of Shaki and
Vilna. The only daughter of Rabbi Jeremiah Flansburg, she received a broad
Hebrew and secular education under her father's tutelage. Esther was proficient in Hebrew language, Bible, *Aggadah*, talmudic law, and Jewish philosophical works. She organized Zionist youth groups among the girls of her
town, Shaki. After her marriage to Rabbi Isaac Rubinstein in 1905, Esther

---

131. See Epstein, *Mekor Barukh*, p. 1958. See also Ashkenazi, *Ha-Ishah be-Asplakaria
ha-Yehudit*, vol. 1, p. 133.

132. For elaboration of the responsum, see Epstein, *Mekor Barukh*, pp. 1957–1958.
See also Jacob Gellis, *Mi-Gedolei Yerushalayim* (Jerusalem, 1967), p. 118.

133. For an autobiographical account of Puah Rakowski, see "A Mind of My
Own," in *The Golden Tradition*, ed. Lucy Dawidowicz (New York: Holt, Rinehart &
Winston, 1967), pp. 388–393. For a brief biography of Puah Rakowski, see Harari,
Ishah ve-Em be-Yisrael, pp. 199–200.

134. Ibid., p. 391. Puah's school, however, was not regarded approvingly by many
in the Orthodox community, who viewed it as not upholding religious standards and,
furthermore, as violating rabbinic strictures against formal instruction of girls (ibid., p.
390).

135. Dawidowicz, *The Golden Tradition*, p. 388.

labored tirelessly on behalf of Hebrew education for girls. She was instrumental in establishing the Hebrew gymnasium for girls in Vilna and rejuvenated the *Yehudiah* school in that city. She was an active founder of several Hebrew journals, in which she wrote prolifically. Her articles on the rights of Jewish women demonstrated her keen knowledge of rabbinic law and impressed the rabbis of her day. Esther was renowned for her Hebrew oratorical skills. She died relatively young and was memorialized in the *Rabbanit Esther Rubinstein Memorbuch*, published in Vilna in 1926.[136]

Women Scholars Around the World

Other regions of the nineteenth-century Jewish world also boasted their notable women religious scholars and writers. In India, Flora (Farha) Gabbai Sassoon (1859–1936),[137] daughter of the distinguished scholar Ezekiel Gabbai and his wife, Aziza of Bombay, and wife of the philanthropist and Hebraist Solomon Sassoon, achieved renown as a Hebrew scholar, well versed in Bible, Talmud, Jewish thought, and the Hebrew language. She was often consulted by distinguished rabbis on questions of Jewish law. A witness to her erudition testified that when discussion at Flora's table centered on a halakhic difficulty, Flora would summon her granddaughter to bring her the relevant volume of the Talmud, pointing to the various interpretations of the commentators and expressing her opinion on the matter.[138] Another admirer commented, "She penetrated all the hidden recesses of the Torah, searching for the essence of Judaism's greatness, strength, and spirit."[139] After her husband's death in 1894, Flora managed the family firm in Bombay for some years and in 1901 settled in England, where she entertained scholars and public personages in a grand style. Strictly Orthodox in her observance of Judaism, she included a *shohet* and a *minyan* in her entourage when traveling. In 1924, at Jews' College in London, she delivered a learned discourse on the Talmud, the first woman to do so at the college, and in 1930 she published an essay on Rashi in the *Jewish Forum*. "She was recognized in England as a leading authority on all matters of Sephardic doctrine and practice, and the Chief Rabbi referred to her as a 'living well of Torah and piety.' "[140]

In *Eretz Israel* (Palestine), Sarah (Sonia) Diskin (1818–1898), wife of Rabbi

136. See Scharfstein, *Toldot ha-Hinukh*, vol. 2, pp. 168–169.

137. See Ashkenazi, *Dor Dor u-Minhagav*, pp. 208–209; Shulamit Flaum, *Bat Yisrael Nodedet* (Jerusalem, 1935), pp. 328–329; Stanley Jackson, *The Sassoons* (New York: E. P. Dutton, 1968), pp. 58, 104–111, 120–121, 208–209; and Cecil Roth, *The Sassoon Dynasty* (London: Robert Hale, 1941), pp. 92, 137–141. Also see Walter J. Fischel. *Encyclopaedia Judaica*, vol. 14, p. 899.

138. See Ashkenazi, *Dor Dor u-Mingahav*, p. 209.

139. Flaum, *Bat Yisrael Nodedet*, p. 328.

140. Jackson, *The Sassoons*, p. 208.

Joshua Judah Leib Diskin, was considered learned in Bible, Talmud, the codes, and many ethical treatises.[141] Known as the *Brisker Rebbitzen* ("the rabbi's wife from Brisk," the city in Lithuania where her husband served as rabbi prior to the couple's settling in Palestine), she dedicated her life in Jerusalem to preventing dangerous inroads in traditional life. She headed efforts to save orphans from the hands of missionaries and oversaw the education of those who were rescued, establishing, together with her husband, the Diskin Orphanage in 1880. Along with her husband she was in the vanguard of Orthodox activism, leading the fight against all expressions of modernity and modern culture in *Eretz Israel*. In some circles it was believed she dominated her husband, leading him to the adoption of extreme views or overriding him in the application of greater stringencies in halakhic matters.

Another learned woman active in the revival of settlement in *Eretz Israel* in the nineteenth century was Sarah Bayla Hirschenson (1816–1905).[142] She and her husband, Rabbi Jacob Mordecai Hirschensohn, played a prominent role in preserving Jewish life in Jerusalem against the forces of secularism, although it was not progress per se that they opposed as much as innovations foreign to the spirit of Judaism. Sarah Bayla "was given full freedom to exert her influence"[143] and was equally responsible, along with her husband, for the establishment and administration of *yeshivot* in both Safed and Jerusalem. It is recorded that whenever she entered a place where the great Rabbi Samuel Salant, chief rabbi of Jerusalem, was present, he would rise and say, "Double respect should be paid to the wife of our revered colleague, highly regarded in her own right."[144] Sarah Bayla had received a solid Jewish education from her father, a scholar and man of affairs, and was thoroughly competent in Bible studies and the Hebrew language. She read many books of an ethical nature, knew much of the *Pirkei Avot* (Sayings of the Fathers) by heart, understood liturgical poetry, and was able to quote numerous passages from Bahya's *Duties of the Heart*. She cherished the poems of Judah Halevi and may have even studied the *Kuzari* (Halevi's philosophical work). When talmudic discussion went on in her presence, she became deeply absorbed and would startle the scholars by her pertinent questions. Sarah Bayla is given a prominent place in publications on outstanding Palestinian women of the nineteenth and twentieth centuries, and she figures in contemporary periodicals in relation to events of her day.

---

141. See Harari, *Ishah ve-Em be-Yisrael*, pp. 266–268, for elaboration.

142. For elaboration, see Nima H. Adlerblum, "Sara Bayla and Her Times," *Jewish Leaders, 1750–1940*, ed. Leo Jung (Jerusalem: Boys' Town, 1964), pp. 345–391.

143. Ibid., p. 346.

144. Ibid., quoted on page 346.

WOMEN WRITERS

A number of women writers–authors of religious poetry, prayers, and other Jewish works–left their imprint on nineteenth-century Jewish literature.[145] Prominent is the name of Rachel Morpurgo of Trieste, Italy,[146] heiress to the literary tradition of Deborah Ascarelli and Sarah Copia Sullam of two centuries earlier. A cousin of the illustrious Samuel David Luzzatto, who powerfully stimulated the development of Jewish scholarship and belles lettres in the nineteenth century, Rachel attained in her verses perhaps a higher poetical level than Luzzatto's, as she became one of the foremost exponents of modern Hebrew poetry in Italy at the time of its final flowering. Her uncles, Hezekiah and David Luzzatto, both competent scholars, were her first teachers, giving her instruction in the Hebrew language, the Bible and commentaries, and Bahya's *Duties of the Heart*. At the age of fourteen, she was inducted into the study of Talmud by a teacher from Mantua. She was also well versed in medieval Hebrew literature and studied the *Zohar*, the most important literary work of the *Kabbalah*. As early as 1816, she and her cousin, Samuel David, who strongly influenced her and fostered her wide-ranging Hebrew education, had been in the habit of exchanging verses. Later, through his encouragement, she became a regular contributor to the Hebrew periodical *Kokhavei Yitzhak*. Her verses, with their beauty of style and depth of emotion depicting Jewish historical values and traditions, were extremely popular with Hebrew readers, many of whom "deemed it incredible that in the nineteenth century a woman could wield the pen with so masterly a skill."[147] Occasionally, a blending of expressions from the Talmud and even from the *Zohar* bears witness to the broadness of the Jewish education that Rachel Morpurgo had early received. Her poems and letters were collected and published as an anthology entitled *Ugav Rachel* by Vittorio (Hayim Isaac) Castiglioni (1890).[148]

Another writer of note was an Englishwoman of Portuguese Marrano

---

145. The proceeding list is by no means exhaustive. I have chosen merely a representative sample from various countries; for additional women writers see, for example, Remy, *Das Juedische Weib*, chap. 16, pp. 270f.

146. For a biographical sketch of Rachel Morpurgo's life and selections of her poetry, see the following sources: Harari, *Ishah ve-Em be-Yisrael*, pp. 124–128; J. L. Landau, *Short Lectures on Modern Hebrew Literature* (London: Edward Goldston, 1938), p. 160; Sabato Morais, *Italian Hebrew Literature* (New York: Jewish Theological Seminary of America, 1926), pp. 199–202; and N. Salaman, *Rachel Morpurgo and Contemporary Hebrew Poets in Italy* (London, 1924), pp. 34–52.

147. Morais, *Italian Hebrew Literature*, p. 199.

148. A later edition of *Ugav Rahel* was published by Y. Zmora (Tel Aviv, 1943).

extraction, Grace Aguilar (1816–1847),[149] who wrote a number of novels on Jewish themes and some religious works, addressed primarily to Jewish women. Her achievement is marked principally by the "phenomenal popularity of her productions, the immense circulation, and the amazing volume of literary labor she achieved in a span of life extending to no more than thirty-one years."[150] In her youth Grace amassed a wealth of knowledge in the seclusion of her home, from her own voracious reading; from the constant instruction she received from her mother, a woman of education (who established a Jewish boarding school for boys in Hackney); and from the encouragement she received from her father in her choice of books and subjects.[151] Though she published prose and verse of a general nature, her reverence for the faith of her ancestors is reflected in her Jewish writings, the best known of which was *The Vale of Cedars* (1850), a romantic, highly idealized picture of the Marranos in Spain. Twice translated into German and twice into Hebrew, it retained popularity for a long time. In a more serious vein, she translated from French the apologetic work of the ex-Marrano, Orobio de Castro, *Israel Defended* (1838). She herself wrote *The Spirit of Judaism: In Defense of Her Faith and Its Professors* (1842) and *The Jewish Faith* (1846). The latter takes the form of letters addressed to a friend wavering in her religious conviction. Her *Women of Israel* (1845) was a series of biographical sketches of biblical and talmudic women, intended to arouse the pride of young Jews in their heritage. Admiration for the young author "whose love for her people and faith shone through every page of her [Jewish] works"[152] extended a generation and as far as the Russian steppes, where a brilliant talmudic scholar and Torah commentator of no less importance than Rabbi Barukh Epstein (1860–1940) praised her as "a shining star in Jewish literature . . . a remarkable vision among the generations."[153] In truth, remarks her biographer, Beth-Zion Abrahams, "the concentration on spirituality and religious submissiveness [as noted in Aguilar's writings] does not in her case go together with profound knowledge of Rabbinical Judaism, or Jewish lore." A great deal of her Jewish knowledge was derived from secondary, sometimes Christian, studies of Jewish learning, rarely from original sources, and certainly never

---

149. For a biographical sketch of Aguilar and selections of her writings, see Beth-Zion Abrahams, "Grace Aguilar: A Centenary Tribute," *Jewish Historical Society of England Transactions* 16 (1945–1951): 137–148; Montagu Modder, *The Jew in the Literature of England* (Philadelphia: Jewish Publication Society of America, 1944), pp. 182–188; and Barukh Epstein, *Mekor Barukh*, p. 1957.

150. Abrahams, "Grace Aguilar," p. 137.

151. Ibid., p. 138.

152. Ibid., p. 143.

153. Epstein, *Mekor Barukh*, p. 1957.

from a direct study of the Talmud or the codes.[154] In 1847, the women of London honored Grace with the title of "the first woman who appears in Jewish literature as a defender of Judaism."[155] Grace Aguilar's collected works appeared in eight volumes in 1861.

A fellow countrywoman, Charlotte Rothschild,[156] wife of Baron Lionel de Rothschild, was another popular English Jewish writer. Raised in Naples by her parents, Baron Karl and Adelaide von Rothschild, she was given a broad Jewish and secular education. In London, active in community affairs on behalf of the poor, she founded a girls' school at Bell Lane, where she herself lectured on religious topics on the Sabbath and holidays. Three of these lectures on the fundamentals of Judaism were published in 1864 and were so well received by the public that a second edition soon appeared, containing another twenty-four of her sermons. Both works were eventually translated into German and French. Many rabbis incorporated her lectures into their Sabbath and holiday sermons. Another of Charlotte's literary efforts included a book of *tehinnot*, entitled *Prayers and Meditations for the Entire Year*, written especially as a means of uplifting the spirits of the impoverished women among whom she worked. Each of these prayers concluded with a verse from the Bible. She also translated a book of thoughts on prayer, entitled *Imrei Lev* (Words of the Heart), into English. Her final literary contribution consisted of a book of poems and fables written for youth, which was later translated into German.

Fani Neuda-Samidal (1828–1894),[157] wife of the rabbi of Leopoldstadt, Austria, composed a book of prayers and supplications in German (Prague, 1870), written especially for Jewish women. It consisted of prayers for occasions throughout the year, as well as singular prayers for an orphan girl, for a bride on her wedding day, for mother of the bride, for mother of the groom, for a woman during pregnancy, and so on. This book appeared in seven printings and was translated into English and Yiddish. In addition, Neuda-Samidal authored a number of essays in German on historical topics relating to the Jewish experience.

In Jerusalem, Liphali composed a volume of prayers for women, entitled *Supplications from the Holy City of Jerusalem*. A contemporary, Rabbi Isaac Jacob Yellin, praised her first as a woman, second as a *talmid hakham* ("a Torah scholar"), and third, as a daughter of Jerusalem who "interspersed her prayers

---

154. Abrahams, "Grace Aguilar," p. 142.

155. Epstein, *Mekor Barukh*, p. 1957.

156. For elaboration, see Ashkenazi, *Dor Dor u-Minhagav*, pp. 220–221, and Harari, *Ishah ve-Em be-Israel*, pp. 151–152. See also Cecil Roth, *The Magnificent Rothschilds* (New York: Pyramid, 1939), p. 165.

157. See Ashkenazi, *Dor Dor u-Minhagav*, p. 221.

with the words of the Torah and the sages, radiating the holiness of Jerusalem and the glory of the holy places."[158].

A nineteenth-century American Jewish writer of note, also commended by the distinguished Russian Torah scholar of her day, Rabbi Barukh Epstein, was the poet Emma Lazarus,[159] best remembered for her sonnet engraved on the Statue of Liberty. Born into a New York Sephardic family, she began writing verse in her teens. Her verses were of a general rather than a religious nature, as "the religious side of Judaism had little interest for Miss Lazarus."[160] Indeed, she received a minimal religious upbringing including some Bible study, the bulk of her education consisting of the "reading of European masters in their original languages and browsing in selected American poets."[161] Emma Lazarus's interest in Judaism was awakened by George Eliot's novel *Daniel Deronda*, with its call for a Jewish national revival, and was reinforced by the Russian pogroms of 1881–1882. "Hers was not a religious conversion but a historical and cultural one."[162] Inspired by a new and sacred cause, she began publishing translations of the great medieval Spanish Jewish poets such as Judah Halevi and Solomon ibn Gabirol (1879), basing herself mainly on the German adaptations of Michael Sachs and Abraham Geiger.[163] Deeply impressed with the Russian Jewish refugees whom she encountered when she joined immigrant relief workers on Wards Island, she energetically defended these "foreigners" against their detractors. Her essay in *Century Magazine* (1882) in reply to anti-Semitic attacks praised her fellow Jews as pioneers of progress and expressed her joy in belonging to a people that was the victim of massacres rather than their perpetrator.[164] The theme of anti-Semitic persecution now rose as a major motif in her work, and she published two poems on this subject in 1880 – "Raschi in Prague" and its sequel, "Death of Raschi."[165] Emma Lazarus's next important work was *The Dance to Death*, a verse tragedy about the burning of the Jews in Nordhausen, Germany, during the Black Death. This appeared in an anthology of poems, *Songs of a*

---

158. Quoted in Ashkenazi, *Dor Dor u-Minhagav*, p. 222.

159. For a biographical sketch of Emma's life, and selections of her poetry, see H. E. Jacob, *The World of Emma Lazarus* (New York: Schocken, 1949); Harold Ribalow, *Autobiographies of American Jews* (Philadelphia: Jewish Publication Society of America, 1965), pp. 27–37; and Dan Vogel, *Emma Lazarus* (Boston: Twayne, 1980). See also Epstein, *Mekor Barukh*, p. 1957.

160. Ribalow, *Autobiographies*, p. 33.

161. Vogel, *Emma Lazarus*, p. 15.

162. Ibid., p. 19.

163. Ibid., see pp. 127–132.

164. Ibid., see pp. 139–141. See also Jacob, *The World of Emma Lazarus*, pp. 112–119.

165. See Vogel, *Emma Lazarus*, pp. 132–135.

Semite (1882), which also included other passionate Jewish poems such as "The New Year: Rosh Hashana 5643" and the Zionist "Banner of the Jew."[166] "An Epistle to the Hebrews" (1882–1883), consisting of fourteen essays, set forth her ideas and plans for the reinvigoration and deepening of Jewish life by a national and cultural revival in the twin centers of America and the Holy Land. One of the more fascinating aspects of these pieces is the fact that Lazarus berates her fellow American Jews for traveling on the path of assimilation, a path that she had just left.[167] The prose poems in *By the Waters of Babylon* (1887), in which she reviewed the millennia of the Jewish exile, were a further demonstration of her prophetic insight.[168] These and other poems of a Jewish nature that Emma Lazarus wrote prompted the literary critic Van Wyck Brooks to comment: "How far a cause could vitalize and magnify a talent one saw in the case of . . . the Jewess Emma Lazarus."[169]

We have looked not only at women whose achievements represented a continuation of the past but also at women who, in the breadth of new outlooks, could assume more public roles than in the past. This very breadth, if viewed positively, allowed some to think progressively about educational opportunities for women; even if viewed negatively, it still spurred these greater opportunities to fruition to save women from the lures of the new tones sweeping Europe. We shall see the impetus to finally create schools for Orthodox women arises in reaction to the nontraditional establishments of the *Haskalah* rather than as an ideal to aspire to in its own right. The stage is set for Sarah Schenirer, a woman of vision and courage, to effect the necessary changes, thereby heralding a new reality for Jewish women worldwide.

---

166. Ibid., see pp. 144–153. See also Jacob, *The World of Emma Lazarus*, pp. 146–155.
167. See Vogel, *Emma Lazarus*, pp. 141–143.
168. Ibid., pp. 154–156.
169. Quoted in Vogel, *ibid.*, p. 152.

9

The Establishment of Universal Jewish Education for Women: The Beth Jacob Educational Movement

The inauguration of Jewish schools for girls in the late nineteenth and early twentieth centuries, particularly by Sarah Schenirer, was a major turn of affairs in the history of Orthodox Jewish women's education. It was she who founded the Beth Jacob movement with a view to bridging the ever-widening social and cultural chasm that separated young Jewish girls in eastern Europe from their religious and spiritual roots.[1] To most of the Jewish world today, the name *Bais Ya'akov* ("Beth Jacob"; alternatively pronounced *Beit Ya'akov*) connotes "religious orthodoxy, strict observance of modesty requirements, and uncompromising adherence to traditional behavior. Few realize that this network of schools and youth organizations for girls and young women began as a rather radical innovation within the Polish Jewish community."[2] The Beth Jacob

---

1. Paraphrasing Naomi Cohen in "Women and the Study of Talmud," *Tradition* 24:1 (Fall 1988): 30.

2. Deborah Weissman, "Bais Yaakov: A Historical Model for Jewish Feminists," *The Jewish Woman: New Perspectives*, ed. Elizabeth Koltun (New York: Schocken, 1976), p. 139. In an unpublished dissertation, Deborah Weissman has examined, in considerable depth, the rise and development of the Beth Jacob movement, as a case study in tradition and modernity. I am grateful to the author for permission to incorporate some of her material into my work. Readers interested in viewing the history and development of the Beth Jacob movement within the framework of sociological theory regarding tradition and social change may wish to scrutinize Weissman's work in its entirety. See *Bais Ya'akov – A Women's Educational Movement in the Polish Jewish Community:*

movement of Poland, during the short span of its existence, before its untimely destruction by Nazi Germany, carved out a pattern for the religious education of girls that was later to be emulated, continued, and adapted in Israel and North America as well as in other countries throughout the world.

BACKGROUND

The realization of universal religious education for Jewish women had its roots in the Jewish Enlightenment, which, as noted in the previous chapter, included as its key agendas both the social and political equality of the Jews as citizens and exposure of the community to Western culture. One of the responses to Enlightenment in the West was the rise of religious movements whose goals were to achieve an accommodation between Judaism and modernity. These included the Reform movement, Neo-Orthodoxy, and the Historical School.

The onset of the Enlightenment movement also saw a progressive change in the Western Jewish communities' attitude toward formal Jewish education for women. The founder of the Neo-Orthodox movement in Germany, Samson Raphael Hirsch, encouraged the establishment of schools for girls, in which most branches of traditional learning, excluding Talmud, as well as secular studies, including the arts and sciences and practical skills, were taught. At the close of the nineteenth century, we find Prof. David Kaufman advocating a full curriculum for Jewish girls and teacher-training programs for Jewish women. Kaufman (Austrian scholar, 1852–1899), an accomplished historian, was politically active in defending Jewish culture against the attacks of anti-Semites. In that regard, he projected the need to bolster the self-image of Jews in the educational sphere.

In a well-reasoned treatise, Kaufman observes that Jewish women have always been the mainstays of Jewish faith and holiness.[3] He begins by relating the spiritual contributions of biblical women as mothers, prophets, judges, and generals. He laments the erosion of religious spirit in contemporary women and wishes to lay the groundwork for revitalizing the essential role of women by implementing concrete educational programs. In the past, he argues, Jewish women, through their strong spiritual constitution, were able to absorb everything necessary for a meaningful Jewish life. But times change. Women are now faced with the allure of trends that run against the grain of Jewish tradition, especially in smaller communities. Kaufman be-

---

A Case Study in Tradition and Modernity, unpublished dissertation (Master of Arts in Sociology), New York University, 1977.

3. The importance of this treatise can be seen by its being translated into Hebrew in 1909 and circulated in eastern Europe: Bameh Narim et Ruah ha-Dat be-Kerev Nasheinu u-Venoteinu? trans. M. Kamianski (Zhitomir: Horozinski, 1909).

lieved schools must be established to counter these trends, complete with prizes for outstanding women teachers and students. Women must be encouraged to formally study their faith before it is lost. The curriculum would comprise Scriptures, Jewish literature, Jewish values, an appreciation of Jewish tradition past and present, major prayers, and, above all, Hebrew language. Girls must be encouraged from early ages to attend the synagogue on Sabbath and festivals. Kaufman's justification for these changes was his claim that it is better to educate women to serve God than for them to be immersed in the shallow values of contemporary society.

In Kaufman's view, it is essential to train superb women teachers to whom no one would object entrusting their children. Herein lies the key to building the social and religious fabric of future generations. Women, he suspected, will quickly develop a strong love and attachment to Jewish wisdom and its literature and so attain proficiency in Jewish learning as they now do in secular studies. It is important to develop a healthy literature for young women to read. Insofar as Scriptures are concerned, he found it desirable to have linear translations free from errors, with precise notations. In this way, women will be able to participate in the synagogue liturgy and appreciate the Torah readings. Kaufman advocated subsidized printings of prayer books that were clearly legible so as to instill confidence in beginning students. He also desired history books that would impart piety as well as excitement for the past. He would have liked to rejuvenate the vast and rich legacy of Jewish poetry together with the storehouses of folklore, which were filled with religious reverence. He saw in the revitalization of education for women a renaissance in Jewish culture as a whole.

This trend toward formal Jewish education for women was not initially supported by the Eastern Jewish communities, which, unlike their peers in the West, resisted attempts to synthesize Judaism with modernity. Enlightenment did bring with it the development of various national ideologies but without corresponding movements for synthesis within the religious sphere. Conceivably because of the strength of the hasidic movement (it has been estimated that no less than two-thirds of Polish Jews were *hasidim*[4]), the bulwark of learning in the traditional *yeshivot*, and the influence of certain renowned leaders such as Moses Sofer (known as the *Hatam Sofer*; 1762–1839), a Hungarian rabbi who taught that "anything new is forbidden by the Torah,"[5] Reform Judaism did not succeed in making inroads within eastern European Jewry, which instead split into religious and secular camps.[6] Ironically, in many Orthodox circles it was more acceptable for girls to study in the public Catholic schools than to be formally taught traditional Judaism in a school. Though the *hasidim* were

4. Weissman, *Bais Ya'akov – A Women's Educational Movement*, p. 30.

5. Moshe Shraga Samet, *Encyclopaedia Judaica*, vol. 15, p. 78.

6. Weissman, *Bais Ya'akov – A Women's Educational Movement*, p. 30.

unyielding in their opposition to *Haskalah* and no secular subject was allowed to penetrate the walls of the *yeshivah*, they were more lenient with their daughters, who read whatever they wished. Indeed, by the beginning of the twentieth century, many hasidic parents now encouraged their daughters to study and gloried in the not inconsiderable intellectual attainments of their eager and receptive daughters. In small Polish towns, private tutors were in great demand, and music, Polish, French, mathematics, and science were favorite subjects. In the larger towns, the daughters of hasidic families were permitted to attend the Gentile gymnasium, where a number even completed the curriculum of "eight classes" and graduated. Beyond academic considerations, a secular education was also viewed in utilitarian terms as a means of enabling young women to deal intelligently with the non-Jewish world so that they could eventually earn a living. The idea of formal Jewish education for girls, however, was regarded as being not in consonance with Jewish tradition and not an issue to be concerned with at the time.[7]

This difference in attitude between western and eastern Europe is exemplified in the famous visit in 1916 of two German Neo-Orthodox rabbis to Warsaw.[8] The Germans had taken over Poland during World War I, whence German Jewry discovered its brethren, the so-called *Ostjuden*. The two rabbis, Dr. Pinchas Kohn of Bavaria and Dr. Emanuel Carlebach of Cologne (their academic titles are significant as they attest to the incorporation of the religious and the secular so characteristic of German Jewry but entirely atypical of their brethren in Poland), had come eastward on a mission to reform the educational and organizational frameworks of the Jewish community. The two belonged to *Agudat Israel*, a nascent organization that had been founded in 1912 in Kattowitz, Upper Silesia.[9] The bulk of the original members of *Agudat Israel* were products of Hirsch's secessionist community in Frankfurt, who had formed the Association for the Interests of Orthodox Judaism. They represented an Orthodox accommodation with modernity, which strove for a synthesis of Torah and secular culture. In 1907, German Jewish leader Jacob Rosenheim had proposed a plan for broadening the scope of the association to include like-minded Jewish groups in other lands. This

7. See Harry M. Rabinowicz, *Hasidism: The Movement and Its Masters,* (Northvale NJ: Jason Aronson, 1988), pp. 347–348. See also Abraham Atkin, *The Beth Jacob Movement in Poland: 1917–1939,* unpublished dissertation (Doctor of Philosophy in education), Yeshiva University, 1959, p. 13, and Aryeh Bauminger, *Sefer Cracow: Ir ve-Em be- Yisrael* (Jerusalem: Mossad Harav Kook, 1959), pp. 369–376, cited in Weissman dissertation, p. 31.

8. See Alexander Carlebach, "A German Rabbi Goes East," *Leo Baeck Institute Year Book* VI (1961), pp. 60–121. See especially p. 62. See also Weissman dissertation, pp. 31–32.

9. For elaboration, see David Rudavsky, *Modern Jewish Religious Movements* (New York: Behrman House, 1967, 1969), pp. 244f.

international organization would be committed to addressing the internal needs of the Jewish community as well as representing Orthodox Jewish interest to the outside world, in competition with the burgeoning (and predominantly secular) Zionist movement. At its 1912 inception, *Agudat Israel* constituted three groups: German Neo-Orthodoxy, Hungarian Orthodoxy, and the Orthodox Jewries of Poland and Lithuania.

The two rabbis had hoped to make inroads into the Polish Jewish community but were met with a great deal of opposition. The Eastern Jews were suspicious of the dress, manner, customs, and secular enlightenment of their German counterparts, whom they considered to be "walking in the ways of the Gentiles." Furthermore, although the eastern European Jews, for the most part, opposed the Zionist movement for its secular character, they could never bring themselves to accept the antinationalistic stance of Hirsch and his group, who defined Judaism in strictly religious categories.[10] Similarly, they met with opposition from the eastern European Zionists and indifference from the assimilationists. Only one large body of Polish Jews supported their cause— the *Hasidim* of Ger—led by their *rebbe*, Avraham Mordekhai Alter.[11] This sect was a more broad-minded group, which published newspapers in both Hebrew and Yiddish and which became the most influential center of Orthodoxy in Poland. It was the *Gerer Hasidim* who initially endorsed the creation of the Beth Jacob Schools for the education of Orthodox girls.[12]

Kohn and Carlebach eventually did meet with a measure of success, buttressed by the support of the German occupational government.[13] They succeeded in organizing an *Agudat Israel* party in the Polish *Sejm* (parliament) and initiated some reforms in the curricula and teacher training of the Polish *heder*. Some of these reforms included separating students according to age and ability, better lighting facilities, higher salaries in order to attract more qualified teachers, a more formal structure with a trained pedagogue as principal, and, finally, a broader curriculum that would include philosophical and ethical works in addition to the traditional Talmud and study of the Bible. They also set up Jewish schools for girls. The largest school they established was the *Havazelet* girls' semivocational high school in Warsaw. Carlebach recruited

10. See Carlebach, "A German Rabbi Goes East," pp. 64 and 65. Carlebach relates an amusing story: when the two rabbis walked through the streets of certain Jewish communities in their Western garb, they were followed by groups of young boys in kaftans with *peyot* (side-curls) who shouted scornfully, *"Nor a Religie?"* ("only a religion?").

11. Ibid., p. 63.

12. See Rabinowicz, *Hasidism: The Movement and Its Masters*, p. 350.

13. Carlebach, "A German Rabbi Goes East," p. 63. See also the letters of Rabbi Emanuel Carlebach from Warsaw in the years 1916–1918, published in this article, pp. 68–121.

Rabbi Dr. Moses Auerbach, another follower of Hirsch, to become its first headmaster. Thus, prior to the founding of the Beth Jacob movement, there was a Jewish girls' school in Poland under Orthodox auspices, albeit German Neo-Orthodox in ideology. However, the *Havazelet* school became the domain of the daughters of the well-to-do, whereas the broader masses of the community were ultimately served by *Bais Ya'akov*.

The *Bais Ya'akov* movement, which was to establish a vast network of religious schools for women that exists to this day, originated in the community of Cracow. Its inception was the result of a number of economic, as well as historical-sociological, realities that led to an acknowledgment, albeit reluctant, of the need for a school system that would provide a secular and religious education for girls within the framework of traditional ideology.

During the interbellum period, the Jews formed the second-largest national minority in Poland (second only to the Ukrainians).[14] There were three million Jews, who lived mainly in the large urban centers. In some cities, the Jews accounted for one-fourth to one-third of the total. They were involved primarily in middle-class occupations, trades, and commerce, whereas the vast majority of the non-Jewish population were agrarian.[15] As the twentieth century progressed, Polish peasants became increasingly more urbanized and bourgeois. Gradually they became competitors in fields that were previously almost exclusively Jewish. The emerging Polish middle class, as well as the growing incidence of anti-Semitism, resulted in less business for Jews in commerce and led to economic hardship for many of them. In 1919, a Sunday Rest Law was passed, preventing stores from being opened on Sunday, which meant that Jewish businesses could not compete on an equal basis with those of their Gentile peers. The worldwide economic depression of the 1930s also was a factor in the increasing economic woes of the Jewish community.[16] As a result of their financial insecurity, members of the Jewish community had a much later average age of marriage and a considerably lower fertility rate than the rest of the population.[17]

14. For population figures, see S. Bronsztejn, "The Jewish Population of Poland in 1931," *Jewish Journal of Sociology* 6 (1964): 3–29; see especially pp. 5–7; Miriam Eisenstein, *Jewish Schools in Poland, 1919–1939: Their Philosophy and Development* (New York: King's Crown Press [Columbia University], 1950), p. 1; and Weissman, "Bais Yaakov: A Historical Model for Jewish Feminists," p. 140.

15. See Bronsztejn, "The Jewish Population in Poland in 1931," pp. 19–28, and Jacob Lestchinsky, "The Industrial and Social Structure of Interbellum Poland," *YIVO Annual of Social Science* 11 (1956–1957): 243–269. See also Hugh Seton-Watson, *Eastern Europe Between the Wars, 1918–1941* (Hamden, CT: Anchor, 1962), cited in Weissman, *Bais Ya'akov–A Women's Educational Movement*, pp. 34–35.

16. See Bronsztejn, "The Jewish Population in Poland in 1931," p. 24

17. Ibid., p. 13. See also Weissman, *Bais Ya'akov–A Women's Educational Movement*, pp. 35f.

In the context of our discussion, what is of particular interest is the effect economic changes wrought on the culture and social structure of the Jewish community, particularly with regard to the educational and vocational roles of the women. Initially, states Jacob Lestchinsky: "It can be unhesitatingly asserted that the orthodox Jewish family preferred to live in a poorer dwelling or to cut its food consumption rather than have the wife or daughters enter the factory labor market. It was far more acceptable to the Jewish family to do sewing or stocking-making at home than to have the daughter work in a factory."[18] However, during the period under discussion, there were 117 women between the ages of 15 to 49 for every 100 men.[19] Of the total number of women of childbearing age in Poland, 55.4 percent were married, whereas this was true of only 48.2 percent of their Jewish counterparts.[20] Therefore, owing to the increasing impoverishment of the Jewish community (to illustrate, in 1929, on the average, 50 percent of Polish Jews were excused from paying synagogue dues, while another 30–35 percent paid token dues[21]) and the large pool of unmarried women in their prime, it became economically disadvantageous to keep this large reservoir of potential wage earners out of the market. Consequently, and particularly during the decade of the 1920s, there were, so to speak, breaches in the fortress of Orthodoxy, as many women began to enter the labor market under the pressure of economic necessity.[22] Entrance into the labor market required the attainment of certain linguistic and vocational skills. Hence, a comprehensive education for girls that would lead to gainful employment had now become an economic necessity.

The Minorities Treaty signed at the end of the First World War promised support for the schools of all cultural minorities in eastern Europe, but in Poland, each year, subventions to the Jewish schools dwindled.[23] In 1927, for example, the municipality of Warsaw granted 60,000 zlotys for support of the Jewish schools in its area; in 1928, only 17,000 zlotys; and by 1934, nothing.[24] Originally, there had been public schools catering to the children of heavily Jewish neighborhoods. These schools would be closed on the Sabbath and Jewish holidays and open on Sundays and, using state funds, would provide

---

18. Lestchinsky, "The Industrial and Social Structure of Interbellum Poland," p. 249. Also quoted in Weissman, Bais Ya'akov–A Women's Educational Movement, p. 36.

19. Bronsztejn, "The Jewish Population in Poland in 1931," p. 14; Weissman dissertation, p. 36.

20. Ibid.

21. Bornstein, "The Budgets of Jewish Denominational Congregations in Poland," Statistical Quarterly (1929): 380, cited in Weissman dissertation, p. 35.

22. Lestchinsky, "The Industrial and Social Structure of Interbellum Poland," p. 250. See also Weissman dissertation, p. 36.

23. See, further, Atkin, The Beth Jacob Movement in Poland, pp. 2–5.

24. See Eisenstein, Jewish Schools in Poland, pp. 4 and 5; and Weissman, "Bais Yaakov: A Historical Model for Jewish Feminists," p. 140.

instruction in Jewish religion. But gradually they were closed down. About three-quarters of Jewish children subsequently attended secular Polish schools, chiefly because their parents could not afford private schooling. Many did attend afternoon religious instruction in Jewish schools, and the rest, Jewish schools of different ideological orientations in which the language of instruction was, variously, Hebrew, Yiddish, or Polish.[25] Within the Orthodox community (which initially constituted the majority of Polish Jews but whose strength began to wane by the 1930s), emphasis was placed on schools for boys.

Thus many of the daughters of Orthodox parents came to be sent to Polish gymnasiums. Gradually, from a religious viewpoint, it became apparent that this was a potentially dangerous situation, as the naive and sheltered Jewish girls were being exposed to modern, secular culture and being seduced by the attractions of non-Jewish ideologies. Many of the girls began to question the religious values and traditions of their parents, because they were influenced by Marxist or other revolutionary ideologies or even being swept into the small but growing feminist movement in Poland (in 1919, Polish women had achieved political emancipation). Young girls would appear at their families' Sabbath dinner attired in stylish, immodest garb and would respond brazenly to their elders. The traditional reading matter for Jewish women, the *Tze'enah u-Re'enah*, was discarded in favor of the epic *Pan Tadeusz*, by the Polish poet Adam Mickiewicz (1798-1855).[26] Matchmakers and parentally arranged marriages were no longer accepted willingly. Many now regarded the *yeshivah* student as unworldly and parochial. Often, newly emancipated young women fled from fatherly reproofs with a husband of their own choosing. "The legendary intergenerational harmony of the Jewish household was being undermined,"[27] and the traditional continuity of Jewish religious life seriously threatened.[28]

---

25. Some examples of such schools were the Tarbut network of Hebrew-speaking, coeducational schools, with a pro-Zionist orientation (see Eisenstein, *Jewish Schools in Poland*, pp. 40–58, and Scharfstein, *Toledot ha-Hinukh be-Yisrael ba-Dorot hu-Aharonim* (Jerusalem: Rubin Mass, 1960–1966), vol. 2, pp. 163–183); the Yiddish-speaking, anti-Zionist schools, the *Cyscho* (Eisenstein, pp. 18–39; Scharfstein, pp. 183–193); the Yiddish-speaking Zionist schools, the *Shulkult* (Eisenstein, pp. 59–70; Scharfstein, pp. 193–195); the *Horev* boys' schools and the *Bais Ya'akov* girls' schools, the educational arm of *Agudat Israel* (Eisenstein, pp. 78–88; Scharfstein, pp. 131–156); and the *Yavneh* schools, run by the *Mizrahi* religious Zionists, coeducational through grade four only (Eisenstein, pp. 88–93; Scharfstein, pp. 156–160). See also Atkin, *The Beth Jacob Movement in Poland*, pp. 5–11, and Weissman dissertation, pp. 36, 42–43.

26. Rabinowicz, *Hasidism: The Movement and Its Masters*, p. 348.

27. Weissman, "Bais Yaakov: A Historical Model for Jewish Feminists," p. 141.

28. See, further, Atkin, *The Beth Jacob Movement in Poland*, pp. 13–14, and the writings of prominent American lecturer, author, educator, and president of the first World

Even had young Jewish girls not entered secular schools or joined the labor force, it is doubtful whether the home and local Jewish community still retained the ability and the moral force to ensure the continued loyalty of the adolescent girl and, at least initially, the adolescent boy as well.[29] As mentioned in the previous chapter, owing to economic, political, and social factors (grinding poverty, religious persecution, and excessive intellectualism), late-eighteenth-century eastern Europe witnessed the defection of numerous boys and young men from the traditional Jewish educational framework, leaving them in a spiritual vacuum. Subsequently, other young men, thirsting for wider vistas, often filled much of their time "imbibing the heady drink of secular *Haskalah* literature."[30] These defections were alternately countered by two developments: the rise of Hasidism and the establishment of large-scale *yeshivot*, both of which were male oriented—the first, partially, and the latter, exclusively. The reality of Hasidism was, and remains, that if both husband and wife were unable to journey to the *rebbe*'s home due to family responsibilities, it was the woman who remained behind to supervise house and children. The husband, and perhaps older sons, sojourned to the warm, soul-satisfying, and spiritually uplifting environment of the *rebbe*'s court, which provided young and old men alike with wonderful feelings of identity, warmth, and loyalty to Judaism. Sarah Schenirer, founder of the *Bais Ya'akov* movement, vividly describes the feelings of abandonment and spiritual emptiness experienced by the women and girls left behind:

And as we pass through the *Elul* days [the month preceding the High Holidays], the trains which run to the little *shtetlekh* [towns] where the *rebbes* live are crowded. Thousands of *Hasidim* are on their way to spend the *Yamim Nora'im* ["Solemn Holy Days"] with the *rebbe*. Every day sees new crowds of old men and young men in the hasidic garb, eager to secure a place on the train, eager to spend the holiest days in the year in the atmosphere of their *rebbe*, to be able to extract from it as much holiness as possible. Fathers and son travel. . . . Thus they are drawn to Ger, to Belz, to Alexander, to Bobow, to all those places that had been made citadels of concerted religious life, dominated by the figure of a *rebbe*'s personality.

And we stay at home, the wives, the daughters, and the little ones. We have an empty *yom tov* [holiday]. It is bare of Jewish intellectual content. The women have never learned anything about the spiritual content that is concentrated within a Jewish festival. The mother goes to the synagogue, but the services echo faintly into the fenced and boarded-off women's galleries. There is much

Jewish Congress of Jewish Women and National Council of Jewish Women Rebecca Kohut, "A New Morning for the Jewish Girls in Europe," *Bejs Jakob*, ed. Samuel Leo Deutschlander (Vienna: Beth Jacob Central Organization, 1930, original in German), p. 8.

29. See Cohen, "Women and the Study of Talmud," pp. 30–32.
30. Ibid., pp. 30–31.

crying by the elderly women. The young girls look at them as though they belong to a different century. Youth and the desire to live a full life shoot up violently in the strong-willed young personalities. Outside the synagogue, the young girls stand chattering; they walk away from synagogue where their mothers pour out their vague and heavy feelings. They leave behind them the wailing of the older generation and follow the urge for freedom and self-expression. Further and further away from synagogue they go, further away to the dancing, tempting light of a fleeting joy.[31]

Similarly, in non-hasidic circles, it was not easy for an educated or an intellectually curious girl to find fulfillment in her own home. The response of the non-hasidic world to both *Haskalah* and Hasidism had been the development of large-scale *yeshivot*, pioneered by the famous *Yeshivat Volozhin* in 1803, the foremost and most outstanding of its kind. Until the establishment of the academy for higher learning at Volozhin, the young adolescent eastern European scholar generally studied in a *klois*, that is, in the company of a few boys and men of varying ages under the intermittent supervision of the local rabbi.[32] In this new-style *yeshivah*, hundreds of boys were gathered together away from home, organized into groups roughly according to age, and provided with a regular program of daily study. They were also placed under the circumspect supervision of *mashgihim* (spiritual mentors) and were "provided with other educational mechanisms aimed at regulating both their spiritual and intellectual diets and their overt behavior."[33] Thus, owing to changing conditions, it was realized that the home and local community were insufficient to ensure the continued allegiance of the adolescent boy. In order to achieve this, he needed to be provided with a structured educational framework in which the demanding ideal of *Torah Lishmah* ("study of Torah for its own sake") would be striven for and realized. Parallel institutions for girls and women were not provided for. To make matters worse, the new type of *yeshivah* was, in increasing numbers, removing the young men who were not attracted by Hasidism or *Haskalah* from the environs of family and community. Consequently, such young men were leaving their sisters bereft of any kind of spiritual and intellectual stimulation that their presence might have afforded. Indeed, with Orthodox girls' increasing attendance at Polish gymnasiums in the early twentieth century—institutions devoid of meaningful religious experience—and with their brothers immersed in *yeshivot* or

31. Sarah Schenirer's words, as recounted by her young colleague Judith Grunfeld-Rosenbaum in "Sarah Schenirer," in *Jewish Leaders: 1750–1940*, ed. Leo Jung (Jerusalem: Boys' Town, 1953, 1964), pp. 410–411.

32. See, for example, Immanuel Etkes, "Mishpahah ve-Limud Torah be-Hugei ha-'Lomdim' be-Lita be-Me'ah ha-Yud-Tet," *Zion* 51 (1986): 89, cited in Cohen, "Women and the Study of Talmud," p. 31.

33. Cohen, "Women and the Study of Talmud," p. 31.

hasidic institutions, an incongruous situation developed in which boys and girls from the same family were growing up living in totally different worlds.

In summation, a number of factors provided the backdrop from which the *Bais Ya'akov* movement was launched: (1) the economic need for educated Jewish women; (2) parents' fear that their daughters would absorb in the public school system Polish cultural values and knowledge both at variance with their own Orthodox Judaism and alien to the "intellectual universe of discourse"[34] in which their brothers were being raised; and (3) the inability of the home and local community to ensure the continued loyalty to Judaism of the young women owing to the menfolk's living in a world of their own that generally excluded women.

Naomi Cohen, Israeli professor of Jewish thought, advances an interesting rationale as to why the breakthrough in Orthodox circles, respecting the formal Jewish education of girls, did not take place in eastern Europe, which was more "Jewishly Jewish" than Frankfurt am Main, where it actually occurred, under the direction of Samson Raphael Hirsch.[35] Earlier we had attributed the influence of the *Haskalah* and the effects on Jewish life of Reform Judaism as factors in Hirsch's decision to establish high-quality formal Jewish education for girls. Cohen further suggests that differing educational ideals in the *yeshivah* world of eastern Europe and in Hirsch's school system in Germany made the parallel establishment of schools for girls based on the two differing ideals totally unsuitable in the former case, while eminently appropriate in the latter. In Cohen's words:

> The institutional remedy of the Volozhin and later Hungarian and other *yeshivot*, was hardly a solution for girls, even in separate institutions. The problem was the very core of the educational ideal central to this new type of *yeshivah*. In the *yeshivot*, every means possible was brought into play to imbue in the aspiring young scholar an uncompromising dedication to talmudic learning "for its own sake," to the exclusion of all worldly pursuits.
>
> Such an obvious impossible ideal for girls ruled out this framework as a potential model which might somehow be adapted for them. In fact, I would suggest that this very stress upon the boy's duty and privilege, *as a male*, to concentrate on Torah study to the exclusion of all else, may well have contributed to the unduly categorical downgrading of Jewish education for girls.

In contrast to the situation in the hasidic and *yeshivah* worlds, in the school founded by Samson Raphael Hirsch,

> the educational ideal was the creation of a well rounded *"Yisroel-Mensch"* – that is, [a] "Jewish-Person" – an ideal eminently fit for the education of both boys and

---

34. An expression used by Weissman in "Education of Jewish Women," *Encyclopaedia Judaica* Year Book 1986–1987, p. 32.

35. See Cohen, "Women and the Study of Talmud," p. 32.

girls. Further, though the curriculum indeed included a significant amount of Jewish studies of all kinds, it had Talmud only in the upper forms. Thus, neither the educational ideal nor the specific curriculum offered had to be radically altered to adapt it to what was looked upon as appropriate for the parallel girls' classes. Indeed, the girls were here offered a rich Jewish curriculum very similar to that of the boys–one which demanded serious intellectual application in Jewish studies.[36]

It was this prototype that, some sixty years later, a now near legendary seamstress named Sarah Schenirer would transfer to the *yeshivah* and the hasidic world of eastern Europe. Before an examination of the way she engineered this extraordinary feat, a deeper look into the persona of this remarkable woman is warranted.[37]

SARAH SCHENIRER–FOUNDER OF *BAIS YA'AKOV*: A MODEL IN EDUCATIONAL LEADERSHIP

Sarah Schenirer was born in Cracow, Poland, in 1883, the daughter of a prosperous hasidic merchant, an adherent of the *rebbe* of Belz. Both her parents were descendants of illustrious scholars and legal commentators.[38]

Sarah attended a Polish elementary school for eight years, excelling in religious studies, handicrafts, and other subjects. Her religious education consisted of instruction given by a rabbi who visited her school once or twice a week for this purpose. Sarah was the only girl in school who took her religious instruction seriously, although she, too, could not help feeling that

36. Ibid.

37. This profile on Sarah Schenirer, as well as information on the development of the Beth Jacob schools, has been assembled from the following sources: Atkin, *The Beth Jacob Movement in Poland*, pp. 17–33; Joseph Friedensohn, "Batei ha-Sefer le-B'not Beit Ya'akov be-Polin" ("Beth Jacob Schools for Girls in Poland"), *Ha- Hinukh ve-ha-Tarbut ha-Ivrit be-Eiropah Bein Sh'tei Milhamot ha-Olam* ("Jewish Education and Culture in Europe Between the two World Wars"), ed. Zevi Scharfstein (New York: Ha-Histadrut ha-Ivrit be-America, 1957), pp. 61–82; Judith Grunfeld-Rosenbaum, "Sarah Schenirer," in *Jewish Leaders*, ed. Leo Jung, pp. 407–432; Zvi E. Kurzweil, *Modern Trends in Jewish Education* (New York: Thomas Yoseloff, 1964), pp. 266–274; Zevi Scharfstein, *Gedolei Hinukh be-Ameinu* ("Great Hebrew Educators") (Jerusalem: Rubin Mass, 1964), pp. 226–243; Scharfstein, *Toldot ha-Hinukh be-Yisrael*, vol. 2, pp. 142–155; Sarah Schenirer, *Em be-Yisrael: Kitvei Sara Schenirer* (S. Schenirer's diary, essays, and letters) (Tel Aviv: Netzah, 1955), see especially p. 21–42; Weissman, *Bais Ya'akov–A Women's Educational Movement*, pp. 46f.

38. Sarah's mother was a descendant of seventeenth-century rabbi Joel Sirkis, author of the *Bayit Hadash* commentary on *Tur*. Her father, Bezalel ha-Cohen of Tarnow, was a descendant of Rabbi Shabbetai Ben Meir Ha-Cohen, author of *Siftei Cohen*, a seventeenth-century commentary on the *Shulhan Arukh*. (See S. Schenirer, *Em be-Yisrael*, p. 21.)

the rather meager lessons were not very conducive to progress. Throughout her life, her greatest pleasure was to study Jewish sacred texts, and even as a child she spent every evening poring over the Bible, books of Jewish ethical literature, and the popular *Tze'enah u-Re'enah*.[39] She envied her father and brothers, who were permitted to study Talmud, "pitting argument against argument, knowledge against knowledge" in their frequent discussions and debates.[40] It was Sarah's inclination for study coupled with a deep sense of religious devotion that earned for her the nickname, as early as age six, of *"hasidonet"* ("the little pious one" – intended derisively).[41] Sarah's father perceived his daughter's deep craving to study and obtained for her a volume of talmudic legends translated into Yiddish. Sarah read as much as she could find in the areas of biblical commentaries, rabbinic lore, and even more modern Jewish philosophy, being particularly impressed with the works of the German Neo-Orthodox thinkers Hirsch, Breuer, and Hildesheimer. In later life she claimed that one of the most profound influences on her thinking had been Hirsch's work *Horev*.[42]

After Sarah grew to maturity, the family fortunes failed and she was obliged to learn a trade to support herself and help her family. Having served her apprenticeship in sewing and embroidery, she started a small dressmaking business and soon built up a considerable clientele. Her close contact with girls and women of all types gave Sarah food for serious thought. She observed how industriously women pursued the adornment of their bodies while sorely neglecting their spiritual development. She often wondered why Jewish parents who spared no pains to promote the physical well-being of their daughters did so little for their religious education. She grew increasingly disturbed by what she perceived as a growing laxity in religious observance among her contemporaries. A relative once took her to a Friday night meeting of a new organization for Jewish girls, called "Ruth." Sarah was shocked to see daughters of hasidic families desecrating the Sabbath and listening to a lecture replete with heretical remarks.[43] She felt that something must be done to reverse this trend, but as yet she had no practical program for how it could be accomplished.

The most significant turning point in Sarah's life, which crystallized her resolve to take action, occurred in 1914, when, with the outbreak of World War I, she temporarily emigrated with her family, leaving Galicia and spending the war years in Vienna.[44] There Sarah began to attend the services and lectures of Rabbi Dr. Moshe Flesch, who was an adherent of the Samson Raphael Hirsch school of thought. These sermons struck Sarah as modern

---

39. Ibid., p. 22.

40. See Grunfeld-Rosenbaum, "Sarah Schenirer," pp. 409–410.

41. Schenirer, *Em be-Yisrael*, p. 22.

42. Yehezkel Rottenberg, ed. *Sefer Zikaron le-Sarah Schenirer* (Bnei Brak, 1960), p. 31, cited in Weissman dissertation, p. 48.

43. Schenirer, *Em be-Yisrael*, p. 23.

44. Ibid., p. 23.

and progressive, though they were in fact completely traditionalist in spirit. Sarah was greatly influenced by Rabbi Flesch and soon realized the power inherent in Judaism if only it were presented to the people in a way they could understand and in a spirit that was akin to theirs. "I listened intently to Dr. Flesch's inspiring sermon," she recalled, writing about the first Hanukkah service she attended in Vienna. "The rabbi painted a vivid picture of Judith, the heroine of Jewish history. He held her image up as an example to the girls and women of our days and urged them to walk in the footsteps of the illustrious women of Israel in ancient times. . . . I said to myself: 'How I wish that the women of Cracow might hear who we are and who our ancestors were.' "[45] Sarah now regularly attended the study circles of Dr. Flesch and read extensively on Judaism. Judith Grunfeld-Rosenbaum, Sarah Schenirer's young colleague at the *Bais Ya'akov* school in Cracow, writes of Sarah's eagerness to expand her knowledge of Judaism, while in Vienna: "[She] wrote down with painful loyalty every speech, every lesson she heard from Rabbi Flesch during the years in Vienna, when she became his constant and most regular and conscientious pupil. And the thicker the volume of her writings, the more impatient she grew to go back to Cracow to share the treasures she had gathered."[46] In 1917 she returned to Cracow with vague plans for concretizing religious education for women.

ESTABLISHMENT AND DEVELOPMENT OF *BAIS YA'AKOV*

The ideas that shaped the educational activities Sarah was to undertake in Cracow were founded on three convictions based on her perceptive observation of the Jewish scene.[47] First, the anomaly of the situation whereby boys received only a Jewish education and girls only a Polish one was obvious. As future mothers, girls would exercise a decisive influence on their children and therefore required, no less than boys, a Jewish education. Second, Sarah was attracted to the ways of Western Orthodoxy, which paid a great deal of attention to the education of girls. Third, she realized that if Polish became the mother tongue of Jewish girls, then their whole outlook would become Polish rather than Jewish, and they would be drawn into alien cultural circles. Thus, in determining the language of instruction that she would ultimately use in educating her pupils, although admiring of the Hirschian school of thought that had adopted the language of the country, she felt instinctively that this was not feasible in her own country. She regarded the Yiddish language as an effective barrier to assimilation, especially because, as opposed to Germany, where from the days of Mendelssohn

---

45. Ibid., p. 24.
46. Grunfeld-Rosenbaum, "Sarah Schenirer," p. 413.
47. See Kurzweil, *Modern Trends in Jewish Education*, p. 269.

German Jews had spoken German, the majority of Polish Jewry still spoke Yiddish as their mother tongue.[48]

Sarah Schenirer realized that in her endeavor to institute formal religious education for girls she would face severe opposition from a variety of sources.[49] On one hand, the "progressives" of the community would consider traditional Jewish education for women a step backward. Experience had shown Sarah that whenever she admonished her friends that their behavior was not in accordance with tradition, they mocked her and labeled her as old-fashioned. On the other hand, the traditionalists would most likely not be receptive either. Years earlier, in 1903, a conference of Polish rabbis had been held in Cracow.[50] One of the participants, Rabbi Menahem Mendel Lando, the *rebbe* of Zvirtche, had chastised his colleagues for neglecting the education of Jewish girls and had called for the establishment of schools to resolve this problem. His suggestion was almost unanimously rejected, and the conference resolutions stated that Jewish parents should certainly educate their daughters at home but that it would be inappropriate for the community to set up schools for this purpose. Nevertheless, Schenirer decided to make the effort of setting up some format for educating women. However, an initial public meeting in Cracow that Sarah called for this purpose, attended by forty women, resulted only in the founding, several months later, of a Jewish women's lending library.[51]

For a number of years after her return to Cracow, Sarah valiantly struggled to find a way of attracting the young ladies of Cracow, but they snubbed her efforts and displayed a contemptuous attitude to her attempts to bring them back to the traditions of their ancestors. "She assembled them," writes Grunfeld-Rosenbaum, "but she failed to hold them. Her words seemed to come back to her empty, and in spite of the growing determination to acquire a circle of listeners and pupils, she found herself alone for a very long time. But with every failure her determination increased. . . . She was certain that just as she had been granted the language to speak, so would she find the hearts to speak to."[52] Sarah finally concluded that she would have to concentrate her efforts on younger students, who were not yet affected by alien influences, if she were to meet with any measure of success.[53]

---

48. See also Scharfstein, *Gedolei Hinukh be-Ameinu*, p. 241.

49. See Schenirer, *Em be-Yisrael*, p. 25.

50. For a discussion of the conference topics, see Jacob Gutman, *Mekitz Nirdamim* (Piotrokow, 1904; Reprint: Copy Corner, Brooklyn, 1992), see especially pp. 51–56 regarding the topic of girls' education. See also Weissman dissertation, p. 50, citing Aharon Suraski, *Toldot ha-Hinukh ha-Torah be-Tekufah ha-Hadashah* (Bnei Brak: Or Hayim, 1967).

51. Schenirer, *Em be-Yisrael*, pp. 26–27.

52. Grunfeld-Rosenbaum, "Sarah Schenirer," p. 413.

53. Schenirer, *Em be-Yisrael*, p. 28. See also Scharfstein, *Gedolei Hinukh be-Ameinu*, pp. 230–231.

278 "And All Your Children Shall Be Learned"

To begin such a school for young children, Schenirer realized that she would need the advice and moral support of leaders of her generation in order to succeed. She was now about to embark on a radical innovation within the traditional world, and she perceived that there would be many among the Orthodox who would object to her conception of formal religious education for girls. At the advice of her brother, who at first cautioned her not to get involved in politics, she approached the *rebbe* of Belz (the hasidic sect of which her family were members), Issachar Dov Rokeah (1854–1927), at Marienbad, where he was attending a conference of the *Agudat Israel* organization.[54] This *rebbe* headed a very conservative and traditional sect and had innovated the use of the instruments of modernity–the press and politics–to propagate and perpetuate the traditionalist and conservative point of view in religion and politics. Issachar Dov denounced most attempts to innovate within traditional Judaism and considered even the *Agudat Israel* party too progressive.[55] Nevertheless, when Sara Schenirer approached him, eloquently expounding her goals, the *rebbe* of Belz was convinced that, in this instance, innovation was necessary, and he responded with, "Good fortune and blessing."[56] However, he refused to allow the daughters of Belzer *Hasidim* to attend the schools. His blessing was an important coup, considering the ultraconservatism of this sect of Jews, but it remained for the *rebbe* of Ger, Abraham Mordekhai Alter (1866–1948), to extend his blessings and total approval of the endeavor to give it the necessary practical support. As Rabbi Alter was to write at a future date, "It is a sacred duty to work nowadays for the *Bais Ya'akov* movement. The future mothers of Israel are being educated in the true traditional spirit of the Torah and are receiving a sound all-round schooling. The question of a Jewish education for Jewish daughters is more important than the education of our sons, for that has always been taken care of."[57] Rabbi Joseph Isaac Schneerson, the Lubavitcher *rebbe*, was another hasidic leader who actively supported the cause.[58]

The greatest single act of ideological support for women's education may well have been the responsum of Rabbi Israel Meir ha-Cohen (Kagan, 1838–1933; popularly called after his most famous work, *Hafetz Hayim*).[59]

---

54. Schenirer, *Em be-Yisrael*, p. 29.

55. For elaboration, see Itzhak Alfassi, *Encyclopaedia Judaica*, vol. 4, pp. 452–453; Lucy Dawidowicz, *The Golden Tradition* (Boston: Holt, Rienhart & Winston, 1967), pp. 192–195; and Rabinowicz, *Hasidism: The Movement and Its Masters*, pp. 166–168.

56. Schenirer, *Em be-Yisrael*, p. 29.

57. *Beit Ya'akov Journal* (Lodz), Fifteen-Year Issue, no. 150 (Spring 1938), cited in Atkin dissertation, p. 52, and quoted in Rabinowicz, *Hasidism*, p. 350.

58. See Atkin dissertation, p. 65; and *Beit Ya'akov Journal* (Lodz), no. 115 (Spring 1934).

59. See *Likutei Halakhot* (St. Petersburg, 1918), *Sotah* 21. This responsum was

The Hafetz Hayim, a prolific writer, was the outstanding spiritual leader of eastern European Jewry in the first third of the twentieth century and gave moral support to Schenirer's endeavor. Guided by realistic considerations, wherein the withholding of formal Torah education from girls exposed to secular culture might well lead to girls' straying from religion, he stressed the point that full account be taken of girls' aspirations in the spiritual climate of modern society. In response to critics on the religious right, he underscored the propriety of religious education for Jewish women in his day and age, stating that historical practices of the past that ignored women's formal religious education were to be readjusted because times had changed. It was necessary to teach Jewish girls the fundamentals of their religion in order to keep them within their traditional faith. The isolation of Jewish communities in earlier times from the wider world was a thing of the past. Girls now had to be fortified in their belief system if they were to stay in it. Rabbi Kagan advocated a curriculum of limited scope, wherein the emphasis would be on study of Bible and works of an ethical-philosophical nature, as well as on practical halakhic guidance. (The full text of Rabbi Kagan's responsum, and an analysis of it, appears in Chapter Three.) Rabbi Kagan also addressed letters to many Jewish communities in eastern Europe, urging them to establish schools for girls, without any hesitation.[60] Another spiritual leader of Lithuanian Jewry at the time, Rabbi Hayim Ozer Grodzinski (1863–1940), shared the Hafetz Hayim's convictions.[61] A contemporary of both of these illustrious leaders, prominent Lithuanian rabbi and talmudic scholar Zalman Sorotzkin (1881–1966), also strongly encouraged the establishment of schools for girls, considering it a religious imperative (see Chapter Three).[62]

Sarah Schenirer opened her school for young girls in 1918 with twenty-five students.[63] Into the small room on Katarzyna Street, in the Jewish quarter of Cracow, which had previously been used for her work as a dressmaker, she

---

subsequently reprinted in the movement's periodical *Beit Ya'akov*, in the summer of 1933.

60. For a text of two such letters, see Scharfstein, *Gedolei Hinukh be-Ameinu*, pp. 109–110, and Atkin dissertation, p. 65 (quoting from the *Beit Ya'akov Journal* (Lodz), no. 115 [Spring 1934]).

61. For his comments on the subject, see *Beit Ya'akov Journal* (Lodz), Fifteen-Year Issue, no. 150 (Spring 1938), quoted in Atkin dissertation, p. 52. See further Rabbi Grodzinski's comments on *Bais Ya'akov* in which he quotes from the sixteenth-century work *Ma'ayan Ganim* (see Chapter 3) and refers to Beth Jacob as "an institution of savior for the daughters of Israel" and the work of the movement as "holy" in *Beit Ya'akov Journal* (Jerusalem) (December 1960): 3.

62. See Zalman Sorotzkin's homilies in *Ha-De'ah ve-ha-Dibur* (Warsaw, 1937), vol. 1, homilies 3 and 17. See also his book of responsa, *Moznaim la-Mishpat* (Jerusalem, 1955), vol. 1, resp. 42.

63. Schenirer, *Em be-Yisrael*, p. 29.

brought a blackboard and some benches.[64] The name Beth Jacob was originally suggested by a man on the initial committee that granted support to the school in Cracow,[65] and it alluded to the verse that would also become the school's motto: "O house of Jacob, come ye, and let us walk in the light of the Lord" (Isaiah 2:5). The name was chosen because of its instantaneous identification with women. This identification came from the verse (Exodus 19:3) "Thus shall you say to the house of Jacob and tell the sons of Israel." Rashi, commenting on the verse, quotes the *Midrash* to the effect that the phrase "the House of Jacob" denotes the women of Israel.

The majority of girls who initially attended the school came from hasidic families associated with the Ger dynasty,[66] owing to the unqualified support and enthusiasm of the *rebbe* of Ger for this undertaking. At the end of 1918 the number of pupils in Sarah's school rose to eighty, and she was compelled to take a larger flat consisting of three rooms in order to house her school adequately. She did not confine her activities to Cracow alone but visited other towns, addressing Jewish communities at numerous meetings and propagating her ideas, generally with great success,[67] but not always without opposition. From these small beginnings there grew a whole network of day schools, seminars for the training of teachers, and evening schools spreading over the foremost Jewish communities in Europe, America, and Palestine. According to reliable statistics, there were by 1924 in Poland nineteen schools with 2,000 students. By the year 1937–1938, Poland itself boasted 250 Beth Jacob institutions with a student population of 35,585.[68]

How can one explain this phenomenal success? "How," ponders Zvi Kurzweil in *Modern Trends in Jewish Education*, "could this simple woman launch an educational movement that spread to so many Jewish communities and won the approval of a substantial part of Jewish Orthodoxy?"[69] First, Sarah Schenirer's cause spoke for itself; her schools answered a vital need. As eminent American rabbi and chairman of the Beth Jacob World Organization Leo Jung commented during the early years of Beth Jacob's existence:

---

64. See Rabinowicz, *Hasidism: The Movement and its Masters,* p. 168. See also Atkin, *The Beth Jacob Movement in Poland,* pp. 23–24, 36, and Grunfeld-Rosenbaum, "Sarah Schenirer," pp. 414–415.

65. See Weissman dissertation, p. 54.

66. Ibid.

67. See Scharfstein, *Gedolei Hinukh be-Ameinu,* pp. 231–232.

68. Kurzweil, *Modern Trends in Jewish Education,* p. 271; Rabinowicz, *Hasidism: The Movement and Its Masters,* p. 350. Friedensohn, "Batei ha-Sefer le-B'not Beit Ya'akov be-Polin," p. 71, places the number at 38,000. For further statistics, see Eisenstein, *Jewish Schools in Poland, 1919–1939,* p. 84.

69. See Kurzweil, *Modern Trends in Jewish Education,* pp. 271–272. See further Atkin dissertation, pp. 24–25.

"The Beth Jacob movement is the most hopeful indication of a religious reawakening in Eastern Europe. It is the one constructive effort to reassert the authority of the Torah, the one substantial endeavor to safeguard the moral and physical welfare of our womanhood."[70] Second, the character and personality of Sarah Schenirer contributed in no small measure to her success. Her pupils and all those who came into contact with her were moved by her piety, her simplicity, her disarming sincerity, and her integrity. She demanded much of her students, and they produced in kind, responding to her expectations – as her colleague Judith Grunfeld-Rosenbaum writes – as one would "to a mother whom you love too much to have her serenity clouded."[71] Grunfeld-Rosenbaum elaborates:

> This was the greatest mystery, something almost magical, and quite inexplicable; something that will probably evade forever any attempt at psychological or analytic explanation. All the young girls, those from Poland and those from Lithuania, those with a revolutionary rebel spirit and those who were by nature inclined to accept dictatorial leadership, those who had a searching mind, and those who found all answers ready in their own piety, those that came from wealthy homes, and those who had always lived in the squalid basement-dwellings of the Ghetto, the vivacious and progressive as well as the humble types, they all loved Frau[72] Schenirer.[73]

---

70. Quoted in Eisenstein, *Jewish Schools in Poland*, p. 83.

71. Grunfeld-Rosenbaum, "Sarah Schenirer," p. 421

72. One of the most fascinating cases of myth-making in Sarah Schenirer's biography concerns her marital status (see Weissman dissertation, p. 46). She is always referred to as "Frau," but in official publications there is almost never any mention of her having been married. Quite the contrary, much is made of the idea that although she never actually bore children of her own, she was a mother of thousands. Schenirer does note in her diary (*Em be-Yisrael*, p. 36) that in 1911, at the age of twenty-eight, she became engaged. She wrote that her friends wanted to take her to the theater to celebrate the occasion, but she preferred to stay home and learn Torah. According to Weissman, there seem to be no further references to her fiancé or wedding. Indeed, until her obituary, there are only vague hints at some type of personal tragedy and a great disappointment at not having had any children. An obituary written by a secular journalist, Moshe Blat, in Cracow in 1935, when Sarah died of cancer at age 52, solves the mystery. The text (quoted in Weissman dissertation, p. 46) includes the following: "In contrast to her success in the educational realm, in her personal life, Sarah Schenirer knew great suffering. For many years, she was alone, having been divorced from the husband of her youth following a family tragedy, and living only for the sake of the Beth Jacob movement. In the later years of her life, she married Rabbi Landau and desired to live a bit for herself."

73. Grunfeld-Rosenbaum, "Sarah Schenirer," p. 421. For tributes and accolades to Sarah Schenirer from some of the leaders, scholars, writers, and students of her time, see *Em be-Yisrael*, pp. 12–19. See, further, Atkin dissertation, pp. 25, 26–27. For tales of

Sarah Schenirer's success was, furthermore, due to the reality that she did not have to crusade single-handedly. The Ger branch of the hasidic movement – a large, popular, and by this time already highly politicized organization – formed the bulk of the eastern European base of support for *Agudat Israel*. In 1919, after two years of independent functioning, and with a student body that now numbered 280, the *Bais Ya'akov* School was taken over as the women's educational arm of the *Agudat Israel* movement in Poland. This takeover of the movement by *Agudat Israel* played a significant role in the school's development. Hitherto, classes had been held in Schenirer's own home with the assistance of two 15-year-old girls, who were sent out after a year of experience to establish branches of the school in their own communities. The leaders of the Cracow branch of *Agudat Israel* – Rabbi Asher Shapira, Rabbi Moshe Deutscher (later, an *Agudah* representative in the Polish *Sejm*), and Meir Heitner – offered to "adopt" *Bais Ya'akov*, provided that Schenirer would agree to expand the network of schools she operated.[74]

Sarah Schenirer was somewhat wary of expansion, lest the high standards she had set be lowered. Her principal concern was the difficulty of finding qualified personnel to staff the schools – teachers with pedagogic training and experience who could also combine with that a deep personal commitment to Orthodox Judaism. She was not entirely satisfied with the prospect of hiring teachers from western Europe, fearing that their values and cultural patterns would clash with those of their eastern European students. She preferred whenever possible to employ her own former students. In fact, a former student wrote that one of the conditions of acceptance in *Bais Ya'akov* was that the student become a teacher after leaving the system. Graduates were almost always sent to communities other than their own to teach, in an attempt to prevent family and social commitments from detracting and impeding total dedication to the job.[75] In spite of Sarah Schenirer's reservations regarding expansion, she allowed her project to come under the supervision of *Agudah*, after consulting with the Bobover *rebbe* Ben Zion Halberstam.[76]

The support of the *Agudat Israel* movement significantly benefited the Beth Jacob schools. *Agudah* had set for itself three goals in its educational ventures for both girls and boys: first, to reorganize the schools and raise the educational

---

her extraordinary humanitarian spirit, see Scharfstein, *Gedolei Hinukh be-Ameinu*, pp. 234f.

74. See Atkin dissertation, pp. 36–37, and Weissman dissertation, pp. 55–56. See also J. Friedensohn, "Batei ha-Sefer le-B'not Beit Ya'akov be-Polin," p. 64, and Scharfstein, *Gedolei Hinukh be-Ameinu*, pp. 232f.

75. See Basya Bender, "The Life of a *Bais Ya'akov* Girl," in *Daughters of Destiny*, ed. D. Rubin (Brooklyn, NY: Mesorah, 1988), pp. 178–183.

76. *Beit Ya'akov Journal* (Jerusalem) (June 1959): 10, cited in Weissman dissertation, p. 56.

standards; second, to secure government recognition without compromising the commitment of the schools to traditional Judaism; and third, to provide a sound material basis for the development and expansion of the school system.[77] The second goal was achieved in 1922, when the *Agudah* schools were declared on par with the state schools and given government accreditation. In point of fact, two criteria of the *Agudat Israel* schools made the Polish government more receptive toward them than to most other Jewish institutions: *Agudah* was politically conservative and made no attempt to turn its students toward socialism or other potentially subversive ideologies, as did some of the other Jewish schools; furthermore, because it lacked an ideological commitment to Yiddish or Hebrew (see later), it had fewer reservations than did other school systems about teaching Polish language and literature and using Polish as the language of instruction in the *secular studies* programs of the schools. The positive relationship with the Polish authorities meant that *Bais Ya'akov* received some government financial aid and, in addition, that those girls who chose to attend *Bais Ya'akov* schools in the afternoon, while continuing their secular studies in the public schools in the morning, would be exempt from religious instruction in their public school.[78]

In 1923, at a conference of *Agudat Israel* in Vienna, a decision was made to establish the *Keren ha-Torah*, a worldwide fund for religious education, which would enable the Beth Jacob network of schools to expand and establish schools throughout Poland and also schools in Lithuania, Latvia, Czechoslovakia, Romania, Hungary, and Austria.[79] Although the main foci of the movement remained in Cracow and Lodz (and later also Warsaw), the World Center for Beth Jacob, primarily for the development of curriculum and pedagogical materials, was established in Vienna by the educational philosopher and writer Dr. Samuel Leo Deutschlaender (1888–1935).[80] He ultimately

---

77. *Beit Ya'akov Journal* (Lodz), no. 122 (Winter 1935), cited in Weissman dissertation, p. 57.

78. See Weissman dissertation, p. 57. For a detailed depiction of Beth Jacob's legal and political struggle for recognition, see Atkin dissertation, pp. 134–145. The president of Poland, upon visiting the Beth Jacob summer camp in Rabka in 1929, made the following comments: "Beth Jacob is a blessing for European Jewry, for it saves our maidenhood from moral and religious dangers and from political radicalism" (quoted in Atkin dissertation, p. 119). For other official Polish reaction to the Beth Jacob movement, see the text of a letter sent from Count Ciechanowski, Polish ambassador to the United States, to Rabbi Leo Jung, chairman of the American Beth Jacob movement, quoted in Atkin dissertation, p. 48.

79. See Eisenstein, *Jewish Schools in Poland,* p. 84; Friedensohn, "Batei ha-Sefer le-B'not Beit Ya'akov be-Polin," p. 66; Kurzweil, *Modern Trends in Jewish Education,* p. 272; Scharfstein, *Gedolei Hinukh be-Ameinu,* p. 232; Scharfstein, *Toldot ha-Hinukh be-Yisrael,* vol. 2, p. 147; and Weissman, "Bais Yaakov: A Historical Model," p. 142.

80. For elaboration on Dr. Deutschlaender's contribution to the development of

spent considerable time in Poland, assisting Sarah Schenirer in "lift[ing] the
Beth Jacob from the dream of a dressmaker, from the vision of an untrained
enthusiast, to the level of a systematic, well-planned organization."[81] Deutschlaender sent to Cracow three educational experts: Dr. Judith Rosenbaum
(Grunfeld), Betty Rothschild Vershner, and Eva Landsberg, all western European women who had received an extensive secular education at the Universities of Bonn and Heidelberg. Schenirer would make her peace with the more
liberal personalities from the West, would be ultimately impressed with their
unique type of religiosity, and would learn to accept their positive contributions while rejecting what she felt was negative in their approach.[82]

With Deutschlaender's appearance in the central leadership role, Beth
Jacob became a methodical, well-planned organization. As Grunfeld-
Rosenbaum testifies about Deutschlaender's contribution:

> He saw the tender beginnings, he recognized the latent forces, and he set himself
> to work. He reared the child he had found in its promising infancy. And he
> found scope for his foresight and educational talents. Leo Deutschlaender made
> of Beth Jacob a well-organized movement. The syllabus, curriculum, examina-
> tions, continuation courses, as well as the financial foundation of the whole
> work, the building of the beautiful Seminary—all these were the result of his
> wisdom and effort. . . . The spark that was kindled by a daughter of the hasidic
> tradition was fanned by the methodical manner of a man who had been
> educated in the best schools of modern European training, who had picked up
> what was best in European culture, and had blended it with the Jewish stores of
> his mind.[83]

Rabbinical support was still an important factor in the struggle for ever-
widening support. A movement publication during the winter of 1924–1925
includes the following responsa—one from a hasidic *rebbe*, the other from a
Lithuanian talmudic scholar and *yeshivah* head. They deal primarily with the
question of the propriety of men's involving themselves in a girls' educational
institution: "The Boyaner *rebbe*, Abraham of Cracow, calls *Bais Ya'akov* a holy
institution. He says that men can be present at the school registration and
collect tuition monies, provided there are at least two of them present and
neither is a bachelor. Married men may lecture in the schools."[84] Similarly:
"The rabbi and scholar Elhanan Wasserman of Baronowicze says that men

the Beth Jacob movement, see Grunfeld-Rosenbaum, "Sarah Schenirer," pp. 426f.
Also see Atkin dissertation, pp. 38f.

81. Grunfeld-Rosenbaum, "Sarah Schenirer," p. 426.

82. See Friedensohn, "Batei ha-Sefer le-B'not Beit Ya'akov be-Polin," p. 66. Also
see Atkin dissertation, p. 73, and Weissman dissertation, pp. 58–59.

83. Grunfeld-Rosenbaum, "Sarah Schenirer," pp. 426–427.

84. *Beit Ya-akov Bulletin*, no. 9, quoted in Weissman dissertation, p. 59.

may be appointed to run a [Beth Jacob] school. Not only would this be permitted to them, but it would consitute a *mitzvah* of great magnitude – the act of "saving souls." Certainly, men may give lectures to groups of women."[85]

The Beth Jacob publications themselves are indicative of the new trend toward professionalism within the movement.[86] Eliezer Gershon Friedensohn, a noted journalist within the Polish Jewish community at that time, took over as editor of the *Beit Ya'akov Journal*, and publication, which had been intermittent, became more regular. Indeed, this journal was to become an important publication in the homes of observant Jews throughout Europe for sixteen years (after World War II it was to resume publication in Jerusalem in 1959).[87] Because there was a lack of suitable textbooks in Yiddish for the students of Beth Jacob, as most of the available Yiddish books had been written by secular, often socialist, and even antireligious authors, the *Beit Ya'akov Journal* became an oft-used text in the schools.[88] The editor of the *Beit Ya'akov Journal* strengthened the movement center in Lodz, while Joel Unger, Rabbi Abraham Mordecai Rogovy, and Alexander Zusha Friedman, an anthologist of religious literature, became its leaders in Warsaw.[89] In time, the Beth Jacob movement established its own publishing house, the Beth Jacob Press, which printed, during the fifteen years of its existence, a large number of pamphlets, textbooks, and miscellaneous writings for use in the *Bais Ya'akov* schools.[90]

In the fall of 1929, at an *Agudat Israel* convention, the organization came out with a decisive statement on the Beth Jacob movement: "The *Agudat Israel* conference affirms that the Beth Jacob movement has proven that it is the only solution to the question of education for girls, which is of significant concern nowadays. Therefore the conference demands of all Orthodox elements in Poland that they support these schools unequivocally [in both moral and financial terms].[91]

---

85. Ibid. See Weissman dissertation, pp. 59–60.

86. For elaboration on the *Beit Ya'akov Journal* and other literature of the movement, see Atkin dissertation, pp. 99f.

87. Another popular Beth Jacob publication was *The Kindergarten*. It was a newspaper for girls in the elementary grades of the Beth Jacob schools and first appeared as a supplementary section to the *Beit Ya'akov Journal*. See Atkin dissertation pp. 69, 103.

88. See Friedensohn, "Batei ha-Sefer le-B'not Beit Ya'akov be-Polin," pp. 76–79, for elaboration. See also Atkin dissertation, p. 100. During Sarah Schenirer's first years as a teacher, she prepared her own texts for use by her students (ibid., pp. 28–30). Later, writers were commissioned to create material for the Beth Jacob schools (ibid., p. 43).

89. Weissman dissertation, p. 60.

90. For elaboration on the variety of literature published by the Beth Jacob Press, see Atkin dissertation, pp. 102f. See especially pp. 110–111.

91. Quoted in Scharfstein, *Gedolei Hinukh be-Ameinu*, p. 233, and Scharfstein, *Toldot ha-Hinukh be-Yisrael*, vol. 2, p. 147. Although there was opposition to Sarah Schenirer's

Meanwhile, Sarah Schenirer had started a school for the training of Beth Jacob teachers in Cracow, but Leo Deutschlaender found it tiny and inadequate.[92] The old building was too crowded, containing twenty girls to a room, with two sharing a bed. Although the girls, imbued with Sarah Schenirer's idealism, did not seem dissatisfied, Deutschlaender felt that a new seminar building was one of the most urgent needs of the movement. At a conference in Warsaw in 1926, two decisions of great importance were reached. The first was to establish a new seminar, funding to be provided by the mobilization of support on an international scale toward maintenance of the movement. The second was to start summer training courses to which prominent Jewish leaders from throughout Europe could be invited. During that season they would be free from their regular responsibilities in their own community.[93] From then on a kind of summer camp was held in the Carpathian Mountains. Seminar students attended, as did those Beth Jacob teachers who had already found teaching positions in various schools but were required to take an inservice training course once every three years. Grunfeld-Rosenbaum, an early participant in the summer camp, describes the kind of education that took place there:

For two months, our schoolrooms would be meadows and woods and the fields of lonely country places. We marched out, at 6 A.M., in the cool morning air for physical training, we learned Psalms in the rays of the rising sun . . . we learned Hebrew grammar while the bells of the cows grazing by tinkled to the conjugation of verbs. We read [books of a philosophical and ethical nature], whilst the scent of the Carpathian vegetation filled the air. We listened to lectures of learned men who came to us after they had become used to the fact that there was a colony of girls who were themselves already young scholars and intelligent listeners. We would sit in the meadows and have debates on education. . . .[94]

endeavor as the 1929 convention statement insinuates, I was unable to find written documentation of such opposition. In personal communication with Joseph Frieden-sohn, son of Eliezer Gershon Friedensohn, currently a member of the World Agudath Israel Organization, and editor of its journal, Dos Yiddishe Vort, Rabbi Friedensohn claimed that the degree of opposition was exaggerated, to further romanticize the legend of Sarah Schenirer. I suspect that opposition to the cause was not documented, since some of the greatest leaders of eastern European Jewry, such as the Hafetz Hayim and Gerer rebbe, had endorsed it. It would have been unfitting of those Hasidic groups who opposed it to come out with written statements, delineating their opposition.

92. For elaboration on the Beth Jacob Teachers' Seminary in Cracow, see Atkin dissertation, pp. 73f.

93. Atkin dissertation, p. 40; Weissman dissertation, p. 60; and Scharfstein, Toldot ha-Hinukh be-Yisrael, vol. 2, p. 147.

94. Grunfeld-Rosenbaum, "Sarah Schenirer," p. 425. For an in-depth description of

Testimony to the "young scholars'" achievements comes from Eliezer Friedensohn, editor of the *Beit Ya'akov Journal* at the time. Following a visit to the Rabka summer camp in 1929, he described the examinations of the seminar students that took place there:

> The examinations included tests on the Five Books of Moses, from beginning to end, with a deep and comprehensive understanding of [their] entirety. The graduates knew the commentaries of the Torah, as well as the homiletics of the rabbis. They are thoroughly acquainted with all cross-references and can compare and contrast various sources of the Torah dealing with many topics. Most astonishing of all is that all this knowledge was displayed orally and with great feats of recollection. The same applies to the study of Prophets and to all the other studies. Everything is studied systematically, reviewed, and committed to memory. . . . We note here, as we acquaint ourselves with the knowledge of the teachers, to what extent the Beth Jacob movement possesses a mind, a heart, and an understanding of all problems, whether they be pedagogic in nature or those pertaining to a knowledge of Judaism. . . .[95]

Also in 1926, Sarah Schenirer was responsible, along with Eliezer Friedensohn, for founding two youth organizations – *Batya* and *B'not* (popularly pronounced *B'nos*) – for students and graduates of *Bais Ya'akov*.[96] She had come to the realization that Beth Jacob graduates aged 14–15 who did not go on to the teachers' seminary would continue to require peer support in order to successfully confront any challenges to their religious commitment. She organized a convention in Lodz that founded *B'nos* ("Daughters of" [*Agudat Israel*]). For girls under the age of fourteen, she established *Batya*. These organizations conducted social, cultural, and fund-raising activities to augment the more formal educational work of the schools. They derived their funds from membership dues, support from *Agudat Israel*, and various fund-raising activities on the part of the members and their parents. The youth organizations were not supported by *Keren ha-Torah*, which was earmarked for more formal educational projects. Before the outbreak of World War II, there were some three hundred *B'nos* groups in Poland, with a total membership of more than fifteen thousand. The third convention of *B'nos* was held in Lodz in 1937. More than two thousand delegates attended, making this the largest gathering of Jewish women in the history of Poland.[97]

---

the in-service summer camps, see Atkin dissertation, pp. 113–120.

95. Eliezer Friedensohn, "Pictures and Notes," *Beit Ya'akov Journal* (Lodz), no. 46 (Summer 1929). Quoted in Atkin dissertation, p. 118.

96. See Atkin dissertation, pp. 31–32, 129–132, and Weissman dissertation, pp. 61–62. Also see Scharfstein, *Gedolei Hinukh be-Ameinu*, p. 241, and Scharfstein, *Toldot ha-Hinukh be-Yisrael*, vol. 2, p. 154.

97. Friedensohn, "Batei ha-Sefer le-B'not Beit Ya'akov be-Polin," p. 76.

On September 16, 1927, an impressive cornerstone-laying ceremony was held for the new teachers' seminar building at 10 Stanislava Street in Cracow, near the shores of the Vistula River. Funds for the seminary had been provided by the American Beth Jacob Committee, composed of Cyrus Adler, Sue Golding, Leo Jung, Rebekah Kohut, and Frieda Warburg.[98] The construction of the big, multistory building, into which the teacher trainees moved in June 1931, was the crowning achievement of Sarah Schenirer's life as well as a great source of pride for Polish Jewry. It housed two kitchens, a large dining hall, classrooms, lecture halls, and living quarters for students and faculty.[99] In addition to those from eastern Europe, students came to the seminary from Belgium, France, Switzerland, the United States, and Canada.

For those wishing to enroll in the teachers' seminary, there were stringent entry requirements to meet.[100] Candidates for acceptance into the school had to be at least sixteen years old; all would-be students were required to offer proof of having successfully completed seven grades in the Polish school system, as well as to furnish recommendations regarding their moral character; they had to know how to pray, had to read and write Yiddish, had to indicate a knowledge and understanding of the Book of Genesis, had to demonstrate an understanding of certain major prayers and benedictions, and had to have read a prescribed three-volume account of Jewish history (Stern-Boimberg). Finally, they were required to possess the following books: the Pentateuch, a prayer book, history books by Boimberg and Kottek, *The Nineteen Letters of Ben Uzziel* (a work of modern Jewish philosophy by Samson Raphael Hirsch), and the abridged version of the Code of Jewish Law. Shortly before World War II, vigorous entrance examinations were introduced as a requirement for admission, prepared by the Beth Jacob Central Organization.[101]

In 1933, when the leadership of the movement had been taken over by Judah Leib Orlean, a new section was added to the seminary. Younger girls, aged 13–16, who had finished their elementary training through the *Bais*

---

98. See Grunfeld-Rosenbaum, "Sarah Schenirer," p. 422 (note). It is interesting to note that support for the Beth Jacob schools spread far beyond the limited partisan realm of *Agudat Israel* and included liberal Jews such as those in the American Beth Jacob Committee, as well as non-Jews. Indeed, for a time, the honorary chairperson of the American committee was Mrs. Sara Delano–Franklin D. Roosevelt's mother. Despite their differing ideologies, the more liberal Jewish elements obviously viewed the movement as an important bulwark against assimilation and perhaps against other movements (e.g., leftist ideologies and Zionism). (See Weissman dissertation, pp. 63–64.)

99. See Grunfeld-Rosenbaum, "Sarah Schenirer," p. 424.

100. *Beit Ya'akov Journal* (Lodz), no. 44 (Summer 1929), cited in Weissman dissertation, p. 62.

101. Atkin dissertation, p. 31.

Ya'akov, were invited to live, study, and play in the building, where they would be supervised by the seminarists, who would thus benefit from practical teaching experience as part of their background while the young girls would be raised in a completely traditional Jewish environment. Many of these younger students themselves later entered the seminary.[102]

Testimony to the kind of ideals imbued into the hearts of young seminary trainees comes from an article entitled "The Graduation – Impressions of the Graduation at the Beth Jacob Seminary," written by one of its graduates of 1936:

> We have lived under the influence of the Torah and Judaism. . . . Here the very walls were breathing that spirit; the atmosphere was filled with it. Now, as we part with this institution, we know that the outside environment is indifferent or perhaps even hostile to such ideals. . . . But we must transfer that which we have received. . . . We must create among Jewish children the type of atmosphere we have been living in. Till now we have been the recipients; now it is time to be the givers. . . . We are facing the world with much strength and energy to propagate that which we have received.[103]

The man who took over as leader of Beth Jacob in 1933, Orlean, was himself a *hasid* of Ger and one of the leading ideologues in the *Poalei Agudat Israel* (the workers' movement within *Agudat Israel,* more leftist and more pro-Zionist than its parent body).[104] He had been involved with the movement for a number of years and had written many articles for the *Beit Ya'akov Journal* on the women's role in Judaism, social questions, and educational thought. After Sarah Schenirer's premature death from cancer at the age of fifty-two in 1935, Orlean was the movement's central figure and certainly its greatest leader during the period of the Holocaust. Statistics are difficult to obtain, but it has been estimated that between 1917 and 1939, on the eve of the destruction of European Jewry, the movement encompassed over eighty thousand young Jewish women in eastern and central Europe.[105]

IDEOLOGY AND CURRICULUM OF THE BETH JACOB SCHOOLS

In discussing the establishment of the Beth Jacob movement, which universalized formal religious education for girls, it would be useful to examine, at

---

102. Weissman dissertation, p. 63.

103. Quoted in Eisenstein, *Jewish Schools in Poland,* p. 85, from *Beit Ya'akov Journal* (Lodz), no. 137 (Fall 1936): 14.

104. For a biography of Orlean and his educational philosophy, see Scharfstein, *Toldot ha-Hinukh be-Yisrael,* vol. 2, pp. 153–154. See also Atkin dissertation, pp. 32f.

105. Weissman dissertation, pp. 65–66, and Friedensohn, "Batei ha-Sefer le-B'not Beit Ya'akov be-Polin," p. 71.

some length, the curriculum offered at these schools. This furnishes us with a conception of what was to be, henceforth, a basic curriculum (with certain variations such as, e.g., language of instruction, complement of religious studies, content of secular studies[106]) in the many similar and differing institutions that were to develop in Beth Jacob's wake. The curriculum in many subsequent schools of a more liberal nature was to be broader in scope, if not necessarily in quality, than that offered in Sarah Schenirer's *Bais Ya'akov*, as were their educational ideologies to differ. However, Beth Jacob's Jewish studies curriculum provides us with an idea of what was to become acceptable among every segment of traditional Jewry worldwide, with the possible exception of the ultraright hasidic sect – Satmar – and its corresponding ideologues in Israel – the *Neturei Karta*.

The curriculum of the *Bais Ya'akov* schools[107] was designed to realize the movement's goal of producing well-integrated religious graduates, knowledgeable about the world, but fortified by a deep religious identity to protect them from succumbing to external temptation. Both secular and Jewish studies were geared to strengthening the girls' knowledge of and commitment to Judaism and its values. All courses of study were designed to inculcate respect for the tradition and for traditional authorities; to foster parental respect, modesty, patience, polite behavior, correct speech, identification with the Jewish community, unity of the Jewish people, and love of God. It was felt that simply teaching a girl to read the prayers and follow certain basic laws was inadequate; she had to be given a broad, conceptual approach to Judaism. Attempts were often made to draw modern parallels to historical situations; for example, the Hellenistic Jews in the time of the Maccabees were compared to contemporary assimilationists. The curriculum was built, in a classically Jewish manner, from the specific to the general. In the first year, specific laws and blessings were taught, and in the sixth year, these were treated on a more sophisticated level in general philosophical discussions of "Jewish Chosenness," "Exile and Redemption," and the like. The Hafetz Hayim's influence was noticeable in the emphasis placed on such seemingly "irrelevant" topics as Jerusalem Temple sacrifices and on commandments that could be performed only in the land of Israel, such as agricultural laws or laws relating to Jewish monarchs.[108] Orlean felt that information about systems of monarchy, slavery, war, and so on should be taught to girls, because though not currently

---

106. We shall include a brief description of the secular curriculum offered in Sarah Schenirer's schools. In certain respects, the secular curriculum of her era differs and/or seems broader than that offered by contemporary Beth Jacob schools.

107. For a more in-depth look at the Beth Jacob curriculum and educational goals, see Atkin dissertation, pp. 76f., and Weissman dissertation, chap. 6, from which the following was essentially derived.

108. Weissman dissertation, p. 72.

relevant, they served as suitable examples of the contrast between Jewish values and the ethical practices of other nations.[109]

Within the Beth Jacob movement there was a tendency to adopt modern forms and methods and to reject many of the concomitant concepts and ideas of modern education. As Weissman states, "The pedagogic philosophy taught in the teacher's seminar or written about in movement publications tended to be reaffirmations of traditional theories from the classical sources of Judaism. The ideological influence of the Talmud was thus felt far more strongly than that of Dewey, Montessori, or others."[110] Nevertheless, there were a number of noteworthy innovations: formal curriculum; teacher training; improved textbooks; emphasis on the kindergarten as a unit; introduction of secular studies—particularly of vocational training—and physical education; use of modern facilities such as gymnasia and laboratories; exposure to world literature and art, and, finally, conceptualization of "Judaism" as a subject area.[111]

It should be noted that the conceptualization of "Judaism" as a subject area, apart from study of the classical biblical or talmudic sources, was a novel approach in Jewish education. A synthetic approach to Jewish thought and culture, whereby the intellectual and emotional components of Judaism were integrated and transmitted, was never taught to boys in the traditional Jewish educational frameworks. "To this day," states Weissman, "general discussions of 'Judaism' as a conceptualized entity and articulations of 'What Judaism Has to Say About . . .' are far more common among the liberal and progressive elements within the Jewish community, while the traditionalists still cling to the specific study of laws and texts."[112] But in the *Bais Ya'akov* schools of Schenirer's and Orlean's time, we find units on, for example, the fame and importance of the Bible among the nations in the modern world, a theme that presumably should be of little relevance to a traditionally believing Jew.[113]

If the goal in the Beth Jacob schools was to produce integrated Jewish human beings in the fullest sense of integration—Hirsch's ideal of the *"Yisrael-Mensch,"* then attention would have to be paid to worldly as well as religious pursuits. At the very least, it was felt that a young girl who had never been exposed to secular culture could become overly impressed with it and swayed away from the tradition. Thus, in keeping with its purpose of strengthening girls' knowledge of and commitment to Judaism, secular aspects of the

109. J. L. Orlean, "Yahadut-Programme" (*Fun Ershter Biz Zekster Bateilung*), Hebrew University Library, cited in Weissman dissertation, p. 72.

110. Weissman dissertation, p. 69. See also H. Ormian, *Ha-Mahshavah ha-Hinukhit Shel Yahadut Polania* (Tel Aviv: Yavneh, 1939), p. 57.

111. Many of these innovations are discussed by Ormian, pp. 56–57, 181.

112. Weissman dissertation, p. 73. See also Scharfstein, *Toldot ha-Hinukh be-Yisrael*, vol. 2, p. 154.

113. See Orlean's "Yahadut-Programme."

curriculum would be presented in such manner as to serve the central goal of
the school.[114] In other words, literature would not be taught for its own sake
but rather to illustrate positive values and attitudes worthy of transmission to
students.[115] Science would be taught only insofar as it would serve to enhance
the sense of wonder at God's creations. "Questionable" sciences, whose
assumptions and findings might contradict the Torah (e.g., archaeology and
the social sciences) would be avoided.[116] As Grunfeld-Rosenbaum testifies,
"All our secular studies were taught with the view that everything in the
world is a product of God's wisdom. There was no concept of Torah's being
Jewish and all other subjects secular. [Therefore] we did not have the partition
between Jewish and secular studies that exists today [in some educational
institutions]."[117] As examples of secular knowledge that Beth Jacob considered to be in line with the spirit of Judaism, the journal (which was often used
as source material within the schools) published a series called "Pearls of
World Literature," which included stories and poems from such far-flung
places as China and ancient Egypt.[118] There were other articles on "The
Shylock Legend in the Middle Ages,"[119] "Dulcinea and the New Woman in
Modern Literature,"[120] Pascal,[121] Gandhi,[122] Tolstoy,[123] Judaism and
Esthetics,[124] and so forth. A poll taken among readers showed their interest in
music, dance, poetry, and painting.[125] A quiz included in one issue asked
readers to identify the terms albino, pariah, Amerigo Vespucci, and Julius
Caesar, among others.[126]

114. See Ormian, *Ha-Mahshavah ha-Hinukhit Shel Yahadut Polania*, p. 56.

115. *Beit Ya'akov Journal* (Jerusalem), no. 84 (Summer 1966), cited in Weissman
dissertation, p. 69; see also p. 80.

116. *Beit Ya'akov Journal* (Jerusalem), no. 3 (Summer 1959), cited in Weissman
dissertation, p. 70.

117. Judith Grunfeld-Rosenbaum, "Her Legacy Lives On," in *Daughters of Destiny*,
ed. D. Rubin, p. 120. See further the writings of Baila Z. Gross, lecturer in secular
studies at the Cracow Bais Ya'akov Seminary, on the role of secular studies in the
curriculum, in the *Beit Ya'akov Journal* (Lodz), no. 100 (Summer 1933), quoted in Atkin
dissertation, p. 88.

118. See *Beit Ya'akov Journal* (Lodz), nos. 53–54 (Spring 1930), cited in Weissman
dissertation, p. 80.

119. *Beit Ya'akov Journal* (Lodz), no. 53 (Spring 1930), Weissman, ibid.

120. *Beit Ya'akov Journal* (Lodz), no. 119 (Fall 1934), ibid.

121. *Beit Ya'akov Journal* (Lodz), nos. 75–76 (Fall 1931), ibid.

122. *Beit Ya'akov Journal* (Lodz), no. 82 (Winter 1932), ibid.

123. *Beit Ya'akov Journal* (Lodz), no. 36 (Fall 1928), ibid.

124. *Beit Ya'akov Journal* (Lodz), no. 122 (Winter 1935), ibid.

125. *Beit Ya'akov Journal* (Lodz), no. 83 (Winter 1932), ibid.

126. *Beit Ya'akov Journal* (Lodz), no. 75 (Fall 1931), ibid.

There were three types of *Bais Ya'akov* schools: the all-day (elementary and high) schools—located mainly in large cities—which would offer a joint program of religious and secular studies; the afternoon schools, mainly in the smaller towns and in which only Jewish studies were taught, since the girls attended Polish state schools in the morning; and the vocational and business high schools, of which there were only a few, all of them in the bigger cities, such as Warsaw and Lodz.[127]

In the two-year teachers' training program at the Cracow seminary, there were about thirty-six hours of instruction weekly,[128] six of which were devoted to the study of the Pentateuch, with commentaries, including those of Samson Raphael Hirsch. The young women also studied the Prophets and Hagiographia, specifically the historical sections, thirty chapters of Isaiah, the sections of Jeremiah and other Prophets read in the synagogue, fifty chapters of Psalms, and the Five Scrolls. In the classes on prayer, they learned the weekday, Sabbath, and Festival liturgies and the mishnaic tractate *Ethics of the Fathers*, with commentaries. The Jewish history curriculum was entitled "From Creation to the Present." A course on Jewish law and thought examined responsibility as human beings, as Jews, and particularly as women; treated the daily and yearly life cycle; and included the philosophical works of Hirsch and Breuer, along with ethical works. A course in Hebrew grammar and written and oral expression was also given. On the secular side, written expression in German was taught, along with the writings of Schiller, Goethe, Lessing, and several other authors and philosophers. The courses in Polish language, literature, history, and geography followed the prescribed state curriculum. For the teachers in training, there were also courses in general psychology, the history of education, important pedagogical principles, talmudic statements with regard to education, moral education, general methods of teaching, methods of teaching specific subjects, hygiene, and bibliographical guidance for the teacher. Two minor subjects were handicrafts and gymnastics, the latter emphasizing recreational leadership among children. Finally, guest lecturers were brought in from time to time to teach religious and cultural themes to the seminary students.[129]

In the standardized curriculum introduced by Orlean for the Beth Jacob schools—a month-by-month and week-by-week breakdown of the "Judaism Program" over the course of six years—there was little if any emphasis on

127. Friedensohn, "Batei ha-Sefer le-B'not Beit Ya'akov be-Polin," p. 69. See also Scharfstein, *Toldot ha-Hinukh be-Yisrael*, vol. 2, p. 152. For elaboration, see Atkin dissertation, pp. 49f.

128. See *Beit Ya'akov Journal* (Lodz), nos. 39–40 (Spring 1929), cited in Weissman dissertation, p. 70, and Atkin dissertation, p. 76.

129. See Eisenstein, *Jewish Schools in Poland,* pp. 84–85; Atkin dissertation, pp. 77–78, 88–90; and Weissman dissertation, pp. 70–72.

hasidic lore. This is interesting, considering that the hasidic tradition was a major influence on the movement. The standardized curriculum for the young Jewish girls of *Bais Ya'akov* exhibits, in Weissman's words, "a masterful balance between the mythical, mystical approaches to Judaism and the rationalism of Maimonides, between learning by rote basic prayers and blessings and understanding their meaning and interpretation, between learning to fulfill commandments between man and God and those between man and his fellow . . . and between the intellectual and emotional components of religious faith."[130]

Earlier, we had spoken of Sarah Schenirer's insistence upon Yiddish, rather than Polish, as being the language of instruction in the Judaic program of her schools. Her attitude is reflected in a thought expressed in the *Beit Ya'akov Journal* in 1930: "Speaking Polish is not a sin, but speaking Polish because one is ashamed to speak Yiddish is a great sin!"[131] Nevertheless, Yiddish was seen only as a tool to strengthen the girls' sense of their Jewishness.[132] It was not an end in itself, as it was to the secular Yiddishists, whose commitment to Judaism was manifested through their devotion to the language of their ancestors. In an attempt to distance themselves as much as possible from the Yiddish secular movement, Beth Jacob instituted the special Orthodox system of Yiddish spelling, which had been developed by Dr. Solomon Birnbaum, a noted philologist and son of Nathan Birnbaum, one of the founders of *Agudat Israel*.[133]

This disassociation from the secular was true of Beth Jacob's attitude toward the Hebrew language and Zionism. Within the Orthodox community, Hebrew was generally regarded as the holy language of prayer, and the speaking of modern, conversational Hebrew the domain of the secular Zionists who had no respect for its sanctity. Initially, *Bais Ya'akov* followed this approach and criticized the schools that taught modern Hebrew for alienating the children from their parents and for making light of the classic Jewish tradition. Still, the seminary students were taught the basic rules of grammar and principles of expression in that language but as a vehicle for the study of biblical sources. Gradually, the schools took a more favorable approach to

---

130. Weissman dissertation, pp. 71, 73.

131. *Beit Ya'akov Journal* (Lodz), no. 54 (Spring 1930), quoted in Weissman dissertation, p. 74.

132. See Scharfstein, *Toldot ha-Hinukh be-Yisrael*, vol. 2, p. 155. At a conference of Beth Jacob schools in Warsaw in 1929, the use of Yiddish as the language of instruction and conversation was emphasized. For a list of conference resolutions, see Atkin dissertation, pp. 46–48. See also pp. 105–107.

133. See Friedensohn, "Batei ha-Sefer le-B'not Beit Ya'akov be-Polin," p. 78. See also Ormian, *Ha-Mahshavah ha-Hinukhit Shel Yahadut Polania*, pp. 54–56; Atkin dissertation, p. 106; and Weissman dissertation, p. 75.

settlement in Palestine, due to the worsening economic conditions and increasing anti-Semitism in eastern Europe. Modern Hebrew was taught to the students. With the establishment of *Beit Ya'akov* schools in Palestine, where the spoken language was always Hebrew rather than Yiddish, the teaching of modern Hebrew was to conflict with more extremist Orthodox sects, such as the *Neturei Karta*.[134]

The love of the Land of Israel as God's promised land, as opposed to the support of a secular, political Zionism, had been stressed by Sarah Schenirer in all of her writings. Under Orlean's leadership this aspect of *Bais Ya'akov* was strengthened even further, and settlement of the land was studied as a commandment in the Judaism curriculum. Eventually, Beth Jacob established schools in Palestine and set up a training center for girls in Lodz (1935) who were contemplating immigration to Palestine. But at no time did the movement support Zionism as a political ideology, in contrast to the Orthodox *Mizrahi* movement that did, and in whose schools political Zionism was a dominant ideology.[135]

Weissman points out that, characteristic of the opposition of Beth Jacob to various kinds of secular ideologies, such as Yiddishism and Zionism, was its feeling that these ideologies were confusing means with ends.[136] In that regard, a similar attitude toward the study of science in *Bais Ya'akov* prevailed. Whereas in the past, no contradiction was believed to exist between Judaism and science – as, for example, Maimonides and other great Jewish thinkers had combined a deep knowledge of and involvement with both – in the present, science had become an end unto itself, a distinct way of viewing the world. It was this worldview that Beth Jacob opposed, not the study of science or Yiddish or Hebrew per se.[137]

Although there were some reservations regarding training Jewish girls for entry into a secular labor market, hard economic necessity triumphed over the reluctance. Vocational studies were as much a part of the curriculum as were the arts and sciences and "Judaism" programs.[138] Initially, young women were prepared for careers in teaching, in clerical work such as bookkeeping

---

134. For elaboration, see Weissman dissertation, pp. 75–77.

135. For an elaboration of differing Orthodox Jewish attitudes toward Zionism and their influence on education, see my unpublished master's research paper on the subject (Ontario Institute for Studies in Education, 1988). Also see Judah Leib Orlean's views on explaining to children the difference between an opposition to Israel and an opposition to Zionism, *Beit Ya'akov Journal* (Lodz), no. 105 (Summer 1933), and Weissman dissertation, pp. 78–79.

136. Weissman dissertation, p. 77.

137. Ibid.

138. See the 1929 Beth Jacob conference resolutions in Atkin dissertation, pp. 46–48.

and typing, and as seamstresses. Gradually, courses were added in home economics, nutrition, hygiene, child care, stenography, nursing, and business and accounting.[139] This aspect of vocational training has been particularly developed in many of the present-day Beth Jacob schools in Israel and, to some extent, in North America, where work roles have been expanded even further.

Matrix of Change

In an insightful analysis of the Beth Jacob movement within the framework of sociological theory regarding tradition and social change,[140] Weissman surmises that the rapid, successful spread of the movement may have been due less to the ideological power of the movement or the charisma of its leaders than to the socioeconomic necessity of vocational training for Polish Jewish girls, supported by the Jewish community. To justify this innovation, which could possibly be seen as challenging the authority of past generations of Jewish sages, the Beth Jacob movement had to develop an ideology and a complicated structural framework. Their ideology was based on the mishnaic principle *"Et la'asot la'Hashem"* ("It is a time to act for God")[141]; this principle has been used at certain times to mean that in a time of crisis, certain specific laws may be set aside. (See Chapter Three.) Invoking this principle at the time in question was based on the realization that women were turning away from the traditional life-style, thereby endangering the future of Judaism. Thus the changing social and historical conditions of Sarah Schenirer's time called for radical action in order to keep women within the tradition.

The pressing need for religious education for Orthodox girls was so pervasive throughout eastern Europe that as the winds of change were sweeping over Poland, Jewish communities in other countries were similarly affected. One excellent network of schools for Orthodox girls in Lithuania — the *Yavneh* educational system (not to be confused with the *Yavneh Mizrahi* schools in Poland[142]) — bears mention, as it paralleled the development of the

---

139. *Beit Ya'akov Journal: Kovetz le-Inyanei Hinukh,* 1945; cited in Weissman dissertation, p. 81. For elaboration on the vocational courses offered by the Beth Jacob movement as well as the trade schools established by them, see Atkin dissertation, pp. 122–127.

140. See Weissman dissertation, chap. 7: "Bais Ya'akov Schools and the Woman's Role in Judaism," pp. 83f, and chap. 9: "Bais Ya'akov as a Social Movement," pp. 106f. Also see her article, "Bais Ya'akov: A Historical Model for Jewish Feminists," in *The Jewish Woman: New Perspectives,* ed. E. Koltun, pp. 139f.; see especially pp. 145–146.

141. *Mishnah Berakhot* 9:5.

142. The *Yavneh Mizrahi* schools in Poland were centralized under the Yavneh

Bais Ya'akov schools in Poland. *Yavneh*, including schools for boys as well as for girls, was founded by a bipartisan group (comprising *Agudat Israel* and *Mizrahi*) called *Tze'irei Yisrael*, which was under the aegis of Rabbi Chaim Ozer Grodzinski of Vilna. *Yavneh* had as its educational mandate the transmission of a broad and deep knowledge of Torah, a thorough knowledge of Jewish history and suitable knowledge of general history, and the proper study of general education. In 1921, a girls' elementary school was opened in Telshe, followed by a girls' gymnasium – the first religious Hebrew high school in all of Lithuania. It was acclaimed throughout Lithuania and beyond for its exceptionally broad Jewish and general studies curriculum, including the study of German and English. Other gymnasiums were established in Kovno (1925) and Ponovich (1928). As opposed to the *Bais Ya'akov* schools, where the language of instruction in the Judaic program was Yiddish, in the *Yavneh* schools the language of instruction was Hebrew. In 1923, a Teachers' Seminary for Women was opened in Telshe, headed by Dr. Y. R. Holzberg. Dr. Holzberg credits the towering personality and genius of Rabbi Joseph Leo Bloch for the success of the *Yavneh* schools. One of the great and more stringent rabbinic figures of Lithuania, Rabbi Bloch was among the first to understand the need for modern Hebrew religious education for both boys and girls. As early as 1915, he had advanced the idea of establishing a modern religious school that would fulfill all government requirements and yet be conducted in the spirit of Torah and godliness. He included secular studies in the curriculum of the preparatory school for the Telshe *Yeshivah*, and when the Lithuanian government agreed not to draft the *yeshivah's* students into the army on the condition that they would receive a secular education commensurate with the four grades of high school, Rabbi Bloch agreed to incorporate such a program in his preparatory school. He was instrumental in the *Yavneh* girls' schools' development and can be credited, along with Sarah Schenirer, as a trailblazer in the establishment of formal religious and secular schooling for girls.[143]

ANALYSIS AND CONCLUSION

Sarah Schenirer lived to see her work expand beyond even her most ambitious dreams and to be acclaimed by Orthodox Jewry the world over. "Her

---

Organization in 1927. For a history of this educational movement, see Eisenstein, *Jewish Schools in Poland*, pp. 88–93, and Scharfstein, *Toldot ha-Hinukh*, vol. 2, pp. 156–160.

143. For elaboration on *Yavneh*, see Isaac Raphael Etzion (Holzberg), "Ha-Zerem ha-Hinukhi 'Yavneh' be-Lita," in *Yahadut Lita*, ed. Jacob Olisky, Mordekhai Elyashuv, et al. (Tel Aviv: Iggud Yotzei Lita be-Yisrael, 1972), vol. 2, pp. 160–165. See also Norman Lamm, *Torah Umadda* (Northvale, NJ: Jason Aronson, 1990), pp. 30–31.

influence," comments Scharfstein, "was not due to her knowledge—many were the women in Israel who were greater than she in erudition—but to her high sense of mission, her selfless devotion to her pupils, and her dedication to God and His Torah."[144] She was one of the pioneers in advocating a combined program of general and religious education for Jewish girls. The religious studies program of the Beth Jacob schools encompassed study of the Bible (Pentateuch, Prophets, and Hagiographia), Jewish history, laws and customs, Jewish thought, Torah ethics, and Hebrew language and grammar. Aside from the study of one (nonlegal) tractate in the *Mishnah* ("Ethics of the Fathers"), it did not seek to encroach on the traditional educational domain of males: study of *Mishnah* and Talmud. This was in keeping with the prevailing view that that world was an unnecessary, if not dangerous, discipline for Jewish girls. Nonetheless, the great service the Beth Jacob movement rendered in eastern Europe was, in the words of one of its admirers, not only in "training Jewish girls in traditional Judaism," but also in "restor[ing] the self-respect of Jewish women, by bringing about a veritable renaissance among them. It revived the ideal of the traditional virtues that Solomon attributed to the Woman of Valor in the Book of Proverbs, so that it could once more be said of Jewish womanhood: 'Give her of the fruit of her hands, and praise her works in the gates.' "[145]

The model of these virtues was Sarah Schenirer herself. The Beth Jacob movement developed a romantic legend around the figure of Sarah Schenirer. Weissman demonstrates how, through the use of psuedokinship terminology (e.g., Sarah Schenirer was called "our mother" and the members referred to each other as "sisters"), Sarah was made to epitomize the traditional ideal of the "Woman of Valor." It was always emphasized that with the virtues of Schenirer as a model, there was no danger of the *Bais Ya'akov* girl's overstepping her bounds as a Jewish woman. Sarah's "feminine" qualities were consistently stressed in descriptions of her (e.g., her modesty, warmth, motherliness), even though she sometimes had to enlist "masculine" aggressiveness in order to withstand shortsighted parents or uncooperative community leaders. Apparently, certain fears were expressed by certain critics of the movement that the girls would learn too much and begin to compete intellectually with the men of the community. Orlean stressed that what was imparted through *Bais Ya'akov* was not so much knowledge as good behavior and the traditional virtues of the Jewish woman: modesty, humility, and love.[146] Nevertheless, young women graduated from the seminary with such

---

144. Scharfstein, *Gedolei Hinukh be-Ameinu*, p. 234.

145. Ari Wohlgemuth, "The Jewish Woman in Eastern Europe," *The Jewish Library: Women*, ed. Leo Jung (London and New York: Soncino Press, 1970), p. 173.

146. Weissman, "Bais Ya'akov: A Historical Model for Jewish Feminists," pp. 146–147.

a broad knowledge of Torah that they often astonished their own fathers and brothers.[147]

In addition, the movement developed a complete system of slogans, mottoes, symbols, special holidays and celebrations, literature, songs, leadership roles, and other organizational techniques. There were international conventions and conferences. Their "total institutions" comprised residential schools, seminaries, and summer camps. Such institutions, says Weissman, are often established for "the purpose of solidifying social movements or strengthening educational frameworks."[148]

The development of the Beth Jacob schools was, in part, an attempt to protect Jewish girls from what many considered to be the subversive influence of the Polish feminist movement. Nevertheless, states Weissman, "through deepening their knowledge of classical Jewish sources, through training them for teaching, secretarial functions, bookkeeping, sewing, home economics, settlement in Palestine, and so on, and through providing a framework for organizational activities and international communications for thousands of young Jewish women, *Bais Ya'akov* was functioning to raise the 'feminist consciousness' of its students."[149] Weissman wonders what might have been the future of the movement, had it not had a truncated life and been unable to develop naturally due to the Holocaust. She is of the belief that the post-Holocaust *Bais Ya'akov* movement made a major shift to the right, as did the Orthodox community in general.[150] She speculates that "[the pre-Holocaust movement] might have developed a new role model for the educated and in certain ways, emancipated, Jewish women."[151] Of course, advocates of the *Bais Ya'akov* movement today see themselves as the torchbearers of Sarah Schenirer's vision and their graduates as the role models Sarah Schenirer foresaw and would contest Weissman's conjecture in this regard.

The heroism and dedication of *Bais Ya'akov* students and teachers during the Holocaust are testimony to the success of *Bais Ya'akov* in repossessing the loyalty of Jewish women to the faith of their ancestors. Until the liquidation of the Warsaw Ghetto, in 1942–1943, Judah Leib Orlean remained at the helm of the movement, corresponding with movement members in other ghettos and occupied areas. Although forbidden by law, educational activity continued in the ghettos of Warsaw, Kovno, Vilna, and elsewhere.[152] The

---

147. Atkin, *The Beth Jacob Movement in Poland*, p. 83.

148. Weissman, "Bais Ya'akov: A Historical Model for Jewish Feminists," p. 146.

149. Ibid.

150. For elaboration, see Weissman dissertation, chap. 8: "Bais Ya'akov Schools: The Holocaust and Its Aftermath," pp. 97f.

151. Ibid., p. 147.

152. Friedensohn, "Batei ha-Sefer le-B'not Beit Ya'akov be-Polin," pp. 80–81. See also Atkin dissertation, p. 93f, and Weissman dissertation, p. 98.

girls would say they were gathering to celebrate a birthday and would secretly meet to study together (reminiscent of Jewish behavior under Roman rule following the destruction of the Temple in 70 C.E.). The most publicized example of devotion and courage on the part of *Bais Ya'akov* girls is the alleged case of the ninety-three students and teachers, aged 14–22, who chose to die a martyr's death rather than be defiled by the Nazi soldiers. A letter in the form of a last will and testament was smuggled out of Poland by one of the students to *Agudut Israel* in New York, and the group has been immortalized in a famous Hebrew poem by the Hebrew poet and educator Hillel Bavli. Whether the incident actually took place is subject to question. Doubts have been raised by some historians as well as by members of *Agudat Israel* about the incident's veracity and the letter's credibility. Nevertheless, with the passage of time this event has become "a symbolic parable woven into the tapestry of Jewish heroism" and has taken its place in the historical/legendary chronicles of the *Bais Ya'akov* movement.[153]

After World War II, the movement was rejuvenated. Today, the world center has been reestablished in Jerusalem, and there are currently several hundred Beth Jacob institutions and teachers' seminaries in Israel, the United States, Canada, England, Belgium, France, Switzerland, Argentina, Uruguay, Brazil, and Morocco.[154] Most remarkably, the concept of schools for girls has been accepted by the right-wing Orthodox groups, which originally were deeply opposed to the *Bais Ya'akov* program. A number of hasidic sects have established their own systems of schools for girls. Undoubtedly, the change of heart among these groups was due to the evidence of several generations of Bais Ya'akov graduates who were fully suited to, and comfortable in, their traditional role as Jewish women.

---

153. For a fascinating treatment of this alleged event, see Judith Tydor Baumel and Jacob J. Schacter, "The Ninety-three Bais Yaakov Girls of Cracow: History or Typology?" in *Reverence, Righteousness, and Rahamanut*, ed. Jacob J. Schacter (Northvale, NJ: Jason Aronson, 1992), pp. 93–129.

154. Weissman dissertation, p. 104.

Afterword

In a recent book Vanessa Ochs sheds considerable light on trends in women's Torah learning taking place in Jerusalem, Israel. Entitled *Words on Fire: One Woman's Journey into the Sacred,*[1] it is an anecdotal observation focusing on Ochs's spiritual odyssey into the study of Jewish sacred texts with other women in Jerusalem. An academic who had taught creative writing at Yale, she accompanied her husband and two young children on a sabbatical year in Jerusalem and decided to explore the written teachings of her religion. Female scholars and seekers became her role models in Israel, making her realize that women can play an active role in Jewish learning and observance if they "open Torah wide and seize it for themselves."[2] Her observations on the developing character of Torah education for women in Israel and her portrayals and the personal narratives of the outstanding Orthodox women Torah scholars she encountered (notably Nehama Leibowitz, biblical commentator and Torah educator par excellence[3]; Aviva Zornberg, Bible teacher; and Malka Bina and Chana Safrai, teachers of Talmud) leave one with little

---

1. Vanessa Ochs, *Words on Fire: One Woman's Journey into the Sacred* (New York: Harcourt Brace Jovanovich, 1990).

2. Ibid., p. 326.

3. Ochs writes, "To have studied with Nehama is to have been in analysis with Freud, to have been educated in nursery school by Maria Montessori, to have been inoculated against polio by Dr. Salk," ibid., p. 268.

doubt that women scholars are vigorously contributing their share to fulfilling the prophetic vision: "For out of Zion shall Torah come forth, and the word of God from Jerusalem" (Isaiah 2:3). Today, indeed, there is a steady growth in opportunities for women to study in Israel under the capable tutelage of other women scholars as well, among them Beruriah David, Tziporah Heller, Chana Henkin, Bryna Levi, Tamar Ross, and until only recently, the late Chana Belenson.

This dynamic development has its immediate origins in the growth of possibilities for Jewish education among women in the early twentieth century. We have already had opportunity to examine the precursors of such growth. By summarizing the background to current times, we will be able to focus on the operative dynamics that have guided the development of modern curricula. The complexities of this development are rooted in the general positionings of women from early times until the present.

The position of women in Jewish society was always far from being monolithic. One may note dramatic differences diachronically from time to time and synchronically from place to place. In certain periods and places in biblical times the position of women (as reflected in cultural attitudes) was fairly high; at other times and places it was relatively lower. Generally, in Hellenistic times women's position ebbed but within the Byzantine empire it heightened, whereas in Arab lands it fluctuated from high to relative low. In the early European experience women enjoyed a degree of freedom in society that was not true of some of the later periods. The effects of general attitudes toward women in the larger, non-Jewish society undoubtedly had its effects on Jewish attitudes (though the status of the Jewish woman was consistently higher), but the rabbinic position in regard to educational possibilities for women seems to have been constant until the nineteenth century. With the dramatic upheavals in Western societies brought about by industrialization, the pressure to allow the entrance of women into the work force became strong. The desire for equal educational opportunities in the West struck secular society and came to be felt in religious groups as well. Those Jewish groups that accommodated themselves to the values of modernization accepted these educational changes as a matter of course: individuals who accommodated themselves to modernity extracted the positive aspects of the changes; those who rejected modernity either repudiated these changes or accepted them with reservation, seeing Torah study as primarily of instrumental value in coping with the alien influences of the outside world.

Let us look now at three models to see the effects of modernity on the religious education of Orthodox Jewish women in this century.[4] In the

———
4. Information for this model was taken from the calendars and the published curricula of schools in New York, Toronto, and Jerusalem. In addition, the information on this section is based on Zvi Adar, *Jewish Education in Israel and in the United States*

	Three Models			
	A		B	C
	Centrist-Orthodox		Right-wing Orthodox	Ultra-Orthodox
Subject	Co-educational	All-girls		
Bible	X	X	X	X
Commentaries[5]	X	X	X	
Halakhah	X	X	X	Very basic
Jewish Thought	X	X	X	
History	X	X	X	Superficially
Hebrew	X	X	X	Reading only
Midrashic Texts	X	X		
Talmud and Codes	X	X*		

*Although not all schools.

above table, Column A represents the curricula of Orthodox high schools in which many of the students' parents are professionals and college educated. Subjects are generally taught in the Hebrew language. Classical texts are studied traditionally. Some of these schools are coeducational, such as Ramaz and Flatbush *yeshivot* in New York, Maimonides in Boston, and Ma'aleh in Jerusalem, where Talmud is taught to boys and girls together although, it may be argued, not with the kind of intensity afforded in the traditional boys' *yeshivot*. Most schools of this type are predominantly all-girls' schools, in which the intensity of study is not as pronounced as in boys' schools, though the study of biblical texts, Hebrew language and literature, and Jewish history is generally superior here. Talmudic texts may or may not be taught in these girls' schools. Some schools may provide their students with selected excerpts from the classic texts, such as the Talmud and the codes, for the study of a particular halakhic or philosophic topic, rather than engage in in-depth, page-by-page study of these texts. These schools are supportive of religious Zionism in Israel. In Column B we find Orthodox girls' high schools that are

(Jerusalem: The Melton Center, Hebrew University, 1977), pp. 105–106, 223–225; Linda Derovan, "Torah Study in Israel for Women," *Ten Da'at* 3:3 (Spring 1989): 22–23; Sylvia Barack Fishman, *Learning About Learning: Insights on Contemporary Jewish Education from Jewish Population Studies* (Waltham, MA: Brandeis University, 1987), pp. 25–29; Jeffrey S. Gurock, *The Men and Women of Yeshiva* (New York: Columbia University Press, 1988), chap. 10; Israel Rubin, *Satmar: An Island in the City* (Chicago: Quadrangle Books, 1972), pp. 196–198, 216–220; Raphael Schneller, "Continuity and Change in Ultra-Orthodox Education," *Jewish Journal of Sociology* 22 (June 1980): 35–45; and Deborah Weissman. "Education of Jewish Women," *Encyclopaedia Judaica Yearbook*, 1986–1987, p. 34. The interested reader may wish to consult these sources for further insight into current trends in religious education for women.
    5. The commentaries include the summarizing of rabbinic sources in *Halakhah* and *Midrash*. Considerable knowledge of the Oral Law is gleaned in this manner.

hesitant toward secularism, although here, too, students' parents are to a fair extent college educated. These high schools are non-Zionist, shun the study of Talmud, and frown on secular education at the college university level. In most schools the language of instruction is the vernacular of the country. Here, too, study of Hebrew language and grammar forms part of the curriculum. Column C represents ultra-Orthodox institutions for high school girls. The language of instruction may be English or Yiddish. Talmud will obviously not be taught; history, if taught at all, will be taught in a very selective manner; Hebrew language, except for reading, will generally not be taught separately as a subject in its own right. However, the very existence of girls' schools demonstrates that the need to educate Jewish women in a formal manner exists in the twentieth century, even if it did not in previous centuries. The parents of these girls will generally not be college educated; they shun Western acculturation and resist modernization as best they can.

Naturally the columns are schematic only. The reality is that there are shades between the columns, but for the most part the schematization represents the situation in New York, Toronto, and Jerusalem, as described in the literature of schools in these cities. Insofar as regional effects are not a major factor here, we may surmise that the same could be said of Paris, London, Geneva, and elsewhere.

It should be emphasized that the purpose of this table is to be descriptive and not evaluative. This schema does not necessarily reflect the intensity of religious observance that ensues after such learning. We note that the more conservative the community (that is, the more resistant it is to change), the more it is prone to exclude women from exposure to the entire range of Jewish studies.

The development of this pattern in the Orthodox movement will shed light on the dynamics that have changed the direction in favor of women's education in this century. That is not to say that the dynamics have not run their course on the one hand or that greater strides are not in the offing on the other.

As discussed previously, in the nineteenth century, the "enlightened" *maskilim* who were abandoning Jewish practices in favor of European customs argued that women should have formal schooling, and they attempted to set up schools for them. When the Orthodox community came to America in the early twentieth century,[6] its members were concerned that its boys were

---

6. We have not attempted to describe the growth and development of girls' education in America (or elsewhere) in the twentieth century, as this would constitute a book in itself. The interested reader may wish to peruse chap. 10 in Jeffrey Gurock's *Men and Women of Yeshiva* for greater insight into this subject matter. What follows is an extremely succinct overview, focusing on New York City.

attending Christmas parties at the public schools, and so they soon organized alternative schools for them. Girls continued to attend public schools. Also at this time, the *heder metukan*, which taught Hebrew language and literature, offered Sunday classes and after-school classes to males and females.[7] In 1918, the Marshaliah Hebrew High School system offered advanced classes to boys and girls, who sat together in these supplementary schools.[8] American Orthodox girls flocked to these schools, which were imitated by the Herzeliah Hebrew High School, with the same results.[9] For Orthodox women interested in a Hebrew teacher's career, the coeducational Teachers' Institute at the (Conservative) Jewish Theological Seminary offered the only viable option.[10]

It became necessary to create schools in which Orthodox girls would not be exposed to nontraditional ideas. In 1928, the Yeshiva of Flatbush in Brooklyn, New York, began coeducational classes.[11] In 1929, the all-girls Shulamith school was founded.[12] Its model was the European Beth Jacob school, although it lay greater emphasis on Hebrew language, Jewish history, and love of Zion, along the lines of the network of schools that was to be established worldwide by the *Mizrahi* Zionist religious party. Soon Orthodox Hebrew Teachers' Colleges for women became necessary. By the 1950s, Jewish schools for girls were becoming acceptable alternatives for public education. Beth Jacob schools spread in America in the 1960s and continued their program along the lines that had been established in Europe. Hasidic sects followed as well, with establishments of their own for the education of their female members. The most right-wing hasidic group, the *Satmar*, also established a school for girls, but because the *Satmar rebbe* has been firm in maintaining the ban on teaching Torah to women, the situation in the *Satmar* community is that boys receive an intensive traditional education with very little secular learning, whereas the girls receive a basic secular background and only a very superficial exposure to Jewish learning. This includes instruction in Hebrew reading, translation of some fundamental prayers into Yiddish, basic Jewish law, biblical stories, and very little else.[13]

Studies on the education of Jewish girls and women in the United States indicate that women from observant homes were more likely than other

7. Ibid., p. 189.
8. Ibid., p. 190.
9. Ibid.
10. Ibid.
11. Ibid., p. 194.
12. Ibid. See also Zevi Scharfstein, *Toldot ha-Hinukh be-Yisrael be-Dorot ha-Aharonim*, vol.3 (Jerusalem: Rubin Mass, 1962), p. 132.
13. This information is based on correspondence with one of the school administrators. See also Israel Rubin, *Satmar: An Island in the City*, pp. 196–197.

Jewish women to have received both formal Jewish schooling and intensive forms of schooling.[14] Two dynamics seem to have guided the course of women's Jewish education in observant, generally Orthodox circles. The first is the desire to keep women from attending nontraditional and public school systems. The second is the realization that women's economic roles in America (and elsewhere) require them to leave the home. Through their deeper understanding of their tradition it is hoped they will want to marry Orthodox men, raise Orthodox children, and remain within the Orthodox fold. With those goals ensured, one might argue that the time is now ripe for a shift to a more positive dynamic: the desire to produce women scholars. So far there is little voice in this direction, but there is some. Two renowned rabbis who have advocated a fuller complement of Torah studies, including the study of *Torah Shebe'al Peh* for women, are Rabbi Joseph B. Soloveitchik and Rabbi Menachem M. Schneerson, the Lubavitcher *rebbe*. Institutions of higher education that are pioneering in producing female Torah scholars within the Orthodox world,[15] and whose syllabi include the full complement of Jewish studies, are the Drisha Institute, Shalhevet Institute, and Stern College for Women in New York; Mikhlelet Beruria (Lindenbaum), Matan Women's Institute for Torah Studies, and Nishmat Institute for Higher Torah Studies for Women in Jerusalem; and the Midrasha of Bar-Ilan University near Tel Aviv. Issues such as How much Torah study for women? and the propriety of teaching women Oral Law are being recurrently addressed in leading rabbinic journals. What were once whispers on this issue became echoes, and what were once echoes have become open discussion in rabbinic literature. Indeed, there are even indications that women Talmud students may be able to turn their theoretical knowledge into practical application. Recently, the Israeli Chief Rabbinate instituted courses in talmudic law for observant women who will eventually fill newly created positions of female rabbinical pleaders in Israel's religious courts.

The study of the Oral Law by women is gaining considerable acceptance among those Orthodox groups that share contemporary modern outlooks. The challenge for women in these groups who are engaged in advocating change in the curriculum is to differentiate between (1) championing change for its own sake and (2) promoting change that will lead to a deepening of Jewish values and knowledge and to elevation in service to God. The Talmud relates that the daughters of Zelophehad who approached Moses asking for change were wise, educated, and righteous women. Rabbi Natan, com-

---

14. See Fishman, *Learning About Learning*, p. 28.

15. In the non-Orthodox world, the educational institutions of the Reform, Reconstructionist, and Conservative movements—Hebrew Union College–Jewish Institute of Religion, Reconstructionist Rabbinical College, and Jewish Theological Seminary—are open to women at all levels.

menting on their action, states, "More beautiful is the strength of women than the strength of men. When men were faced with a new and difficult situation, they demanded the right to return to Egypt. Women, on the other hand, requested an inheritance in the Land of Israel."[16] The challenge facing contemporary Jewish women, then, is that in confronting a new reality they will not turn back – unless it is to take example from the many learned women of the past – but that they will establish an "inheritance" rooted in Torah and fear of God and that it will be said of them as God said of the daughters of Zelophehad: "The daughters of Zelophehad speak rightly."[17]

There remains within Orthodoxy, however, a large, and even growing, contingent that shuns contemporary modern outlooks that are at variance with the life-styles of earlier generations. Will women in these groups ever come to study Talmud? Let me try to draw some inferences from my work and to speculate with information gleaned from common experience and from two recent books describing Orthodox life as it appears to women about to undertake this life-style.[18] In reflecting upon the direction my work has taken me, I find some question to ponder in regard to the present state of Orthodox Jewish education for women among the more right-wing elements. Although it is true that many of these women will be homebound with children for many years, it is also true that these women have received more Jewish education overall than their forebears. The reasons for this are sometimes stated in less than positive terms: "Give them more Judaism or they will get more secularism!" It does not seem, however, that these women are lobbying for anything more than what they already have. Indeed, studies of secular Jewish women who are joining these groups indicate that they are willing to adopt, with successful rationalizations, the current role models in exchange for acceptance in these groups.[19]

Certainly these women are aware that the society they inhabit is male oriented in educational access and power structure. And they accept it as such. In the past, women organized their own modes of prayer and spiritual devotion. To a large extent contemporary culture has been eroded by the onslaught of change in Jewish culture precipitated by the Enlightenment and vastly accelerated by the Holocaust. The question can be raised here if there is need to reach back and close the open seam by reestablishing the past culture. Does it make sense to try to revive what has died and been forgotten? Perhaps

16. *Sifrei* on Numbers 27:4, *piska* 133.

17. Numbers 27:7.

18. See Debra Renee Kaufman, *Rachel's Daughters: Newly Orthodox Jewish Women* (New Brunswick and London: Rutgers University Press, 1991), and Lynn Davidman, *Tradition in a Rootless World: Women Turn to Orthodox Judaism* (Berkely, CA: University of California Press, 1991).

[19]See Davidman, *Tradition in a Rootless World*, pp. 127–128.

not. To continue the trends of the past means that women's educational roles advance by concession and not by right. What is suggested here is that the rift with the past may well set the stage for a new future. Jewish women can today live with contradictions between the pull and tug of an authority that limits their role as students of texts and can still maintain their own moral authority by the way they "choose" to enact their role. This choice is molded by their motivation. In an earlier chapter we saw how a number of thinkers were able to see the importance of strengthening education for women in order to motivate their moral sensibilities in accord with their life roles.

We noted that while the legal codes did not help to establish formal schooling for women, they did not hamper serious-minded women from mastering the most complex areas of Jewish study. Nevertheless, real gains for these groups came only when pressure from outside the groups threatened to disrupt the traditional cohesiveness, and so concessions were made that gradually became normative. Yet, given this advance we can note that Jewish women, as a result of strides in Jewish education, are more aware of the theoretical underpinnings of their faith and more keen to promote Torah study among their children than before. A generation ago the quest for prosperity, honor, and security was deemed important in right-wing Orthodox Jewish homes, whereas today one witnesses a proliferation of study halls for men and seminaries for women in these communities. It may well be argued that women are seeking more learned husbands and that husbands are seeking more learned women than in past generations. As such, we see that the forces of history that animated past generations have changed—for better or for worse.

The past was able to conceive women's learning things that would not bring them to the point of deciding questions of Jewish practice for themselves, but the present may be able to conceive women's going beyond this. Even though there have always been exceptional women (known to us primarily through the writings of males), today women are more able to understand these women as sisters rather than as creatures from far away. To a large extent, right-wing Orthodox women share the skills that were regarded by past generations as supernatural feats. As was pointed out earlier, in more centrist wings of Orthodox Judaism women have begun the study of Talmud and, indeed, the teaching of it. It is only a matter of time until these trends come to fruition. The wings on the right will undoubtedly resist and even denounce that state of affairs. If the model works and proves to be beneficial, it is not impossible to imagine women's eventual study of Talmud even in right-wing Orthodoxy—again the pressure may come from without rather than from within. But this is not likely. It will not happen by revolution, nor by radical authoritative decision. These groups have amazing resistance to modern trends. It may happen, slowly and quietly, until it is sanctioned by history and no one will consciously perceive the final break with the past. The intragroup pressures are such that no pronouncement this way or that way will radically alter the courses these groups are historically determined to follow. It is not by planned advocacy, not by lobbying, not by rabbinic pronouncement, but only within the working-out of these courses that such breaks may ensue. There have been other breaks, generally moving things more to the right, but also liberal ones such as acknowledging that single Orthodox women might be professionals, college educated, and still accepted in right-wing Orthodox society.

On the other hand, it may not happen. Women will not miss the study of Talmud and may even look down at women in other Jewish groups who are proficient in Talmud and legal codes. Life may continue much as it has done for these women, tending to their roles and cares for which they are cherished and by which they are fulfilled. This study from antiquity to the present is now open—as a backdrop for the future—to gauge the continuous or discontinuous educational trends in Jewish subjects for women.

Bibliography

GENERAL REFERENCES

Babylonian Talmud. New York: Pollack Brothers, 1964. Includes commentaries of Rashi, Tosafot, Rashba, and Hassagot ha-Ravad.
Beit Ya'akov Journal. Lodz (1924–1939) and Jerusalem (1959–   ).
Encyclopaedia Judaica. Jerusalem: Keter, 1971.
Encyclopedia Hinukhit. Jerusalem: Ministry of Education and Culture and the Bialik Institute, 1964. See esp. vol. 4.
Jerusalem Talmud. Krotoszyn, 1866.
Mahzor Vitry. Berlin, 1889.
Midrash Zuta to Ruth, ed. S. Buber. Berlin, 1894.
Mikra'ot Gedolot. New York, 1944. Includes commentaries of Ibn Ezra, Nahmanides, Or ha-Hayim, Rashi, and Sforno.
Mishnah, ed. Pinhas Kahati. Jerusalem: Keter, 1977.
Pesikhta Rabbati, trans. W. S. Braude. Jerusalem, 1968.
Sifre, ed. Louis Finkelstein. New York: Jewish Theological Seminary of America, 1969.
Tosefta, ed. Moshe Samuel Zuckermandel. Vienna and Berlin, 1877.

AUTHORS: ANCIENT AND MODERN

Aaron Berakhiah de Modena. *Ma'avar Yabbok*. Vilna, 1927.
Aberbach, Moshe. *Ha-Hinukh ha-Yehudi be-Tekufat ha-Mishnah ve-ha-Talmud*. Jerusalem: Rubin Mass, 1982.

311

Abohav, Isaac. *Menorat ha-Ma'or*. Jerusalem: Eshkol, n.d.

Abrabanel, Isaac. *Perush al ha-Torah*. Tchernowitz, 1860.

Abraham ben David (Ravad). *Ba-al ha-Nefesh*. Jerusalem: Mossad Harav Kook, 1964.

———. *Hassagot ha-Ravad al Mishneh Torah*. In standard printed editions of Maimonides' *Mishneh Torah*.

Abrahams, Beth-Zion. "Grace Aguilar: A Centenary Tribute." *Jewish Historical Society of England Transactions* 16, 1945–1951.

Abrahams, Israel. *Hebrew Ethical Wills*. Philadelphia: Jewish Publication Society of America, 1926.

———. *Jewish Life in the Middle Ages*. London: Edward Goldston, 1932.

Abramson, Henry. "The Jew in History." *Nishma* 8, 1991.

Abudarham, David ben Joseph. *Sefer Abudarham*. Warsaw, 1878.

Adar, Zvi. *Jewish Education in Israel and in the United States*. Jerusalem: Melton Center, Hebrew University, 1977.

Adelman, Howard. "Rabbis and Reality: Public Activities of Jewish Women in Italy During the Renaissance and Catholic Restoration." *Jewish History* 5, Spring 1991, pp. 27–40.

Adlerblum, Nina H. "Sara Bayla and Her Times." In *Jewish Leaders*, ed. Leo Jung, *1750–1940*. Jerusalem: Boy's Town, 1964, pp. 345–391.

Alon, Menachem. An address delivered in Jerusalem on January, 1, 1990, before the World Emunah Congress.

Alshekh, Moshe. *Torat Moshe*. Warsaw, 1879.

Altmann, Alexander. *Moses Mendelssohn*. Philadelphia: Jewish Publication Society of America, 1973.

Amkin, Hayim. "Limud Torah la-Nashim." *Otzar ha-Hayim* 5, 1928 (h.d. 5689), pp. 15–18.

Amram, David. *The Jewish Law of Divorce*. New York: Hermon Press, 1968.

Arama, Isaac. *Akedat Yitzhak*. Lemberg, 1808.

Asher ben Jehiel. *Responsa*. Vilna, 1881.

Ashkenazi, Shimon. *Yalkut Shimoni*. Vilna, 1910.

Ashkenazi, Solomon. *Dor Dor u-Minhagav*. Tel Aviv: Dan, 1977.

———. *Ha-Ishah be-Asplaklaria ha-Yehudit*. Tel Aviv: Yizra'el, 1955.

Assaf, Simha. *Mekorot le-Toldot ha-Hinukh be-Yisrael*. Tel Aviv: Dvir, vol. 1, 1930, 1954; vol. 2, 1931; vol. 3, 1936; vol. 4, 1947.

Aszdod, Yehudah. *Yehuda Ya'aleh: Responsa*. Lemberg, 1873.

Atkin, Abraham. *The Beth Jacob Movement in Poland: 1917–1939*. Yeshiva University, Doctor of Philosophy dissertation in education, 1959.

Auerbach, David. *Halikhot Beita*. Jerusalem: Machon Sha'arei Ziv, 1983.

Auerbach, Menachem Mendel. *Ateret Zekanim*. In standard editions of Caro's *Shulhan Arukh*.

Azulai, H. J. D. *Birkei Yosef*. Vienna, 1860.

———. *Ma'agal Tov ha-Shalem*, ed. A. Friemann. Jerusalem: Mekitzei Nirdamim, 1934.

———. *Shem ha-Gedolim*. Vilna, 1853.

———. *Tov Ayin*. Husyatin, 1904.

Babad, Joseph. *Minhat Hinukh*. Jerusalem, n.d.

Bacharach, Jair Hayim. *Havot Ya'ir*. Lemberg, 1869.

Baer, Yitzhak. *A History of the Jews in Christain Spain*. Philadelphia: Jewish Publication Society of America, 1966.

_____. *Toledot ha-Yehudim bi-Sepharad ha-Notzrit.* Tel Aviv: Am Oved, 1965.

Bahya ben Asher. *Midrash Rabbenu Bahya.* New York: Keter, 1945.

Bamberger, Zekel. "She'elah be-Inyan Limud Torah la-Nashim." *Otzar ha-Hayim* 4, 1927 (h.d. 5688), pp. 146–148.

Barnett, R. D. "Anglo-Jewry in the Eighteenth Century." In *Three Centuries of Anglo-Jewish History,* ed. V. D. Lippman. Cambridge: Jewish Historical Society of England, 1961, pp. 45–68.

Baron, Salo W. *The Jewish Community.* Philadelphia: Jewish Publication Society of America, 1945.

Baron, Salo W., and Blau, Joseph. *Judaism: Postbiblical and Talmudic Period.* Indianapolis: Bobbs-Merrill, 1954.

Baskin, Judith. "Jewish Women in the Middle Ages." In *Jewish Women in Historical Perspective,* ed. Judith Baskin. Detroit: Wayne State University Press, 1991, pp. 94–114.

_____. "Some Parallels in the Education of Medieval Jewish and Christian Women." *Jewish History* 5, Spring 1991, pp. 41–51.

Basser, Herbert. "The Meaning of 'Shtuth' Gen. R. 11 in Reference to Mt. 5:29–30 and 18:8–9." *New Testament Studies* 31, 1985, pp. 148–151.

Baum, Charlotte. "What Made Yetta Work? The Economic Role of Eastern European Jewish Women in the Family." *Response* 7(2), Summer 1973, pp. 32–38.

Baumel, Judith Tydor, and Schacter, Jacob J. "The Ninety-three Bais Yaakov Girls of Cracow: History or Typology?" In *Reverence, Righteousness, and Rahamanut,* Northvale, NJ: Jason Aronson, 1992, pp. 93–130.

Bauminger, Aryeh. *Sefer Cracow: Ir ve-Em be-Yisrael.* Jerusalem: Mossad Harav Kook, 1959.

Beauvoir, Simone de. *The Second Sex,* trans. H. M. Parshley. New York: Vintage, 1974.

Becker, Carl. *The Heavenly City of the Eighteenth-Century Philosophers.* New Haven, CT: Yale University Press, 1932.

Beinart, Hayim. *Conversos on Trial.* Jerusalem: Magnes Press, 1981.

Belenky, M., Clinchy, B., Goldberger, N., and Tarule, J. *Women's Ways of Knowing.* New York: Basic Books, 1986.

Belkin, Samuel. *In His Image.* New York: Abelard-Scheiner, 1966.

Ben Sira, Simeon. *Sefer Ben Sira ha-Shalem (Ecclesiasticus),* ed. M. Segal. Jerusalem: Mossad Bialik, 1958.

Ben-Dod, Aharon. *Ha-Hinukh ha-Yehudi be-Tzfon Taiman u-Shoreshav ba-Yahadut.* Jerusalem: Leket, 1980.

Ben-Yaacob, Abraham. *Kurdistan Jewish Communities.* Jerusalem: Kiryat-Sepher, 1980.

Benayahu, Meyer. "Rabbi Samuel Barazani, Leader of Kurdistan Jewry." *Sefunot* 9, 1964, pp. 27ff.

Bender, Basya. "The Life of a Bais Ya'akov Girl." In *Daughters of Destiny,* ed. D. Rubin. Brooklyn: Mesorah, 1988, pp. 178–183.

Berkovits, Eliezer. *Jewish Women in Time and Torah.* Hoboken, NJ: Ktav, 1990.

Berlin, Naftali Z. Y. *Ha'amek Davar.* Jerusalem, 1938.

Berliner, Abraham. *Geschichte der Jueden in Rom von der Altesen Zeit bis zur Gegenwart.* Frankfurt am Main: J. Kaufmann, 1893.

_____. *Hayei ha-Yehudim be-Ashkenaz Bimei ha-Beinayim.* Tel Aviv: Tsiyon, 1968.

Berman, Joshua. "Balancing the Bimah: The Diaspora Struggle of the Orthodox Feminist." *Midstream* 36(6), August/September, 1990, pp. 20–24.

Berman, Saul. "The Status of Women in Halakhic Judaism." In *The Jewish Woman: New Perspectives,* ed. Elizabeth Koltun. New York: Schocken, 1976, pp. 114–128.

Bermant, Chaim. *Troubled Eden.* New York: Basic Books, 1969.

Bernfeld, Simon. *Sefer ha-Dema'ot.* Berlin: Eshkol, 1924.

Besdin, Abraham. *Reflections of the Rav,* vol. 1. Hoboken, NJ: Ktav, 1992.

Biale, Rachel. *Women and Jewish Law.* New York: Schocken, 1984.

Bilu, Yoram. "The Woman Who Wanted to Be Her Father: A Case Analysis of Dybbuk Possession in a Hassidic Community." *Journal of Psychoanalytic Anthropology* 8, 1985, pp. 11–27.

Blau, Rivkah."What Are Observant Jewish Women Really Thinking?" *Jewish Action,* Holiday Issue, 1986, pp. 69–70.

Bleich, David. *Contemporary Halakhic Problems.* New York: Ktav, 1977.

_____ . *With Perfect Faith: The Foundations of Jewish Belief.* New York: Ktav, 1983.

Bloch, Joseph Judah. *Shi'urei Da'at,* vol. 3. B'nei Brak: Netzach, n.d.

Blum, Saul. *Gedolei Yisrael: Hayei Rabbenu Akiva Eiger.* Warsaw, 1938.

Bolekhov, Dov. *The Diary of Dov of Bolekhov.* Berlin, 1922.

Bornstein, J. "The Budgets of Jewish Denominational Congregations in Poland." *Statistical Quarterly,* 1929.

Boton, Abraham Di. *Lehem Mishnah.* In standard printed editions of Maimonides' *Mishneh Torah.*

Brauer, E. *Yehudei Kurdistan.* Jerusalem: Israeli Institute for Folklore and Anthology, 1947.

Breuer, Isaac. *Concepts in Judaism.* Jerusalem: Israel Universities Press, 1974.

Breuer, Mordechai. "Jewish Women in the Middle Ages." *Jewish Digest* 29, October 1983, pp. 200–207.

Breyer, Menachem. *The Jewish Woman in Rabbinic Literature: A Psychosocial Perspective.* Hoboken, NJ: Ktav, 1986.

Brickman, William. "Education for Eternal Existence: The Philosophy of Jewish Education." In *Judaism and the Jewish School,* ed. Judah Pilch and Meir Ben-Horin. New York: Bloch, 1966, pp. 200–207.

Bromberg, Batya. "Nashim Mehadshot Dinim ba-Halakhah." *Sinai* 59, 1966, pp. 248–250.

Bronsztejn, S. "The Jewish Population of Poland in 1931." *Jewish Journal of Sociology* 6, 1964, pp. 3–29.

Brooten, Bernadette. *Women Leaders in the Ancient Synagogue.* Chico, CA: Scholars Press, 1982.

Bulka, Reuven. "The Jewish Family: Realities and Prospects." *Jewish Life* 6, Spring-Summer 1982, pp. 25–34.

Carlebach, Alexander. "A German Rabbi Goes East." *Leo Baeck Institute Year Book,* vol. 6, 1961, pp. 60–121.

Caro, Joseph. *Bet Yosef.* In standard printed editions of Jacob ben Asher's *Arba'ah Turim.*

_____ . *Shulhan Arukh.* Vilna, 1875.

Cassuto, Umberto. *Commentary on Genesis.* Trans. Israel Abrahams. Jerusalem: Magnes Press, 1961.

Castle, E. B. *Ancient Education and Today.* Baltimore: Penguin, 1961.

Chajes, Zevi Hirsh. *Kol Sifrei Maharitz Chajes.* Jerusalem: Divrei Hakhamim, 1958.

_____ . *The Student's Guide Through the Talmud.* New York: Philipp Feldheim, 1960.

Chavel, Chaim D., ed. *Sefer Ha-Hinukh.* Jerusalem: Mossad Harav Kook, 1961.

Chesler, Phyllis. *Women and Madness.* New York: Avon, 1973.

Cohen, Gerson D. "The Rabbinic Heritage." In *Great Ages and Ideas of the Jewish People*, ed. Leo W. Schwarz. New York: Random House, 1956, pp. 133–212.

Cohen, Jeremy. *"Be Fertile and Increase, Fill the Earth and Master It": The Ancient and Medieval Career of a Biblical Text.* Ithaca, NY, and London: Cornell University Press, 1990.

Cohen, Naomi G. *Hinukh ha-Bat ve-ha-Ishah.* Pamphlet of a lecture delivered at a symposium on the topic of women's education in Tel Aviv, 1980.

_____. "Women and the Study of Talmud." *Tradition* 24 (1), Fall 1988, pp. 28–37.

Crenshaw, James L. "Education in Ancient Israel." *Journal of Biblical Literature* 104(4), December 1985, pp. 601–615.

Crescas, Hasdai. *Or Hashem.* Vilna, 1904.

Davidman, Lynn. *Tradition in a Rootless World: Women Turn to Orthodox Judaism.* Berkeley, CA: University of California Press, 1991.

Dawidowicz, Lucy. *The Golden Tradition.* Boston: Holt, Rinehart and Winston, 1967.

Dewey, John. *Democracy and Education.* New York: Macmillan, 1916.

Dinberg, Zion. *Yisrael ba-Golah.* Tel Aviv: Dvir, 1926.

Donin, Hayim. *To Be a Jew.* New York: Basic Books, 1972.

Drazin, Nathan. *History of Jewish Education from 515 B.C.E. to 220 C.E.* New York: Arno Press, 1979.

Dubnow, S. M. *History of the Jews in Russia and Poland,* trans. I. Friedlaender. New York: Ktav, 1975.

Duran, Simeon ben Tsedek. *Responsa of Tashbetz.* Lemberg, 1891.

Durr, Lorenz. *Das Erziehungswesen im Alten Testament und im Antiken Orient.* Leipzig: J. C. Hinrichs, 1932.

Dushkin, Alexander. *Jewish Education in New York City.* New York: Bureau of Jewish Education, 1918.

Dushkin, Alexander, and Engelman, Uriah. *Jewish Education in the United States.* New York: American Association of Jewish Education, 1959.

Ebner, Eliezer. *Elementary Education in Ancient Israel.* New York: Bloch, 1956.

Eby, Frederick, and Charles F. Arrowood. *The History and Philosophy of Education: Ancient and Medieval.* New York: Prentice-Hall, 1940.

Edels, Samuel. *Maharsha.* In most printed editions of the Babylonian Talmud.

Eger, Akiva. *Responsa.* Vienna, 1889.

Eisenstadt, Israel T. *Da'at Kedoshim.* St. Petersburg, 1897–1898.

Eisenstein, Miriam. *Jewish Schools in Poland, 1919–1939: Their Philosophy and Development.* New York: King's Crown Press (Columbia University), 1950.

Eisenstein, J. D. *Otzar Masa'ot.* Tel Aviv, 1969.

_____. *Otzar Midrashim.* New York, 1915.

Elbaum-Dror, Rachel. *Ha-Hinukh ha-Ivri be-Eretz Yisra'el.* Jerusalem: Isaac ben Tzvi, 1986.

Elbogen, I. M. *Ha-Tefilah be-Yisrael.* Tel Aviv: Dvir, 1972.

Eliav, Mordechai. *Ha-Hinukh ha-Yehudi be-Germanyah b'Ymei ha-Haskalah ve-ha-Emanzipaziah.* Jerusalem: Jewish Agency, 1960.

Eliezer ben Natan. *Sefer Raban,* ed. S. Albeck. Warsaw, 1905.

Eliezer ben Judah of Worms. "Elegy of Rabbi Eliezer, Ba'al ha-Rokeah." In *Shomer Zion ha-Ne'eman,* ed. J. Ettlinger. Altona, 1849, p. 1586.

Elijah ben Solomon of Vilna. *Be'ur ha-Gra.* In standard printed editions of Caro's *Shulhan Arukh.*

Ellinson, Getzel. *Serving the Creator: Women and the Mitzvot.* Jerusalem: World Zionist Organization, 1986.

Emden, Jacob. *Migdal Oz.* Warsaw, 1882.

Endelman, Todd. *The Jews of Georgian England, 1714-1830.* Philadelphia: Jewish Publication Society of America, 1979.

Epstein, Abraham. *Kitvei Abraham Epstein,* ed. A. Habermann. Jerusalem: Mossad Harav Kook, 1950.

Epstein, Barukh. *Mekor Barukh.* Vilna, 1928.

_____ . *Torah Temimah.* Vilna, 1904.

Epstein, Yehiel M. *Arukh ha-Shulhan.* Warsaw, 1884.

Etkes, Emmanuel. "Mishpahah ve-Limud Torah be-Hugei ha-'Lomdim' be-Lita be-Me'ah ha-Yud-Tet." *Zion* 51, 1986, pp. 87-106.

Etzion (Holzberg), Isaac Raphael. "Ha-Zerem ha-Hinukhi 'Yavneh' be-Lita." In *Yahadut Lita,* ed. Jacob Olisky et al. Tel Aviv: Iggud Yotzei Lita be-Yisrael, 1972, pp. 160-165.

Falk, Joshua. *Derishah.* In standard printed editions of Jacob ben Asher's *Arba'ah Turim.*

Falk, Zev. *Law and Religion.* Jerusalem: Mesharim, 1981.

Feinstein, Moshe. *Responsa Igrot Moshe.* 7 vols., 1959-1985.

Fink, Greta. *Great Jewish Women.* New York: Bloch, 1978.

Fiorenza, Elisabeth Schussler. "In Search of Women's Heritage." In *Weaving the Visions: New Patterns in Feminist Spirituality,* ed. Judith Plaskow and Carol P. Christ. San Francisco: Harper Collins, 1989, pp. 29-38.

Fishbane, Simha. "In Any Case, There Are No Sinful Thoughts: The Role and Status of Women in Jewish Law as Expressed in the *Arukh ha-Shulhan,*" *Judaism* 43 (3), Summer 1993.

_____ . "A Response to the Challenge of the Modern Era as Reflected in the Wording of Rabbi Yechiel Mechel Epstein." In *Social Scientific Study of Jews and Judaism,* ed. Simha Fishbane, vol. 2. Hoboken, NJ: Ktav, 1992, pp. 96-112.

Fishelis, Abraham. *Kol Ram,* vol. 3. New York: Moriah, 1969.

Fishman, Isidore. *The History of Jewish Education in Central Europe (16th to 18th Centuries).* London: Edward Goldston, 1944.

Fishman, J. L. *Arim ve-Immahot be-Yisrael.* Jerusalem: Mossad Harav Kook, 1948.

Fishman, Sylvia Barack. *Learning About Learning: Insights on Contemporary Jewish Education from Jewish Population Studies.* Waltham, MA: Brandeis University Cohen Center for Modern Jewish Studies, 1987.

Flaum, Shulamit. *Bat Yisrael Nodedet.* Jerusalem, 1935.

Fleischer, Ezra. "On Dunash ibn Labrat, His Wife and His Son: New Light on the Beginning of the Hebrew Spanish School." In *Jerusalem Studies in Hebrew Literature,* vol. 5, 1984, pp. 189-202.

Frank, Ray. "Women in the Synagogue." *Papers of the Jewish Women's Congress, 1893.* Philadelphia: Jewish Publication Society of America, 1894, pp. 52-65.

Frankiel, Tamar. *The Voice of Sarah: Feminine Spirituality and Traditional Judaism.* San Francisco: Harper Collins, 1990.

Freehoff, Solomon. *The Responsa Literature and a Treasury of Responsa.* New York: Ktav, 1973.

Fried, M. J. *Yamim ve-Shanim.* Tel Aviv, 1939.

Friedensohn, Joseph. "Batei ha-Sefer le-B'not Beit Ya'akov be-Polin." In *Ha-Hinukh ve-ha-Tarbut ha-Ivrit be-Eiropah Bein Sh'tei Milhamot ha-Olam,* ed. Zevi Scharfstein. New York: Ha-Histadrut ha-Ivrit be-America, 1957, pp. 61-82.

Fuerer, Benzion. "Limud Torah la-Nashim." *Noam* 3, 1960, pp. 130-131.

Gamoran, Emanuel. *Changing Conceptions in Jewish Education*. New York: Macmillan, 1924.

Gellis, Jacob. *Mi-Gedolei Yerushalayim*. Jerusalem, 1967.

Ghirondi, Mordekhai Samuel. *Toldot Gedolei Yisrael*. Trieste, 1853.

Glazer, Nathan. *American Judaism*. Chicago: University of Chicago Press, 1972.

Gluckel of Hameln. *The Life of Gluckel of Hameln*, trans. and ed. Beth-Zion Abrahams. New York: Thomas Yoseloff, 1963.

Goitein, Solomon D. "Jewish Women in the Middle Ages." *Hadassah* 55, October 1973, pp. 14–15

_____ . *Jews and Arabs: Their Contacts Through the Ages*. New York: Schocken, 1955.

_____ . *A Mediterranean Society*. Berkeley, CA: University of California Press, 5 vols., 1967–1988.

_____ . *Sidrei Hinukh Bimay ha-Geonim u-Bet ha-Rambam*. Jerusalem: Hebrew University Press, 1962.

Goldfeld, Anne. "Women as Sources of Torah in the Rabbinic Tradition." *Judaism* 24, Spring 1975, pp. 245–256.

Gombiner, Abraham. *Magen Avraham*. In standard editions of Caro's *Shulhan Arukh*.

Goodblatt, David. "The Talmudic Sources on the Origins of Organized Jewish Education." *Studies in the History of the Jewish People in the Land of Israel* 5, 1980, pp. 83–103.

Goodspeed, Edgar J., ed. and trans. *The Apocrypha*. New York: Vintage Books, 1959.

Gordis, Robert. "Valeria Beruriah." *Universal Jewish Encyclopedia*, vol. 2. New York, 1940, p. 243.

Greenberg, Blu. *On Women and Judaism*. Philadelphia: Jewish Publication Society of America, 1981.

Greenberg, Simon. "Jewish Educational Institutions." In *The Jews: Their History, Culture and Religion*, ed. Louis Finkelstein. Philadelphia: Jewish Publication Society of America, 1949, pp. 916–949.

_____ . "Lifetime Education as Conceived and Practiced in the Jewish Tradition." *Religious Education* 68(3), May-June 1973, pp. 339–347.

Greenspahn, Frederick E. "A Typology of Biblical Women." *Judaism* 32(1), Winter 1983, pp. 43–50.

Greenwald, Toby Klein. "Wise Women: Is There a Women's Approach to Torah Study?" *Kol Emunah*, Winter/Spring 1991, pp. 10–13, 25.

Grossman, Abraham. "The Historical Background for the Ordinances on Family Affairs Attributed to Rabbenu Gershom Me'or ha-Golah." In *Jewish History: Essays in Honour of Chimen Abramsky*, ed. Albert A. Rapoport and S. Zipperstein. London: Halban, 1988, pp. 3–23.

Grunfeld-Rosenbaum, Judith. "Her Legacy Lives On." In *Daughters of Destiny*, ed. D. Rubin. Brooklyn: Mesorah, 1988, pp. 178–183.

_____ . "Sarah Schenirer." In *Jewish Leaders*: 1750–1940, ed. Leo Jung. Jerusalem: Boys' Town, 1953, pp. 407–432.

Guedemann, Moritz. *Quellenschriften zur Geschichte des Unterrichts und der Erziehung bei den Deutschen Juden*. Amsterdam: Philo Press, 1968.

Gunzberg, Aryeh Leib. *Sha'agat Aryeh*. Warsaw, 1869.

Gurock, Jeffrey S. *The Men and Women of Yeshiva*. New York: Columbia University Press, 1988.

Gutman, Jacob. *Mekitz Nirdamim*. Piotrokow, 1904. Reprint: Copy Corner, Brooklyn, 1992.

Habermann, Abraham. *Nashim Ivriyot be-Tor Madpisot, Mesadrot, Motsiot le-Or, ve-Tomkhot be-Mehabrim*. Berlin, 1933.

Hackett, JoAnn. "In the Days of Jael: Reclaiming the History of Women in Ancient Israel." In *Immaculate and Powerful. The Female in Sacred Image and Social Reality*, ed. Clarissa W. Atkinson, Constance H. Buchanan, and Margaret R. Miles. Boston: Beacon Press, 1985, pp. 15–38.

Halevi, A. A. *Olamah Shel ha-Aggadah*. Tel Aviv: Dvir, 1972.

Halevi, David. *Turei Zahav*. In standard printed editions of Caro's *Shulhan Arukh*.

Halivni, Ephraim B. "Nashim ve-Talmud Torah." *Hadarom* 61, Elul 5752 (1992), pp. 25–34.

Halperin, Yehiel. *Seder ha-Dorot*. Warsaw, 1881.

Hannover, Nathan. *Yeven Metzula*, intro. J. Fichman, notes by J. Halperin. Tel Aviv, 1945.

Harari, Judith. *Ishah ve-Em be-Yisrael*. Tel Aviv: Massada, 1959.

Hartman, David. *A Living Covenant: The Innovative Spirit in Traditional Judaism*. New York: Free Press, 1985.

Harvey, Warren. "The Obligation of Talmud on Women According to Maimonides." *Tradition* 19(2), Summer 1981, pp. 122–130.

Hassan, Abraham, and Kupetz, Moshe. "The Use of Midrash in Adult Education." *The Jewish Observer* 26(4), May 1993, pp. 37–41.

Hayyot, Ephraim. *Mikra'ei Kodesh*. Ortakoy, Turkey, 1729.

Heaton, E. W. *Everyday Life in Old Testament Times*. London: B. T. Batsford, 1956.

Hecht, Benjamin. "Crisis in Jewish Identity." *Nishma* 4–7. Toronto, April 1988–April 1990.

_____. "Emotional Identity and Halacha." *Nishma* Update, June 1991.

_____. "Examining the Ideal." *Nishma* Update, December 1992.

_____. *Study Materials on Kabbalat Ha-Torah*. Toronto and New York: Nishma, 1991.

_____. "Torah Shebe'al Peh." *Nishma* 6. Toronto, Fall 1989.

_____. "Women and Judaism: The Question of Learning." *Nishma*, September 1992.

Henkin, Judah H. "Amirat Kaddish Al Yidei Eshah." *Hadarom* 54, Sivan 5745 (1985), pp. 34–48.

_____. "Limud Torah le-Nashim." *Hadarom* 61, Elul 5752 (1992), pp. 11–19.

Henry, Sondra, and Taitz, Emily. *Written out of History: Our Jewish Foremothers*. Sunnyside, NY: Biblio Press, 1988.

Herrin, Judith. "In Search of Byzantine Women: Three Avenues of Approach." In *Images of Women in Antiquity*, ed. Averil Cameron and Amelie Khurt. London and Canberra: Croom Helm, 1983, pp. 157–189.

Herring, Basil F. *Jewish Ethics and Halakhah for Our Time*. New York: Ktav and Yeshiva University Press, 1984.

Hezekiah ben Manoah. *Hizkuni*. Vilna, 1875.

Himmelfarb, Harold. "The Non-Linear Impact of Schooling: Comparing Different Types and Amounts of Jewish Education." *Sociology of Education* 50(2), April 1977, pp. 114–132.

Hirsch, Samson Raphael. *Chapters of the Fathers: Translation and Commentary*. Jerusalem and New York: Feldheim, 1972.

_____. *The Hirsch Siddur*. Jerusalem and New York: Feldheim, 1978.

_____. *Horeb: A Philosophy of Jewish Laws and Observances*, trans. and intro. Dayan I. Grunfeld. New York, London, and Jerusalem: Soncino Press, 1962.

_____. *Judaism Eternal*, trans. Dayan I. Grunfeld. London: Soncino Press, 1960.

_____ . *Commentary on Genesis*. Vol. 1 of *The Pentateuch: Commentary on the Torah*, trans. Isaac Levy. London: Judaica Press, 1989.

Hisiger, Chaim. "Roots and Legends." *Nishma* 5, June 1989.

Horodezky, Samuel A. *Ha-Hasidut ve-ha-Hasidim*. 4 vol. Berlin, 1919–1922.

_____ . *Leaders of Hasidism*, trans. Maria Horodezky-Magasanik. London: Hasefer Agency for Literature, 1928.

Hutner, Isaac. "Shiur be-Hilkhot Hinukh" (Yiddish). *Divrei Rabbotainu*. New York: Torah U'Mesorah, 1959, pp. 11–16.

Hyamson, Albert M. *The Sephardim of England*. London: Methuen, 1951.

Ibn Aderet, Solomon ben Abraham. *Hidushei ha-Rashba*. Warsaw, 1922.

Ibn Latif, Yitzhak. "Tzror ha-Mor," ed. Adolph Jellinek. *Kerem Hemed* 9, 1856, pp. 154–159.

Ibn Yahya, G. *Shalshelet ha-Kabbalah*. Warsaw, 1928.

Isaac ben Joseph of Corbeil. *Amudei Golah: Sefer Mitzvot Katan*. Satmar, 1935.

Isaac ben Moses of Viena. *Or Zarua*. Frankfurt, 1911.

Isaac ben Reuben of Duren. *Sha'arei Dura*. Soslov, 1907.

Isaiah de Trani. *Tosafot Rid*. New York, 1945.

Isserles, Moses. *Hassagot Ha-Remah*. In standard editions of Caro's *Shulhan Arukh*.

_____ . *Responsa of Rema*. Warsaw, 1883.

Isserlin, Israel. *Terumat ha-Deshen*. Warsaw, 1882.

Jackson, Stanley. *The Sassoons*. New York: E. P. Dutton, 1968.

Jacob ben Asher. *Arba'ah Turim*. Warsaw, 1875.

Jacob, H. E. *The World of Emma Lazarus*. New York: Schocken, 1949.

Jellinek, Adolph. *Beit ha-Midrash*. Leipzig, 1878.

Johnson, Paul. *A History of the Jews*. London: Weidenfeld and Nicolson, 1987.

Joseph ben Moses. *Leket Yosher*, ed. J. Friemann. Berlin, 1903.

Joseph Hayim ben Elijah. *Rav Pe'alim*. Jerusalem, 1901.

Josephus, Flavius. *Against Apion*, trans. H. St. J. Thackery. Cambridge, MA: Harvard University Press, 1926.

_____ . *Antiquities*, trans. William Whiston. Grand Rapids, MI: Kregel, 1981.

Jospe, Raphael. *Torah and Sophia: The Life and Thought of Shem Tov ibn Falaquera*. Cincinnati: Hebrew Union College Press, 1988.

Judah ben Samuel he-Hasid. *Sefer Hasidim*, ed. J. Wistinezki. Frankfurt am Main: Wahrmann, 1924.

_____ . *Sefer Hasidim*, ed. R. Margolius. Jerusalem: Mossad Harav Kook, 1957.

Jung, Leo, ed. *Judaism in a Changing World*. New York: Holt-Rinehart, 1954.

Kagan, Israel Meir ha-Cohen. *Mishneh B'rurah*. Vilna, 1896.

_____ . *Likutei Halakhot*. St. Petersburg, 1918.

Kahn, Moshe. "Jewish Education for Women." *Ten Da'at* 3(3), Spring 1989.

Kamelhar, I. *Rabbenu Eleazar mi-Germiza: ha-Rokeah*. Rzeszow, 1930.

Kaplan, Aryeh. *Handbook of Jewish Law*. New York and Jerusalem: Maznaim, 1979.

Kaplan, Lawrence. "The Religious Philosophy of Rabbi Joseph Soloveitchik." *Tradition* 14(2), Fall 1973, pp. 43–64.

Katz, Jacob. *Exclusiveness and Tolerance*. New York: Schocken, 1961.

_____ . *Out of the Ghetto*. Cambridge, MA: Harvard University Press, 1973.

_____ . *Tradition and Crisis*. New York: Schocken, 1971.

Katz, Joseph. *She'erit Yosef*. Cracow, 1893.

Kaufman, David. *Ba-Meh Narim et Ruah ha-Dat be-Kerev Nasheinu u-Venoteinu?*, trans. M. Kamianski. Zhitomir: Horozinski, 1909.

Kaufman, Debra Renee. *Rachel's Daughters: Newly Orthodox Jewish Women*. New Brunswick, NJ, and London: Rutgers University Press, 1991.

Kayserling, M. *Die Juedischen Frauen in der Geschichte, Literatur und Kunst*. Leipzig, 1879.

Kellner, Menachem. *Maimonides on Human Perfection*. Atlanta: Scholars Press, 1990.

Kimhi, David. *Perushei Rabbi David Kimhi al ha-Torah*, intro. notes and ref. by Moses Kamelhar. Jerusalem: Mossad Harav Kook, 1970.

Kobler, Franz. *Letters of Jews Through the Ages*. London: Ararat, 1953.

Kohut, Rebecca. "A New Morning for the Jewish Girls in Europe." In *Bejs Jakob*, ed. Samuel Leo Deutschlaender. Vienna: Beth Jacob Central Organization, 1930.

Kook, Abraham Isaac. *Igrot Reiyah*. Jerusalem, 1922.

_____ . *The Lights of Penitence, Lights of Holiness, Essays, Letters and Poems*, trans. Ben Zion Bokser. New York and Toronto: Paulist Press, 1978.

Kraemer, Ross S. "Jewish Women in the Diaspora World of Late Antiquity." In *Jewish Women in Historical Perspective*, ed. Judith Baskin. Detroit: Wayne State University Press, 1991, pp. 43–67.

Kramer, Joel L. "Spanish Women in the Cairo Genizah." *Mediterranean Historical Review* 6(2), December 1991, pp. 236–267.

Kranzler, Gershon. "The Changing Orthodox Jewish Family." *Jewish Life* 3, Summer-Fall 1978, pp. 23–36.

Krauss, Esther. "Educating the Jewish Woman of the Twenty-First Century." *Ten Da'at* 3(3), Spring 1989, pp. 12–15.

Kurzweil, Zvi E. *Modern Trends in Jewish Education*. New York: Thomas Yoseloff, 1964.

Lacks, Rosalyn. *Women and Judaism: Myth, History and Struggle*. New York: Doubleday, 1980.

Lamm, Maurice. *The Jewish Way in Love and Marriage*. San Francisco: Harper and Row, 1980.

Lamm, Norman. *A Hedge of Roses*. New York: Feldheim, 1966.

_____ . *Torah Lishma: Torah for Torah's Sake in the Works of Rabbi Hayim of Volozhin and His Contemporaries*. Hoboken, NJ: Ktav,1989.

_____ . *Torah Umadda*. Northvale, NJ: Jason Aronson, 1990.

Landau, Jacob. *Sefer Ha-Agur*. St. Petersburg, 1884.

Landau, J. L. *Short Lectures on Modern Hebrew Literature*. London: Edward Goldston, 1938.

Landshuth, L. *Amudei ha-Avodah*. Berlin, 1857.

Lattes, Isaac de. *Responsa*. Vienna: Friedlander, 1860.

Leibowitz, Nechama. *Studies in Genesis*. Jerusalem: World Zionist Organization, 1985.

Leneman, Helen. "Sara Coppio Sullam, 17th-Century Jewish Poet in the Ghetto of Venice." *Response* 15(3), 1987, pp. 13–22.

Lenowitz, Harris. "Women Saints in Early Hasidism." *Explortions: Journal for Adventurous Thought* 3(3), 1985, pp. 27–34.

Lestchinsky, Jacob. "The Industrial and Social Structure of Interbellum Poland." *YIVO Annual of Social Science* 11, 1956–1957, pp. 243–269.

Levi, Leo. "Man and Women in Torah Life." *Jewish Life*, Spring 1974, pp. 36–57.

Levinsohn, Isaac Ber. *Te'udah be-Yisrael*, ed. Emmanuel Etkes. Jerusalem: Mercaz Zalman Shazar, 1977.

Levitats, Isaac. *The Jewish Community in Russia, 1772–1844*. New York: Octagon, 1970.

Lew, Myer S. *The Jews of Poland*. London: Edward Goldston, 1944.

Lichtenstein, Aaron. "Fundamental Problems Regarding the Education of Women." *Ten Da'at* 3(3), Spring 1989, pp. 7–8.

Lifschitz, Aryeh L. *Avot Atarah la-Banim*. Warsaw, 1927.

Lipman, V. D. *Social History of the Jews of England, 1850–1950*. London: Watts, 1954.

_____. *Three Centuries of Anglo-Jewish History*. Cambridge: Jewish Historical Society of England, 1961.

Lipscheutz, E. M. "Rashi." In *Sefer Rashi*, ed. Y. L. Maimon. Jerusalem: Mossad Harav Kook, 1956, pp. 175–176.

Lipshutz, Israel. *Tiferet Yisrael*. Berlin, 1862.

Loew, Judah ben Bezalel (Maharal). *Sifrei Maharal*. New York: Judaica Press, 1969.

Lookstein, Joseph H. "Goals for Jewish Education." In *Judaism and the Jewish School*, ed. Judah Pilch and Meir Ben-Horin. New York: Bloch, 1966, pp. 213–219.

Lubinsky, Menachem. "Jewish Education in the 80s." *Religious Education* 75(6), November-December 1980, pp. 654–658.

Lunel, Armand. *Juifs du Languedoc de la Provence et des États Francais du Pape*. Paris: Albin Michel, 1975.

Luntchitz, Solomon Ephraim. *Amudei Shesh*. Lemberg, 1865.

Luria, Solomon. *Responsa of Maharshal*. Lemberg, 1859.

Luzzatto S. D., and Leopold Zunz. See their correspondence in *Otzar Nehmad*, ed. S. Blumenfeld. Vienna, 1856.

Maimon, I. L. *Sarei ha-Me'ah*. Jerusalem: Ahiasaf, 1961.

Maimonides, Moses. *Guide of the Perplexed*. New York, 1944.

_____. *Mishnah with the Commentary of Rabbi Moses ben Maimon*, trans. from the orig. manuscript by Joseph David Kafah. Jerusalem: Mossad Harav Kook, 1963.

_____. *Mishneh Torah*. Vilna, 1900.

_____. *Teshuvot ha-Rambam*, ed. Joshua Blau. Jerusalem: Miketse Nirdamim, 1957.

Malbim, Meir Loeb Ben Yehiel Michael. *Ha-Torah ve-ha-Mitzvah*. New York: MP Press, 1974.

Malka, Moshe. *Mikveh ha-Mayim*, vol. 3. Jerusalem, 1975.

Maller, Julius B. "The Role of Education in Jewish History." In *The Jews: Their History, Culture and Religion*, ed. Louis Finkelstein. Philadelphia: Jewish Publication Society of America, 1949, pp. 896–915.

Mann, Jacob. *Text and Studies in Jewish History and Literature*. Cincinnati: Hebrew Union Press, 1931.

Marcus, Jacob. *The Jew in the Medieval World*. New York: Atheneum, 1975.

Margoliot, Moshe. *P'nei Moshe*. Warsaw, 1837.

Marrou, H. I. *History of Education in Antiquity*. New York: Sheed and Ward, 1956.

Matzner-Beckerman, Shoshana. *The Jewish Child: Halakhic Perspectives*. New York: Ktav, 1984.

Meir ben Barukh of Rothenburg. *Responsa of Maharam*, ed. R. N. Rabinowitz. Lemberg, 1860.

_____. *Teshuvot Maharam*, ed. Yitzhak Cahana. Jerusalem: Mossad Harav Kook, 1957.

Meiri, Menahem. *Bet ha-Behirah*. New York, 1944.

Meiselman, Moshe. "Women and Judaism: A Rejoinder." *Tradition* 15(3), Fall 1975, pp. 52–68.

_____. *Jewish Women in Jewish Law*. New York: Ktav, 1978.

Meyer, Michael A. *The Origins of the Modern Jew: Jewish Identity and European Culture in Germany, 1749–1824*. Detroit: Wayne State University Press, 1967.

Miller, Yisrael. *In Search of the Jewish Woman*. New York: Feldheim, 1984.

Millet, Kate. *Sexual Politics*. Garden City, NY: Doubleday, 1970.

Minkin, Jacob S. *The Romance of Hasidism.* New York: Macmillan, 1935.

Minkoff, Harvey, and Evelyn B. Melamed. "Was the First Feminist Bible in Yiddish?" *Moment* 16(3), June 1991, pp. 28–33.

Modder, Montagu. *The Jew in the Literature of England.* Philadelphia: Jewish Publication Society of America, 1944.

Moellin, Jacob Halevi. *Responsa Maharil.* Cracow, 1881.

_____. *Sefer Maharil: Minhagim.* Jerusalem: Makhon Yerushalayim, 1989.

Morais, Sabato. *Italian Hebrew Literature.* New York: Jewish Theological Society of America, 1926.

Mordekhai ben Hillel. *Piskei ha-Mordekhai.* In standard printed editions of the Babylonian Talmud.

Morpurgo, Rachel. *Ugav Rahel,* ed. Y. Zmora. Tel Aviv, 1943.

Morris, Nathan. *The Jewish School.* New York: Jewish Education Committee Press, 1937.

_____. *Toldot ha-Hinukh Shel Am Yisra'el.* Jerusalem: Rubin Mass, 1977.

Mouan, L. *Quelques Recherches sur l'état des Juifs en Provence au Moyen-Age.* Paris, 1879.

Mueller, Joel, ed. *Massekhet Soferim.* Leipzig, 1878.

Munk, Eli. *The World of Prayer.* New York: Feldheim, 1953.

Nahmanides, Moses. *Commentary on Genesis.* In *Mikra'ot Gedolot.* Jerusalem, 1972.

_____. *Responsa.* Warsaw, 1883.

Nave-Levinson, Pnina. "Women and Judaism." *European Judaism* 15(2), Winter 1981, pp. 25–28.

Niditch, Susan. "Portrayals of Women in the Hebrew Bible." In *Jewish Women in Historical Perspective,* ed. Judith R. Baskin. Detroit: Wayne State University Press, 1991, pp. 25–42.

Ochs, Vanessa. *Words on Fire.* New York: Harcourt Brace Jovanovich, 1990.

Orlean, J. L. "Yahadut-Programme (Fun Ershter biz Zekster Bateilung)." Hebrew University Library.

Ormian, H. *Ha-Mahshavah ha-Hinukhit Shel Yahadut Polaniah.* Tel Aviv: Yavneh, 1939.

Ovchinski, Levi. *Toledot ha-Yehudim be-Kurland.* Latvia, 1908.

Perlow, T. *L'Éducation et l'enseigment chez les Juifs a l'époque talmudique.* Paris, 1931.

Philo. "On a Contemplative Life." In *The Essential Philo,* ed. Nahum N. Glatzer. New York: Schocken, 1971.

Plaskow, Judith. "Jewish Memory from a Feminist Perspective." In *Weaving the Visions: New Patterns in Feminist Spirituality,* ed. Judith Plaskow and Carol P. Christ. San Francisco: Harper Collins, 1989.

_____. *Standing Again at Sinai.* San Francisco: Harper, Collins, 1990, pp. 39–50.

Pool, David de Sola. "Judaism in the Synagogue." In *The American Jew,* ed. Oscar Janowsky. New York: Harper & Row, 1972, pp. 28–55.

Posner, Arthur. "Literature for Jewish Women in Medieval and Later Times." In *The Jewish Library: Women,* ed. Leo Jung. London and New York: Soncino Press, 1970, pp. 213–243.

Poupko, Chana K., and Devorah L. Wohlgelernter. "Women's Liberation – An Orthodox Response." *Tradition* 15(4), Spring 1976, pp. 45–52.

Powers, Eileen. *Medieval Women.* London: Cambridge University Press, 1975.

Rabinowicz, Harry M. *Hasidism: The Movement and Its Masters.* Northvale, NJ: Jason Aronson, 1988.

_____. *The World of Hasidism.* London: Valentine, Mitchell, 1970.

Rakowski, Puah. "A Mind of My Own." In *The Golden Tradition*, ed. Lucy Dawidowicz. New York: Holt, Rinehart and Winston, 1967, pp. 388–393.

Rapoport-Albert, Ada. "The Maid of Ludmir." *Kabbalah: A Newsletter of Current Research in Jewish Mysticism* 2(2), 1987, pp. 1–3.

_____. "On Women in Hasidism: S. A. Horodezky and the Maid of Ludmir Tradition." In *Jewish History: Essays in Honor of C. Abramsky*, ed. Ada Rapoport-Albert and Steven J. Zipperstein. London: Halban, 1988, pp. 495–525.

Reinman, Yaakov. *Menoras Hamaor: The Light of Contentment*. Lakewood, NJ: Chinuch, 1982.

Remy, Nahida. *Das Juedische Weib*. Leipzig, 1892.

Ribalow, Harold. *Autobiographies of American Jews*. Philadelphia: Jewish Publication Society of America, 1965.

Riskin, Shlomo. "Women and Judaism: The Key Issues." In *Orthodoxy Confronts Modernity*, ed. Jonathan Sacks. Hoboken, NJ.: Ktav, 1991, pp. 86–96.

Rosensweig, Michael. "Personal Initiative and Creativity in Avodat Hashem." *Torah U-Madda Journal* 1, 1989, pp. 72–90.

Rossi, Azariah dei. *Me'or Eini'em*. Jerusalem: Makor, 1970.

Rottenberg, Yehezkel, ed. *Em Be-Yisrael: Sefer Zikkaron le-Sarah Schenirer*. B'nei Brak, 1960.

Roth, Cecil. *Essays and Portraits in Anglo-Jewish History*. Philadelphia: Jewish Publication Society of America, 1962.

_____. "The European Age: The Success of the Medieval Jewish Ideal." In *Great Ages and Ideas of the Jewish People*, ed. Leo Schwarz. New York: Random House, 1956, pp. 267–312.

_____. *The History of the Jews of Italy*. Philadelphia: Jewish Publication Society of America, 1946.

_____. *The Jews in the Renaissance*. Philadelphia: Jewish Publication Society of America, 1959.

_____. *The Magnificient Rothschilds*. New York: Pyramid, 1939.

_____. "Outstanding Jewish Women in Western Europe." In *The Jewish Library: Women*, ed. Leo Jung. London and New York: Soncino Press, 1970, pp. 247–268.

_____. *The Sassoon Dynasty*. London: Robert Hale, 1941.

Rubin, Israel. *Satmar: An Island in the City*. Chicago: Quadrangle, 1972.

Rudavsky, David. *Modern Jewish Religious Movements*. New York: Behrman House, 1967, 1979.

Salaman, N. *Rachel Morpurgo and Contemporary Hebrew Poets in Italy*. London, 1924.

Sarna, Nahum. *The Torah Commentary*. Philadelphia and New York: Jewish Publication Society of America, 1989.

Sassoon, David. *Me'at Devash*. Oxford, 1928.

Scharfstein, Zevi. *Gedolei Hinukh be-Ameinu*. Jerusalem: Rubin Mass, 1964.

_____. *Toldot ha-Hinukh be-Yisrael ba-Dorot ha-Aharonim*, 5 vol. Jerusalem: Rubin Mass, 1960–1966.

Schechter, Solomon. *Studies in Judaism*. Philadelphia: Jewish Publication Society of America, 1917.

Schenirer, Sarah. *Em be-Yisrael: Kitvei Sarah Schenirer*. Tel Aviv: Netzah, 1955.

Schimmel, H. Chaim. *The Oral Law*. Jerusalem and New York: Feldheim, 1978.

Schneerson, Joseph Isaac. *Lubavitcher Rebbi's Memoirs*, trans. N. Mindel. Brooklyn: Kehot, 1956.

Schneerson, Menachem M. "Me-Sihat Shabbat Parshat Emor, Erev Lag ba-Omer 5750: Al Devar Hiyuv Neshei Yisrael be-Hinukh u-ve-Limud ha-Torah." *Likutei Sichot* (Hebrew version) 5750. New York: Mercaz le-Inyanei Hinukh, 1990.

_____ . "A Woman's Place in Torah." An adaptation of addresses of the Lubavitcher Rebbe given on May 12 and 19, 1990. New York: Mercaz le-Inyanei Hinukh, Sihot in English, 1990.

Schneller, Raphael. "Continuity and Change in Ultra-Orthodox Education." *Jewish Journal of Sociology* 22, June 1980, pp. 35–45.

Seton-Watson, Hugh. *Eastern Europe Between the Wars, 1918–1941.* Hamden, CT: Anchor Books, 1962.

Sforno, Ovadiah ben Jacob. *Commentary on Genesis,* trans. Ralph Pelcovitz. New York: Mesorah, 1987.

Shneur Zalman of Lyadi. *Shulhan Arukh ha-Rav.* Warsaw, 1875.

Shoub, Mary. "Jewish Women's History: Development of a Critical Methodology." *Conservative Judaism* 35, Winter 1982, pp. 33–46.

Shulman, Nisson E. *Authority and Community: Polish Jewry in the Sixteenth Century.* Hoboken, NJ: Ktav, 1986.

Shulvass, Moses A. *Jewish Culture in Eastern Europe.* New York: Ktav, 1975.

_____ . *The Jews in the World of the Renaissance.* Chicago: E. J. Brill, 1973.

Silver, Arthur. "May Women Be Taught Bible, Mishnah and Talmud?" *Tradition* 17(3), Summer 1978, pp. 74–85.

Sirkis, Joel. *Bayit Hadash.* In standard printed editions of Jacob ben Asher's *Arba'ah Turim.*

Slonik, Benjamin. *Responsa.* Vilna, 1894.

Smalley, Beryl. *The Study of the Bible in the Middle Ages.* Oxford: Basil Blackwell, 1952.

Smith, William A. *Ancient Education.* New York: Philosophical Library, 1955.

Soloveitchik, Joseph B. "Confrontation." *Tradition* 6(2), Spring 1964, pp. 5–29.

_____ . "Ish ha-Halakhah." In *Talpiot,* vol. 1. New York, 1944, pp. 651–735. Trans. into English by Lawrence Kaplan, *Halakhic Man.* Philadelphia: Jewish Publication Society of America, 1983.

_____ . "The Lonely Man of Faith." *Tradition* 7(2), Summer 1965, pp. 5–67.

_____ . "A Tribute to the Rebbitzen of Talne." *Tradition* 17(2), Spring 1978, pp. 73–83.

Sorotzkin, Zalman. *Ha-De'ah ve-ha-Dibur.* Jerusalem, 1955.

_____ *Moznaim la-Mishpat.* Jerusalem, 1955.

Sosevsky, M. "The Lonely Man of Faith Confronts the Ish ha-Halakhah." *Tradition* 16(2), Summer 1976, pp. 73–89.

Stanislawski, *Tsar Nicholas I and the Jews.* Philadelphia: Jewish Publication Society of America, 1983.

Steinberg, Milton. *Basic Judaism.* New York: Harcourt Brace Jovanovich, 1947.

Steinhardt, Joseph. *Zikhron Yosef.* Fuerth, 1773.

Steinsaltz, Adin. *Biblical Images: Men and Women of the Book.* New York: Basic Books, 1984.

_____ . *The Essential Talmud.* New York: Bantam Books, 1976.

_____ . *The Strife and the Spirit.* Northvale, NJ: Jason Aronson, 1988.

_____ . *The Talmud, the Steinsaltz Edition: A Reference Guide.* New York: Random House, 1989.

_____ *The Thirteen Petalled Rose.* New York: Basic Books, 1980.

Suraski, Aharon. *Toldot ha-Hinukh ha-Torah be-Tekufah ha-Hadashah.* B'nei Brak: Or Hayim, 1967.

Symposium. "Does Judaism Need Feminism?" *Midstream* 32, April 1986, pp. 39–43.

Taitz, Emily. "Kol Ishah – The Voice of Woman: Where Was It Heard in Medieval Europe?" *Conservative Judaism* 38, 1986, pp. 46–61.

Tallan, Cheryl. "Medieval Jewish Widows: Their Control of Resources." *Jewish History* 5, Spring 1991, pp. 63–74.

Talmage, Frank. *David Kimhi: The Man and the Commentaries*. Cambridge, MA: Harvard University Press, 1975.

Trible, Phyllis. "Depatriarchalizing in Biblical Interpretation." In *The Jewish Woman: New Perspectives*, ed. Elizabeth Koltun. New York: Schocken, 1976, pp. 217–240.

Twersky, Isadore. *Introduction to the Code of Maimonides (Mishneh Torah)*. New Haven, CT, and London: Yale University Press, 1980.

Ulich, Robert. *Three Thousand Years of Educational Wisdom*. Cambridge, MA: Harvard University Press, 1954.

Urbach, Ephraim. *Ba'alei ha-Tosafot*. Jerusalem: Bialik Institute, 1980.

Vaux, Roland de. *Ancient Israel: Its Life and Institutions*. London: Darton, Longman and Todd, 1961.

Vogel, Dan. *Emma Lazarus*. Boston: Twayne, 1980.

Wahrman, Solomon. "Mitzvat Talmud Torah be-Nashim." *Hadarom* 46, 1978, pp. 55–62.

Waldenberg, Eliezer. *She'alot u-Teshuvot Tzitz Eliezer*. Jerusalem, 1985.

Waxman, Chaim. *America's Jews in Transition*. Philadelphia: Temple University Press, 1983.

Wegner, Judith Romney. "The Image and Status of Women in Classical Rabbinic Judaism." In *Jewish Women in Historical Perspective*, ed. Judith Baskin. Detroit: Wayne State University Press, 1991, pp. 68–93.

Weinberger, Moshe. "Teaching Torah to Women." *Journal of Halacha and Contemporary Society* 9, Spring 1985, pp. 19–52.

Weinryb, Bernard D. *The Jews of Poland: A Social and Economic History of the Jewish Community in Poland from 1100 to 1800*. Philadelphia: Jewish Publication Society of America, 1973.

Weiss, Avraham. *Women's Prayer Groups: A Halakhic Analysis of Women's Prayer Groups*. Hoboken, NJ: Ktav, 1990.

Weiss, Isaac. *Avnei Bet ha-Yotser*. Paks, Hungary, 1900.

Weiss-Rosmarin, Trude. *Jewish Women Through the Ages*. New York: Jewish Book Club, 1940.

Weissler, Chava. "For Women and for Men Who Are Like Women: The Construction of Gender in Yiddish Devotional Literature." *Journal of Feminist Studies in Religion* 5(2), Fall 1989, pp. 7–24.

_____. "Prayers in Yiddish and the Religious World of Ashkenazic Women." In *Jewish Women in Historical Perspective*, ed. Judith Baskin. Detroit: Wayne State University Press, 1991, pp. 159–177.

_____. "The Traditional Piety of Ashkenazic Women." In *Jewish Spirituality*, ed. Arthur Green. London: Routledge and Kegan Paul, 1987, pp. 245–275.

_____. "Woman as High Priest: A Kabbalistic Prayer in Yiddish for Lighting Sabbath Candles." *Jewish History* 5, Spring 1991, pp. 9–26.

Weissman, Deborah. "Bais Ya'akov: A Historical Model for Jewish Feminists." In *The Jewish Woman: New Perspectives*, ed. Elizabeth Koltun. New York: Schocken, 1976, pp. 139–148.

_____ . *Bais Ya'akov–A Women's Educational Movement in the Polish Jewish Community: A Case Study in Tradition and Modernity.* Unpublished dissertation (Master of Arts in Sociology) at New York University, 1977.

_____ . "Education of Jewish Women." In *Encyclopaedia Judaica Yearbook, 1986–1987.* Jerusalem: Keter, 1987, pp. 29–36.

Wessely, Naphtali H. *Divrei Shalom ve-Emet.* Warsaw, 1886.

Winkler, Gershon. *Maiden of Ludmir.* New York: Judaica Press, 1990.

Winkler, Michael. "Limud Torah la-Nashim." *Otzar ha-Hayim* 5, 1928 (hid. 5689), pp. 14–15.

Wohlgemuth, Ari. "The Jewish Woman in Eastern Europe." In *The Jewish Library: Women,* ed. Leo Jung. London and New York: Soncino Press, 1970, pp. 399–415.

Wolowelsky, Joel B. Letter to the editor. *Hadarom* 57, Elul 5748 (1988), pp. 157–158.

_____ . "Modern Orthodoxy and Women's Changing Self-Perception." *Tradition* 22(1), Spring 1986, pp. 65–81.

Wolpert, N., A. Braunspiegel, M. Willig, J. Parnes, and Z. Schachter. "Teshuvah be-Din Nashim be-Tefilah, be-Kri'at ha-Torah, be-Hakafot." *Hadarom* 54, Sivan 5745 (1985), pp. 49–53.

Wurzberger, Walter S. "Plural Models and the Authority of the Halakhah." *Judaism* 20(4), Fall 1971, pp. 162–174.

Yiftah, Yehezkel. *Ha-Hinukh ha-Yehudi be-Iraq be-Dorot ha-Aharonim.* Nahalal: Hotsa'at Yad Eli'ezer, 1983.

Yom Tov ben Avraham Ishbili. *Hiddushei ha-Ritva.* Warsaw, 1879.

Yuttar, Abraham Y. "Nashim ve-Talmud Torah: Iyun Halakhati Tahbiri." *Hadarom* 61, Elul 5752 (1992), pp. 38–41.

Zacuti, Abraham. *Yuhasin ha-Shalem,* ed. A. Freiman. Frankfurt am Main: M. A. Wahrmann Verlag, 1924.

Zedekiah ha-Rofeh. *Shibolei ha-Leket.* Vilna, 1887.

Zevin, J. *Le-Or ha-Halakhah Ba'ayot u-Verurim.* Tel Aviv: Abraham Zioni, n.d.

Zinberg, Israel. *A History of Jewish Literature.* Cleveland: Press of the Case Western Reserve University, 12 vol. 1972–1978.

Zohar, Noam J. "Women, Men and Religious Status: Deciphering a Chapter in Mishnah." In *Approaches to Ancient Judaism,* ed. Herbert Basser and Simha Fishbane, vol. 5. Atlanta: Scholars Press, 1993, chap. 2.

Zunz, Leopold. "Rashi." In *Zeitschrift fuer die Wissenchaft des Juedentums,* ed. L. Zunz. Berlin, 1825.

Index

Abahu, 80
Abelard, 178
Abohab, Isaac, 202
Abrabanel, Bienvenida, 156
Abraham ben David (Rabad), 24, 61
Abraham ben Hayim, 183
Abudarham, David ben Yosef, 42, 43, 45
Adam, Michael, 200
Adelman, Howard, 157
Adler, Cyrus, 288
Adler, Nathan Marcus, 232
Advanced studies, Babylonian hegemony, 133, 134
Aguilar, Grace, 257–259
Agunah (deserted wife), *Halakhah* and, 41
Akiva, 116
Alliance Israélite Universelle, 241–242
Alon, Menachem, 47, 49
Alter, Avraham Mordekhai, 267, 278
Amkin, Hayim, 69
Amoraic era. *See* Talmudic (Amoraic) era

Amsterdam, Babylonian hegemony, 169
Anshel, Asher, 201
Antiochus Epiphanes (k. of Syria), 109
Anti-Semitism
    Beth Jacob movement and, 299–300
    French Revolution and, 228
    Poland and, 268
Arak, Meir, 252
Arama, Isaac, 35, 36
Archivolti, Samuel ben Elhanan Jacob, 63–64, 169
Arpino, Anna d', 158–159
Ascarelli, Deborah, 163, 257
Ascarelli, Joseph, 163
Asenath (Barazani) Mizrahi, 140, 141–146
Asher, Jacob ben, 61, 73–74
Asher ben Jehiel, 147, 150
Ashkenazi, Jacob ben Isaac, 202, 209, 249
Ashkenazi, Rachel, 249
Assaf, Simha, 146–147, 151

Assimilation
  French Revolution and, 228
  Jewish Enlightenment and, 230
Aszdod, Yehudah, 64
Auerbach, David, 70–71
Auerbach, Menahem Mendel, 60
Auerbach, Moses, 268
Azulai, Hayim Joseph David, 27, 64,
  216

Ba'al Shem Tov, 248
Babad, Joseph, 64
Babylonian exile
  synagogue and, 105
  women's education and, 110
Babylonian hegemony, 131–170
  Amsterdam, 169
  Geonic, post-Geonic, and Islamic
    periods, 131–146
    Asenath (Barazani) Mizrahi,
      141–146
    generally, 131–136
    women scholars during, 140
    women's education during,
      137–140
  London, 169–170
  Palestine, 169
  Sephardic centers, 146–169. See also
    Sephardic centers (Babylonian
    hegemony)
Bacharach, Abraham Samuel, 203–204
Bacharach, Hava, 202–206
Bacharach, Jair Hayim, 203
Baer, Yitzhak, 148
Bahur, Elijah, 162
Bahya ibn Pakuda, 198
Balkan states, Europe (19th century),
  241–242
Bamberger, Zekel, 67–68
Bar Kokhba's insurrection, 124
Bass, Shabbtai, 213
Bas-Tovim, Sarah, 220–222
Bavli, Hillel, 300
Becher, Fortuna, 243
Belenson, Chana, 302
Belinfante, Cohen, 169
Belisaro, Miriam Mendes, 233
Belkin, Samuel, 2

Benjamin ben Aaron, 201
Ben Sira, 102
Berekhiah, Aaron, 159, 219
Berkovits, Eliezer, 111
Berlin, Isaiah, 216
Berlin, Reyna Basya, 253
Berman, Saul, 43, 52–53
Bernfeld, Simon, 236
Beruriah, 64, 116, 117–124
Beth Jacob movement, 66, 67, 252,
  263–300
  analysis of, 297–300
  background of, 264–274
  establishment and development of,
    276–289
  ideology and curriculum of, 289–297
  Schenirer, Sarah and, 274–276
Biale, Rachel, 30, 40, 42–43
Biblical era
  education of women during,
    101–105
  images of women during, 98–101
Bina, Malka, 301
Birkenthal, Dov Ber, 218
Birnbaum, Nathan, 294
Birnbaum, Solomon, 294
Bleich, David, 8
Blitz, Jekuthiel ben Isaac, 225
Bloch, Joseph Leo, 297
Blum, Saul, 217
Bonifaccio, Baldassar, 165
Brauer, Erich, 143–144
Bresch, Judah Leib, 200, 201
Brickman, William, 18
Brooten, Bernadette, 107
Bulka, Reuven, 28, 39
Bunim, Akiva ben Simha, 217
Burckhardt, Jacob, 156
Business. See Secular factors
Byzantine Empire, women's status in,
  137

Caesar, Julius, 292
Carlebach, Emanuel, 266–268
Caro, Joseph, 61
Cassuto, Umberto, 22
Castiglioni, Vittorio, 257
Castle, E. B., 105

Catholic Church, ghetto creation and,
    171. *See also* Christianity
Ceba, Ansaldo, 164–165
Chasan, Bella Hurwitz, 219, 223
Chesler, Phyllis, 38
Children
    Biblical era and, 99–100
    family ideal and, 29
Christianity
    ghetto creation and, 171
    Judaism isolated by, 227–228
    misogyny and, 173
    Sephardic centers (Babylonian
        hegemony), Spain, 153
    women's education and, Europe
        (12th–13th centuries), 173
Coeducation
    Babylonian hegemony, 138
    Orthodox Judaism and, 305
    sexuality and, 79–80
Cohen, Gerson, 6–7
Cohen, Hendelin, 185
Cohen, Naomi, 177, 273
Communal education, Sephardic centers
    (Babylonian hegemony), 166–169
Compulsory education, Mishnaic
    (Tannaitic) era and, 113–114
Conat, Abraham, 161
Conat, Estellina, 161
Control, of women, 44
Creation, women and, 20–26
Cromwell, Oliver, 169
Cultural factors. *See also* Social factors
    school establishment and, Second
        Temple era, 109
    women's education and, 307–308
Curriculum, Beth Jacob movement,
    289–297
Cuzi, Meshullam, 161

Da Pisa family, 156–157, 159
David, Beruriah, 302
David ibn Yahya, 156
David of Imola, 159
Deborah (daughter of Samuel Nahum of
    Minsk), 206–208
Deserted wife (*agunah*), *Halakhah* and, 41
Deutscher, Moshe, 282

Deutschlaender, Samuel Leo, 283–284,
    286
Dewey, John, 1n1, 291
Díaz, María, 153
Diskin, Joshua Judah Leib, 256
Diskin, Sarah, 255–256
Divorce law, women and, 40–41
Donin, Hayim, 3, 10
Drazin, Nathan, 13, 109, 110, 111, 113
Dubnow, Solomon, 193
Dulce of Worms, 175, 181–183
Dunash ibn Labrat, 152
Duran, Simeon ben Tsedek, 184
Dushkin, Alexander, 243

Eastern Europe
    Beth Jacob movement, 266
    immigration from, to United States,
        245–246
    16th century, 189–193
    19th century, 229, 238–241
Ebner, Eliezer, 109, 111
Economic factors. *See also* Secular factors
    Babylonian hegemony, 135
    Beth Jacob movement and, 268–269,
        271, 295–296
    school establishment and, Second
        Temple era, 108–109
Edels, Israel, 194
Education. *See* Jewish education
Eger, Akiva, 217–218
Eger, Gittele, 28, 217
Eger, Wolf, 217
Elazar, Daniel, 38
Eleazar ben Judah Rokeah of Worms,
    181
Eleazar ben Samuel of Mayence,
    187–188
Elementary schools and education. *See
    also* Schools
    Babylonian hegemony, 133, 134,
        147–148
    14th–15th centuries, 187–188
    Mishnaic (Tannaitic) era and,
        113–114
    16th century, 190
Eliezer, 57, 79, 80, 81–82, 116
Eliezer ben Hyrcanus, 125

Eliezer ben Joel ha-Levi, 180
Elimelekh of Lyzhansk, 249
Eliot, George, 260
Elisha ben Avuyah, 125
Emden, Jacob, 224
England
  Europe (19th century), 232–234
  London, Babylonian hegemony,
    169–170
Engleman, Uriah, 243
Epstein, Baruch, 80–81, 127, 253, 254,
  258, 260
Epstein, Yehiel Michel, 65–66
Equality
  creation and, 25–26
  exemption of women from *Halakhah*
    and, 47–48
  Maimonides and, 76–77, 78
Esther of Cracow, 205
Europe (12th–13th centuries), 171–184
  exclusion of women, 176–177
  generally, 171–173
  House of Rashi and contemporary
    scholars, 178–183
  information education and women
    scholars, 177–178
  synagogue as educational institution,
    173–176
  testimony concerning Jewish law,
    183–184
Europe (14th–15th centuries), 184–188
  education in, 187–188
  prominent women in, 184–187
Europe (16th century), 189–202
  Eastern European ascendancy,
    189–193
  prominent women of, 193–196
  religious literature for women,
    196–202
Europe (17th century), 202–215
  devotional prayers for women, 213
  literature and attitudes during,
    208–212
  women printers, 213–215
  women scholars of, 202–208
  women's education during, 212–213
Europe (18th century), 215–225
  devotional literature, 219–223

  educational forms, 223–225
  women scholars of, 215–218
Europe (19th century), 227–261
  general background, 227–231
  Jewish education, 231–246
    Balkans, Islamic States, and
      Alliance Israélite Universelle,
      241–242
    Eastern Europe, 238–241
    England, 232–234
    France, 231
    Germany, 234–238
    Italy, 231–232
    Palestine, 242–243
    United States, 243–246
  women scholars, 246–256
    generally, 246–247
    Hasidic women, 247–252
    Lithuania and Russia, 252–255
    worldwide, 255–256
  women writers, 257–261
Europe (20th century), Beth Jacob
  movement, 266
Exemption of women, *Halakhah* and, 42

Falk, Bella, 194–196
Falk, Joshua, 63, 64, 72, 77
Falk, Zev, 4, 8, 12
Family
  attitudes toward women and, 31–35
  Babylonian hegemony, 133–134
  Biblical era and, 99–100
  creation and, 22–25
  as educational institution, during
    Biblical era, 103–104
  exemption of women from *Halakhah*
    and, 42, 43, 50, 80–81
  ideal form of, 28–30
  Torah study by women and, 83–84
Fano, Izota da, 160
Fano, Jacob da, 157
Fargis, Rachel Reidnitz, 223
Father–daughter relationship, Torah
  education and, 63–64
Feinstein, Moses, 70
Feminism
  Beth Jacob movement and, 299
  male exclusivity and, xiii

Fink, Greta, 251
Fishels, Roizl, 213
Fishman, Isidore, 212–213
Flansburg, Jeremiah, 254
Flavius Josephus, 13
Fleischer, Ezra, 152
Flesch, Moshe, 275–276
France. *See also* Europe
    14th-15th centuries, 184–188
    19th century, 231
    Provence, Sephardic centers
        (Babylonian hegemony),
        154–155
    12th–13th centuries, 171–184
Frankiel, Tamar, 50, 90, 111, 252
French Revolution, Judaism and, 228
Fried, M. J., 240
Friedensohn, Eliezer Gershon, 285, 287
Friedman, Alexander Zusha, 285
Frummet of Ahrweiler, 186
Fuerer, Ben Zion, 70

Gabbai, Ezekiel, 255
Gamba, Bartolomeo, 166
Gandhi, Mahatma, 292
Gaon, Elijah (Vilna Gaon), 225
Gedaliah Ibn Yahya, 152
Geiger, Abraham, 260
Gender role. *See also* Sex differences
    exemption of women from *Halakhah*
        and, 47
    women's education and, 85
Genizah documents, women's status and,
    131–132, 137, 138–139
Germany. *See also* Europe
    14th–15th centuries, 184–188
    19th century, 234–238
    12th–13th centuries, 171–184
Gershom ben Judah of Mayence, 41
Ghettos
    Christianity and, 171
    French Revolution and, 228
Ghirondi, Benvenida, 159–160
Ghirondi, Mordekhai, 159
Ginzberg, Louis, 133
Gluckel of Hameln, 210, 211–212
God
    creation and, 21

    family ideal and, 30
    Halakhic system and, 11
    husband's rights and, 42–43
    Jewish education and, 16
    marriage and, 22
    Orthodox Judaism and, 3–4
Goitein, Solomon Dov, 135
Golding, Sue, 288
Gordis, Robert, 120
Graetz, Heinrich, 243
Granada, San Luis de, 165
Gratz, Rebecca, 245
Greenberg, Simon, 16, 103–104
Grodzinski, Hayim (Chaim) Ozer, 279,
    297
Grunfeld-Rosenbaum, Judith, 276, 277,
    281, 284, 286, 292
Gunzenhausen, Joseph, 161

Habermann, Abraham, 214
Hafetz Hayim, 74–75
Halakhah and Halakhic system
    described, 8–12
    Europe (12th–13th centuries),
        183–184
    Torah study and, 60, 71–89
    women and, 39–53
Halberstam, Ben Zion, 282
Halevi, Judah, 152
Halevy, David, 60
Halivni, Ephraim, 87, 88
Haninah ben Teradyon, 117
Hannover, Nathan, 190
Hasidism
    Beth Jacob movement and, 280,
        293–294
    Europe (19th century), women
        scholars, 247–252
    Jewish Enlightenment and, 230,
        265–266, 271
    origins of, 229
Haskalah. See Jewish Enlightenment
Hayim ben Isaac of Vienna, 183
Hayyot, Ephraim, 223
Hecht, Benjamin, 46, 72
Heilbronn, Jacob, 163, 201
Heitner, Meir, 282
Hellenism, 109, 111

Heller, Tziporah, 302
Henkin, Chana, 302
Henkin, Judah, 71, 87–88, 89
Henochs, Moses, 201
Heschel, Abraham Joshua, 249
Heschel, Joshua, 205
Hirsch, Fiola Shlenker, 215
Hirsch, Samson Raphael, 8, 21, 23, 45,
    91–92, 120, 236–238, 246, 264,
    267, 268, 273–274, 288, 293
Hirschenson, Jacob Mordecai, 256
Hirschenson, Sarah Bayla, 256
Hoeschel, Joshua, 196
Holocaust, Beth Jacob movement and,
    299–300. See also World War II
Holzberg, Y. R., 297
Horodezky, Samuel Aba, 247, 248
Horowitz, Abraham ben Shabtai
    ha-Levi, 210
Horowitz, Isaiah, 204
Horowitz, Joshua, 253–254
Horowitz, Sarah Rebecca Rachel Leah,
    219–220
Horowitz, Sheftel, 210
Horowitz, Yokil Segal, 219
Husband's rights, God and, 42–43
Hutner, Isaac, 111, 112

Ideology, Beth Jacob movement,
    289–297
Ima Shalom, 125
India, 255
Intellectual abilities. See Mental abilities
Isaac, Moses, 224
Isaac ben Eliakim of Posen, 201–202, 210
Isaac ben Menahem the Great, 180
Isaac of Basra, 140
Isaac of Corbeil, 61, 172
Isaac of Vienna, 174
Isaiah ben Elijah di Trani, 56
Isaiah of Montaniena, 167
Islam
    Genizah documents, 131–132
    Jewish education, Europe (19th
        century), 241–242
    women's status in, 77, 135
Israel of Czortkov, 252

Isserles, Moses, 61, 63
Isserlin, Israel, 184–185
Italy. See also Europe
    Jewish education, Europe (19th
        century), 231–232
    Sephardic centers (Babylonian
        hegemony), 155–169
        communal education, 166–169
        generally, 155–157
        religious literature for women,
            162–166
        Torah study by women, 157–158
        women in synagogue, 158–159
        women scholars, 159–162
    women's education in, 152

Jacob ben Asher, 215
Jacob Mizrahi of Amadiyah, 140
Jewish education
    background of, 1–2. See also Torah
        study
    Beth Jacob movement, 263–300. See
        also Beth Jacob movement
    Europe (19th century), 231–246. See
        also entries under Europe
        Balkans, Islamic States, and
            Alliance Israélite Universelle,
            241–242
        Eastern Europe, 238–241
        England, 232–234
        France, 231
        Germany, 234–238
        Italy, 231–232
        Palestine, 242–243
        United States, 243–246
    French Revolution and, 228–229
    philosophy of, 13–18
    Torah study by women, 55
Jewish Enlightenment
    assimilation and, 228–229
    Beth Jacob movement and, 264
    Hasidism and, 230, 265–266, 271
    Jewish education and, 239
Jewish law. See Halakhah and Halakhic
    system
Jewish survival
    education of women and, 80–81

French Revolution and assimilation, 228
Jewish education and, 13
Roman Empire and, 113
Jonah ben Abraham Gherondi, 148–150
Joseph ben Johanan, 184
Joseph Hayim ben Elijah Al-Hakam, 144–145
Joseph ibn Aknin, 147
Joseph ibn Migash, 151
Joshua ben Gamla, 108, 111, 113
Judah ha-Hasid, 61, 62
Judah Halevi, 260
Judah ha-Nasi, 32, 79
Judah Loew of Prague, 45–46
Judaism
defined, 2–3, 8
French Revolution and, 228
isolation of, Middle Ages, 227–228
theological principles in, 3–4
women and, 19–53. See also Women
Jung, Leo, 4, 280, 288

Kagan, Israel Meir (Israel Meir ha-Cohen), 66–67, 88, 278–279
Kaidenover, Zvi Hirsch, 202
Kaplan, Marion, 50
Katz, Hannah, 213
Katz, Isaac ben Simeon, 202
Katz, Joseph ben Mordekhai Gershon ha-Kohen, 191
Katznellenbogen, Hirsch, 216
Katznellenbogen, Marla, 216
Kaufman, David, 264–265
Kaufman, Debra Renee, 50–52
Kempner, Sprintza, 205
Kimhi, David, 200
Kobler, Franz, 137
Kohn, Pinchas, 266–268
Kohut, Rebekah, 288
Konitz, Moses, 205
Kurzweil, Zvi, 280

Lamm, Maurice, 22
Landau, Ezekiel, 195
Landau, Jacob, 61, 62
Landau, Menachem Mendel, 66

Lando, Menahem Mendel, 277
Landsberg, Eva, 284
Landsofer, Yonah, 201
Language. See also Literature
Beth Jacob movement and, 270, 276–277, 288, 293, 294–295
Europe (16th century), 189, 190, 193, 197, 198, 200–202
Europe (18th century), 224–225
Europe (19th century), England, 232
Jewish education and, 239
United States (19th century), 244, 245
Lattes, Isaac Immanuel de, 160
Lazarus, Emma, 260–261
Legitimacy, Halakhic system and, 10
Leib, Aryeh, 217
Leibowitz, Nechama, 36, 301
Lenowitz, Harris, 249
Levi, Bryna, 302
Levi, Leo, 34
Levinsohn, Isaac Baer, 239
Lichtenstein, Aaron, 89, 95
Lilienthal, Max, 244
Lipkin, Isaac, 253
Lipkin, Leah, 253
Lipman, V. D., 234
Literacy, Babylonian hegemony, 135, 145–146
Literature. See also Language
Europe (16th century), 196–202
Europe (17th century), 208–212
Europe (18th century), 219–223
Sephardic centers (Babylonian hegemony), 162–166
Lithuania
Europe (19th century), women scholars, 252–255
Jewish education and, 240
Litte of Regensburg, 213
Loew, Judah, 193, 202
Loew, Pearl Reich, 193–194
London, Babylonian hegemony, 169–170
Lookstein, Joseph, 15, 16, 17
Luria, David Hayyim, 159
Luria, Miriam, 159, 185–186
Luria, Solomon, 61, 192, 214

Luzzatto, David, 257
Luzzatto, Hezekiah, 257
Luzzatto, Samuel David, 257

Maccabbean revolt, 109
Maharil, 61
Maimonides, 3, 16, 31, 58–59, 60, 61,
    63, 64, 68, 70, 72, 74, 75–77, 78,
    80, 88, 137, 139, 159, 233
Male exclusivity
    Europe (12th–13th centuries),
        176–177
    feminism and, xiii
    patriarchal society and, xiii–xiv
Maliha, 137
Malka, Moshe, 81–83
Maller, Julius, 13
Manoscrivi, Jehiel, 163
Margoliot, Moshe, 116
Marriage
    creation and, 22–25
    family ideal and, 28–30
    Mishnaic era, 116
Marriage age
    Babylonian hegemony, 135
    Europe (12th–13th centuries), 177
Massarani, Isaiah, 158
Matzner-Beckerman, Shoshana, 17
Meir of Rothenburg, 175, 183
Meiselman, Moshe, 24, 27, 45, 78
Meisels, Tcharna, 214
Mendel, Isaiah Menahem, 214
Mendels, Eidel, 223
Mendelssohn, Moses, 218, 228,
    276–277
Mendes, Doña Gracia, 157, 161
Mendes, Reyna, 161
Mental abilities, 76–79, 92, 94
Michals, Mordecai, 219
Mickiewicz, Adam, 270
Midwives, 33
Miller, Yisrael, 27
Minkin, Jacob, 247
Minorities Treaty, Beth Jacob
    movement and, 269
Minyan, exemption of women from
    Halakhah and, 49
Minz, Judah, 155–156

Mirabeau, Comte de, 228
Mishnaic (Tannaitic) era, 113–124
Misogyny, Christianity and, 173
Modena, Aaron Bereckiah da, 159
Modena, Abraham ben Yehiel, 159
Modena, Fioretta da, 159
Modena, Leon da, 157, 166
Modena, Mordekhai da Solomon da,
    159
Modena, Pomona da, 159
Modena, Solomon da, 159
Modernism
    Orthodox Judaism and, 307
    women's education and, 81–82,
        302–303
Modesty, women and, 26–27
Moellin, Jacob ben Moses, 184
Moellin, Jacob Halevi, 61
Montesquieu, 228
Montessori, Maria, 291
Mordekhai ben Hillel of Nuremburg,
    172
Mordekhai of Chernobyl, 251
Morpurgo, Elijah, 168–169
Morpurgo, Rachel, 257
Morris, Nathan, 103, 107
Moses ben Abraham of Nicholsburg and
    Prague, 214
Mother–daughter relationship, women's
    education and, 105
Murada of Gunsberg, 202
Mysticism, women denied education in,
    62

Nahman of Bratzlav, 249
Nave-Levinson, Pnina, 29
Neo-Orthodox Judaism, Beth Jacob
    movement and, 264, 266, 268, 275
Neuda-Samidal, Fani, 259
Nissim ben Jacob of Kairouan, 140

Ochs, Vanessa, 301
Oppenheim, David, 223
Oppenheim, Sara, 223
Oral Law
    recording of, 73
    women's study of, xv, 57, 75, 306–307
    Written Law contrasted, 59–60

Oral Torah
  described, 5–6. *See also* Torah
  women's study of, 58
Orlean, Judah Leib, 288–289, 290, 291,
    293, 298, 299
Orthodox Judaism
  Beth Jacob movement and, 282,
    296–297
  coeducation and, 305
  modernism and, 307
  Neo-Orthodox Judaism, Beth Jacob
    movement and, 264, 266, 268,
    275
  19th century, conflict within, 229
  patriarchal society and, xiii
  politics and, xiv–xv, 308–309
  secularism and, 303–304
  women's role and, 39, 50–51, 70,
    308–309

Palestine
  Babylonian hegemony, 169
  Beth Jacob movement and, 295
  Jewish education (19th century),
    242–243, 255–256
Pascal, Blaise, 292
Patriarchal society
  male exclusivity and, xiii–xiv
  Orthodox Judaism and, 50–51
  power structures and boundaries in,
    89–90
  women's political role in, 90–91
Pelliken, Conrad, 186
Petahiah of Regensburg, 134, 140
Philo, 112
Phinehas of Prague, 185
Plato, 165
Poland
  Beth Jacob movement, 252, 266,
    268–269
  16th century, 190, 191, 192
Politics
  Jewish isolation and, 228
  Orthodox Judaism and, xiv–xv,
    308–309
  school establishment and, Second
    Temple era, 109
  women's role in, 90–91

Prayer books
  Europe (17th century), 213
  Sephardic centers (Babylonian
    hegemony), religious literature
    for women, 162–166
Prayer groups
  establishment of, 49
  Europe (12th–13th centuries), 174
Printers
  Europe (17th century), 213–215
  women as, Babylonian hegemony,
    160–161
Private sphere
  exemption of women from *Halakhah*
    and, 43–44
  Mishnaic era, 114–115
  women and, 26–27
Provence (France), Babylonian
    hegemony, 154–155
Psychology, women's political role and,
    90–91
Public sphere
  exemption of women from *Halakhah*
    and, 43–44
  women and, 27–28
  women's exclusion from, Mishnaic
    era, 114
Public worship
  Biblical era and, 100–101
  exemption of women from *Halakhah*
    and, 49
Publishing, Beth Jacob movement and,
    285
Pumbedita academy, 133

Rabbinate, attitudes concerning women,
    Sephardic centers, 148–151
Rabinowicz, Harry, 247, 249
Rabinowitz, Rebecca, 254
Rabinowitz-Teomim, Elijah David, 254
Rakowski, Puah, 240, 254
Ramanover, Yekele, 252
Rappaport, Mordecai Katz, 219
Rappaport, Serel Segal, 219
Rechenza, 175
Reuven, Rebecca, 242
Reuveni, David, 158, 159
Rieti, Hezekiah, 158

Rieti, Moses, 163
Rogovy, Abraham Mordecai, 285
Rokach, Eidel bat Shalom, 249
Rokeah, Issachar Dov, 278
Roman Empire, 113, 124
Rosanes, Judith, 215
Rosanes, Zevi Hirsch, 215
Rosenheim, Jacob, 266
Rosenthal, Tcharna, 218
Ross, Tamar, 302
Roth, Cecil, 158, 166–167
Rothschild, Charlotte von, 232–233,
    259
Rothschild, Lionel de, 259
Rousseau, Jean-Jacques, 235
Rubinstein, Esther, 254–255
Rubinstein, Isaac, 254
Rudavsky, David, 7, 124
Russia, 19th century, 252–255

Saadiah Gaon, 32
Sachs, Michael, 260
Safrai, Chana, 301
Salanter, Israel, 253
Samuel Barazani of Kurdistan, 140
Samuel ben Ali of Baghdad, 140
Samuel ben Natronai, 180
Samuel ben Yehudah the Maghrebi, 140
Samuel Nachum of Minsk, 205
Samuel of Falaise, 183
Saraval, Sorellina, 158
Sarna, Nahum, 25–26
Sassoon, Flora Gabbai, 255
Sassoon, Solomon, 255
Scaliger, Joseph Justus, 155
Scharfstein, Zevi, 298
Schechter, Solomon, 174
Schenirer, Sarah, 252, 263, 271,
    274–276, 277, 278, 279, 282, 284,
    286, 289, 290, 294, 297–298
Schimmel, Chaim, 6, 12
Schneerson, Joseph Isaac, 278
Schneerson, Menachem, 83–86, 88,
    306
Schools. See also Elementary schools and
    education
  Babylonian hegemony, 133

    Biblical era and, 102–103
    Mishnaic (Tannaitic) era and,
        113–114
    Second Temple era and, 108–113
    Sephardic centers (Babylonian
        hegemony), 166–169
Schoolteachers. See Teachers
Schwartz, Tsertel Horowitz, 253
Scribes
    Babylonian hegemony, 145–146,
        160–161
    Europe (14th–15th centuries), 186
Second Commonwealth, synagogue
    and, 105
Second Temple era
    education of women during,
        105–106
    education of women during (formal
        education), 107–113
    women's religious roles during,
        106–107
Secular factors. See also Economic
    factors
    Beth Jacob movement and, 291–292,
        295–296
    Europe (12th–13th centuries),
        172–173
    Europe (16th century), 191–192
    French Revolution and, 228–229
    Orthodox Judaism and, 303–304
    women's education and, 66, 75,
        81–82, 85, 88–89, 95
Segal, Dina, 217
Segal, Ephraim, 222
Segal, Jacob Halevi, 219
Segal, Saul ben Isaac, 217
Self-fulfillment, women and, 35–39
Sephardic centers (Babylonian
    hegemony), 146–169
    Italy, 155–169
        communal education, 166–169
        generally, 155–157
        religious literature for women,
            162–166
        synagogue, 158–159
        Torah study by women, 157–158
        women scholars, 159–162
    Provence, 154–155

Spain, 146–154
  generally, 146–148
  Rabbinic attitudes concerning
     women, 148–151
  women's education, 151–154
Sex differences. *See also* Gender role
  areas of study and, 95
  mental abilities and, 79, 92
  school establishment and, 111–112
Sexuality
  Orthodox Judaism and, 51
  teachers and, 62
  women's education and, 79–80
Sforno, Ovadia, 25
Shapira, Asher, 282
Shifra bas Joseph, 222–223
Shoub, Mary, 49–50
Shulvass, Moses A., 157–158, 163
Silver, Arthur M., 71, 74–75
Simeon ben Shetah, 108, 110
Single women, exemption of women
  from *Halakhah* and, 45
Sirkis, Joel, 59–60, 80, 196
Slonik, Aaron Ben Abraham, 192
Slonik, Benjamin, 201
Smith, William, 103
Social factors. *See also* Cultural factors
  Babylonian hegemony, Sephardic
     centers, 147–148, 152, 156
  Europe (12th–13th centuries), 173
  Europe (14th–15th centuries),
     184–187
  Europe (16th century), 191, 193
  exemption of women from *Halakhah*
     and, 43–44
  Jewish education and, 16–17
  modesty and, 27
  school establishment and, Second
     Temple era, 108–109
  Torah and, 7–8
Sofer, Moses, 65, 265
Sofer, Rachel, 219
Sofer, Yudel, 185
Solomon, Amelia, 233
Solomon ben Adret, 151
Solomon ben Isaac (Rashi), 80, 176,
     178–181
Solomon ibn Gabirol, 260

Soloveitchik, Joseph Ber, 12, 22, 88,
     92–95, 306
Sommi, Leone da, 163
Sorotzkin, Zalman, 68–69, 70, 279
Spain, Sephardic centers (Babylonian
     hegemony), 146–154
  generally, 146–148
  Rabbinic attitudes concerning
     women, 148–151
  women's education, 151–154
Spira, Shlomo, 186
Steinhardt, Joseph ben Menahem,
     215–216
Steinhardt, Krendel, 215–216, 216
Steinsaltz, Adin, 7, 8, 14–15, 46, 116,
     117
Stendal, Moses, 213
Sullam, Sarah Copia, 164–166, 257
Sura academy, 133
Survival. *See* Jewish survival
Synagogue
  Babylonian exile and, 105
  Babylonian hegemony, 133, 136
  Europe (12th–13th centuries),
     173–176
  Sephardic centers (Babylonian
     hegemony), 158–159
  United States (19th century), 244
  women leaders in, during Second
     Temple era, 107

Talmudic (Amoraic) era, 124–129
Talmudic jurisprudence, Torah study
  and, 55–57
Tannaitic era. *See* Mishnaic (Tannaitic)
  era
Teachers
  Alliance Israélite Universelle, 242
  Babylonian hegemony, 139,
     143–144, 152, 169
  Beth Jacob movement, 265, 288
  Mishnaic era, 116
  Orthodox Judaism and, 305
  Second Temple era and, 106
  sexuality and, 62
  of Torah to boys, 70
Technology, women's education and,
     81–82

Tevel, Nahum, 208
Therapeutae sect, 112
Tiktiner, Rebecca, 198–200
Tolstoy, Lev, 292
Torah
   described, 4–8
   halakhic system and, 8–12
   Jewish education and, 13–14
Torah study, 55–95
   extra-halakhic sources, 89–95
   halakhic processes and, 71–89
   Israel and, 301–302
   obligation of, 14–15, 56
   overview of, 55
   pre-twentieth-century legal sources,
      57–65
   talmudic jurisprudence and, 55–57
   twentieth-century legal sources,
      65–71
Tosafists
   12th–13th centuries, 180
   14th–15th centuries, 184–188
Trani, Isaiah de, 161, 169
Treves, Mattityahu, 184
Trujillo, Fernando de, 153, 154
Twersky, Hannah Haya, 249
Twersky, Mordekhai, 249
Tzedek, Joseph Cohen, 186

Ulich, Robert, 13, 14
Unger, Joel, 285
United States
   Jewish education (19th century),
      243–246
   Jewish education (20th century),
      305–306
Universal education. See Beth Jacob
   movement
University education, women and, 95
Urania of Worms, 174–175

Valeria the Proselyte, 125
Values, halakhic system and, 11
Vershner, Betty Rothschild, 284
Vespucci, Amerigo, 292
Villareal, Isaac da Costa, 170

Wagenseil, Johann Christophe, 200
Wahl, Dinah, 196
Wahrman, Shlomo, 86–87
Waldenberg, Eliezer, 57, 70
Warburg, Frieda, 288
Wasserman, Elhanan, 284–285
Waxman, Chaim, 28
Wegner, Judith Romney, 114–115,
   122–123, 127
Weil, Jacob, 160
Weinberger, Moshe, 71
Weissler, Chava, 197–198, 219, 222
Weissman, Deborah, 98, 291, 295, 296,
   298, 299
Werbermacher, Hannah Rachel,
   250–252
Werbermacher, Monesh, 250
Wetzler, Isaac, 224, 225
Winkler, Michael S., 68
Wisdom, defined, 94
Wolowelsky, Joel, 95
Women, 19–53
   attitudes toward, 31–35
   creation and, 20–25
   family ideal and, 28–30
   Halakhah and, 39–53
   as individual, 25–28
   Islam and, 77
   mental abilities of, 76–79, 94
   overview of, 19–20
   political role of, 90–91
   work and self-fulfillment, 35–39
Women's prayer groups. See Prayer
   groups
Workplace, women and, 35–39
World War I, Beth Jacob movement
   and, 269, 275
World War II, Beth Jacob movement
   and, 285, 288, 299–300
Writers, Europe (19th century), 257–261
Written Law, Oral Law contrasted,
   59–60
Written Torah. See Torah
Wurzberger, Walter, 10, 11, 12

Yalta, 126–129
Yavetz, Joseph, 150

Yellin, Isaac Jacob, 259
Yeosha of Worms, 217
Yiftah, Yehezkel, 145
Yochanan Ben Zakkai, 16
Yuttar, Abraham Jacob, 87, 88
Yuzpa, Joseph, 194

Zakheim, Feigel, 252
Zakheim, Joseph, 252
Zalman, Shneur, 64–65, 249

Zeltner, George, 200
Zinberg, Israel, 209, 221
Zionism
    Beth Jacob movement and, 295
    Eastern Europe and, 267
    Europe (19th century), 239
    women leadership and, 254, 261
Zohar, Noam, 44–45
Zornberg, Aviva, 301
Zunz, Leopold, 184

About the Author

Shoshana Zolty, a Toronto educator, has been active in the field of Jewish education in a variety of capacities. She has taught children in mainstream and special-education classes and has helped to found a school for children with special needs. She has received a doctorate in education from the University of Toronto and currently lectures to adults and studies Torah herself. She and her husband are the parents of six children.